E–Portfolios and Global Diffusion:

Solutions for Collaborative Education

Darren Cambridge
American Institutes for Research, Washington, DC

Managing Director:	Lindsay Johnston
Senior Editorial Director:	Heather A. Probst
Book Production Manager:	Sean Woznicki
Development Manager:	Joel Gamon
Development Editor:	Development Editor
Acquisitions Editor:	Erika Gallagher
Typesetter:	Jen McHugh
Cover Design:	Nick Newcomer, Lisandro Gonzalez

Published in the United States of America by
Information Science Reference (an imprint of IGI Global)
701 E. Chocolate Avenue
Hershey PA 17033
Tel: 717-533-8845
Fax: 717-533-8661
E-mail: cust@igi-global.com
Web site: http://www.igi-global.com

Library of Congress Cataloging-in-Publication Data

E-portfolios and global diffusion: solutions for collaborative education /
Darren Cambridge, editor.
      p. cm.
   Includes bibliographical references and index.
   Summary: "This book addresses the emerging requirements, concerns and
applications for e-portfolios, offering real-world business uses, educational
experiences, and ideal design"--Provided by publisher.
   ISBN 978-1-4666-0143-7 (hbk.) -- ISBN 978-1-4666-0144-4 (ebook) -- ISBN 978-
1-4666-0145-1 (print & perpetual access) 1. Electronic portfolios in
education. 2. Employment portfolios. 3. Business and education. I.
Cambridge, Darren, 1974-
   LB1029.P67E22 2012
   371.39--dc23
                                          2012002233

British Cataloguing in Publication Data
A Cataloguing in Publication record for this book is available from the British Library.

Editorial Advisory Board

Table of Contents

Section 1
Europe

Gordon Joyes, University of Nottingham, UK
Elizabeth Hartnell-Young, University of Nottingham, UK

Gerd Bräuer, University of Education Freiburg, Germany
Brady Spangenberg, Purdue University, USA

Joanne Nakonechny, University of British Columbia, Canada
Shona Ellis, University of British Columbia, Canada

Igor Balaban, University of Zagreb, Croatia
Blazenka Divjak, University of Zagreb, Croatia
Darko Grabar, University of Zagreb, Croatia
Bojan Zugec, University of Zagreb, Croatia

Kevin Kelly, Wiley Learning Institute, USA
Ruth Cox, San Francisco State University, USA

Detailed Table of Contents

Section 1
Europe

Chapter 1

Gordon Joyes, University of Nottingham, UK
Elizabeth Hartnell-Young, University of Nottingham, UK

This chapter outlines the European context of lifelong learning and educational cooperation across member states and the relationship of eportfolios to current development. It focuses specifically on the priority given to portfolio developments in higher education in the UK through reports and policy documents and particularly through the extensive funding distributed via the Joint Information Systems Committee of the Higher Education and Further Education Funding Councils (JISC). A model is presented that was developed by analyzing current practice and a matrix for identifying eportfolio developments in relation to purposes and learning processes, useful also for mapping key areas for future work.

Chapter 2

Gerd Bräuer, University of Education Freiburg, Germany
Brady Spangenberg, Purdue University, USA

The professional field of primary and secondary education can through reflective practice become visible and serviceable when the field itself is open to systematic research and exploration. Facilitating the development of such competencies stands at the center of instructional and pedagogical efforts, and portfolios in particular are currently enjoying a swell of interest. This chapter works to describe the Anglo-American concept of reflective practice in more detail in order to come up with suggestions on how to adapt this concept to the specific needs of education in Europe in general and in specific regard to electronic portfolios. When learners experience that working with a portfolio—a writing portfolio, for example—contributes to their continued long-term development as writers and readers, then they are able to better understand the reason for the portfolio work instead of merely mimicking some sort of predetermined model.

Joanne Nakonechny, University of British Columbia, Canada
Shona Ellis, University of British Columbia, Canada

Throughout this chapter, the authors trace how the theoretical and practical understanding, interpretation, and interactions with e-portfolios and their implementation support, both individually and through group work, students' abilities to engage in deeper structure learning, and their resulting growth as authentic science scholars. The bryofolio, an individual and group course e-portfolio, begins this online journey to facilitate deeper structure learning for 31 students in Biology 321, Bryophytes: Mosses, Hornworts and Liverworts. ("Bryfolio" is a contraction of "bryophytes" and "e-portfolio.") Initially, the authors give a short introduction to science education and how constructivist learning theory can include the use of e-portfolios as a teaching method. Following this, e-portfolios are situated within the learning context by providing a definition, a condition, and discussion on the key e-portfolio element, of critical reflection. The authors continue by introducing the bryofolio, its major components, and our analysis of how the bryofolio encourages deep structure learning at both individual and group levels.

Igor Balaban, University of Zagreb, Croatia
Blazenka Divjak, University of Zagreb, Croatia
Darko Grabar, University of Zagreb, Croatia
Bojan Zugec, University of Zagreb, Croatia

This chapter presents the most important steps in the process of ePortfolio implementation at the Faculty of Organization and Informatics (FOI) at the University of Zagreb. Stemming from an announcement by 11 faculties from the University of Zagreb, the Centre for E-Learning at the University of Zagreb reports that eportfolio is now used by over 500 students. The University of Zagreb adopted the E-learning Strategy in 2007 and this chapter covers the period 2007-2010. During this time, the response to ePortfolios greatly improved, which the authors suggest are due to changes discussed in this chapter.

Kevin Kelly, Wiley Learning Institute, USA
Ruth Cox, San Francisco State University, USA

For centuries, educators have been experimenting with the art and science of promoting, collecting, and assessing student work—just as horticulturalists have explored improvements in the cultivation of fruits, vegetables, flowers, or ornamental plants. While horticultural practices have evolved into an extremely complex science, so, too, has the use of new tools and technologies to nurture and harvest a wider range of student work. New digital technologies like electronic portfolios have opened the way for profound changes in education. The case can be made that, at the dawn of the 21st century, converging technologies and emerging social trends lay the groundwork for entirely new societal landscapes.

Yi-Ping Huang, University of Maryland Baltimore County, USA

Along with accelerated changes in the economy, culture and polity have become increased demands for global competitiveness and increased urgency to re-envision notions of educational excellence. With the rising focus on accountability by policymakers, accreditation agencies, and the general public, greater expectations are no longer the aspiring ideals of a few educational leaders but the obligations people share for preparing new generations of teachers and learners with the knowledge, skills, and dispositions needed to meet the demands of the 21st century.

Section 2
The Developing World

Chapter 7

Hédia Mhiri Sellami, University of Tunis, Tunisia

Researchers propose different structures for the ePortfolio. To examine the extent of portfolio use in Africa, the author conducted an experiment using google.com with four results that were less illuminating than originally hoped. Although this kind of experiment is not a rigorous one, it points to the range of significance of portfolios in Africa in relation to other places.

Chapter 8

Candyce Reynolds, Portland State University, USA
Judith Patton, Portland State University, USA

The use of eportfolios in American universities has proliferated over the last ten years as administrators and educators have discovered the rich opportunities that they provide for both promoting and assessing student learning. However, too often institutions of higher education prioritize assessment over student learning, creating assignments and protocols that ease assessment of student work while at the same time ignoring the valuable aspects that creating an eportfolio can provide for students, rendering the eportfolio as merely another assignment. This chapter focuses on lessons learned in University Studies, Portland State University's four-level interdisciplinary general education program, about the importance of balancing assessment needs with student learning needs.

Chapter 9

Gabriela Alpírez, Instituto Experimental de la Asunción, Guatemala

For more than 50 years, an all-girls Catholic school located in Guatemala City, Guatemala has aimed to shape the intelligence and the heart of every girl so that they will fulfill their vocation and become strong, resilient women. In accordance with the school's mission, in 2005 the forward-looking school counselors wanted to increase the students' awareness of the importance of exploring and planning their professional careers, as it was recognized by many national and international organizations that women who received a formal education could have a greater impact on the economic, political, and social life of their communities. By starting to use electronic portfolios at an earlier age, students are better equipped to make more informed choices in terms of the direction they would like to take their careers.

This chapter highlights the types of portfolios most frequently used in the business world or in preparation for entering a career. It shows that content in each area can be cumulative or separate. It will describe ideas for the types of artifacts to compile along with how to format them effectively and digitize them creatively. Compiling a digital portfolio is a strong contribution to a student's learning path as well as providing a business professional with a means of collecting and preserving valuable projects. Continual reflection upon their work provides individuals with more confidence in their own worth as they embark upon their professional careers or justify their desires for advancement.

Section 3
Australasia

This chapter provides an overview of ePortfolio practice in Australia where a national research project has successfully documented ePortfolio practice in Australian higher education, and a parallel study has investigated emergent practice in the vocational education and training (VET) sector. It examines the policy context for ePortfolio activity in Australia, introduces the Australian ePortfolio Project and then presents a review of the research findings. This chapter discusses how ePortfolios offer the potential to be a meaningful medium for convergence and integration of education and training. This is done in order to support innovation and productivity, ensuring ongoing national economic development and growth.

This article discusses the issues of and solutions to ePortfolio adoption in the Hong Kong higher education context. Over the past few years, all eight government-funded universities in Hong Kong have been piloting different types of ePortfolios for different purposes. However, the piloting and use of ePortfolios have been rather fragmented. This article discusses the issues of and solutions to ePortfolio adoption in the Hong Kong higher education context. The aim of this project is to develop an ePortfolio culture which will encompass both the academic/course-based, self-learning approach and the support/personal development/professional approach.

Chapter 13

Gary Brown, Portland State University, USA
YoonJung Cho, Oklahoma State University, USA
Ashley Ater-Kranov, ABET, USA

The advent of open knowledge and open source and the ubiquity of the phenomenon identified as Web 2.0, as evidenced by the phenomenal growth of Facebook, Google, and hundreds of other open and social Internet applications, have ramifications for education. At the same time, educators have been slow to understand that it is how a technology is implemented, not the technology itself, that most influences learning. This article examines how ePortfolios are being and will be used, depending in large measure on the teaching beliefs that guide their implementation and the quality of learning that follows.

Chapter 14

Royce Robertson, Walden University, USA

Today, higher education institutions need to prepare for technology integration into even the most sacred of rituals: promotion and tenure for faculty members. A holistic approach is necessary to extract the practices and dispositions of the faculty and support providers. This chapter aims to define the Electronic Teaching Portfolio and to describe some conditions to satisfy before implementing a support system. Furthermore, the chapter describes the design and content of an ideal support system that is feasible to implement, given that the institution is willing to commit necessary resources.

Chapter 15

Yu-Fen Yang, National Yunlin University of Science and Technology, Taiwan
Hui-Chin Yeh, National Yunlin University of Science and Technology, Taiwan

Over the past decade, e-portfolios have been widely used for different purposes in education. However, specific issues, such as whether students will upload and organize their documents in the language e-portfolio without incentives or whether the language e-portfolio will increase students' cognitive load, remain unaddressed. A range of challenges faces eportfolio use in Taiwanese universities. The definitions, purposes, and advantages of e-portfolios described in this article provide readers with background for the further discussion of challenges in developing online language portfolios.

Preface

INTRODUCTION: THE FLAT WORLD OF GLOBAL EPORTFOLIOS

In *The Geography of Thought*, Richard Nisbett draws on philosophy, cultural psychology, and his own laboratory research to argue that people of European and of East Asian origins differ not only culturally but cognitively. They enact distinctively different ways of understanding the world. For example, central to the Western worldview are the agency of the individual and the discrete categorization of reality. In contract, the Eastern worldview values harmony and elevates context as the key understanding. Although these are familiar generalizations, they seem to have sufficient scholarly grounding to take seriously. From this body of research, Nisbett and others suggest that thriving in globalized society means that people need to become familiar with, and be able to make use of, the multiple ways of making sense offered by regional cultures.

This book offers a snapshot of the diffusion of eportfolios—an innovation in learning technology originating in the United States—in higher education across several global regions during the period from about 2008 to 2010. When I assumed the editor's role for this book from the first editor who was unable to complete the project he had originated, most chapters were already written, including some from countries with which I had no previous direct experience. I expected to see in the manuscripts the kinds of differences in thinking and valuing Nisbett and others have documented. I expected to find that the eportfolio concept was being transformed through these global lenses.

However, what emerged is much more a story of adaptation than transformation. Similar concerns and priorities appear throughout these pages. Implementing eportfolios across an academic program involves similar essential governance challenges whether one is in Baltimore or Zagreb. Helping students become reflective practitioners requires careful curricular integration whether it is happening in Freiburg or Vancouver. Professors across Africa struggle with the same challenge of balancing the use of eportfolios for learning and assessment that faculty members in Portland and staff members in Sydney confront. Given the parallels that abound, my predecessor was right in using the word *diffusion* in this volume's title. This book is more a record of the spread of North American educational practices across several global regions and of significant enrichments of those practices as they are integrated into national and local educational systems than it is of a syncretic reimagining of the eportfolio tradition.

Of the multiple possible explanations for this relative global homogeneity, I here highlight three. First, an obvious limitation of this collection is the overrepresentation of countries that were once European colonies. Neither the previous editor nor I successfully solicited chapters from countries such as Japan or Russia where the influence of the larger Western models of higher education, in contrast to the specific innovation of eportfolios, might be less evident. With more examples from such countries, greater differences might have presented themselves. Second, because the eportfolio has been recently introduced in most countries, homogenous diffusion may be a first stage in its global development. As learners and scholars around the world move beyond the surface issues of implementation and gain in-depth experience, the limits of the received models in their contexts may come into focus, and practitioners and researchers may undertake a more fundamental reconceptualization attuned to them.

A third possibility is that eportfolio practices may move across national and regional boundaries relatively intact because of their internal heterogeneity and protean nature. At international events focused on eportfolios in which I have participated over the last ten years, the emphasis of the eportfolio genre on individualization is a common concern. Is promoting a means for abstracting and categorizing individual experience and expertise a form of cultural domination? Is celebrating agency and difference an imposition of a value system and way of understanding the world that many people do not and should not be compelled to share? The individualizing strand of eportfolio practice is undeniable, and so not unproblematic. However, as I have argued elsewhere at length, the strongest eportfolio models foreground the establishment of what I have termed integrity, the integration of multiple dimensions of identity and experience through a rich representation of context (Cambridge, 2010). The ability to place reasoned, categorical analysis of individual agency within a rich representation of social context that acknowledges complexity and dependency may turn out to be the key reason that eportfolios have such a global appeal.

OVERVIEW OF THE COLLECTION

This book is organized into three sections: Europe, the Developing World, and Australasia. Each section consists of one or more chapters of each of three types: overview chapters, which survey the use of eportfolios at the time of their writing in a region or country; case chapters, which focus on practice or research at a particular institution; and North American companion chapters, which focus on themes important in one or more of the cases.

Europe

The Europe section begins with Chapter 1, an overview of eportfolio use in the United Kingdom as of 2008 and its relationship to work on the European continent, a piece written by researchers at the International Centre for ePortfolio Development at the University of Nottingham. The authors explain how policy drivers such as the Bologna Process, the Widening Participation agenda, and the Higher Education Achievement report, linked to funding from the Joint Information Systems Committee, have led to widespread use of eportfolios that emphasizes their role in personal development planning, the development of employability skills, and e-assessment, particularly through emphasizing reflection. At the time of the writing of Chapter 1, there was growing interest in using eportfolios for continuing professional development, work based learning, and supporting transitions between different levels of education and education and the workplace.

Chapter 2 shifts focus to the European continent, deepening the focus on reflection to examine theoretical and practical issues involved in supporting the development of reflective practice in both students and professionals within German universities, with a particular emphasis on writing instruction. Particularly notable are the multiple "discourses" of reflective practice that come into play, organized along a continuum from private to public, challenging the assumption that reflection is done primarily in social isolation. Chapter 3 offers a North American perspective on the role of reflection in learning, examining through both constructivist learning theory and observation of educational practice how introducing critical reflection activities through an eportfolio into a biology course at the University of British Columbia deepens students' scientific understanding, leading to "deep structure learning." Information Processing Sheets are one structured form of reflection that instructors and students found particularly powerful for achieving this deeper knowledge.

Chapter 4 introduces the theme of implementation. It returns to Europe, detailing the process of implementing eportfolios in an organization and informatics program at the University of Zagreb in Croatia. Considering technology, pedagogy, and assessment, the authors offer evidence based on course outcomes that students who chose to complete optional eportfolio assignments are more likely to gain credit for courses based on their class work rather than on an exam. Chapter 5 presents a complementary North American perspective on eportfolio implementation, advocating that colleges and universities develop "eporticulture," that is, the custom of supporting student learning and assessment with eportfolios so that a healthy diversity of teaching and learning practices is well supported. Examples of programs at San Francisco State University illustrate this approach. Chapter 6 presents another North American implementation model, detailing the process through which the University of Maryland Baltimore County's School of Education, implemented eportfolios not only for teacher education but for supporting the professional development of graduates as they move into the classroom, enabling both alignment with standards and cultivation of 21st century learning. "Five-R" processes guided the implementation: re-envisioning, re-organization, re-engineering, realization, and renewal.

The Developing World

The Developing World section begins with Chapter 7, an initial effort to survey eportfolio use throughout Africa. The author provides a range of examples of individual eportfolios and faculty projects and outlines four cases, one from Tunisia, two from South Africa, and one joint project of a French agency and the University of Montreal involving faculty from universities in a range of sub-Saharan countries. These examples illustrate the wide range of applications of eportfolios of interest to African teachers and scholars, encompassing both assessment and support of learning. Chapter 8 provides a North American perspective on how assessment and learning applications of eportfolios can be balanced, drawing on the mature eportfolio processes in place at Portland State University in the United States. The authors outline principles that have guided successful use of eportfolios in their first-year general education program, including such practices as scaffolding the experience, integrating collaborative learning experiences, using rubrics, and compensating faculty evaluation of eportfolios for programmatic assessment independent of the contexts in which the portfolios were created.

Chapter 9 focuses on one of many uses of eportfolios in the developing world, supporting employability. The author describes the use of portfolios at Instituto Experimental de la Asunción in Guatemala in conjunction with job shadowing, achieved through working closely with mentors in the workplace. Eportfolios are intended to help secondary school girls explore their capabilities, sharpen their career interests, and increase their self-esteem. Chapter 10 explores the use of eportfolios for employability in a North American context. It offers detailed guidance to creators of career portfolios, arguing that such advice is relevant not just to students but also to people already in the professional workforce. Eportfolios can play an important role in performance appraisal and may help workers demonstrate their indispensability in the face of downsizing.

Australasia

The Australasia section begins with Chapter 11, an overview of eportfolio use in the higher education and vocational education and training sectors in Australia, drawing on surveys conducted as part of a national study in 2007 and follow up work in 2010. The authors examine the policy context, considering alignment with the Bologna Process in support of student mobility; an imperative to strengthen employability that suggests the need for stronger connections between higher and vocation education and a renewed commitment to lifelong learning; and an increased emphasis on the development and assessment of "generic skills." The surveys suggest a range of understandings and uses of eportfolios across Australian universities, with responsibility for eportfolio work becoming more distributed across organizational units from 2007 to 2010. The cases, of the Queensland University of Technology and of Curtin University, illustrate how the national patterns map onto local practice.

Chapter 12 presents the state of eportfolio practice in Hong Kong, focusing particularly on the dynamics of eportfolio adoption at the City University of Hong Kong. Universities are examining the potential role of eportfolios as they expand their undergraduate degree programs from three to four years to integrate new general education courses, which create the imperative to define and assess associated graduate attributes. Universities seeking to implement eportfolios face challenges related to perception, motivation, pedagogy, technology, and, perhaps most crucially, funding. Their experiences suggest that substantive and sustained support from institutional leaders and funders is essential to successful implementation at scale. Chapter 13 presents North American research that sheds light on the challenges of perception and motivation introduced in the previous chapter. As part of the Inter/National Coalition for Electronic Portfolio Research, researchers at Washington State University surveyed faculty about their teaching beliefs. Faculty held views that were teaching-centered, learner-centered, or learning-centered, with many instructors holding views that intersected with two of the three categories. Teaching beliefs correlated with perceptions of eportfolios. For example, teaching-centered beliefs inversely correlated with a perception that eportfolios could be valuable for documenting growth over time, while learner-centered beliefs strongly correlated with that perception. Learning-centered beliefs also positively correlated with growth over time, but also correlated with the perception that eportfolios could be useful in building community, to which the other two belief categories were less strongly related. Chapter 14 also presents results of North American research, in this case focused on the potential role of eportfolios in documenting teaching as part of the tenure and promotion process. Experience with such a process could powerfully shape faculty members' perceptions and use of eportfolios in their teaching.

The book concludes with Chapter 15, which examines an eportfolio system created to support language learning at the National Yunlin University of Science and Technology in Taiwan. Unlike many eportfolio systems, this language learning platform combines domain-specific learning tools that adapt based on student performance to allow for personalized learning, thereby reducing cognitive load, with tools for both individual reflection on learning and social reflection on student work. Particularly notable are self-assessment tools that allow students to examine specific aspects of their language learning in the service of self-reflection. Perhaps more than any other contribution to this collection, this chapter begins to show hints of the influence of a non-Western worldview. In focusing on the integration of individual learners into an externally structured, social process of learning while deemphasizing their articulation of distinctiveness or exercise of independent agency, it may be an early contribution to a next phase in the global evolution of eportfolio practice.

Darren Cambridge
American Institutes for Research, Washington, DC

REFERENCES

Cambridge, D. (2010). *Eportfolios for lifelong learning and assessment*. San Francisco, CA: Jossey-Bass.

Nisbett, R. (2003). *The geography of thought*. New York, NY: Free Press.

Acknowledgment

Thanks to George Mason University and the American Institutes for Research, where I worked during the editing of this volume; Phil Jones, who initiated the project; the authors, who patiently endured the transition to my editorship; the reviewers, who generously donated their time; Lisa Jones, Danielle Griffin, and Barbara Cambridge, who assisted with editing; Serge Ravet, for his work over the past decade cultivating a global community of eportfolio practitioners; and my wife Kara Gotsch and my son Oliver Cambridge, who have graciously tolerated all the travel needed to participate fully in that community.

Darren Cambridge
American Institutes for Research, Washington, DC

Section 1
Europe

Chapter 1
Mapping UK ePortfolio Developments within a European Context

Gordon Joyes
University of Nottingham, UK

Elizabeth Hartnell-Young
University of Nottingham, UK

ABSTRACT

This chapter outlines the European context of lifelong learning and educational cooperation across member states and the relationship of eportfolios to current development. It focuses specifically on the priority given to portfolio developments in Higher Education in the UK through reports and policy documents and particularly through the extensive funding distributed via the Joint Information Systems Committee of the Higher Education and Further Education Funding Councils (JISC). The chapter provides an overview of current eportfolio use and points to future trends for technical and pedagogical development, drawing on the extensive JISC project archive, which covers examples from many disciplines and for a range of purposes. The authors are JISC expert consultants in eportfolios and have an in depth knowledge of completed and ongoing work in this area. In this chapter we present a model that we developed by analyzing current practice and a matrix for identifying eportfolio developments in relation to purposes and learning processes, useful also for mapping key areas for future work.

INTRODUCTION

This chapter outlines the European context of lifelong learning and educational cooperation across

member states and the relationship of eportfolios to current development. It focuses specifically on the priority given to portfolio developments in higher education in the UK through reports and policy documents and particularly through the extensive funding distributed via the Joint

DOI: 10.4018/978-1-4666-0143-7.ch001

Information Systems Committee of the Higher Education and Further Education Funding Councils (JISC). The chapter provides an overview of current eportfolio use and points to future trends for technical and pedagogical development, drawing on the extensive JISC project archive that covers examples from many disciplines and for a range of purposes. The authors are currently JISC expert consultants in eportfolios and have an in-depth knowledge of completed and ongoing work in this area. In this chapter, we present a model that we developed by analyzing current practice and a matrix for identifying eportfolio developments in relation to purposes and learning processes, useful also for mapping key areas for future work.

THE EUROPEAN CONTEXT

The 1999 Bologna declaration of Ministers of Education in Europe emphasized the importance of education and educational cooperation in the development and strengthening of stable, peaceful and democratic societies (http://www.bologna-bergen2005.no/Docs/00-Main_doc/990719BOLOGNA_DECLARATION.PDF). Since then, the aim has been to create a European Higher Education Area and to promote the European system of higher education worldwide. The Bologna Process, as it is known, demonstrates a commitment to lifelong learning in Europe, seen as essential to meet the challenges of increased global competition and the spread of new technologies. Lifelong learning is defined as:

all learning activity undertaken throughout life, with the aim of improving knowledge, skills and competences within a personal, civic, social and/or employment-related perspective (Commission of the European Communities, 2001, p. 9).

Institutions in Europe are now encouraged to develop courses and curricula with significant European content and to engage in joint partnership activities and curriculum development, including joint degrees. The purpose of these activities is to improve quality and ensure standards of higher education, to remove obstacles to student and academic mobility within Europe and beyond and to simplify comparisons between qualifications by adopting a European approach to degrees at bachelor, master and doctoral levels. This will be aided by the establishment of a European Credit Transfer System and the Diploma Supplement, a document for students that provides a description of the nature, level, context, content and status of studies successfully completed.

Although the UK has played an active part in the development of the Bologna Process, and its qualification framework broadly matches the three cycle system (up to the degrees of master's and doctorate), the general level of awareness of Bologna and its implications is lower than in many other European countries. Implementation of the European Diploma Supplement is not widespread, and the Europass scheme, which promotes mobility and aims to make skills and qualifications clearly and easily understood in Europe, underpins Bologna's objectives, yet relatively few UK institutions are actively promoting it (UK HE Europe Unit).

However, other developments are occurring in the UK to encourage students to record, reflect and build on their achievements systematically in a process known as Personal Development Planning (PDP). This is defined as:

a structured and supported process undertaken by an individual to reflect upon their own learning, performance and/or achievement to plan for their personal, educational and career development (Dearing, 1997).

In order to increase the range of students participating in post-16 education, including at university level, the Widening Participation agenda (Department for Education and Skills, 2003), promotes recognition of learning in both formal and informal settings. Such policies have influenced the development of eportfolios in the UK as a means of recording learning. The Burgess report (Universities UK, 2007) recommended introducing a Higher Education Achievement Report (HEAR) in England that would be the primary vehicle for measuring and recording achievement. Supported by the Higher Education Funding Council (HEFCE), the HEAR would provide employers with a richer picture of a student's competencies and experiences, containing information on areas such as work-based learning, and would incorporate the Diploma Supplement. UK research (Fielden, 2007) has shown the importance employers place on international skills of graduates. In particular, time spent abroad for study or work and language competencies are highly valued, and it is thought that eportfolios will provide a means of presenting these skills.

EPORTFOLIO DEFINITIONS

The term "eportfolio" sometimes refers to a container, or repository of material, and to a selection of artifacts presented for some purpose. Recent work on eportfolios has attempted to both clarify and expand the definition of personal repositories and eportfolios to incorporate both form and processes. Expanding on an earlier definition promoted and developed by the EDUCAUSE National Learning Infrastructure Initiative, Ravet (2007) has suggested that an eportfolio is:

a collection of authentic and diverse evidence, drawn from a larger archive, representing the capital developed by a reflective person or organization designed to exploit/valorize their assets in a particular context (2).

This definition acknowledges the selection of evidence from a larger repository or archive, the importance of both individual and collective reflection and the need to be mindful of the context

or purpose, which implies audience. However, while it refers to the processes of collection, selection and reflection that are often seen at the core of eportfolio work, it does not focus on the other processes of learning that are increasingly supported by online tools. In contrast, references to the term in policy documents in England (e.g., Department for Education and Skills, 2005) indicate that eportfolios are part of a personal online space, where learners can store their work, record their achievements (a repository function) and access personal course timetables (an organizing function), digital resources relevant to their own study (personalized information) and links to other learners (for collaboration and feedback). These references sometimes ignore the presentation function of eportfolios. On the other hand, JISC takes the view that eportfolios are "a purposeful aggregation of digital items, ideas, evidence, reflections, feedback, etc., which 'presents' a selected audience with evidence of a person's learning or ability." These "presentational" eportfolios are created through the use of systems or tools, which can include a range of functionality (i.e., repositories) enabling the storage and organization of material for planning, reflecting and giving feedback.

A study conducted by the authors for the British Educational Communications & Technology Agency (Becta) was commissioned to consider the uses and potential impact of eportfolios on learning and teaching. This involved literature review and an in-depth study of eight projects in the early stages of eportfolio use within the primary, secondary, FE, HE and Adult and Community Learning sectors.

The model developed from the data included repositories and a range of tools for storing and organizing material for planning, reflecting, giving and receiving feedback and collaborating and presenting discrete selections (eportfolios) to various audiences for assorted purposes. Figure 1 shows how the components relate to each other.

Figure 1. Components of an eportfolio system

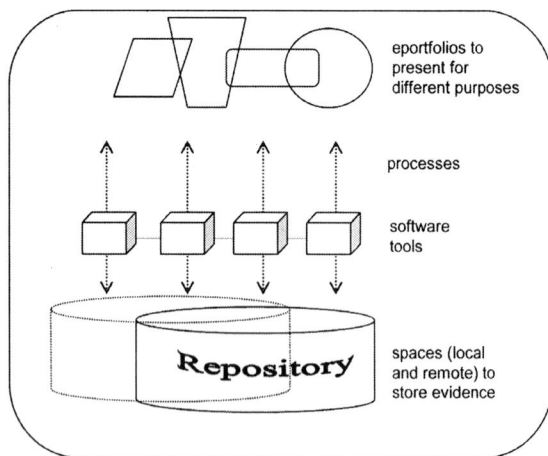

The repository in Figure 1 consists of any places where digital material is stored, including learner-generated items (assignments, images, reflective journals) and resources or links to resources that the learner requires. With web services, these can be stored on various servers, personal or institutional, and brought together when needed. In the middle of Figure 1, the software tools that support the differing processes are represented. For example, tools that support planning, collaboration, reflection, selection and so on feed into the repository as well as enable items to be drawn into an eportfolio for a particular purpose. Eportfolios are currently used for many reasons, including formative and summative assessment, employment applications, professional accreditation, transition between institutions and/ or employment and less high-stakes purposes, such as recording personal growth and learning. Therefore, the top level of the diagram shows multiple eportfolios containing purposeful material for a range of audiences.

Recently, and in conjunction with the spread of Web 2.0 tools such as social networking, blogging, and wiki sites, opportunities to engage in eportfolio processes have expanded. For example,

while a blog is not an eportfolio, it is an expression of the process of reflection. Similarly, MySpace and Facebook are repositories that also support communication, collaboration in groups, and presentation of identities. It is the processes involved in developing eportfolios that users have found to be most valuable (Hartnell-Young et al., 2007).

JISC

JISC is a body of the UK Higher and Further Education Funding Councils, established to support the further and higher education sectors in the use of information communications technology (ICT), particularly though funding projects in single institutions or partnerships as well as services such as the JISC infoNet. Its vision is a world where learners, teachers, researchers and wider institutional stakeholders use technology to enhance the overall educational experience by improving flexibility and creativity and by encouraging comprehensive and diverse personal, high-quality learning, teaching and research. JISC's e-Learning program takes the view that technology should be exploited in order to free time from those activities that can be efficiently automated and should be used to support innovative and creative approaches to teaching and learning. Under this program, JISC has funded more than thirty projects that involve eportfolios and has provided an infokit to support dissemination (JISC, 2008a). In addition, JISC infoNet, an advisory service that provides resources to promote good practice and innovation within the UK education sector, has been working with the European University Information Systems Organization (EUNIS) and others on a capacity-building project: Preparing for Bologna (http:// www.jiscinfonet.ac.uk/bologna/index_html).

Interestingly, we have found in our work for JISC that projects in these developments may not necessarily adopt the term "eportfolio," referring more to the processes of collection, selection, collaboration, reflection, presentation, and so on, and the purposes for which they use these processes. Several that have been explored within the HE context in the UK—such as information retrieval, planning, reflection, feedback, collaboration, and assessment—are described and explored within this chapter, as well as in the main contexts in which eportfolios have been applied. These contexts are:

- Assessment
- Personal Development Planning/ Continuing Professional Development
- Transition/Application
- Work Based Learning/Employment

The distinction between purpose or context of portfolio use and the processes involved in developing a portfolio is often confused in the literature. As a result of a recent review of eportfolio use, we propose the matrix in Table 1 as a means of illuminating the diversity of eportfolio contexts and processes and distinguishing between them. This is a work in progress, and, as we are exploring use within JISC projects, there may be additions to both purposes and processes. Certainly, from a JISC perspective, many projects also have a technical purpose, but, as this is not directly related to pedagogy, it has not been included in the matrix shown here.

Eportfolio use within UK higher education institutions has been promoted extensively as part of the strategy for e-learning in higher education, implemented by HEFCE. JISC was asked to investigate the use of eportfolios across institutions and sectors, and this resulted in the funding of approximately thirty projects (2005-8). Further JISC funding for twelve curriculum projects (2008 -10) will potentially involve portfolios. We have used the portfolio purpose-process matrix as a means of informing the evaluation of the project reports as well as supporting current eportfolio projects to identify areas in which they can contribute to knowledge in this area. This work is providing interesting insights into issues involved in integrating eportfolios within the curriculum.

By their nature, eportfolio projects have been working with embryonic software products and have often focused on technical issues. In addition, the eportfolio use has tended to be treated as a project activity - as a pilot where use is often not adequately integrated within the curriculum. The JISC, in its recent call for two-year curriculum delivery projects (JISC, 2008b), is aiming to support greater integration, and the Inter/National Coalition for Electronic Portfolio Research (I/NCEPR) community has recognized that integration of eportfolio use in HE is a change management issue. Projects can buy in technical solutions and expertise for pilot work; however, sustainable use impacts institutional strategy. Who decides on the product or products? Who funds these? Which eportfolio solution/s are suitable for which contexts? The matrix provides some insight into the nature of the difficulty. An eportfolio tool suited to personal development planning may not be suited to application. One that is suited to presentation may not be ideal for collaboration. Decision making in this area is becoming even more complex as institutions rethink their Learning Management System strategies as they recognize the need to support the use of Web2.0 and student-preferred applications alongside their institutionally-delivered ones.

One future is the Personalised Learning Environment (PLE) in which learners engage with a range of processes involved in learning to use their chosen web applications in a desktop "mashup." The PLE links to institutionally provided information and services as well as to personal biodata, qualifications, etc., held in other locationsor repositories. Decisions about which eportfolio product/tool to support in this context are likely to be seen as short-term and temporary while technologies mature and institutions engage with the process of advancing their technology infrastructures. In spite of this complexity, there are lessons to be learned about eportfolio purposes

Table 1. The portfolio purpose- process matrix

Purpose/ Context	Process	Information retrieval	Planning	Reflection	Feedback	Collaboration	Presentation
Assessment							
Personal Development Planning/ Continuing Professional Development							
Work Based Learning/ Employment							
Transition/ Application							
Other purpose							

and processes that can inform future practice, and the rest of the chapter will focus on these. The initial focus will be on eportfolios for assessment.

ASSESSMENT

It is helpful to consider assessment as a continuum of recognizing, valuing and judging something rather than purely as measurement. Knight and Yorke (2003) suggest that if assessment is judgment, then anything that provides data for judgment is an assessment method. Eportfolios clearly enable data in many forms to be presented to others for assessment. Boud and Falchikov (2007) suggest that considering "informed judgment" as the central idea of assessment incorporates both the judgment of others in processes of certification and informing the judgment of learners in presenting themselves. It thus encompasses summative and formative assessment purposes and values the development of the learners' own capacity to make judgments. Further, they argue, it contextualizes assessment as judgment which always has to be for a particular purpose. These aspects are particularly relevant to eportfolio development, where purpose and audience are key considerations. In his book entitled *Assessing Students: How Shall We Know Them?* Rowntree (1977) suggests five dimensions of assessment: Why assess? What

to assess? How to assess? How to interpret? and How to respond? The "why" demands clear purpose, but addressing the other questions is quite problematic. Eportfolios and their disaggregated contents can provide those making judgments with the materials to know learners better, but some formats enable this more than others. Eportfolios are judged in various ways, whether by self-assessment, peer assessment, tutor assessment or university admissions officers. There are also other contexts, such as employment applications, in which audiences must recognize, acknowledge, and value material in new forms.

Eportfolios are part of a broader scheme of e-assessment in the UK, which is defined as "the end-to-end electronic assessment processes where ICT is used for the presentation of assessment activity and the recording of responses" (Qualifications and Curriculum Authority, 2004). The official documents suggest that some forms of e-assessment may be used for diagnostic purposes, such as assessment of a learner's knowledge and skills at the outset of a course, for formative purposes, providing developmental feedback to a learner on his or her current understanding and skills (JISC, 2007a, p. 6) and for summative or final assessment of a learner's achievement, usually leading to a formal qualification or certification of a skill. The QCA Blueprint for e-Assessment (2007) proposed that all awarding bodies should be set up to accept and assess e-portfolios by 2009, and, among others, HEFCE and JISC are supporting the work required to achieve this.

Some industry sectors (notably health) have seen rapid development in the use of eportfolios to support personal reflection, in planning and recording lifelong learning and as a means of accreditation or review. The National Health Service Education for Scotland (NES) uses eportfolios for high-stakes assessment of all Foundation (junior) doctors in Scotland and has influenced the development of eportfolios for over 25,000 healthcare professionals across the UK in medicine, dentistry, and pharmacy. The eportfolio innovation was introduced at the same time as the Modernizing Medicine initiative, a major reconfiguration of postgraduate training and its associated processes of assessment. Although junior doctors had previously been required to keep a portfolio, the electronic format and the detailed structure of the recording necessary for an eportfolio were new. The purpose of the activity in this case is to record developing competence and reflection as a means of assessment. All trainees are now required to keep this record, reflect and build upon their own learning experiences, identify learning needs, support involvement in planning education and training and evaluate the effectiveness of their own learning experiences.

The NES eportfolio provides a space to record relevant assessments, training records, educational agreements, and required declarations that give evidence of competency for General Medical Council registration and satisfactory completion of Foundation Programs. The categories of artifact include a personal development plan, supervisors' reports, a certificate of performance, multi-source feedback, workplace assessments, log entries, and significant event analyses. Educational supervisors are required to sign a learning agreement which includes a commitment to visit the training website at least once a week in order to collect emails and other documents. Effectively, there is an assessment about every four months. The

eportfolio is structured to solicit evidence that the student has taken part in a number of clinical engagements and has shown success in a number of basic clinical competencies and includes tick box questions and open text fields for free responses. It is available online and is integrated with the Doctors' Online Training Scheme (DOTS) system, an online electronic resource database which supports trainees' general educational needs. Due to the nature of doctors' work, the eportfolio is designed for individual use rather than collaboration, but completion of the requirements depends on the involvement of nurses and other clinical colleagues who need to confirm that certain experiences have occurred and that competencies have been achieved. However, there is also an area of the portfolio that is reserved for private, unshared reflection.

Incorporating reflection has often been seen as the aspect that sets eportfolios apart from mere collections of material. Training in medicine has a long tradition of reflective practice, yet documenting reflection around clinical matters is highly sensitive. As one tutor expressed, "the idea of self-reflection is so ingrained that I don't need to be taught how to do it." However, our research also found some reluctance to write reflections down, "because you might be in court one day" (Hartnell-Young et al., 2007). In an increasingly litigious world, there may be serious professional consequences as a result of access to documented reflection by known or unknown parties. The study found that most tutors, supervisors and administrators saw the value of the NES eportfolio in terms of streamlining the necessary tasks of assessment, with a strong scaffolding structure to assist recording of competencies. The students themselves knew it was compulsory to their success in gaining registration and complied, although one commented:

More often than not it has felt like a chore and an exercise in "jumping through hoops," but it is compulsory in my job, so it simply has to be done.

Having said that, it should come in useful when providing evidence of competencies achieved, so I can see some benefit in the exercise.

The input is in text form, via the Internet, and there are no facilities as yet for uploading other digital artifacts (for example, media files or images).Thus, the design of the technology tool constrains the ways in which eportfolio users can present themselves and their identities, as the same doctor noted in our survey:

However, it does provide limited opportunity to discriminate between individuals as we are all filling in the same pro formas, completing the same modules... so it may be difficult to "stand out" using the eportfolio at interview.

PERSONAL DEVELOPMENT PLANNING (PDP) AND CONTINUING PROFESSIONAL DEVELOPMENT

The report by the National Committee of Inquiry into Higher Education (Dearing, 1997) has been influential in establishing PDP within both policy and practice agendas at a national and an institutional level in the UK. However, work on recording Professional Development Planning in higher education based on "progress files" predated the Dearing Report (Dearing, 1997). An example is the HEFCE-funded PADSHE (Personal and Academic Development for Students in Higher Education) project (http://www.nottingham.ac.uk/padshe). This project, involving seven universities, informed the development of electronic PDP approaches and an early version of an ePDP was developed by the electronic Personal and Academic Records (ePARs) project funded by the Department for Education and Skills (1998-2002) and involved the Universities of Nottingham and Newcastle. Both these universities went on to establish centers for eportfolio developments and have been influential both nationally and

internationally. Many other PDP developments have included digital space for eportfolios integrated into a virtual learning environment (VLE) or in purpose-built commercial or open-source software.

This early PDP work was developed in a climate of increased accountability of higher education institutions to government and society. The government-led subject review process from 1993-2001 (QAA, 2003), where each institution had to make transparent its Quality Assurance (QA) processes and was inspected by teams of peer reviewers, is indicative of this period. This assessment looked at student learning experience and student achievement, and each subject area was judged as "excellent," "satisfactory" or "unsatisfactory" for the quality of its teaching and learning, and this was made publicly available in order to inform students and parents in the application process. Institutionally-agreed approaches to PDPs became a useful way of ensuring not only a means of providing students with a centrally supported approach to recording progress but also evidence to demonstrate the quality of academic support and guidance. The support for personal development planning in this QA approach has tended to be provided by an undergraduate personal tutor system where progress is discussed and reflected upon. The purpose is intended to be wider than building an academic record as it is also designed to include skills and career development. Though the focus here seems to be on the product, it is the process that tends to be valued.

Issues related to the use of PDPs in HE in the UK are many and are well-documented (QAA, 2001; JISC, 2008). Some of these relate to the use of eportfolios in general, but some are PDP specific. For example:

- PDP, in many institutions, relies on a personal tutoring system that involves timetabled yet infrequent meetings as well as the enthusiasm of the individual tutor, which can be problematic;

- The process can seem burdensome for tutors in many subject areas with large numbers of students;
- Tutors may not see any added value for them in completing an online form, because it is the process that seems more important. It can be perceived as looking at a screen rather than at the student;
- Many students, particularly high achievers and school dropouts, may not perceive the process to be valuable and see this as something being done to them - another institutional requirement. They may not see the link between the PDP and employment prospects. However, there is evidence that mature students view the PDP process more favorably.

The PDP4XL project has successfully tested the feasibility of transferring the data of learner records securely between institutions and from institutions to a repository and has conducted research into the perceptions of students, academics and employers on the value of PDP and lifelong learner records, particularly in the creative industries. The project found that students had difficulty projecting their lifelong learning needs and were very focused on presenting their "best work" in their CV for their first job. They also reported that a hard copy portfolio was very important to them. The employers surveyed reported that they would not be interested in the detail in the PDP record, since they would not have time to read the material. Academic staff members were not convinced of the value of PDP, since it appeared to involve additional work for both tutors and students.

Some JISC projects such as ISLE (Individualised Support for Learning through e-Portfolios) (JISC, 2007c) have been designed to build foundations for transforming staff perceptions of PDP where there is a genuine conviction that it is a worthwhile process for students. ISLE was

a large-scale project involving three universities and seven further education colleges, ninety staff and nearly a thousand students across 35 subjects including undergraduate degree courses. These courses included audiology, media, legal studies, information technology, computing and multimedia, social engineering, science, performing arts, costume design, built environment, nursing studies, biomedical sciences, sport, and fitness. The project noted differences between the ways different types of learners value personal development planning, but, with the increasing use of PDP at school level, this effect may be a temporary one. However, the influence of a competency approach to learning is being felt:

This could be a reflection on education as a whole, which encourages specialization at an early age and, as a result, learners take "a jumping through hoops" perspective on education to obtain their qualification, and hence, recording their learning through an eportfolio is not something that seems immediately relevant to gain better marks for an assessment (JISC, 2008a).

The result can be a tokenistic use of the PDP: it becomes a quality assurance and curriculum requirement. There is evidence to suggest that where key performance standards are set, such as in teacher or nursing education within the UK, the link between PDP and entry into the profession is transparent, as it is a requirement of accreditation, and hence is perceived to be valuable by both academic tutors and their students.

JISC projects have also explored the use of eportfolios to organize evidence for application for professional accreditation. For example, the myWorld (Wider Opportunities for Reflective Learning & Development) project found that maintaining an eportfolio could allow members to record their Continuing Professional Development (CPD), set targets and demonstrate how they have applied their skills in preparation for membership of the Chartered Management Institute. In addition, there is growing recognition of the ways eportfolios can be used to support professionals' continuing development. All 300,000 further education lecturers in the UK are now required to complete 30 hours of CPD, and the Institute for Learning is introducing the optional use of eportfolios to record this statutory requirement.

Another JISC-funded project, Flourish, is exploring the use of eportfolios to support learning, teaching and research practitioners at the University of Cumbria for a variety of professional purposes, including career review, academic qualification, professional accreditation and personal development. This project is also exploring the use of eportfolios for staff appraisals and has found that the move from a paper-based to an electronic approach leads to deeper analysis by the pilot participants of the nature of appraisal itself.

WORK BASED LEARNING/ EMPLOYMENT

Early work on portfolios to support employability in the UK began during the 1990s as part of the government's Enterprise in Higher Education (EHE) initiative which placed emphasis on the need for the undergraduate curriculum to prepare students for the world of work and for lifelong learning. The focus was on active learning, transferable skills development, and flexibility and adaptability. A major UK research project sponsored by the Quality Assurance Agency in 2000 obtained input from a sample of eighteen major graduate employers and seven professional and statutory bodies to inform the development of progress files in higher education. This provided important evidence of employer expectations in relation to the nature of graduate skills:

Overall, employers emphasized that PDP skills learned by students in their undergraduate years are crucial (and indeed constitute the first concrete step) for lifelong learning, management of their

own careers and to enable the widest possible contribution to performance improvement in organizations (Edwards, 2000, p. 6).

As a result, the UK government's University for Industry (Ufi) adopted these findings by providing opportunities for employees to fit learning into their professional lives through reflective work-based learning. The Ufi, now known as Learndirect, is based on a distributed campus with multiple hubs (1000 centers) connecting individual purchaser-learners to HE providers.

New developments in the senior school curriculum, in line with the widening participation agenda, include diplomas that are intended to provide an alternative route to the established qualifications of GCSEs and A levels for students aged 14-19. The University of Nottingham's JOSEPH Project, funded by JISC, is developing web services to link eportfolios and information, advice and guidance for those studying or considering studying engineering.

Other JISC projects in work-based settings include the sharing of reflections with mentors and peers in HE courses. For example, the WoLF project, a collaboration between Leicester University and Leicester College, is investigating how Pocket PCs support portfolio development by primary school teaching assistants in foundation degree courses. Ensuring that all assistants are professionally qualified is a priority for the UK government, and a foundation degree is the main route for assistants wanting to gain HE qualifications. Thirty students involved in a Foundation Degree in Educational Studies are using Pocket PCs to systematically record activities and develop a portfolio of evidence of their work in classrooms. Normally, they would rely on pen and paper, because it is too awkward to use laptops in a hectic classroom. WoLF is exploring new ways of recording learning experiences, such as reflective logs and personal development profiles through the redesign of course content for mobile learning devices and through integration with institutional online learning environments. It is also exploring how mobile devices can be used to provide learning resources in a mobile digital "briefcase," enabling learners to integrate learning occurring in multiple spaces (i.e., workplace (classrooms), college, home, and on the move) and to record their classroom observations.

TRANSITION/APPLICATION

Using portfolios to support movement between educational institutions, or between work and education, is a long-term aim for many projects. Work has been done on the development of presentational portfolios for different audiences. For example, the JISC-funded myWorld project included the use of an eportfolio to support transition from FE to HE and from HE to employment. Plumpton Further Education College enabled students in their final year of the Viticulture BSc to take a career development module. An eportfolio was included to encourage learners to reflect on their personal skills and to collect and select evidence to support their job applications. Rather than producing a standard CV, the learners were encouraged to use it as a development tool to track skills and experience. They could see the benefits of enriching their CVs in this way and felt it could give them a competitive advantage with employers. By providing potential employers with a link to supplementary information about their experiences in their eportfolio, applicants could help differentiate themselves and give "a better insight into what [they're] about" (JISC, 2007d, p. 16).

Evaluation of the MyWorld project indicates the value of developing an eportfolio in supporting reflection on current achievements and strengths and in mapping areas for further development. For these users, of key importance was the assurance that the data was secure, transferrable and would be valued by employers (Hartnell-Young

et al., 2007). Interestingly, users were already demanding Web2.0 type functionality of eportfolio tools in 2006.

It is intriguing to note that unlike recent focus groups with employers conducted by several JISC projects, the 2001 QAA study found that most employers put the:

strongest emphasis on the process of PDP because it adds value ... by helping students reflect on their experiences and improve their ability to articulate and demonstrate resulting competencies during recruitment activities (Edwards, 2001, p. 3).

Yorke and Knight (2004) affirm the findings of this study, arguing that employers want to appoint staff who can demonstrate "employability skills," such as critical thinking, self-evaluation/assessment, teamwork, adaptability, flexibility and interpersonal skills.

The recent JISC funded HEEPSS (Higher Education E-Portfolio Scenario Study) project set out to examine the possibility of an academic providing an eportfolio CV that contained validated qualification information as well as applicant-provided evidence for the job specification to a future employer. While it found that it would be possible to provide the "eportfolio CV" that would allow validation and verification of qualifications and achievements and confidential sharing of information with referees, the issue remained as to whether this would be of additional value to the employer who was necessarily controlled by employment regulations and had a limited amount of time to read applications. The HEEPSS project raises the question as to how this information can be usefully implemented for an application purpose even if it was captured as part of PDP and assessment.

The ways that audiences such as employers value and incorporate eportfolios seem critical at this stage in their development. For example, the JISC funded Epistle project's final report in July 2007 stated that:

Users need to have a clear demonstration of the longer term benefits of using an e-Portfolio, beyond immediate applications. The key driver would seem to be whether the concept is adopted wide-scale by employers, to pull through demand along the whole chain (JISC, 2007c, p. 14).

Other JISC projects have focused on the use of e-portfolios to support the transition from further to higher education in order to support students as they move from a high-support environment to a low-support environment. The TransPortALL project (Transfer of Portfolios Assisting Lifelong Learning), which supports the development of key skills, and the Kent PLPP (Personal Learning Portal Pilot) project are two examples. These JISC-funded projects faced technical challenges in relation to transition, as the act involves the transfer of learner data and its security. A Shibboleth-based authentication system for eportfolios has been developed and tested, and lightweight standards, i.e., UK LeaP2.0, have been developed through the JISC Portfolio SIG as a response to the low uptake of other approaches to eportfolio standards, e.g., IMS.

What is clear from this work is that, given resources, JISC projects are able to transfer data between systems, i.e., between school and FE college, FE and HEI, school and HEI, etc. The possibility of achieving this across a region, rather than between single institutions, has also been explored. A key project in this area has been the RIPPL project (Regional Interoperability Project on Progression for Lifelong Learning). This set out in 2005 to pilot the transfer of data directly from the City of Nottingham Passport, the main post-16 PDP system within the City of Nottingham, into the different HE PDP systems at the University of Nottingham and Nottingham Trent University to support learner admissions and transitions, thus joining successive phases of study, pre-HE

and HE. The project was able to demonstrate a single learner journey across five transitions from school to work and prototyped an electronic FE application process.

Current regional projects, as with other JISC projects, are mapping and testing the scenarios for use of eportfolios. The JISC e-Portfolio Reference Model project scoped the eportfolio domain with a focus on eportfolios for transition. This project was influential in the JISC exploration of an eFramework that is mapping the web services required for the eportfolio scenarios of use. This is seen as a key requirement if Web 2.0 thin eportfolio approaches, which involve the user drawing on data from multiple, distributed online repositories, are to be a reality.

CONCLUSION AND IMPLICATIONS

The development and widespread implementation of eportfolios in the UK, while encouraged and funded by the government, is not without difficulties. The report of a northeast regional collaboration around eportfolio progression pathways with illustrative studies (the EPICS project (2005-6) illuminates some of the key issues that need to be addressed in order for wider uptake of eportfolios to occur. It recognizes that these changes are highly disruptive in that they:

throw up needs for organizational change; changes to governance; changes in the roles of many staff, and the consequent need for staff development, changes to pedagogy, and hence to the nature and shape and form of courses, and the consequent need for educational development support; changes to the student's "contract" with their HEI or FE College.... (JISC, 2006, p. 4).

We must wonder how effective short-term projects can be in shaping sustainable change. We recognize that developing collaboration on a regional scale takes time, and a focus on a number of long-term projects could be more effective than short-term ones. JISC projects can provide an impetus for change and support the recognition of the need for change, but, for it to be sustainable, the major resource has to come from the key life-long learning partners themselves. This requires a change to a more collaborative culture than the traditionally competitive organizational culture.

This chapter has provided an overview of UK eportfolio developments in the areas of assessment, personal development planning/continuing professional development, transition/application and work based learning/employment. These appear in the purpose-process matrix set out in Figure 1 that was developed as a result of exploring current work in this area. The matrix is a work in progress, and there are likely to be other contexts of use of portfolios that are not represented here, such as the possibility that its use to directly support the curriculum may be another discrete context. Mapping the processes involved has revealed that information retrieval, capturing evidence, planning, reflection, feedback, collaboration and presentation are the key processes involved in e-portfolio work. However, the purpose/context influences the processes involved, and it is clear that available eportfolio systems tend not to be flexible enough to meet these. It appears that a key drive for change in relation to the use of eportfolios is whether they can be shown to add value to the learners' and other users' experiences, and there is more work to be done to demonstrate this within the four purposes/contexts identified in this chapter. This calls for a more systematic approach to supporting projects to explore the evidence for this "added value."

The challenges involved with more widespread use of eportfolios are likely to continue to be influenced by the changing nature of the technologies in everyday use, currently being shaped by Web2.0, and the need to provide institutional, regional, national and international approaches to storing, organizing and delivering information to meet user needs. The nature of these developments requires sustained collaboration and changes to established practice that may be problematic.

REFERENCES

Boud, D. (2006). Foreword. In Bryan, C., & Clegg, K. (Eds.), *Innovative assessment in higher education*. London, UK: Routledge.

Boud, D., & Falchikov, N. (Eds.). (2007). *Rethinking assessment in higher education*. London, UK: Routledge.

Boud, D., Keogh, R., & Walker, D. (Eds.). (1985). *Reflection: turning experience into learning*. London, UK: Kogan Page.

Bryan, C., & Clegg, K. (Eds.). (2006). *Innovative Assessment in higher education*. London, UK: Routledge.

Commission of the European Communities. (2001). *Making a European area of lifelong learning a reality*. Brussels, Belgium: Author.

Dearing, R. (1997). *Higher education in the learning society - The report of the National Committee of Inquiry into higher education*. London, UK: HMSO. Retrieved July 20, 2008, from http://www.leeds.ca.uk/educol/ncihe

Department for Education and Skills. (2005). *Harnessing technology: Transforming learning and children's services*. London, UK: Department for Education and Skills.

Edwards, G. (2000). *Connecting PDP to employer needs and the world of work* (Project Report to QAA). Retrieved July 20, 2008, from http://www.qaa.ac.uk

Fielden, J. (2007). *Global horizons for UK universities*. London, UK: Council for Industry and Higher Education. Retrieved September 9, 2008, from http://www.cihe-uk.com/docs/PUBS/0711IntHEsumm.pdf

Gibbs, G. (2006). How assessment frames student learning. In Bryan, C., & Clegg, K. (Eds.), *Innovative assessment in higher education* (pp. 23–36). London, UK: Routledge.

Hartnell-Young, E., Harrison, C., Crook, C., Joyes, G., Davies, L., & Fisher, T. (2007). *The impact of e-portfolios on learning.* Coventry, UK: British Educational Communications and Technology Agency (Becta).

Irons, A. (2008). *Enhancing learning through formative assessment and feedback.* London, UK: Routledge.

JISC. (2006). *Epics project final report.* Retrieved August 22, 2008, from http://www.jisc.ac.uk/whatwedo/programmes/programme_edistributed/epics.aspx#downloads

JISC. (2007a). *Effective practice with e-assessment.* Retrieved August 22, 2008, from http://www.jisc.ac.uk/media/documents/themes/elearning/effpraceassess.pdf

JISC. (2007b). *ISLE: Individualised support for learning through e-portfolios: All roads lead to enhanced learning?* Retrieved August 22, 2008, from http://www.jisc.ac.uk/media/documents/programmes/elearningsfc/sfcbookletisle.pdf

JISC. (2007c). *epistle: Individualised support for learning through e-portfolios: All roads lead to enhanced learning?* Retrieved August 22, 2008, from http://www.jisc.ac.uk/media/documents/programmes/elearningsfc/sfcbookletisle.pdf

JISC. (2007d). *myWorld final report.* Retrieved August 22, 2008, from http://www.jisc.ac.uk/whatwedo/programmes/programme_edistributed/myworld.aspx

JISC. (2008a). *eportfolios Infokit.* Retrieved August 22, 2008, from http://www.jiscinfonet.ac.uk/infokits/e-portfolios/

JISC. (2008b). *Circular 08/08: Projects in the areas of curriculum delivery, assessment and course advertising.* Retrieved August 22, 2008, from http://www.jisc.ac.uk/fundingopportunities/funding_calls/2008/06/circular808.aspx

Knight, P., & Yorke, M. (2003). *Assessment, learning and employability.* Maidenhead, UK: Open University.

Pellegrino, J., Chuowsky, N., & Glaser, R. (Eds.). (2001). *Knowing what students know: the science and design of educational assessment.* Washington, DC: National Academy Press.

Qualifications and Curriculum Authority. (2004). *A proposed blueprint for delivering e-assessment.* Retrieved July 20, 2008, from http://www.qca.org.uk/libraryAssets/media/6995_blueprint_for_e-assessment.rtf

Quality Assurance Agency for Higher Education (QAA). (2003). *Learning from subject review 1993-2001.* Retrieved July 20, 2008, from http://www.qaa.ac.uk/reviews/subjectReview/learningfromSubjectReview/learningFromSubjectReview.pdf

Ravet, S. (2007). *For an ePortfolio enabled architecture.* Retrieved June 11, 2007, from http://www.eife-l.org/publications/eportfolio/documentation/positionpaper

Rowntree, D. (1977). *Assessing students: How shall we know them?* London, UK: Harper and Row.

Universities, U. K. (2007). *Beyond the honours degree classification: The Burgess Group final report.* Retrieved September 10, 2008, from http://bookshop.universitiesuk.ac.uk/downloads/Burgess_final.pdf

Yorke, M., & Knight, P. (2004). *Learning, curriculum and employability in higher education.* London, UK: Routledge Falmer.

Chapter 2
Reflective Practice:
Political Paper Tiger, Bone of Contention in the Professions, or Pedagogical Challenge?

Gerd Bräuer
University of Education Freiburg, Germany

Brady Spangenberg (translator)[1]
Purdue University, USA

ABSTRACT

This chapter discusses the theoretical, practical, and institutional foundations of reflective practice through two frames of reference: How to initiate, organize, and use reflective practice in the classroom as a form of meta-cognitive learning; and how to initiate, organize, and use reflective practice and its theoretical implications for professionals at an institution.

INTRODUCTION

As part of the discussion about a new learning and achievement culture in the systems of primary, secondary and higher education within the German-speaking countries, there has been much said about documenting, evaluating, and reflecting on learning processes (cf. Gläser-Zikuda & Hascher, 2007). Facilitating the development of such competencies stands at the center of instructional and pedagogical efforts, and portfolios in

particular are currently enjoying a swell of interest. However, there is a sense that portfolios are used because they are en vogue or because they have been ordered from above, and one must weather this craze. This contrasts with the more earnest approach that emphasizes the use of portfolios because they express a growing and maturing culture of learning and achievement whose possibilities will be discussed in more detail in the following sections. When the former sense prevails, the behavior of the portfolio-maker remains relatively unchanged, as if he or she only wants to use the portfolio as a means to achieve a better

DOI: 10.4018/978-1-4666-0143-7.ch002

grade or professional recognition (Bräuer, 2006a). But when used as part of a culture of learning and achievement, portfolios can serve as a means to transition between learning processes.

The following discussion will work to describe the Anglo-American concept of reflective practice in more detail in order to come up with suggestions on how to adapt this concept to the specific needs of education in Europe in general and in specific regard to electronic portfolios. The motivation for this article stems from an understanding of reflection as a situated, meta-cognitive activity that not only enhances competencies in documenting, analyzing, interpreting, comparing, and evaluating learning (Bräuer, 2007a, p. 48, 2009, p. 162), but also directly augments the particular activity being observed. When learners experience that working with a portfolio—a writing portfolio, for example—contributes to their continued long-term development as writers and readers, then they are able to better understand the reason for the portfolio work instead of merely mimicking some sort of predetermined model. In Anglo-American literature on social constructivist writing pedagogy, this type of process-oriented textual work is characterized as "meaning making," an expression that triggers not only personal involvement but also stronger motivation on the part of students and instructors alike.

The following sections will more closely examine the implied connections between reflection, situated learning, and qualified practice. Major areas of focus will be the theoretical, practical, and institutional foundations of reflective practice observed from the two frames of reference noted below. These frames of reference simultaneously embody, in my understanding, core objectives of teacher education and professional development:

a. How to initiate, organize, and use reflective practice in the classroom as a form of meta-cognitive learning?

b. How to initiate, organize, and use reflective practice, and its theoretical implications, for professional development within an institution?

An altered culture of learning and achievement must not only begin in a school-based professional context but must equally be integrated in the whole university curriculum particularily in teacher education programs. Nevertheless, this essay will not discuss the use of reflective practice at the university-wide level. The author has considered this perspective elsewhere, from a writing research perspective (Bräuer, 2006b), from the perspective of research on institutional development (Bräuer et al., 2012), and from the stance of second language acquisition (Bräuer, 2009).

TERMS AND CONCEPTS

Reflective Practice

The term "reflective practice" stems from the work of Schön (1987), Hillocks (1995), and Bolton (2005), and it denotes a process of perceiving and taking advantage of stimuli for perceiving or reflecting back on one's own activity, which can occur, for example, when students are asked to write or read a text about writing or reading competencies. An individual can ignore these stimuli for various reasons, but this would mean that the acting individual will hardly, if at all, be aware of the effectiveness of his or her actions. In this way, the individual stands to repeat the ineffective strategy, ultimately allowing it to become routine. The acting individual will learn to accept these ineffective patterns of behavior as given and thus become less motivated to relearn different and perhaps more effective ways of doing things. When students in such situations are confronted with alternative strategies, they often react negatively, not infrequently in connection with the excuse: This is the way I always do it! The repeated behavioral pattern conveys a sense of flow to the individual, an air of familiarity, regardless of any inefficiencies perceived by an outside observer. The pattern facilitates the growth of a positive emotional attachment, which inevitably provides these students with reinforcement. An intuitive departure from the routine would here require first a conflict of such a degree that the students can no longer avoid or ignore the discrepancy. Based on these circumstances, the students would have to react not in the sense that they want to alter such habitualized behaviors but rather feel themselves forced to do so. In contrast, an *action* that stems from critical reflection about a particular behavioral pattern can, on an intrinsic motivational level, lead to a progressive and lasting development.

As long as non-reflective behavioral routines and extrinsically imposed behavioral changes dominate in learning and teaching processes, they will continue to impede not only attempts to optimize current behaviors but also attempts to transfer effective strategies into other fields of activity. If it remains unclear why a particular strategy is unsuccessful, then it will also be difficult to identify other conditions under which this strategy will contribute to the failure or success of an activity.

Within itself, practice already carries reflective elements according to Hillocks (1995), whereby these elements must necessarily be made known and operable in order to methodically optimize any given behavior. Based on these conditions, changes to already routinized behavior would be possible, because the actor still retains control of the "decision switch" and, with the help of a critical perspective, may be able to break the routine (Hillocks, 1995, p. 31).

For a description of the learning potential inherent in reflective practice, Hillocks borrows from North (1987, p. 33): One speaks of practice as inquiry, (altered) practice as a stimulus for its own habituation, when the basic situation of the routinized activity, oral reading in the classroom for example, becomes "alienated." In other words,

the routinized activity is confronted with an unfamiliar context (e.g., oral reading outside of the classroom) or with different standards (oral reading as a form of artistic recitation), so that the previously used skills, in this case, oral reading skills, must be adapted or supplemented in some way. This example of how to break up students' behavioral routines also creates an incentive to critically consider any routinized professional attitude that the instructor may have developed in connection with oral reading. Thus, in the new context of oral reading outside of the classroom or as a form of artistic recitation, it also becomes necessary for the instructor to consider modifying the content, approach, or pedagogy of a particular lesson plan. In this way, one can create incentives on both sides for continued and even expanded oral reading work in the classroom.

By critically questioning changes to one's practice, one seeks to examine, among other items, the basic ideas, beliefs, and values embedded within a particular behavior. Also included in this list are derivatives of the behavior, such as decision making processes and possible courses of action. Action, when used in conjunction with reflective practice, can thereby become an ever-opening field of learning that stimulates the continued development of a person's knowledge, skills, and personality.

Schön (1987, p. 157), nevertheless, emphasizes the enormous challenge posed by the openness and possible strangeness of strategies of action removed from their traditional routines. Frame experiments can determine the strength with which learning stimuli affect the students' individual capabilities and any available instructional assistance. These experiments are conducted by selecting and then producing a known quantity of behavioral demands in different contexts (e.g., oral reading activities first in front of familiar small groups, then in front of a larger peer audience, and finally in front of an unknown public audience outside of the school). The extent to which these demands fall within the participant's "zone of proximal development" (Vygotsky, 1987)—this goes both for learners as well as instructors—largely determines the amount of motivation he or she has to reflect and work on his or her learning processes. Educators are often asked to take learners as they are and yet maintain professional standards in the classroom, but this can only successfully happen within a framework of situated learning, namely a context of performance in which the individual, school, and society continuously negotiate solutions to their respective needs. The following discussion will describe the conditions of situated learning in more detail by looking at reflective writings assignments as part of portfolio work.

Situated Learning

School writing assignments are often characterized by an excess of didactic directedness, an expression that points to the efforts of instructors and administrators to achieve educational goals as defined by a discipline's traditional "canon" of methods and content. Neglected in this effort is the situatedness of learning (Lave & Wenger, 1991; Mandl, Gruber, & Renkl, 2002), namely the fact that learning occurs in a concrete, individual context that neither an educational canon nor a pedagogical concept can fully anticipate or model. In other words, when learning stems from a concrete social context, in particular from the social interaction between learners and their personal quests for information, it can only partially be directed from "outside" (cf. Wenger, 1998).

Historical Background

The didactic directedness of writing assignments has been significantly strengthened recently by attempts to turn traditional writing pedagogy, largely oriented on the criteria of individual genres, into a portfolio concept. The reason for this tendency lies in differing approaches to writing at the grade school and university levels in both German-speaking areas as well as Anglo-American educational environments. Without being able to delve into this point in more detail (for more on grade school differences see Bräuer, 1998, and on university differences Kruse, 2006), one should note at this point the following: The fundamental objectives of German-speaking writing pedagogy from the 1980's, which were largely process-oriented, have only now begun to gain acceptance in the language arts curriculum. While this change is occurring slowly at best, other disciplines have not even taken these steps. One example of this change is the idea of supplementing written corrections on a student's text with oral feedback and the possibility for revision (cf. Fix, 2006). The author's own experience with teacher education has shown that many instructors are not yet adequately prepared to integrate the objectives of process-oriented writing pedagogy into their classroom instruction practices.

In contrast, Anglo-American writing pedagogy since the 1980's, in particular the American composition approach, is able to draw from decades of professional experience and pedagogical research. Most importantly, it has not only recognized but also worked to address the need to integrate adequate forms of evaluation into writing instruction, which is largely based on the writers' individual processes of text production (cf. Belanoff & Dickson, 1991). In this case, the portfolio concept was adapted as a holistic measure to meet the needs of interdisciplinary and cross-curricular writing pedagogy. Here, the emphasis lies on both the process and the product (text production and genre), on learner-centered rather than text-centered reflection and evaluation (cf. Graves & Sunstein, 1992).

Terminology: Situated Learning—Authentic Learning

As a result of social interaction among learners, part of the aforementioned definition of situated learning, so-called "communities of practice" emerge (Wenger, 1998), namely groups of individuals with compatible information needs, collective spheres of activity, and growing collective identities. The members of these communities of practice (such as students collectively publishing a school newspaper) are, to each others' mutual advantage, generally willing to help each other. This takes place either as so-called "cognitive apprenticeship"—mental instruction in contrast to mechanical instruction—between experts and novices with regard to a particular activity or subject. Or it can also take place as "peer learning," which occurs between partners of similar knowledge and ability who are working on the same assignment. At different stages of the assignment, these partners then provide each other with critical feedback.

Lave and Wenger (1991), when speaking of situated learning, also speak of "negotiation of meaning," namely figuring out personal meaning for both parties: What does this (particular experience) actually have to do with me? With this type of open-ended assignment, there exists a strong motivating stimulus for learners. For example, it exists when the current, individual needs of students are molded into the subject of competency acquisition in schools, such as when students use language arts class time to report on their community engagement with the local press in reaction to recent destruction of public property. The situatedness of this type of instruction not only cultivates students' identities, but it also conveys a sense of belonging. Therefore, students experience situated learning as authentic learning. They can identify with their actions in a context of knowledge acquisition, peer interaction, and problem-solving and continue to do so as part of a collaborative process throughout and hopefully beyond the term of the assignment.

When the situatedness of the learning can be consciously perceived and didactically employed, authentic occasions for portfolio work as a mode of reflective practice will emerge through a multiplicity of ways: making sense of the subject ("negotia-

tion of meaning"), gaining a sense of belonging among learners, working within a community of practice, enhancing individual competencies for both learner and instructor, and improving future professional practice.

The following section will discuss how situated learning can be achieved through reflective practice in the center of portfolio work.

LEVELS OF REFLECTIVE PRACTICE

Before discussing reflective practice and some examples of how to implement situated reflection in the classroom, this section will first point to the levels at which reflective practice on a language level occurs and can therefore be observed and evaluated. Between 2003 and 2005, evidence was collected through research on application portfolios as part of the project, *Neue Wege in die Ausbildung* (New Paths to Education) (Iwan, 2006). The project was initiated and established through the *Perpetuum Novile* School Project GmbH at the BVJ Mannheim *Berufsvorbereitendes Jahr* (one year of vocational preparation for students without high school diploma). Up until then, very little research existed in the German-speaking community of portfolio practice that would explain why the more complex levels of reflective practice were hardly ever achieved in students' written accounts. Results of conversations with the BVJ students, which were intended to assess student knowledge levels during the project, suggested that the levels of reflection missing in students' written or oral accounts do not appear, or are only weakly defined, in their cognitive perception as well.

At the first level of reflective practice, characterized by documenting and describing, the individual collects and personally formulates impressions of the activity in a journal or portfolio folder. Those who do not pursue their reflections any further remain at the level of private discourse and are therefore only able to discuss conditionally their experiences with other learners and, therefore, receive fragmented evaluation about the quality of their own work. Here is a project journal entry from a student in a work experience program (Bräuer, 2005):

We had to drill holes.

[The student presents the activity without reference neither to broader importance nor to his individual performance or capabilities.]

In response to another student's inquiry, the student, later on, supplied the following addition:

We had to drill holes needed for the screw connected to the holder.

[The student describes his activity as part of a broader scheme but does not relate it to his individual performance or capabilities.]

Beginning at the second level of reflective practice, characterized by analyzing and interpreting what has been documented or described, the individual starts to question the quality of his or her performance and give meaning to what he or she has experienced. Newly acquired knowledge is connected to existing knowledge, which also leads to new insights. The quality of reflective practice achieved here also serves to deepen the individual's current learning process, and it also allows for his or her learning to become visible and also comparable to other peers' achievements. In this light, here is some expanded commentary from the above-cited student's project journal:

I drilled holes for the screws connected to the holder.

[The student understands the activity as part of a broader scheme and relates it to his individual performance; however there is no mention of the quality of the student's performance.]

In response to another student's inquiry, the student added the following:

Unfortunately, the screws did not fit after the first try, so I had to re-drill the holes.

[The student understands the activity as part of a broader scheme and relates it to his individual performance. The student discusses the quality of his performance but does not mention any possible alternatives.]

The third level of reflective praxis, characterized by comparing what has been learned with one's own goals and audience expectations, allows individuals to evaluate not only what has been accomplished but also the path they have taken to get there. Standards and competency descriptions, understood as the collected experiences and knowledge from a particular discipline, help students and instructors alike to classify their performance capabilities in an educational and professional-oriented context, to create new goals, and to plan further efforts. Here again is an excerpt from the student's revised commentary, which is now part of an extended application portfolio:

I drilled holes for the screws connected to the holder. Unfortunately, the screws did not fit after my first try, and I had to re-drill the holes. The next time, I will check the size of the drill before drilling.

[The student understands the activity as part of a broader scheme and relates it to his individual performance. The student discusses the quality of his performance and mentions some possible alternatives.]

In response to another student's inquiry, the student supplied the following addition:

I drilled holes for the screw connected to the holder. Unfortunately, the screws did not fit after my first try, and I had to re-drill the holes. The next time, I will check the size of the drill before drilling. ... As my problems with drilling show, the work of a manufacturing mechanic requires foresight and attention to detail. Sometimes, I show these capabilities, for example, when driving my car. But I also want to apply these skills to my future professional training.

In this didactically arranged interplay between the writer and the peer tutor across the above mentioned levels of reflective practice within a portfolio, the student writer effectively improves his reflection capabilities based on scaffolding questions provided by his peer. These reflection capabilities can ultimately contribute to the development of transfer competencies. These are related to what Betty K. Garner, an American expert on lifelong learning, has referred to as "metability," namely a person's ability to alter his or her practice through a continuous interactive cycle of thinking, feeling, and creating (Garner, 2007).

DISCOURSES OF REFLECTIVE PRACTICE

In the context of the above-mentioned levels of reflective practice, the following section will introduce the different discourses that are necessary for illustrating and developing reflective practice competency (Bräuer, 2003, 2009). The discourses and levels of reflective practice are deeply interconnected, whereby actual reflection is conditioned and bounded by the level and type of discourse that can be achieved. The learning potential of reflective practice can only be exploited through the interplay of all discourses and levels.

Private Discourse

Self-reflection in a journal or portfolio or feedback among peers are forms of private discourse that provide writers with a protected space in which they can begin to engage critically with what they have achieved so far. The subject of this discourse is largely that which has been documented or described. Through reflection, the student becomes more aware of his or her working and learning processes by perceiving the traces of his or her actions. The student thereby constructs a foundation of understanding upon which he or she can later build when moving on to the next level of reflection.

Semi-Private Discourse

Writing consultations, group project discussions, and feedback on journal work from less well-known or trusted peers are all forms of a discourse that require additional motivation on the part of the reflecting person, because these reflective forms provide less predictable results. Among other reasons, writers often enter this type of discursive space in order to gain additional information, ideas, and support but also to test the quality and potential success of their work. Because individuals with different levels of experience and knowledge come together in these spaces, one must determine in advance the framework of the exchange and provide a vocabulary understood by all participants. Such shared points of reference or vocabulary may stem from feedback criteria inherent in a particular lesson, from a specific learning phase, or desired finished product

Public Discourse

The portfolio can be understood as a medium of public discourse insofar as it presents knowledge gained through reflective practice completed at both the private and semi-private levels. The portfolio serves as the window into both the foundation and context(s) of learning processes and products. The creator of the portfolio demonstrates his or her command of the collected artifacts by presenting them alongside evaluation standards—both of his or her own and those of others. In this way, the portfolio can also be understood as the potential sum of all three discourse forms of reflective practice, out of which future plans of action inevitably grow.

Practical Excursus

The following is an example of how the different levels and discourses of reflective practice interact based on a user description of Web 2.0 media for an electronic platform. The previous excerpts from the application portfolio of a student at the BVJ-Mannheim showed how the student qualified his reflective practice; this example will serve to emphasize the interplay among the different discourses of reflective practice. The discussion will focus on four main points, namely how these discourses a) lead the individual learner to form knowledge based on peer feedback, b) create multiple linguistic and visual frameworks with which the learner can express this knowledge, c) provide a continuous forum for "shared knowledge" (Mandl, Gruber, & Renkl, 2002, p. 167), and d) sustain a "community of practice" that will allow participants to find a sense of belonging among learners and thereby facilitate the expansion and refinement of their knowledge. A study conducted at the University of Salzburg (Austria) revealed how learning with Web 2.0 tools not only facilitates the interplay within a learning community but also affects the behavior and actions of individual community members in complex ways (Paus-Hasenbrink, Jadin, & Wijnen, 2007). In conjunction with the learning arrangements proposed by the Salzburg Project, it would be interesting to investigate how the elements of reflective practice used in the study (Weblog and Wiki) affected the learners' insights. In addition, this investigation may also reveal the learning potential of other reflective media, such as the e-portfolio.

Here is an excerpt from the information about creating e-portfolios for the Comenius Project 2.1, "Scriptorium," that illustrates three discourses.

The information can be found on the program's electronic learning platform at http://www.scriptorium-project.org (Bräuer, 2007b):

By using the course Website and tools named in parentheses (see upper and left-hand menu bars), one can find support for your writing and portfolio work. During this process, users will interact through a combination of private, semi-public, and public discourses that are all intended to promote the writing process. Different kinds of texts will emerge in this process, particularly those that belong to the so-called "helping genres" (texts that facilitate the collection and processing of information necessary for a more complex target text) and "transfer genres" (texts composed for a separate purpose but that can nevertheless add to the development or conceptualization of another text). Through this type of "text recycling," ideas can be developed and tested. This exchange of ideas can lead to further insights, and the procedures and results can eventually be reflected upon and presented in different discourses:

Private Discourse

Personal planning ("My Calendar", upper menu bar): *There is not much space available. Therefore, formulate your concerns as concretely and concisely as possible.*

Devising and developing ideas ("Personal Blog," upper menu bar): *How to maintain your ideas, impressions, and evaluations together in a learning journal? What happens when, how, why, and with what consequence? What is the next step?*

Communicating impressions ("Personal Blog," upper menu bar): *How do you perceive the results from the last few sessions? In your opinion, what would you do differently?*

Individual exchange in real-time ("Chat," left menu bar): *Discuss any questions you currently* have with a trusted colleague. Formulate these questions in concise, individual statements in order to retain the flow of your discussion.

Semi-Public Discourse

Creating a working group: *search out partners with whom you can discuss your portfolio work. Build a group with these partners and inform the workshop director/facilitator of this group and its members.*

Continuously collecting and commenting on the materials in your portfolio ("Groups," "Documents/Links"): *Comment on each entry in the portfolio: What type of document is it? Where did I get it from? What is the most important aspect about the content? How does this document relate to other material in the portfolio? What have I learned through interacting this new portfolio entry?*

Synchronic exchange about time-sensitive concerns ("Group," "Chat," cf. private discourse): *Reduce your discussion to a single person. Discuss only specific, limited concerns.*

Asynchronous exchange about complex inquiries as well as feedback on ideas and drafts ("Group," "Forum"): *Formulate focused, procedure-oriented inquiries. Explain the context of your inquiry. For what purpose do you need the information?*

Collective composition of texts through cooperative writing ("Group," "Wiki"): *Arrange a clearly defined working/writing contract with a definitive objective and transparent distribution and description of the roles involved (Who works on which focal points? Who takes over from whom at which stages of text production?).*

Collective definition of a portfolio about the workshop: *Which strategies, methods, and tech-*

niques have proven to be valuable in our group practice? How can these be described so that other users can easily understand them? (see also "Wiki, "Group Forum," "Tool-Box")*

Public Discourse

Documentation of current instruction and commentary: *("Blog," left menu bar)*

Continual collection and storage of group materials: *("Documents/Links," left menu bar)*

Presentation and review of texts in the final phase of composition and commentary from workshop leaders or experts: *("Assignments," left menu bar)*

Collective adherence to fundamental principles and knowledge (e.g., portfolio for writing tutoring): *("Wiki," left menu bar)*

Organizational conversations: *("Dates," left menu bar) After having created your portfolio based on the framework of the professional development session/workshop, you can save it in one of the following formats—depending upon how you intend to use the material later.*

E-Portfolio*: if you are writing an introductory text for your readers and would like to list the links to selected material on the learning platform. This format also allows you to comment briefly on the material.*

ZIP-Hypertext*: if you are assembling the selected material (platform and any additional materials) in a Word document and would like to organize individual main points into some type of sensible order for your readers. As a ZIP-file, you can send this portfolio to other persons at your discretion.*

Printed Folder or Reader*: if you are printing off material from the learning platform (and* *elsewhere) or possibly reformatting the materials visually and would like to present the information in a folder or reader.*

MEASURES FOR ENHANCING THE QUALITY OF REFLECTIVE PRACTICE

When working toward developing students' reflective practice one should move slowly by scaffolding the writing process based on the different levels of reflective practice (cf. the portfolio example from BVJ-Mannheim). These levels should be applied within changing discourses and through interaction with changing feedback partners (peer, writing tutor, instructor, external expert). Questions relating to "what," "how," and "why," related to the reflected experience, are the most suitable for feedback. These questions can also serve to orient expectations and/or conditions inherent in the different discourses in which the learners will have to convey their reflections.

In the sense of situated learning, which was defined in the introduction, one should consistently strive to work in an audience-oriented fashion within the framework of a particular level or discourse of reflective practice. This means reflecting individuals should be able to recognize a specific and justifiable purpose in each reflective assignment. At the semi-private or public levels, diverse feedback opportunities should be addes, so that learners can experience the effectiveness of their reflection from different perspectives.

Facilitators of reflective practice should also remember not to focus too closely on one type of reflection only. Oral and written reflection can be usefully combined because each type creates different possibilities for enhancing reflective abilities. Individual reflection, such as in a journal, should consistently occur in connection with the entire portfolio work, so that reflection performed in a private discourse can address the challenge of meeting the expectations of a growing and more complex audience.

ORGANIZATIONAL COMPONENTS OF REFLECTIVE PRACTICE

In order to unlock the learning potential of reflective practice, the following components should be considered when including portfolio work in school education or professional training:

- Have the parameters for the particular form of reflective practice been defined?
  - **Example:** Do the participants know how to keep a journal, give feedback to their peers, or create a portfolio? Do they have the time and opportunity to use reflective practice effectively?
- Is the targeted level and medium of reflective practice realistic in the sense of Vygotsky's "zone of proximal development?"
  - **Example:** Do the participants have enough experience working with journal writing, or would a dialogue journal, in which two persons write back and forth to each other, scaffold individual reflection?
- Is there a justifiable reason for reflection, particularly as it relates to the current learning process and educational development of the participants?
  - **Example:** Students create an internship portfolio with the knowledge that it can in the near future be used as material for a job application portfolio.
- Is the reflective work set in a larger social context that obliges students to assume responsibility within a clearly defined public space?
  - **Example:** An entry in the internship journal about a particular assignment at work is also sent as an eMail to peers who have to take over the same assignment at work on the following day of the internship.

- Have the evaluation standards of the desired reflection been clearly defined and communicated?
  - **Example:** The peer mentioned above must be able to completely understand the reflective email and the conditions and requirements described there in order to be able to succeed at work on the following day of the internship.

OUTLOOK: REFLECTIVE PRACTICE AND ACTION RESEARCH

The professional field of primary and secondary education can through reflective practice become visible and serviceable when the field itself is open to systematic research and exploration. The approach named "action research" is most suitable for such an analysis (cf. Altrichter, Posch, & Somekh, 1993) because its methodology focuses on changes in practice over a given time period. Burns (2007) understands action research as "practice as inquiry," which is similar to Stephen North's assessment of reflective practice: Activating stimuli gleaned from practice within others in the field and using research questions and the responsibility that these create as a means to change individual practice (cf. Burns, 2007, p. 11). Darling-Hammond and McLaughlin (1995, p. 597) demand that up-to-date professional development offer regular opportunities for self-reflection: "Occasions for teachers to reflect critically on their practice and to fashion new knowledge and beliefs about content, pedagogy, and learners." Smith and Sela (2005) see in action research the additional potential for a successful transfer of knowledge and ability from one discourse community (teacher education programs) to another (in-service teachers). This can happen in multiple ways, but Smith and Sela argue that through reflective practice student teachers will not only be able to adapt what they have learned at the university but also develop a foundation for an investigative, self-conscious attitude throughout their professional careers. Thus, they will be able to investigate the needs, problems, and questions that exist in their particular educational context, and the potential answers will enhance these instructors' awareness of their own professional practice and thereby contribute to the continued development of a specific professional field.

Below is a list of suggestions combining ideas by Levin and Rock (2003) and Smith and Sela (2005) for undertaking action research in a way that meaningfully mingles university studies and professional work within the framework of reflective practice:

- Observe a particular aspect of instruction and individually analyze it in a research journal.
- Identify a central problem in the observed instructional aspect.
- Search current scholarship on and reported professional experiences with the identified problem.
- Create an action plan to overcome the identified problem in practice.
- Implement and document the process of problem-solving.
- Conceptualize or write out what you have learned in terms of your own professional practice.

For the analysis of primary and secondary education as a professional field, York-Barr et al. tested the following means of enacting reflective practice, which they termed the "reflective practice spiral" (2006, p. 19). When using the approach, insights gained from individual reflection are then tested and developed in dialogue with (learning/working) partners, a team, an institution, and the entire professional field:

- Journal writing
- Dialogue journal

- Structured dialogue
- Instructed storytelling
- Reflective minutes of a meeting
- School-wide steering committee
- School development portfolio

The listed assignments and media integrate the different levels of reflective practice in a didactically effective manner because these learning arrangements enable participants to proceed step-by-step as they formulate specific responses to observed practice, connect what they have observed to their pre-existing knowledge, and generate and implement new and professionally necessary knowledge. However, it is not yet clear how much of an actual, lasting effect new insights gained from action research will have on the professional practice of students and teachers alike, but researchers are currently looking into the educational impact of particular media on reflective practice, such as the research journal (cf. Zuckermann, 2007). Still, many questions remain. Perhaps in the future we will be able to grant the phenomenon of reflective practice a more prominent place both in the classroom and in education as a whole due to its focused emphasis on human learning.

REFERENCES

Altrichter, H., Posch, P., & Somekh, B. (1993). *Teachers investigate their work*. London, UK: Routledge.

Belanoff, P., & Dickson, M. (1991). *Portfolios: Process and product. Portsmouth, NH: Boynton/ Cook, Heinemann. Bolton, G. (2005). Reflective practice: Writing and professional development* (2nd ed.). Thousand Oaks, CA: Sage.

Bräuer, G. (1998). *Schreibend lernen: Grundlagen einer theoretischen und praktischen Schreibpädagogik*. Innsbruck, Austria: Studienverlag.

Bräuer, G. (2003). *Schreiben als reflexive Praxis: Tagebuch, Arbeitsjournal, Portfolio* (2nd ed.). Freiburg, Germany: Fillibach.

Bräuer, G. (2005). *Analyse der Portfolio-Arbeit im Projekt "Neue Wege in die Ausbildung"* (unpublished project report). Mannheim, Germany: BVJ/perpetuum novile.

Bräuer, G. (2006a). Keine verordneten Hochglanz-Portfolios, bitte! Die Korruption einer schönen Idee? In Brunner, I., Häcker, T., & Winter, F. (Eds.), *Das Handbuch Portfolioarbeit. Konzepte, Anregungen, Erfahrungen aus Schule und Lehrerbildung* (pp. 257–261). Seelze-Velber, Germany: Kallmeyer.

Bräuer, G. (2006b). Eine andere Schreibkultur für die Schule bereits im Studium erleben. *Journal für LehrerInnenbildung, 3*(6), 8–13.

Bräuer, G. (2007a). Portfolios in der Lehrerausbildung als Grundlage für eine neue Lernkultur in der Schule. In M. Gläser-Zikuda & T. Hascher (Eds.), *Lernprozesse dokumentieren, reflektieren und beurteilen* (45-62). Bad Helbrunn, Germany: Klinkhardt.

Bräuer, G. (2007b). *Lernplattform und Portfolio* (Arbeitsmaterial, Projekt Scriptorium). Retrieved January 12, 2011, from http://www.scriptorium-project.org/claroline/claroline/document/document.php

Bräuer, G. (2009). Reflecting the practice of foreign language learning in portfolios. *German as a Foreign Language*. Retrieved January 1, 2012, from http://www.gfl-journal.de

Bräuer, G., Keller, M., & Winter, F. (Eds.). (2012). *Portfolio macht Schule. Unterrichts- und Schulentwicklung mit Portfolio.* Seelze-Velber, Germany: Klett-Kallmeyer.

Burns, D. (2007). *Systemic action research: A strategy for whole system change.* Bristol, UK: The Policy Press.

Darling-Hammond, L., & McLaughlin, M. L. (1995). Policies that support professional development in an era of reform. *Phi Delta Kappan, 76*(8), 587–604.

Fix, M. (2006). *Texte schreiben: Schreibprozesse im Deutschunterricht.* Paderborn, Germany: Schöningh.

Garner, B. K. (2007). *Getting to got it! Helping struggling students learn how to learn.* Alexandria, VA: Association for Supervision and Curricukum Development.

Gläser-Zikuda, M., & Hascher, T. (Eds.). (2007). *Lernprozesse dokumentieren, reflektieren und beurteilen. Lerntagebuch und Portfolio in Bildungsforschung und Bildungspraxis.* Bad Helbrunn, Austria: Klinkhardt.

Hillocks, G. Jr. (1995). *Teaching writing as reflective practice.* New York, NY: Teachers College Press.

Iwan, R. (2006). Wie man schreibend den Weg von der Schule in die Ausbildung finden kann. In Bräuer, G. (Ed.), *Schreiben(d) lernen: Ideen und Projekte für die Schule* (2nd ed., pp. 71–83). Hamburg, Germany: Edition Körber-Stiftung.

Kruse, O. (2006). The origins of writing in the disciplines. *Written Communication, 23*(3), 331–352. doi:10.1177/0741088306289259

Lave, J., & Wenger, E. (1991). *Situated learning: Legitimate peripheral participation.* New York, NY: Cambridge University Press.

Levin, B. B., & Rock, T. C. (2003). The effects of collaborative action research on preservice and experienced teacher partners in professional development schools. *Journal of Teacher Education, 54*(2), 135–149. doi:10.1177/0022487102250287

Mandl, H., Gruber, H., & Renkl, A. (2002). Situiertes Lernen in multimedialen Lernumgebungen. In Issing, L. J., & Klimsa, P. (Eds.), *Information und Lernen mit Multimedia und Internet* (3rd ed., pp. 138–148). Winheim, Germany: Beltz Psychologie Verlags Union.

North, S. (1987). *The making of knowledge in composition: Portrait of an emerging field.* Portsmouth, NH: Heinemann.

Paus-Hasebrink, I., Jadin, T., & Wijnen, C. (2007). *Aktualisierter Bericht zur Evaluation des Projekts "Web 2.0-Klasse."* Retrieved January 19, 2008, from http://beat.doebe.li/bibliothek/b03924.html

Schön, D. A. (1987). *Educating the reflective practitioner: Toward a new design for teaching and learning in the professions.* San Francisco, CA: Jossey-Bass.

Smith, K., & Sela, O. (2005). Action research as a bridge between pre-service teacher education and in-service professional development for students and teacher educators. *European Journal of Teacher Education, 28*(3), 293–310. doi:10.1080/02619760500269418

Vygotsky, L. S. (1978). *Mind in society: The development of higher psychological processes.* Cambridge, MA: Harvard University Press.

Wenger, E. (1998). *Communities of practice: Learning, meaning, identity.* New York, NY: Cambridge University Press.

York-Barr, J., Sommers, W. A., Ghere, G. S., & Montie, J. K. (2006). *Reflective practice to improve school: An action guide for educators* (2nd ed.). Thousand Oaks, CA: Corwin Press.

Zuckermann, T. (2007, June 29-July 1). *From journal writing to action research: A step toward systematic reflective writing*. Paper presented at the EATAW Conference, Bochum, Germany.

ENDNOTE

[1]   Brady Spangenberg translated this chapter from German.

Chapter 3
Bryofolios:
Individual and Group E-Portfolio Learning Spaces for Developing Authentic Science Scholars

Joanne Nakonechny
University of British Columbia, Canada

Shona Ellis
University of British Columbia, Canada

ABSTRACT

Throughout this chapter we trace how our theoretical and practical understanding, interpretation, and interactions with eportfolios and their implementation support, both individually and through group work, students' abilities to engage in deeper structure learning and their resulting growth as authentic science scholars. The bryfolio, an individual and group course eportfolio, begins this on-line journey to facilitate deeper structure learning for 31 students in Biology 321, Bryophytes: Mosses, Hornworts and Liverworts. Initially, we give a short introduction to science education and how constructivist learning theory can include the use of eportfolios as a teaching method. Following this, we situate eportfolios within our learning context by providing a definition, a condition, and discussion of the key e-portfolio element, critical reflection. We continue by introducing the bryofolio, its major components, and our analysis of how the bryofolio encourages deep structure learning at both individual and group levels.

DOI: 10.4018/978-1-4666-0143-7.ch003

SETTING THE SCENE: CURRENT SCIENCE TEACHING

In science teaching, "the dominant orientation [is] toward isolated, nonsituated facts, which are seldom applied to real-life situations" (Giest & Lompsche, 2003, p. 63). This deliver-the-facts mode of teaching tends to facilitate rote memory that also negatively impacts students' ability to learn the procedural and conceptual knowledge required in science. Several Biology 321 focus group participants[1] demonstrate this belief that facts equals science when recounting that they "only need to memorize" course facts. These participants articulate what many other students believe and use as a base for studying, learning and practicing science. These students, unable to see the necessity of learning or generalizing their scientific knowledge from this course to other courses, are interested in retaining facts, not the scientific principles behind them. Unfortunately, as Kaparov (2003, p. 71) notes, "students' mastery of rote meaningless skills also results in spontaneous (and often wrong) concepts." Students use these concepts–often inaccurate–to build their knowledge nets, feeding a reinforcing cycle through which students integrate information into increasingly incorrect knowledge nets that become more dysfunctional the more they are elaborated. This lack of accurate knowledge also hinders students' ability to think within the subject domain and engage in appropriate problem solving approaches (Karpov, 2003). This learning approach often results in student failure, a rise in instructor frustration, and despair for both groups.

CHANGING THE SCENE: CONSTRUCTIVIST LEARNING THEORY

While the processes of knowing are complex and still not fully understood, it is generally accepted that "people construct new knowledge and under-standings based on what they already know and believe" (Bransford, Brown et al., 2000, p. 10). Constructivism, emphasizing cognitive development in reasoning, problem-solving, and prior conceptions (Bertrand, 1995), situates the learner within a complex contextualized learning environment. Constructivist instructional approaches combine three factors: paying attention to students' knowledge and beliefs; using these knowledge and beliefs as a beginning for instruction; and checking on what the students are learning (Bransford et al., 2000, p. 11). Acknowledging the student as the locus of learning (Brooks, 1993) changes the dynamic of how the learning occurs. It is now the student working with both prior knowledge concepts and new information, not the instructor, who constructs new knowledge by integrating the new information into previous knowledge nets. After learning about e-portfolios, we saw the possibility of further implementing constructivist instructional approaches in Biology 321 by providing an online contextually and conceptually scaffolded e-portfolio space to facilitate students' knowledge construction and integration, the Bryofolio.

E-PORTFOLIOS AS A LEARNING ENVIRONMENT

To explain our theoretical approach, development, and implementation of the bryofolio, we offer our definition of an e-portfolio, then illustrate how social learning is an important implementation factor, and conclude by giving some background on how critical reflection is the key transformative element of an e-portfolio. The discourse about e-portfolios and learning is steadily growing and now occupies a settled space in the learning landscape. Discussions by Yancey (1996, 2004), Shulman (1998), Barrett (2003), and Jafari (2004), amongst others, provide the frame for defining an e-portfolio. Yancey's (1996) definition of a portfolio as a selected collection of work that documents diversity, presumes development, requires reflection, and is both evaluative and communicative as it shares with observers what is valued by the participants, establishes broad parameters for a wider application of the portfolio idea across all disciplines. The Office of Learning Technology's definition, at our institution, the University of British Columbia (UBC), mirrors the above elements: "e-Portfolios are personalized, online collections, responses to work and reflections that are used to demonstrate key skills and accomplishments for a variety of contexts and time periods" (http://www.olt.ubc.ca). These portfolio definitions describe how both students and instructors can engage in a learning discourse in ways not limited to one-time representations of learning. During meaningful portfolio development, the learning discourse becomes multi-dimensional and interpretive, providing both learners and instructors with various opportunities to negotiate meanings and construct new, more meaningful understandings of what constitutes discipline knowledge and how it is learned.

A major criterion for an e-portfolio site is that it contains students' collected experiences from a variety of circumstances which can be constantly revisited so the experiences, "can be planned, articulated, interrogated, reflected upon, [and] made sense of" (Yancey, 2004, p. 751). The portfolio, and in this case the e-portfolio site, provides students and instructors with a learning space that permits multi-encounters with the discipline subject matter for both personal and social learning. After one semester, Biology 321 students' responses to the question, "What is your understanding of what e-portfolio is?" substantiate these criteria:

Student B: "a place online where you can organize previous work, submit present work and prepare for future work (job interviews)"

Student C: "a place on-line to organize, store, and share work"

Student D: "An online storage area and an 'e-space' for our bryo-enlightened 'e-musings.'

Also somewhere to make our projects available to other years [of students]. A system of reflection meant to solidify course in our brains after lecture."

Student F: "A place to store and publish ideas and projects; share and showcase work; a way to communicate these ideas – allows for feedback and changes over time."

The possibility of social learning is another important aspect of the e-portfolio structure, as it can enable and facilitate students' interaction with their peers and instructors that helps them to negotiate meaning from new concepts they encounter (Watters & Watters, 2007) and integrate these meanings with their existing conceptual knowledge. While engaged in social learning, the students are practicing meaningful learning: a state which requires the learner to possess some anchoring knowledge, to have potentially meaningful material to learn, and to not learn the material by rote (Novak, 1988). (Novak cites Ausubel's work on the Assimilation Theory of cognitive learning for this definition of meaningful learning.) Socially constructed meaningful learning requires an environment that provides adequate scaffolding, reflective opportunities, and access to social networks. The e-portfolio site, by providing students with the opportunity to engage in this meta-reflective process from various positions within the learning process, more accurately represents authentic scholarship and contributes to the construction of the students' academic identity. Yancey (2004, p. 739) alludes to this when she says, "what we ask students to do is who we ask them to be."

CRITICAL REFLECTION: A TRANSITIONING PROCESS

Conceptually, reflection weaves together the parts of the e-portfolio together and it is this central condition or process that facilitates students' development from novice to more expert learners. Without critical reflection, portfolios become repositories of documents or displays of work that do not show how the individual or group has integrated the discipline concepts into their own cognitive knowledge maps or how they can now apply these new conceptual tools and ideas. Before detailing how our e-portfolio construction was designed to facilitate student reflection and their responses to it, the following short overview of significant critical reflection elements provides some theoretical background for the course construction choices we made.

Rodgers (2002) notes that Dewey's idea of critical reflection is to make meaning not only between the elements of an experience but also through a continuing chain between the initial meaning to meaning already held by the individual and then outwards to meaning held by others. Additionally, critical reflection, systematic and rigorous with its base in scientific inquiry, needs to occur in interaction with others and requires attitudes that value personal and intellectual growth. This meaning making process requires students to contrast and compare new information with previously integrated knowledge and create or add it to existing cognitive structures. The analytic practices, whether comparative, organizational, integrative, or inter-relational, used while processing the information and its relationship to existing or newly created concepts also encourages students to assess the discipline knowledge with which they are working. This re-structuring facilitates students' crucial ability to distinguish one discipline from another, a process that Shulman (1988) believes requires understanding how the discipline questions are formulated, what is considered content and its organization, and how to engage in research and substantiation.

The meaning making that occurs during critical reflection still needs to be learned. At this point in the learning process, the two major components of metacognition, self-appraisal and self-management (Paris & Winograd, 1990), are required if students are to effectively engage in studying and learning the material. The constructs of self-monitoring, self-evaluation and goal oriented behaviors are important for understanding the self-management feature in the context of critical reflection, as enacted in the learners' plans for a task, their evaluation and adjustments to the plans as they work and their subsequent revisions (Paris & Winograd, 1990). These goal-oriented behaviors, as Kuiper and Pesut (2004) ascertain, are linked within the literature on reflection. This linkage between critical reflection and metacognitive factors broadens the importance and impact of critical reflection, as it is no longer an isolated learning element but one which acts as a merging function between meaning making and learning meaning.

Metacognitive components are important for helping novice learners develop learning strategies and discipline-based problem solving approaches. Metacognition requires students to be aware of how they cognitively function, the importance of which many students are not aware and which contributes to their continuing failure in certain areas or their lack of achievement in others (Ayersman, 1995). Students' study approaches, often unconsciously constructed on the ground rules used to achieve previous successes in other courses, frequently do not incorporate metacognitive components such as goal clarification, progress monitoring, and regulation of effort, which are so essential to successfully accomplishing what Thomas and Rohwer denote as the ill-defined task of studying (Campbell et al., 2001). Significantly, we and others (Sternberg, 1998) find that students are often not enthusiastic about or open to learning about metacognitive processes that could ameliorate their current studying outcomes, because past success without metacognition has been effective in more rote learning based courses. From focus group discussions, it became clear that many students dislike the requirements of reflection and felt tricked into doing something they perceived as valueless. These students' objectives are often more short-term–obtaining at least passing grades for course-related requirements and exams–and are not tied to deeper conceptual learning, a requirement for scientific problem solving. One student's comments express this general feeling quite eloquently: "The only way to cause everyone to participate is to make the reflections worth some marks (but only for participation) and to have them accounted for at the end of every week."

BRYOFOLIO GOALS

Group and individual workspaces in this third year botany course e-portfolio were a structure through which students begin to make sense of the complex bryological world. The course e-portfolio, as with the more generic portfolio, became a place where students could reflect upon the many different components within the field of bryology and, more generically, of science. Although the course e-portfolio does not cast as wide a net for reflection and integration as does the traditional e-portfolio, it does provide students with the practice of critical reflection for deep structure learning and practice in integrating component parts of discipline knowledge within science. Bryofolio use resulted in more engaged students who better supported each other's learning and were more capable of discussing discipline knowledge and approaches to scientific research. In addition, students' deeper understanding of bryophytes facilitated by peer learning through the course portfolio led to greater subject matter confidence which was demonstrated by more scholarly bryophytic communications on the public course website and a report to a community group. The following student responses from the focus group sessions illustrate these points.

Student B: "The organization is better; it's more current and being online makes it convenient."

Student C: "Organization is easier and I have something to take away at the end. It's good for communication."

Student D: "Reflection after lecture can facilitate memorization if it actually happens. It's a good way to deal with class projects; to make them easy to view."

Student E: "You can easily change what is on it for different purposes."

Student F: "It gives everyone an online presence and allows publication of work."

Student G: "It's easy access to other people's ideas and it doesn't take up physical space. It's a way to communicate these ideas – allows for feedback and changes over time. It's an on-line collection of work - thoughts, ideas etc. There is a better coordination of class material."

Structuring Bryofolio Space to Enhance Deep Structure Learning

Although interested in having students work within this type of learning environment, we realized that students would generally be constrained to using an e-portfolio for only one course given the funding and technological support available. We hoped that by students' participating in at least one e-portfolio course they would become more aware of how useful these techniques were and begin to apply them in other courses. Given these constraints and goals, we embarked on designing an e-portfolio that includes elements of Vygotsky's zone of proximal development and what Greenberg (2004) calls learning, structured, and showcase e-portfolios to facilitate students' learning in the bryophyte course. The instructor, prior to implementing the e-portfolio component, was already incorporating interactive lecturing, many field-trips, a term-long research project, laboratory activities, and a non-interactive course website.

Vygotsky's zone of proximal development is the pivotal learning point where learners require strategic input, ideally from peers (Novak, 2004), to help them gain the next level of learning. Greenberg's three components of the bryofolio, learning, structured, and showcase, supplied students in their zones of proximal development with a learning environment that invited peer and instructor scaffolding. The following components of Greenberg's e-portfolio types are used to demonstrate how the bryofolios constructed by each student and student group provided a pathway for them to explore a variety of learning dimensions at the university in ways they seldom, if ever, had before. The frame for the bryofolios was strategically chosen to help students more closely achieve the working atmosphere of scientists at their third year level, in effect to become authentic scholars doing active research. Comments from student focus groups indicate the e-portfolios successfully achieved this effect as students valued the opportunity to publish individually and in groups. It made them feel like scientists.

1) Learning Section

Although Greenberg (2004) contends that learning e-portfolios "extend beyond the time frame of the courses" (p. 34), we maintain that individual course-limited e-portfolios can serve as a gateway for students to begin building their own virtual- or paper-learning environments, where academic critical reflection becomes possible and productive. To help facilitate this development, the first bryofolio component focused on helping students learn about bryophytes by supporting exchanges between students and the instructor and amongst students. These exchanges are in alignment with Greenberg's (2004, p. 34) contention that learning portfolios "support private exchanges between the author and teachers" and "facilitate

shared discussions about work in progress for formal and informal peer review." This learning section was intended to facilitate the development of collegial learning, reflective analysis of discipline knowledge and the process of science, and integration of students' scientific knowledge with their knowledge of bryophytes. WebCT was chosen as the preferred environment given its presentation tool, discussion board and chat rooms, which provided on-going spaces for these interchanges. All the components of WebCT were well-used by the students. In particular, we noted that the development of peer-supported collegial learning grew over the semester. From the start, students had their own private presentation area to upload files and work on materials, as well as group space for small group collaborations. We did not encourage students to use either site, but by the term's end, we found students were far more interested in participating in the group site. Exploring this trend the next year, we assigned students group areas and gave them the option of a private site, in which only one student expressed interest. Given this strong preference for group space, we now continue to only offer the option of a private site while assigning group space for laboratory work, such as a tissue culture project or field work, such as the Camosun Bog and Forest Vegetation Survey projects. During the focus group sessions, students' comments on how they gained ways to synthesize information, developed better study skills, and used concept maps for learning and study indicated they used the learning spaces as we had hoped.

2) Structured Section

Focusing students' time and attention on particular tasks – a requirement for the structured e-portfolio (Greenberg, 2004) was the dominant consideration for the bryofolio's second component. While we wanted to ensure that students kept up with and learned the course material, we also wanted to continue facilitating the development of deep

Exhibit 1. Discussion Board Posting

Student A, 27/02/2006, 7:09 p.m., Subject: Tetraphidae
"I am not sure if I missed it or not but, I don't remember talking much about the tetraphidae in class, so I don't really get the following questions:
1. Describe the protonematal phase of Tetraphis. How does it differ from that of the Bryidae? - protonema > Protonematal flaps > shoot > Gemmae > not fertilized > antheridia (I am not sure if this is correct.)
2. Describe the formation of the peristome teeth in the Tetraphidae. How does this differ from the Bryidae? (I have no idea for this one.)
3. Explain how reproduction (sexual and asexual) is accomplished in the Tetraphidae
- asexual is by gemmae cup, and sexual with gametophyte producing sporophyte, so is there more to this?
Thanks in advance!!!"

Instructor, 27/02/2006, 9:03 p.m., Subject: Re: Tetraphidae
"Hmmmm....well...I seem to recall that we discussed the formation of teeth when we talked about nematodontous tooth development in polytrichidae....You should go into more detail when asked to 'explain.'
Cheerio, Shona"

Student B, 28/02/2006, 7:55 p.m., Subject: Re: Tetraphidae
"Hey STUDENT A, did you get the information about the tooth formation in
tetraphidae? If not, then this is what I understand. There is no division of the inner ampithecial layers, rather they, along with the rest of the ampithecium are thickened and form four massive teeth out of the entire ampithecium. Is this right Shona? Thanks!"

Instructor, 28/02/2006, 10:31 p.m., Subject: Re: Tetraphidae
"You betcha!"

structure learning and encourage the habit of learning analysis and reflection. To meet these objectives, we chose three different learning activities: discussion boards, information processing sheets (IPS), and study questions.

i) Discussion Boards

To foster genuine discussion about specific syllabus topics, we decided to use the online WebCT discussion board as a time-bounded space for communication amongst students and between students and the instructor. The following discussion involving both students and the instructor reflects the nature of the postings to the discussion board. (See Exhibit 1)

Students used the discussion boards to find out information, test the accuracy of their knowledge, and help other students learn the material. Students would often begin to answer the instructor's posted question, indicate where they were having problems, and then continue with their explanations. Their peers would venture explanations or give advice on where to find information that might be useful. This peer-to-peer interaction within a group learning space helps students learn how to suitably respond to queries and provide appropriate information, mirroring patterns useful during interchanges in scientific research. The instructor's interactions in this section, and throughout most of the postings, are ones that scaffold student learning and seldom provide information. For example, the instructor provides a hint as to where to find the information by reminding Student A where she has learned about the topic. The instructor also provides the student with information on how to better answer a question when asked to "explain" and provides reassurance for Student B that the information given is accurate.

ii) Information Processing Sheets (IPS)

We wanted to provide a model for students on how to think about the subject at hand and, more generally, about any subject material they might encounter in subsequent courses. Given student concerns about time constraints, we also wanted the completed activity to provide students with a set of study sheets that would aid them in learning the material for their exams. To attain this goal, we developed an information processing sheet, based on Zajchowski's (1999) work that included the following questions:

1. What is the concept?
2. Write down the concept in your own words.
3. Where/how does this fit into the big picture of this system/theory/function?
4. Where/how does this fit/interact with the specific system under consideration?
5. Where/how does this link to a close-up view of the system/function/element being studied?
6. Vocabulary/definitions:
7. What might cause problems in understanding the concept?
8. What are the important steps/elements to remember?
9. Make a diagram/picture/chart of the concept

Students responded in a variety of ways to these sheets. Almost all students saw value in completing the sheets, but some expressed frustration with various questions and the time it took to complete them. A number of students realized that the IPS could change the way they approached the subject material and how it was more efficient for retention to start transforming and integrating the new course material as soon as possible after class.

Student D: "Reflecting right after lecture definitely does decrease the amount of rote memorization I'll have to do later on, so it is a more pleasant style of learning."

The value of the concept map (Novak & Gowan, 1984), for learning has been discussed elsewhere (Stoddart et al., 2000; Kinchin & Hay, 2000), and we found once again that students noted its strengths:

Student E: "I like concept maps. It forces me to think about the concepts which causes me to memorize them. So it is a good way for me to study. I also like concept maps because there is something problem-solving about them – they are challenging in a good way."

Student F: "Concept mapping specific ideas in 321 were useful for example, in identifying vocabulary words and where they relate in developmental stages – allows a way to associate things visually, as opposed to just reading a paragraph of text."

Student G: "sort of.....helped gain broader view of overall concepts"

However, we note that not all students found concept mapping useful for a variety of reasons, ranging from lack of understanding course material, confusion in how to construct a concept map, time it took to construct a concept map, through to disliking the process.

Some students wanted the IPS questions to be more specifically linked to the course.

Student B: "Reflections were too abstract to be beneficial; reflections could be based on specific or practical knowledge, like study questions."

For these students, our hope that the IPS would be seen as a way to approach any discipline material did not hold true. However, we were encouraged to see that other students did find the idea of the IPS relevant to their learning.

Student C: "I like the idea of synthesizing ideas, but ideas should be course related."

iii) Study Questions

Our third learning activity for the bryofolio structured section asked students to post non-trivial (deeper level) study questions for their fellow students. Students were graded on their contributions—a necessary "carrot" given the institutional and therefore student focus on marks—and knew that some of these questions could be used on exams. This learning activity, as did the discussion board, encouraged students to work with one another, to encounter learning as an interactive developmental process rather than a solely individuated one. Students were generally very positive about the activity as they saw it was directly beneficial for learning the course material:

Focus group notes*: "Students responded with a unanimous 'yes.' They recognized the study questions as a way of reflecting on course content. They liked seeing other people's study questions, too. They felt they had more control over their studying by knowing that some of these questions would be asked on exams."*

To provide students with an overview of the material required for exams, the instructor posted a selection of students' study questions, accompanied by some of the instructor's questions, in the group bryofolio area. The students had discussion board space where they could discuss the answers amongst themselves. The instructor did not answer questions directly but scaffolded the students' learning by providing non-information feedback and re-assuring students' that their responses were on track. Students were strongly engaged in developing challenging study questions as they were aware that some of them would then be used on mid-term and final exams if they were appropriately in-depth. This use of students' questions in mid-term and final exams provided a new assessment strategy, an acknowledged possibility when using e-portfolios.

The study questions activity provided two unexpected deeper structured learning benefits. The first benefit related to how the questions were asked as many questions were asked in different ways than presented in the lecture. The different question forms highlighted various facets of the subject under discussion and provided students with alternate ways of engaging with the material. In some cases, the questions were in greater depth than had been discussed in class, so students had to do some research to develop a complete answer. The second benefit related to information integration. Some students' questions integrated

information they were learning in other classes with Biology 321, and the responses required the same type of integration. This cross-course informational and conceptual integration is very hard to achieve, and we were reassured about the learning activity validity when we saw students being able to achieve it.

3) Showcase Section

The third bryofolio component is the showcase section. As Greenberg (2004, p. 32) states, "they should provide a stimulating context for reflecting on a body of work in order to make new connections, personalize learning experiences, and gain insights that will influence future activities." Students were asked to contribute their work to an online public bryophyte website, such as bryophyte photographs taken during fieldtrips, at other times, or through microscopes in the laboratory. They also contributed appropriate semester projects to the site, ranging from annotated maps for bryophyte walks in city parks and games people could play to become more familiar with bryophytes to information about the life cycle of bryophytes and their importance ecologically. Small research projects, such as the Camosun Bog project where each group was assigned a bog plot and inventoried the bryophytes in their plot, were included in the site and shared with the relevant community group, in this case, the Camosun Bog Restoration Group. Throughout the semester, often in groups, students used the course e-portfolio site to work on their projects, view other students' work, and make comments. The instructor noted that this process of being able to see others' work significantly raised educational standards as students encouraged better scholarship by providing feedback to each other on their term project goals, suggesting where to find readings on particular bryophytes and how to use the available technology, whether in the laboratory or on the website.

TECHNOLOGY

Although students in this class were familiar with text messaging, iPods, and e-mail, they experienced ongoing technical difficulties with WebCT and various online tools provided for them. These technical difficulties formed an unintended barrier for students using the bryofolio, a barrier which Tosh, Light, Fleming, and Haywood (2005) also document. We provided a two-hour introduction to the bryofolio space, handouts, and ongoing technical support, but from student interviews and surveys, we were aware of their ongoing technological difficulties. These difficulties did abate somewhat as the term progressed, but they still interfered with the learning space and student interest in maintaining e-portfolios. The following student's comment is fairly representative of the underlying frustration level that many students evinced: **Student C:** "Yes, I liked learning how to put it together and if I could get good at it, would find it more effective than files (hardcopy)."

Student feedback on what type of help they needed included having more handouts on technical aspects, more in-class time to learn how to use the technology, and better tools. For example, the WebCT HTML editor scrambled formatting, and URL links had to be added by typing the file name rather than browsing and clicking; plus, the system was often very slow.

An unexpected positive effect of these technical difficulties was the sense of course identity students gained as they helped each other with the technical difficulties. Further, while not contributing directly to science learning, these technical challenges and the discussions amongst the students about how to solve them provided clear examples of peer aided social learning in the zone of proximal development and also provided students with better levels of technical literacy, which they appreciated.

CONCLUSION

By combining three different e-portfolio forms, learning, structured and showcase, the bryofolio allowed us to successfully implement our constructivist pedagogical goals in Biology 321. We were also able to incorporate both individual and group learning activities that led to a stronger course identity, which engendered better student engagement and interactive learning amongst the students. Further, we saw students involved in deeper structure learning, resulting in better understanding of bryology as well as how the process of science occurs.

Students generally positively responded to the different learning environments provided by the individual and group levels within the bryofolio. The individual bryofolio spaces were seen to be good places for posting study questions, assignments, etc. The group bryofolio spaces were acknowledged as being more "fun." Students in the focus groups said they learned a lot from collaborating with one another and agreed the best thing about the bryofolio was the potential to share information and ideas.

Although the emphasis in the literature and in educational contexts of student e-portfolio development has often stressed the individual nature of the portfolio for reflection and integration of learning, we have found the e-portfolio structure useful at both the individual and group level to facilitate students' metacognitive skill development and critical reflection of disciplinary knowledge. Students involved in the semester-long bryofolio project came away with better learning skills, more understanding about the process of science, and products that demonstrated their abilities. The course instructor continues to use bryofolios as she perceived significant positive change in students' levels of engagement, deeper levels of questions asked in the course, and overall student performance whether in the study questions, responses to questions on exams, or individual and course projects. The last words are from the students:

What was the value of e-portfolio to Biology 321?

Student A: "Collaboration; group projects were easier – could add to some sites."

Student B: "Sharing: – people could see what projects other were building; working together; it was an easier way to submit homework."

Student C: "Questions – a place to put ideas and know where they are to revisit and revise later (project ideas); learning computer skills (never knew what html was before)."

Student D: "It was a good way to see everyone's photos from fieldtrips and the like."

Student E: "Being able to communicate with classmates easily; an opportunity for creativity – as much work as you want to put into it."

Student F: "Communication between users."

Student G: "Can get instant replies - ease of contact (sometimes); WebCT was a hassle at times."

REFERENCES

Ayersman, D. (1995). Effects of knowledge representation format and hypermedia instruction on metacognitive accuracy. *Computers in Human Behavior*, *11*(3-4), 533–555. doi:10.1016/0747-5632(95)80016-2

Bertrand, Y. (1995). *Contemporary theories and practice in education*. Madison, WI: Magna.

Brooks, J. G., & Brooks, M. G. (1993). *In search of understanding: The case for a constructivist classroom*. Alexandria, VA: Association for Supervision and Curriculum Development.

Campbell, J., Smith, D., Boulton-Lewis, G., Brownlee, J., Burnett, P., & Carrington, S. (2001). Students' perceptions of teaching and learning: The influence of students' approaches to learning and teachers' approaches to teaching. *Teachers and Teaching: Theory and Practice*, *7*(2), 173–187.

Fleet, J., Goodchild, F., & Zajchowski, R. (1999). *Learning for success: Effective strategies for students* (3rd ed.). Toronto, ON, Canada: Harcourt, Brace.

Giest, H., & Lompscher, J. (2003). Formation of learning activity and theoretical thinking in science teaching. In Kozulin, A., Ginidis, B., Ageyev, V., & Miller, S. (Eds.), *Vygotsky's educational theory in cultural contexts* (pp. 267–288). Cambridge, UK: Cambridge University Press.

Greenberg, G. (2004). The digital convergence: Extending the portfolio model. *EDUCAUSE Review*, *39*(4), 28–34.

Jafari, A. (2004). The "sticky" eportfolio system: Tackling challenges and identifying attributes. *EDUCAUSE Review*, *39*(4), 38–45.

Karparov, Y. V. (2003). Vygotsky's doctrine of scientific concepts: Its role for contemporary education. In Kozulin, A., Ginidis, B., Ageyev, V., & Miller, S. (Eds.), *Vygotsky's educational theory in cultural context* (pp. 65–82). Cambridge, UK: Cambridge University Press.

Kinchin, I., & Hay, D. (2000). How a qualitative approach to concept map analysis can be used to aid learning by illustrating patterns of conceptual development. *Educational Research*, *42*(1), 143–157. doi:10.1080/001318800363908

Novak, J., & Gowin, D. (1984). *Learning how to learn*. Cambridge, UK: Cambridge University Press.

Prus, R. (2005). Studying human knowing and acting: The interactionist quest for authenticity. In Pawluch, D., Shaffir, W., & Miall, C. (Eds.), *Doing ethnography: Studying everyday life* (pp. 7–23). Toronto, ON, Canada: Canadian Scholars' Press.

Rodgers, C. (2002). Defining reflection: Another look at John Dewey and reflective thinking. *Teachers College Record*, *104*(4), 842–866. doi:10.1111/1467-9620.00181

Sternberg, R. (1998). Metacognition, abilities, and developing expertise: What makes an expert student? *Instructional Science, 26*(1-2), 129–140.

Stoddart, T., Abrams, R., Gasper, E., & Canaday, D. (2000). Concept maps as assessment in science inquiry learning - a report of methodology. *International Journal of Science Education, 22*(12), 1221–1246. doi:10.1080/095006900750036235

Tosh, D., Light, T. P., Fleming, K., & Haywood, J. (2005). Engagement with electronic portfolios: Challenges from the student perspective. *Canadian Journal of Learning and Technology, 31*(3). Retrieved September 24, 2008, from http://www.cjlt.ca/content/vol31.3/tosh.html

University of British Columbia. (n. d.). *Office of learning technology*. Retrieved September 24, 2008, from http://www.olt.ubc.ca

Watters, D., & Watters, J. (2007). Approaches to learning by students in the biological sciences: Implications for teaching. *International Journal of Science Education, 29*(1), 19–43. doi:10.1080/09500690600621282

Yancey, K. (1996). The electronic portfolio: Shifting paradigms. *Computers and Composition, 13*(13), 259–262. doi:10.1016/S8755-4615(96)90014-6

Chapter 4
Implementing ePortfolios:
From Pilot Project to Full Scale Implementation

Igor Balaban
University of Zagreb, Croatia

Blazenka Divjak
University of Zagreb, Croatia

Darko Grabar
University of Zagreb, Croatia

Bojan Zugec
University of Zagreb, Croatia

ABSTRACT

This chapter presents the most important steps in the process of ePortfolio implementation at the Faculty of Organization and Informatics (FOI) at the University of Zagreb. Stemming from an announcement by 11 faculties from the University of Zagreb, the Centre for E-Learning at the University of Zagreb reports that eportfolio is now used by over 500 students. The University of Zagreb adopted the E-learning Strategy in 2007 and this chapter covers the period 2007-2010. During this time, the response to ePortfolios greatly improved, which the authors suggest are due to changes discussed in this chapter.

INTRODUCTION

Within its E-learning strategy developed in July 2007, the University of Zagreb committed to establish and maintain the ePortfolio system at the university and/or at the faculties belonging to the university. According to the report of the Centre for E-Learning at the University of Za-

greb, 11 of its faculties have announced a plan for conducting other activities defined by the E-learning strategy, among which is ePortfolio. To date, several researches within the Centre for E-Learning have dealt with certain professional aspects of ePortfolio, such as the functionalities of tools that support ePortfolio. However, comprehensive research has neither been conducted by the Centre nor any university in Croatia. Therefore,

DOI: 10.4018/978-1-4666-0143-7.ch004

the ePortfolio experience at the Faculty of Organization and Informatics (FOI), which belongs to the University of Zagreb, represents a very valuable contribution to supporting and developing lifelong learning in Croatia. In this chapter, the most important steps in the process of ePortfolio implementation at the Faculty of Organization and Informatics are presented.

E-LEARNING STRATEGY ON THE FACULTY

The E-learning Strategy of the University of Zagreb was adopted in 2007 and covers the period 2007-2010. According to the strategy, technology should be used to improve the quality of teaching and learning to ensure the achievement of learning outcomes, with pedagogical needs always kept in mind rather than the application of modern technologies for their own sake. To support realization of planned activities, a new e-learning support center was established at the central university level. The main tasks of this center are: to provide a standard LMS and e-portfolio platform; to provide support to teachers and students through a help desk and training; to promote and encourage the application of information and communication technologies in university education; and to monitor and analyze e-learning implementation at the university. Since faculties are independent entities in Croatia, it was left to the faculty management to decide whether to use resources provided by this center or to base e-learning on their own resources. A few months later, then, the university-wide strategy, an e-learning strategy developed by the Faculty of Organization and Informatics (FOI), was approved. It acknowledged the goals that were given in the university strategy but also refined them to make them operational and introduced a few new goals that were specific to the Faculty mission.

By implementing e-learning, FOI plans to achieve following strategic goals: to enhance quality of educational process and learning outcomes; to prepare students for lifelong learning; to ensure that potential students have better and wider access to education; and to provide exposure to the international market. The Faculty believes a blended (hybrid) learning approach is the most suitable one in teaching and learning. Such an approach is based on the combination of classic teaching methods and those employed in virtual learning and teaching environments. Choice of the form and intensity of e-learning is left to the teachers of the Faculty. Since it is acknowledged that systematic implementation of e-learning contributes to enhancement of teaching and research processes, the business position of FOI, personnel development and lifelong learning and the fact that FOI is mainly a faculty of information sciences, the faculty decided that entire e-learning infrastructure will be based on internal faculty human and technical resources.

In the FOI E-learning Strategy, there are three different levels pre-defined for e-courses (Figure 1). The main goal of the first level is to increase availability of learning materials and to ease communication with students. The first level means that an e-course includes basic information about curriculum/topics, learning outcomes, references, forums for communication and selected learning materials. This level is obligatory for all courses. The hidden goal of this basic level is to gradually introduce e-learning to teaching staff and to get them more involved. The goal of the second level is to ease the learning process through better integration between e-learning and classic teaching. An e-course that is on the second level should contain learning materials organized according to specific topics, discussion forums for different topics (i.e., student communication), a timetable and calendar for different tasks, and course tools, such as tests, marks, homework, and a glossary. Finally, the goal of the third level is to advance teaching methods by hybrid course organization made according to the principles of instructional design. An e-course on the third level improves upon the second level in terms of design, the inclu-

Figure 1. Levels of E-learning at FOI

LEVEL 1	LEVEL 2	LEVEL 3
Goal: to increase availability of certain educational materials and to improve communication between students and teachers	**Goal:** to improve the process of knowledge acquisition by integrating Learning Management Systems into the ordinary classroom	**Goal:** to improve educational methods and techniques by organizing courses and classes in a blended manner, according to principles of instructional design
• Basic course information • Learning outcomes • Course plan & program • Course literature • Selected educational materials • General discussion forum	**LEVEL 1 + ...** • Calendar of important course events • Selected educational materials organized according to educational units • Homework upload and grading • Self-perception and self-evaluation materials (online exams) • Announcements and notifications (exam results, homework assignments...) • Discussion forum structured in detail • Online dictionary	**LEVEL 2 + ...** • Homework and seminar upload and grading, online questionnaires • Systematical grading of all online student activities (discussions, access to materials, exams...) • All educational materials organized according to educational units and available online • Audio and video educational materials

sion of audio and video materials, and utilization of online evaluation.

All courses at FOI implemented at least the first level of accompanying e-course as required in 2008. Beyond the basic level, teachers have been encouraged to introduced also higher levels of e-learning into their courses whenever it can be justified by the subject's goals and resources available. At the end of 2010, there were around 50% of courses at level 2, 30% of courses at level 1 and 20% of courses at level 3.

In E-learning Strategy at the University as well as Faculty levels, e-portfolio implementation was planned. At FOI, considerable development has been accomplished so far regarding implementation as well as research.

THE PILOT PROJECT

The first phase of ePortfolio implementation was initiated in the winter semester of the academic year 2008/2009, during which an ePortfolio system was implemented in a hybrid course, in Security of Information Systems, and as support for an international Tempus project. For this pilot ePortfolio implementation, the following goals were defined:
1. To choose which ePortfolio system would be the best to use at the Faculty to compliment the course structure, given that most of the courses at the Faculty are organized in a similar manner; and
2. To introduce the ePortfolio concept to students and educators.

One of the first steps prior to implementation of ePortfolio concept was to choose an adequate ePortfolio application. Four main aspects were taken into consideration:

1. **The IMS/GLC ePortfolio interoperability specification**
2. **Organizational/course requirements and possibilities**, which were not so strict, since this was the first case of ePortfolio implementation, and it was not possible to define them completely
3. **Case-examples from the emerging ePortfolio literature**
4. **Available open source ePortfolio applications:** These included the Exabis ePortfolio block within Moodle LMS (which is official LMS at our Faculty); **ELGG** – an open source social networking and social publishing platform; and **Mahara** – an open source ePortfolio and social networking software.

Since Exabis was still in its early phase of development and "showed serious weaknesses concerning the support of portfolio processes, especially in regard to the design of a presentation portfolio" (Himpsl & Baumgartner, 2009), we decided to introduce only the Mahara and ELGG ePortfolio systems to our students.

Mahara is entirely built as an ePortfolio application, while ELGG is foremost a social networking platform which also supports ePortfolio functionalities. Numerous examples of using both of these systems as an ePortfolio can be found in the literature. Although we primarily wanted a system which would support ePortfolio features, we offered the students ELGG, with its social networking functionalities, to see if they would also use those functionalities. Although Mahara supports single-sign-on from Moodle, no such connection has been made in order to preserve the independency of the systems and to avoid giving any advantage to Mahara, since our students are using Moodle LMS and would perhaps prefer to use a system that is interoperable with Moodle.

Once both applications were up and running, the students were given a quick tutorial on using the ePortfolio systems and were also given assignments which they had to complete simultaneously in both ePortfolio systems at the end of each week (Table 1). Since this was the students' first encounter with such a system, a lecture was given as an introduction to the concept of ePortfolio, as well to ePortfolio as a tool that they would use in the course. In addition, an agenda, shown in Table 1, with stages of the ePortfolio implementation and its usage was given to students. Thus, the students had a full insight into the entire process: they knew what their assignments were and what would be expected from them at any moment. In that same week, they were given a quick tutorial on the use of the ePortfolio systems Mahara and ELGG in their laboratory classes. Further details about the pilot project execution can be found in Balaban (2010).

Based on students' feedback received in the end of the pilot project, all aims set for each stage were fulfilled. In Stage 1, students became interested in ePortfolio, and most of them became very enthusiastic about this new concept. In Stage 2, they learned how to reflect and to send and receive feedback on their artifacts. In Stage 3, students were taught how to create an assessment ePortfolio and to get better insight into the new way of assessing their knowledge. Stage 4 was intended to discuss the ePortfolio face-to-face and to fill out the questionnaire designed to select the ePortfolio system that will be used on our Faculty by all students. Based on students' answers, the ePortfolio system Mahara was chosen as the default ePortfolio system at the Faculty as its interoperability enabled very tight integration with the Faculty's learning management system Moodle.

Students' comments about ePortfolio evidence that this new concept was embraced by them:

EPortfolio[s] offer a possibility to find a job much faster and more easily, to work on projects and

Table 1. Stages of the pilot project and instructions for students

Stage	Title and description
1	**Introduction to ePortfolio** 1. Introduction to the ePortfolio concept and systems; The need for an ePortfolio; Power of reflection 2. Logging into the systems and artifact upload: a. Upload course related artifacts: seminar, presentation, practical work b. Personal artifact upload (4-5 artifacts) → "Best of me" section c. Tag the artifacts as follows: i. All course-related artifacts are to be tagged with SIS08 ii. Tag all personal-related artifacts arbitrarily 3. Fill in a personal profile (including the resume) and review at least 5 profiles of your peers
2	**Reflecting on ePortfolio** 1. Monitor progress, problem solving... 2. Reflect by answering the questions according to the template: a. What have I learned about the ePortfolio? b. What was the most interesting thing about using the ePortfolio so far? Explain why. c. What was less interesting in the ePortfolio? Why? d. Where can I apply the ePortfolio in the process of my lifelong learning? 3. Split in groups. Make a view available only to peers from your group in which you will include the reflection made in Step 2. Use the ePortfolio systems to give feedback on reflections made by other peers within your group.
3	**Using ePortfolio to make course-related reflections** 1. Monitor progress, problem-solving... 2. Now a set of tasks has been created. Reflect on all four major units learned in laboratory exercises. For each of them, answer the following questions by using the given template: a. What have I learned in this unit? b. What was the most interesting part of this unit? Why? c. What was less interesting? Why? d. Where can I apply it in the future?
4	**Analysing the results and evaluating the systems** 1. Final conversation about experience and impressions. 2. Analysing and scoring students' work in ePortfolio. 3. Evaluating the ePortfolio systems used during classes.

maintain relationships with other peers that use this system. In any case, I fully support educators in introducing ePortfolio to other students. It is most likely those systems will replace a job interview in the future.

EPortfolio has enabled me to record my qualifications and experience during education. My own ePortfolio could assist me in student mobility, in finding a right job and starting my career. EPortfolio enables me to introduce myself, my competencies, skills and work to potential employers.

EPortfolio has a special purpose in fulfilling personal goals. Namely, when one has one's life goals written out in one place like in an ePortfolio, one will look at them more often and therefore ask oneself whether they are being fulfilled or not. If one of those goals is lifelong learning, it can be assumed that some of the activities in one's life would be directed towards fulfilling that goal.

I see ePortfolio application in lifelong learning primarily as an opportunity to express our soft skills we didn't acquire in formal education but rather through working on projects or in teams or doing some other job... Furthermore I like the possibilities the ePortfolio offers, such as the ability to benchmark with other peers. In that way we can perceive our advantages and disadvantages to work on to improve our own capabilities.

Considering all the aforementioned statements, it can be concluded that both goals defined at the beginning of the pilot-project were accomplished and that the Faculty-wide implementation process can be initiated.

Preparing the Environment and the Students

Based on the results from the pilot project, we initiated a second phase. This phase had a twofold goal: 1. To install and provide support for the needed ICT functionalities; and 2. To prepare students to work with ePortfolio. Among the ICT-related issues, it was necessary to decide on hardware and software requirements, study the possibilities of Moodle and Mahara integration and determine whether changes in the application interface would be needed. Students undertook training tasks that introduced them to the ePortfolio concept within the course Informatics 2. This course, which is taught in the summer semester, is for undergraduate students. They were introduced to the ePortfolio concept and its application in lifelong learning. In addition, Mahara ePortfolio was demonstrated to them with a detailed description of its functionalities and its particular support to lifelong learning concepts. Besides working with the application, students learned how to (self-)reflect and present their artifacts in different ePortfolio views.

ICT Support

Before deciding which Web application to use as an official ePortfolio system, it is essential to analyze the technical requirements and organizational issues related to ePortfolio implementation. From the technical perspective, it is important that the system is reliable and that it does not require constant maintenance. The system should be able run on inexpensive hardware, and it should be easy to scale in case of an increased load. Finally, perhaps one of the most important technical requirements is that the ePortfolio system should be both secure and easy to use.

Introduction to Mahara

Mahara (Kent, Bradbury, Kent, & Hand, 2010) is an open source ePortfolio and social networking Web application. What distinguishes Mahara from other similar systems is that Mahara puts a strong emphasis on the ePortfolio part of the system. Other similar applications like Elgg (Mayank, 2008) are primarily social-networking applications that also can be configured to serve as a kind of ePortfolio solution. Mahara is an open source solution available under the GNU GPL v3 license (2010). Basically, this license permits free usage and modification of the Mahara system by giving:

- freedom to use the software for any purpose,
- freedom to change the software to suit your needs,
- freedom to share the software, and
- freedom to share the changes you make.

It is developed using well-known and reliable open source technologies.

Technical and Organizational Considerations

Mahara is designed to run mainly on the Linux platform. It is written in PHP programming language, so it is mostly run using Apache Web server and PostgreSQL or MySQL database server. There are no special hardware requirements to run Mahara. It can be deployed on any computer capable of running the previously mentioned software. Of course, if Mahara is used in production environment, it should be deployed on a server that has sufficient hardware resources (CPU, RAM) to support usage of its application by a larger number of concurrent users.

Since these are all standard requirements, it should be easy to install Mahara in any higher education institution. The installation of Mahara itself is rather simple and consists of putting the code on the Web server, creating the appropriate database, and running the Web-based installer. After few steps, the system should be up and ready to be used. Of course, in production, Mahara will need some extra configuration to fit into the overall institutional e-learning system.

Although Mahara does not integrally support advanced horizontal scaling methods, it can be scaled horizontally, since it is built on standard open source technologies that offer a variety of plug-ins. As it is an open source application, most potential security problems are likely to be quickly detected by community members and required patches to be quickly available for download. During the last two years (2009, 2010) that we have been running Mahara, the system has proved itself to be reliable, although more bugs were detected in the system than we initially anticipated. The bugs were usually of minor importance and were mostly related to the system's usability. After we filled out a bug report, the development community would quickly respond so that patches were provided in a reasonable time. Since Mahara is a relatively new application that has gone through a few substantial code changes, it is understandable that such bugs will occur in the system. However, it is important to note that there have not been any bugs that could have led to security breaches. It should also be mentioned that the number of bugs has decreased in recent versions of the system due to system maturity and achieving a stable code base.

Besides merely technical considerations, organizational issues and the overall environment in which the ePortfolio will be implemented must be considered. In our case, each student should be given his or her ePortfolio user account at the beginning of the first semester, and students should have access to their ePortfolio until they graduate. Since an ePortfolio is a collection of personal achievements, students should be able to keep those records after finishing their study. Furthermore, besides tracking students' personal achievement records, an ePortfolio should be used

in the everyday learning processes, so teachers must have an option to give students assignments related to using the ePortfolio system. To make those assignments feasible, the ePortfolio system must have export functionality and be able to integrate with the institution's learning management system. Moodle, which is the Faculty's official learning management system, and Mahara can be connected at the authentication level so that users can switch from one system to another while only having to enter their credentials to authenticate themselves once. Moreover, Mahara version 1.2.0 supports import and export of ePortfolio data using the LEAP2A specification and static HTML export. By providing LEAP2A and HTML export support, we can be sure that each student will be able to transfer his or her ePortfolio data after finishing his or her education.

Integration and Customization

Figure 1 shows the overall positioning of the ePortfolio system from both organizational and technical perspectives. To work as part of a fully realized enterprise e-learning infrastructure, an ePortfolio system has to communicate with the institution's LMS, digital library and student information system. At present, the only existing integration is with our LMS, which solely exists at the login level through single sign-on (SSO). Since Mahara currently supports the LEAP2A standard (Grant et al., 2010), there is not much that can be done easily regarding Mahara's integration with LMS on the side of the ePortfolio application itself. For users to be able to export and import their data from LMS to ePortfolio without extensive modification of the Mahara code, the LMS must also support exporting and importing data using the LEAP2A standard. Moodle 2.0, which will be published in July 2010, will fully support importing and, even more importantly, exporting various data (snapshots of forums, assignments, etc.) to the Mahara ePortfolio system. When Moodle 2.0 in implemented, full integration between ePortfolio and LMS will be possible. Nevertheless, the integration of Mahara with other systems like the digital library and student information system will be more difficult since no API is currently available for accessing internal Mahara data using the standard Web services technologies like SOAP, REST or XML-RPC. One option is to leverage the new Moodle 2.0 Web services and use a tight integration between Moodle and Mahara to control user data only on the Moodle side. Although this would make some segments of user administration easier, it does not provide a solution flexible enough to support a wide range of desired functionalities. As a result, it is up to the development community to build Web services support to allow for a full integration of Mahara with external systems on the user level (Figure 2).

Mahara has been designed to be easily pluggable and customizable, and it is exactly for that reason that it is written in the PHP programming language. The entire Mahara architecture is organized around plugins, for everything from content types to user authentication, and each plugin can be modified and customized. In addition, Mahara's core is written in a framework-like fashion, so it easy for developers to develop new functionality on top of the Mahara core system. Since Mahara supports a wide range of functionality, not much configuration was required to fit it in the Faculty's e-learning process. The SSO integration with Moodle, also known as Mahoodle (http://docs.moodle.org/en/mahoodle), is well-documented, and it was easy to set up, because Moodle provides support for integration from its side as well. Visual design is also easily customizable since Mahara uses a standard template system similar to products like Moodle, Drupal and Joomla. For the time being, there is no support for the Croatian language. We are using the interface in English, although it is being translated into Croatian.

Introducing ePortfolio to Students

The course Informatics 2 is taught in the summer semester and taken by most of the students at FOI. This blended course is used:

1. To introduce the ePortfolio to students and to use it as an assessment tool.
2. For students to develop their own profiles and CV and to present themselves to the Faculty staff, potential employers and other peers.

For that purpose, staff delivered several lectures to students accompanied by ePortfolio materials explaining the ePortfolio and its purpose in lifelong learning, along with potential benefits. These introductory actions were almost identical to Stages 1 and 2 in the pilot project. In addition, laboratory sessions were held to make students familiar with Mahara as an ePortfolio application and its functionalities. After that, students had two weeks to try out the application, explore the reflections segment and do their first ePortfolio task. It consisted of making their own reflections about the ePortfolio following the questions provided in the template. The questions were the same as those in stage 2 of the pilot project (Table 1, stage 2, task 2).

Other reflections were related to the remaining three main topics of the laboratory exercises: Linux OS, OpenOffice, and Python programming. Students were asked to reflect on those topics according to the instructions provided in the template (Figure 3). The template for reflection was provided at the end of each topic. Their other task was to develop a "Best of me" profile, similar to a CV, described in Stage 1 in Table 1, and to make it public.

At the end of the semester, the students stated that they had found reflections very interesting. In addition, the reflections gave teachers feedback about the topics and the attractiveness of the content, which enabled them to make slight

Figure 2. Integration with other systems

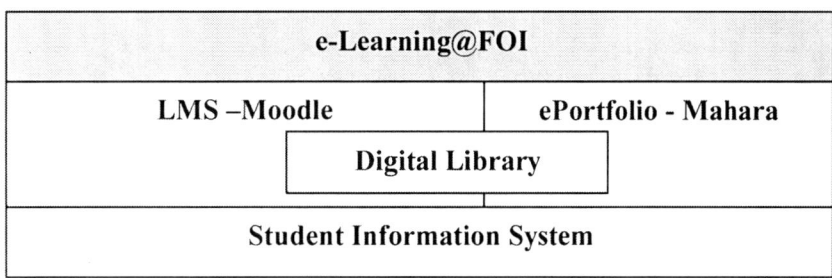

modifications accordingly. Over the course of the semester, the students became familiar with ePortfolio and learned how to use the system. They also learned how to use ePortfolio as a pedagogical tool since their reflections were evaluated. Moreover, they were prepared to show their CV or to create a showcase ePortfolio to present themselves in different contexts. With all this, prerequisites were met for a comprehensive usage of ePortfolio in other courses.

Full Scale Use in Blended Course

In the fourth semester of undergraduate study, students enroll in the course Selected Chapters of Mathematics (SCM), which is quite a complex course consisting of six chapters. In addition to monthly tests, students have to work on many problem-solving exercises that require using mathematical theory as well as ICT tools that support problem-solving. The ePortfolio was therefore introduced in order to fulfill two goals: 1. To enable students to reflect on their progress in the course; and 2. To provide a tool for the assessment of learning outcomes to be used by both students and teachers. At the end of the course, we conducted an evaluation of the ePortfolio implementation.

Course Description

The Faculty introduced ePortfolio as a new element in continuous assessment of students' coursework on the SCM course in the academic year 2008-2009. The course is taught in the fourth semester of the Information Systems study program. It is generally considered a difficult course and not easy to pass since it covers a variety of mathematical topics and a certain level of mathematical pre-knowledge is required. Therefore, one of the goals of ePortfolio implementation was to investigate the problems students encounter during the course and devise possible teaching strategies to overcome them. In order to do so, students were asked to write their reflections on the course itself (topics, the role of the course in the curriculum, possibility of usage and implementation of the course content, etc.), course activities and their performance. Furthermore, students also engaged in discussion on the accomplishments and difficulties arising during the course, involving clarifying course concepts and integration with other courses, as well as reflections on mathematical modelling and the role of mathematics in the IT profession in general.

The Methodology of ePortfolio Use

SCM is structured into six chapters, so students had to reflect on the issues they had learned, referring to the learning outcomes, for each particular chapter at various points throughout the term. Students' reflections in ePortfolio were due two weeks after the lectures on a certain chapter had finished. Students submitted their reflections using Mahara. This system enables

Figure 3. Example of assessment ePortfolio

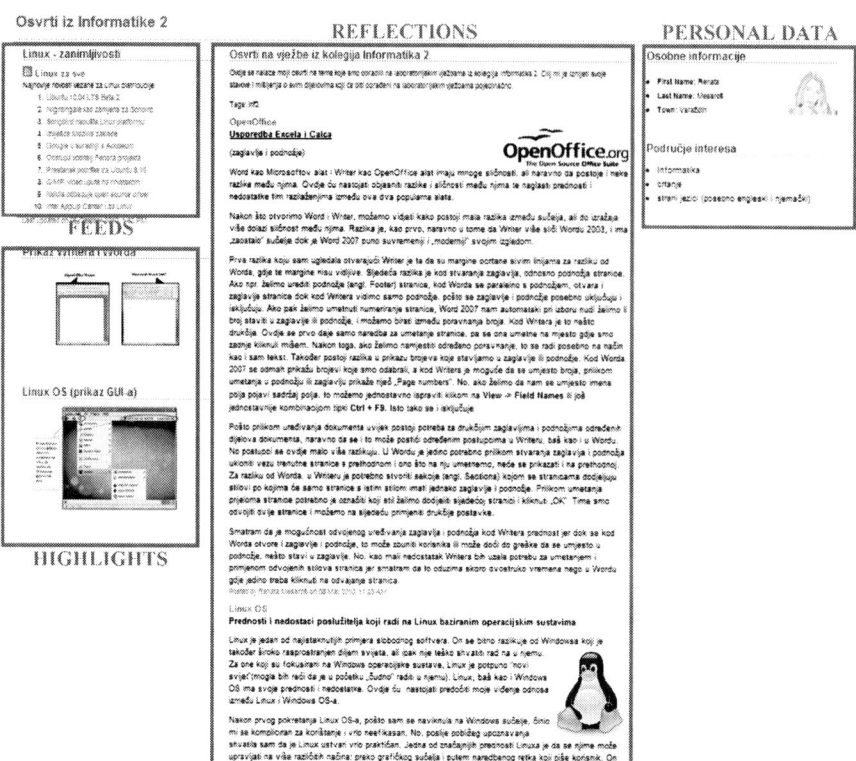

students to write their reflections in the form of a blog with six posts corresponding to each of the aforementioned chapters. This blog system is fairly functional, because one can see the date of the last post edited and the attachments can be commented on separately (i.e., feedback can be given to students for each attachment). Along with every reflection, students also needed to attach an artifact (such as homework solved, a solved test, a solved midterm exam, a solved exercise from a lecture presentation, a model, a description of its possible application, an organized lecture notes collection, or a computer experiment made in Wolfram Mathematica), explaining why they had decided to attach that particular one. The work done in ePortfolio was not an obligatory condition for fulfilling their course requirements and getting the professor's signature on the student's transcript. However, by participating in it, students were able to collect 6% of the total amount of points awarded for coursework in SCM (i.e., 6 points, or one for each chapter). In awarding these points, teachers used the following criteria: student understanding of the basic course concepts presented in the reflection, student achievement evidenced by the attached artifacts, and creativity of their choice. The teachers' motivation for introducing this new kind of assessment was to systematically gather reflections and evaluations of learning outcomes resulting from working with a large group of students (approximately 250 students on SCM and only three teachers – one professor and two teaching assistants). In this teaching environment, there are a significant number of students who do not have the opportunity to express their opinions, and the teachers can hardly manage to monitor their individual achievements. The intention of using ePortfolio was thus to obtain a certain insight into the progress and work of each student. The activity related to ePortfolio represents a contribution to the usage of technology in education and serves in raising the students' awareness about their own work and progress in the course.

Results

Since e-learning is implemented rather intensely at the Faculty of Organization and Informatics, it is common to collect a questionnaire on students' satisfaction with the SCM course at the end of each term, for which Moodle is commonly used. The questions concern the learning and teaching environment in SCM. Two new questions were added to the questionnaire in the academic year 2008/2009 concerning the ePortfolio activity: whether ePortfolio was useful to them and how much time they spent on average working on their reflections. In the sample, approximately 55% answered that ePortfolio was useful or even very useful to them, which is a good result considering the fact that ePortfolio was a novelty to them. Others were indifferent or not so favourable. Among those examinees, there were also students who had not participated in ePortfolio exercise, which may have led to some spurious responses to the eportfolio-related items. The survey also asked students to evaluate the potential useful-

ness of ePortfolio improvements planned for the next academic year. Most criticism was pointed towards the fact that the portfolio exercise is very time-consuming and that six reflections in one semester was too much to write. In the 2009-2010 academic year, the results were better because 80% responded that e-portfolio was useful or even very useful to them. Better results may be due to some organizational changes we introduced in that academic year. First among these is that students have to write their reflections only three times each semester.

The remainder of this section contains a more detailed analysis of students' ePortfolio results and their relation to the total sum of course points awarded to students for their coursework (i.e., ePortfolio together with the all the other activities). In order to determine whether there is any relation between the two, the aforementioned data are shown in a graph (Figure 4).

To fulfill their course obligations and get the professor's signature on his or her transcript, each student needs to collect at least 20 points out of a possible 100. Otherwise, they have to enroll in the SCM course again in the following year. Having collected between 20 and 50 points, students are entitled to take a regular exam. To pass SCM on the account of their coursework, which is continuously assessed, students need to collect at

Figure 4. Relation between ePortfolio points and course total points

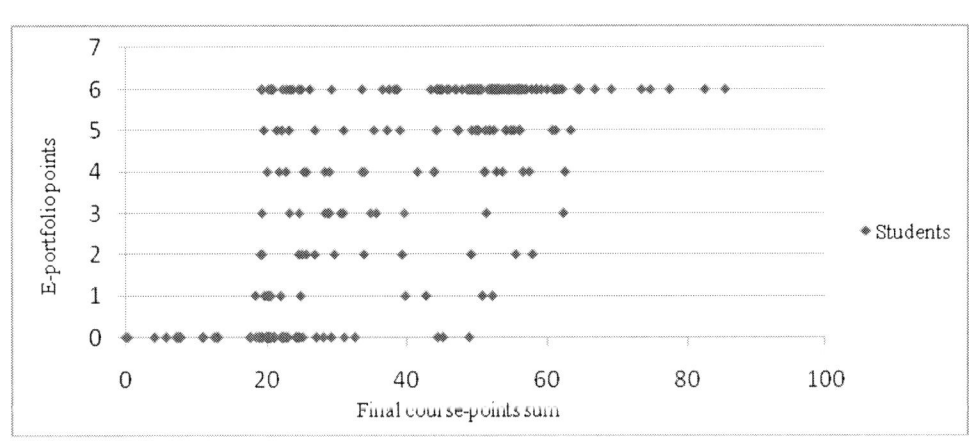

least 50 points. Consequently, there are two thresholds of interest: 20 and 50 points. In Figure 4 it is evident that most students are grouped around those two numbers. The distribution of eportfolio points is as follows: 55% of all students have 5 or 6 points, 25% have 1, 2, 3 or 4 points and 20% of them 0 points. Therefore, this analysis indicates that students can be divided into 3 separate groups for further analysis: students who got 5 or 6 points for their ePortfolio activity (i.e., the "Upper group"), students who received 1-4 points for their ePortfolio activity (i.e., the "Middle group") and those who decided not to do activities in ePortfolio (0 points for ePortfolio activity – i.e., the "Bottom group"). Figures 5, 6, and 7 show the relation between these groups.

The Upper group consists of students who devoted their time to writing reflections following the instructions and did so for every chapter (except perhaps one). They showed a certain level of understanding of the course matter. The results in Figure 5 show that most of them are grouped around 50 points or more. The Middle group is quite different. The majority of students in this group are slightly shifted to the left, which means that most of them did not pass SCM through their coursework and are situated between 20 and 50 points (Figure 6). It can be assumed that they had intended to pass SCM through their coursework

but the assignments turned out to be slightly too difficult for them at the time. Finally, it is obvious that no one from the Bottom group passed SCM through their coursework, the only exception being one student who succeeded in doing so due to additional exercises.

Results in Figure 7 suggest that the students' goal was merely to reach 20 points, so they would not have to take SCM again in the following year. The number of students in each group who eventually passed the course through their coursework is shown in Figure 8. It is evident that a great majority of students who passed the course in this way were in the Upper group. We can therefore use the ePortfolio analysis as a useful instrument to identify students' competences and motivation in the course. As ePortfolio is associated with learning outcomes, a logical next step in evaluating its effectiveness would be to examine the artifacts students attach (notes, short tests, midterm tests, homework etc.). It may be helpful to analyze the nature of their reflections as well (i.e., whether they reveal understanding or are simply copy-and-paste definitions).

These issues provide a possible course of further research and more thorough analysis. Finally, we would like to better document the role of ePortfolio in the process of raising students' awareness and critical thinking about their own

Figure 5. Score distribution in the "Upper group"

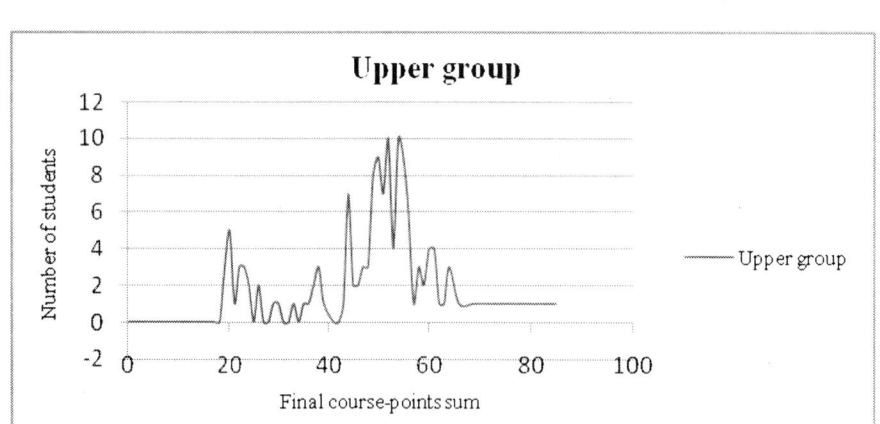

Figure 6. Score distribution in the "Middle group"

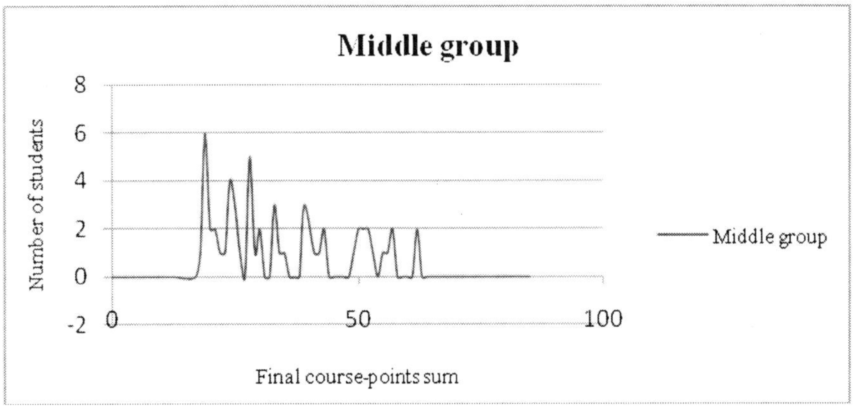

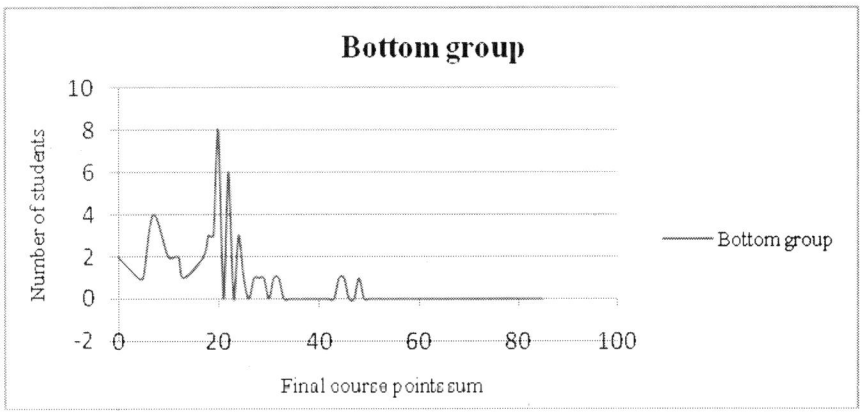

achievements and motivation. We believe that this, along with self-monitoring their learning progress, has a vast influence on their study success.

FUTURE WORK

This chapter described the process of ePortfolio implementation over almost 18 months starting from the pilot project and ending with its full scale implementation. Today more than 500 students are using ePortfolio at the Faculty of Organization and Informatics. This is the second year that ePortfolio has been used in the courses

Informatics 2 and SCM. We intend to introduce ePortfolio in a few other courses, one of which is the Psychology of Teaching. In this course, students will be taught how to use the ePortfolio to set up their own goals and monitor their own progress in achieving those goals. It is clear that, if the potential of ePortfolio is to be entirely exploited, students should also be introduced to lifelong learning and how ePortfolio supports its elements. From the organizational and technical perspective, we plan to use the ePortfolios of all individuals (students and teachers) to create the Faculty's ePortfolio. LMS and ePortfolio will be more tightly integrated so the artifacts could be more easily transferred between them. Special

Figure 7. Score distribution in the "Bottom group"

Figure 8. Comparison between categories regarding the pass rate

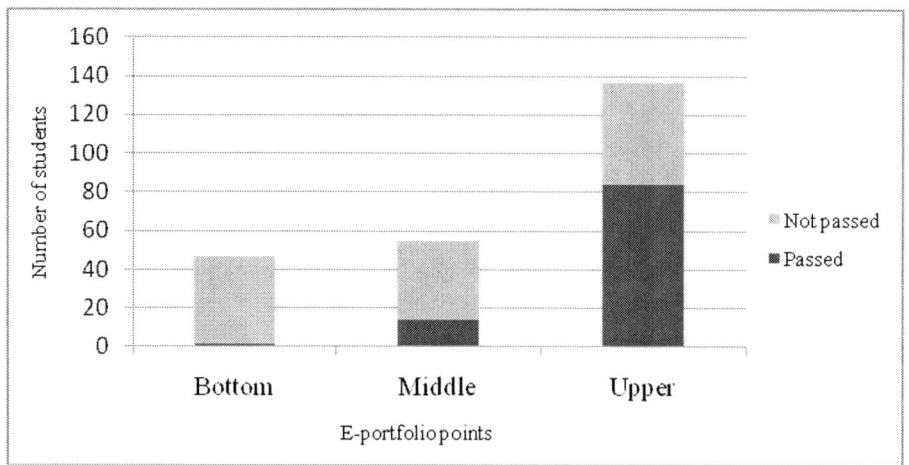

attention will be given to the artifacts' credibility and integrity. Research (Balaban et al., 2010) has shown that most of the artifacts found on a variety of ePortfolios lacks authentication, and little attention is given to intellectual property rights, both of which are important considerations if the ePortfolio is to support employability. In order for artifacts to have broad validity and reliability, the lightweight artifact integrity method described in Balaban and Kisasondi (2009) or a digital signature method will be implemented.

We hope that in a few years we will be able to fully utilize ePortfolio capabilities not only as a pedagogical tool but also as a concept embraced by students, educators and employers. This would enable students to not only become more effective and reflective learners but also to present themselves to future employers and all other stakeholders.

REFERENCES

Balaban, I. (2010). First steps in using eportfolio in a university course. In Landeta Etxeberria, A. (Ed.), *E-learning new tendencies and innovation didactic activities* (pp. 155–164). Madrid, Spain: CEF.

Balaban, I., & Bubas, G. (2009). Evaluating an eportfolio system: The case of a hybrid university course. In *Proceedings of the ICL Conference: The Challenges of Lifelong Learning*, Villach, Austria (pp. 638-643).

Balaban, I., Divjak, B., & Kopic, M. (2010). Emerging issues in using eportfolio. In *Proceedings of the I-Learning Forum*, London, UK.

Balaban, I., & Kisasondi, T. (2009). A lightweight eportfolio artifact integrity method. In *Proceedings of the ICL Conference: The Challenges of Lifelong Learning*, Villach, Austria (pp. 681-686).

Cambridge, D., Cambridge, B., & Yancey, K. B. (2009). Electronic portfolio technology and design for learning. In Cambridge, D., Cambridge, B., & Yancey, K. B. (Eds.), *Electronic Portfolios 2.0: Emergent research on implementation and impact*. Sterling, VA: Stylus.

GNU Operating System. (2010). *Licenses*. Retrieved from http://www.gnu.org/licenses

Grant, S., et al. (2010). *Leap2A specification*. Retrieved from http://wiki.cetis.ac.uk/LEAP2A_specification

Himpsl, K., & Baumgartner, P. (2009). Evaluation of e-portfolio software. *International Journal of Emerging Technologies in Learning, 4*(1).

Kent, D. M., Bradbury, G. G., Kent, M. A., & Hand, R. W. (2010). *Mahara 1.2 ePortfolios: Beginner's guide*. Birmingham, UK: Packt.

Mayank, S. (2008). *ELGG social networking*. Birmingham, UK: Packt.

Wikipedia. (2011). *Mahara architecture introduction*. Retrieved from http://wiki.mahara.org/Developer_Area/Mahara_Architecture_Introduction

Chapter 5

ePorticulture:
Growing a New Culture of Assessment

Kevin Kelly
Wiley Learning Institute, USA

Ruth Cox
San Francisco State University, USA

ABSTRACT

Institutional culture is a critical component in making eportfolios an integral teaching and learning tool. As instructors and students engage in using eportfolios, the campus goes through culture change in several different areas. Institutions may start with questions related to technology and logistics, but buy-in at all levels is critical as campuses begin to shift, redefine or adapt existing cultures of assessment. Namely, these efforts promote the adoption of more diverse and comprehensive assessment strategies— that embody new, learner-centered teaching methodologies—along with traditional strategies. By using more than one method to demonstrate their competencies within the context of the eportfolio process, students can become more reflective learners, make connections between curricular and co-curricular work, and prepare to enter the workforce. This chapter will help readers determine why they might pursue the use of eportfolios within their educational institution, at the course, program, or institutional levels.

ePorticulture *(n.) the act or custom of learning, developing intellectually and professionally, and transmitting knowledge through the creation, review, and assessment of authentic, reflective, and integrative student work that is shared over time via electronic portfolios*

etymology: ***e*** *(electronic)* + ***portfolio*** *(a selection of a student's work compiled over a period of time and used for assessing performance or progress)* + ***culture*** *(the integrated pattern of human knowledge, belief, and behavior that depends upon the capacity for learning and transmitting knowledge to succeeding generations)*

DOI: 10.4018/978-1-4666-0143-7.ch005

- Kelly and Cox (2009)

INTRODUCTION: DESIGNING A NEW EDUCATIONAL LANDSCAPE

For centuries, educators have been experimenting with the art and science of promoting, collecting, and assessing student work—just as horticulturalists have explored improvements in the cultivation of fruits, vegetables, flowers, or ornamental plants. Etymologically, "horticulture" derives from the Latin *hortus* (garden) and *cultus* (tilling/cultivation of land). And while horticultural practices have evolved into an extremely complex science, so, too, has the use of new tools and technologies to nurture and harvest a wider range of student work. It may seem a contrivance to apply a metaphor of horticulture to the cultivation of modern methods for growing and assessing student learning. Yet just as we have been besieged by core instabilities in our systems of agriculture and finance, we are seeing too often that our educational monoculture does not adequately prepare students for the ever-changing future. Our agricultural monocultures have led to an atrophy of knowledge about growing a wider variety of crops and an increased reliance on pesticides, creating a systemic fragility. Similarly, educational institutions are depending on mono-forms of harvesting student knowledge, such as standardized testing.

New digital technologies like electronic portfolios have opened the way for profound changes in education. The case can be made that, at the dawn of the 21st century, converging technologies and emerging social trends lay the groundwork for entirely new societal landscapes—in the very meaning of the work we do and the lives we lead, and ultimately in the what, where, why, and how we learn. Wardlaw (2006) argues that expectations for learning have changed in response to a new global context, requiring students to gain skills in communication, teamwork, problem solving, analysis, reflection, performance improvement, innovation, and lifelong learning. However, curriculum design has changed only marginally since the start of the modern academy in the Renais-

sance period. Emerging socio-technology trends must play a wider role in influencing changes in curriculum design going forward. Darling-Hammond (2009, p. 29) stated that on-demand and curriculum-embedded assessments should be used together to "measure the full range of knowledge and skills represented in standards." We believe that learners must be guided toward clear, concise academic learning outcomes and, like Darling-Hammond, that good practice in comprehensive assessment will require a wider variety of assessment strategies over time.

In this chapter on ePorticulture, we argue for a more educationally bio-diverse, or "edu-diverse," approach to teaching, learning, and assessing. Through our experiences of working "from the ground up" in an academic technology unit at a four-year university, we have worked directly with faculty and departments interested in innovative approaches to adapting the culture of assessment. We have also offered advice and recommendations to administrators and academic senate committees making operational and policy decisions for the institution. We are especially excited about the unique potential that eportfolios are creating and hope to share some cultural changes underway that relate to this new growth.

BACKGROUND: ELEMENTS FOR SUCCESSFUL PLANTING

In 1993, the Coalition of Essential Schools and the Annenberg Institute for School Reform conducted one of the first research projects investigating digital portfolios, also called eportfolios. Researchers identified five core factors to consider when exploring the successful planning and implementation of electronic portfolios: vision, assessment, technology, logistics, and culture. While the eportfolio movement has evolved and grown dramatically over the past 15 years, consideration of all of these basic factors still makes sense. We have learned a lot about what it takes to nurture and harvest a good "crop" of portfolios in our experience of working on eportfolio development within a large public university. And while there are many factors that may determine the success or failure of comprehensive assessment, we believe that the most essential element that needs to be planted is that of shifting, re-defining, or adapting the existing culture of assessment.

Attitudes, values, goals, and practices underlying how disciplines expect students to demonstrate their learning varies radically—from high-stakes testing to observation/demonstration to comprehensive portfolios. Cultivating a common cultural approach to curriculum and assessment has proven to be a significant, ever-present challenge. Yet the Association of American Colleges and Universities (AAC & U, 2009, para. 2) believes that "to achieve a high-quality education for all students, valid assessment data are needed to guide planning, teaching, and improvement" and that "good practice in assessment requires multiple assessments, over time." They also advocate for well-planned electronic portfolios that can "provide opportunities to collect data from multiple assessments across a broad range of learning outcomes while guiding student learning and building self-assessment capabilities and eportfolios" and assert that "assessment of work in them can inform programs and institutions on progress in achieving expected goals" (AAC&U, para. 2).

Eportfolios address a current and emerging need for students to have an environment in which they can collect, select, reflect upon, build, and publish a digital archive of their academic work to selected audiences. Eportfolios represent potential keys to open closed doors between disciplines, making transparent the expectations, values and goals that educators expect of students. Eportfolios also represent opportunities for academia to help students bridge their learning with professional development and workforce readiness.

According to a 2008 study by the Campus Computing Project, over 50% of public and private universities and public four-year colleges now offer some form of an eportfolio to their students. Inevitably, campuses are finding a need to balance tensions between using eportfolios for institutional and program assessment or for student-centered, reflective learning. Many students today are adept at representing themselves informally on the Web through social networking yet few have rarely considered creating a more formal, academic identity through a published Web-portfolio.

Around the world, assessment practices are changing. For example, eportfolio use is becoming more commonplace as project-based learning is adopted more widely. Gulbahar and Tinmaz (2006) from Baskent University in Turkey conducted a small-scale study that found eportfolios were valuable assessment tools when evaluating student projects. Similarly, the COMPORT Project in the United Kingdom analyzed the effectiveness of using eportfolios in courses with work-based learning components (Robinson, 2009). The UK study recommended a flexible approach—not using only one tool to demonstrate students' competencies—and identified implementation issues to resolve, such as gaining faculty buy-in, preparing students for reflective writing, engaging both learners and employers, and creating a sustainable project.

Each campus will have its own unique "growth-pattern" and logistical needs. Again, having a *strong vision and guiding rationale* for the use of comprehensive assessment tools and strategies such as eportfolios will make sharing the concept easier through cultural shifts. J. Elizabeth Clark and Bret Eynon from LaGuardia Community College, successful pioneers in eportfolio development, provided such a rationale in a recent article in the AAC&U publication, *Peer Review*. They wrote that the "e-portfolio movement has grown dramatically in significance over the past decade. Linked to sweeping economic, demographic, political, and technological changes, the e-portfolio is an increasingly salient feature of the changing educational landscape" (Clark & Eynon, 2009, p. 18).

Clark and Eynon also outlined what they consider to be the four major drivers of eportfolio use. The first of these drivers, pedagogical change bolstered by innovative teaching methods in higher education, emphasizes student-centered and integrative learning and the effort to help students develop meta-cognitive skills. New methods in learning may include a role shift for faculty, from being the "sage on the stage" to "guide on the side," working more interactively with students.

Second, using Web 2.0 tools students today have developed informal digital self-portraits on Facebook, MySpace, or Twitter years in advance of their college admission. Web-based eportfolio software has made portfolio creation and sharing easier and more adaptable to multiple audiences. Most millennial students swim easily in the social networking and digital communication waters, intimate with the concept of "user-generated" content.

Third, transparency and accountability in higher education act as additional drivers pushing eportfolio development. On our campus at San Francisco State University, the need to document disciplinary competencies has been a major growth factor in the adoption of portfolios as an alternative to summative exams. For example, in undergraduate programs, such as Liberal Studies and Journalism, and graduate programs in Public Health, eportfolios have been adopted as both formative and summative measurement tools. We offer specific examples of direct measure protocols using eportfolios later in this chapter.

Finally, Clark and Eynon identify student mobility among higher education institutions as a precursor to similar mobility among workforce organizations. Faced with the reality that greater numbers of students than ever transfer between institutions, those students can use portfolios as a proactive "passport" or record of their learning. Moreover, employers are increasingly looking for more comprehensive information in the forms of visual curriculum vitae and eportfolios.

These four drivers validate the elements of culture change we have chosen to cover based on our experiences at San Francisco State University. The first and third drivers described by Clark and Eynon—pedagogical change and the call for accountability—highlight key needs related to changing the culture at an educational institution: balancing tensions between using eportfolios for institutional and program assessment or for student-centered, reflective learning; moving toward project-based, authentic assessment; mapping eportfolio artifacts to objectives at different levels; and changing curriculum based on changes to assessment strategies.

The second and fourth drivers—easy-to-use, emerging technologies; and student mobility during and after their higher education experiences—highlight how educational institutions must support students. Namely, institutions must teach students about formal Web identities and Web reputation, the transitional pathways among educational institutions, and bridging to careers through professional development. At the same time, campuses must manage interactions with other institutions in regional or even statewide eportfolio projects.

This chapter will also help readers determine why they might pursue the use of eportfolios within their educational institution, at the course, program, or institutional levels. While our experience is primarily through the lens of higher education, we hope that the information herein will also be relevant for K-12 educators as well.

ENCOURAGING EDU-DIVERSITY: CHANGING ASSESSMENT = CHANGING CURRICULUM = CHANGING THE CULTURE OF THE INSTITUTION

As instructors and students engage in using eportfolios, campuses may go through culture changes in several different areas. On a decentralized campus like San Francisco State University, finding a set of shared attitudes, values, goals, and practices that characterize a common approach to curriculum, assessment, or eportfolios has been a significant challenge. We have responded primarily by fostering and accommodating growth at the departmental level.

Case Story: Liberal Studies Faculty at SF State Change Curriculum and Assessment Strategy

When faculty who share a common curriculum can agree to work together towards a new culture of assessment, change can be rapid and exponential. For example, a group of new faculty in the interdisciplinary field of Liberal Studies jointly decided that electronic portfolios could provide a way to capture undergraduate student work within sections of their gateway and capstone courses. As a part of their shared curricular planning for the course, they outlined core areas that all Liberal Studies students needed to complete. Within a consensus process, they agreed that the portfolios should all include an Introduction, Mission Statement, Resume, elements of the Liberal Studies Major/Classes and Competencies, as well as sections for Values, Skills, and Leadership. In consulting with this innovative group, we set

up an eFolio "profile" base site and scheduled 90-minute, hands-on training labs for each gateway course section.

Within the training, students sign up online for their electronic portfolio, become familiar with features of the software, and begin uploading "signature" assignments to their sites (see Figure 1 and http://stephenkuhn.efolioworld.com/ for examples). We also introduce our informational website, http://eportfolio.sfsu.edu, with Web-based tutorials to support independent work.

Following our philosophy that students should be the owners of their own content, students control whether to make their portfolios public or share selectively using security features of the software. By the time students enter the capstone course in their final semester, they have created work across many disciplines. The eportfolio provides a shared common "container" and way to track and manage their coursework.

What makes this undergraduate program unique is the ongoing active collaboration of faculty towards a common curricular goal. In returning to work with the group after a year of implementing eportfolios, we are now able to focus on deeper aspects such as keyword "tags" that students will associate with objects in their portfolios. Faculty members collaborate on what the keywords should be to map to departmental,

Figure 1 Eportfolios completed by liberal studies students at SF State

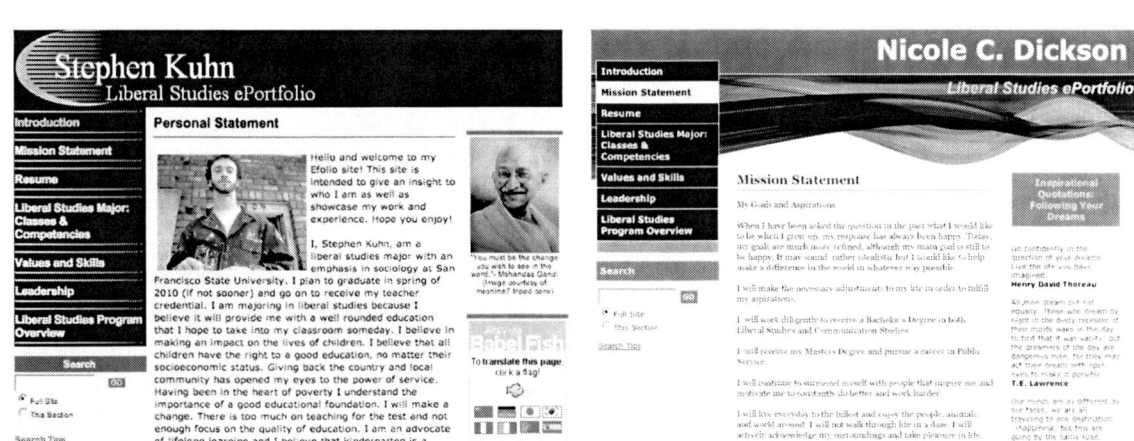

institutional, and even national goals—allowing the department to prepare for its program review cycle and accreditation reporting.

Promoting Project-Based Learning and Assessment

Promoting edu-diversity also means promoting alternative methods of instruction, such as project-based learning (PBL). John W. Thomas (2000) reviewed multiple research studies about PBL, concluding that the method is an effective one. "Project Based Learning designs, because of their emphasis on student autonomy, collaborative learning, and assessments based on authentic performances are seen to maximize students' orientation toward learning and mastery" (Thomas, 2000, p. 6). Thomas also found that students may require additional support with respect to learning how to learn. He prescribed support strategies that point to the use of eportfolios in conjunction with PBL practices, such as formative self-assessment, peer feedback, presentations to external audiences, and the use of computer supported intentional learning environments.

Looking at PBL from a different perspective, Edutopia staff members (2008, para. 4) outlined some of its benefits to the students themselves: "Because students are evaluated on the basis of their projects, rather than on the comparatively narrow rubrics defined by exams, essays, and written reports, assessment of project-based work is often more meaningful to them." Project-based learning situations can also provide opportunities to engage students in group work, service learning, and higher-level thinking.

Balancing Tensions between Institutional Assessment and Student-Centered ePortfolios

Some institutions use eportfolios as a forum to collect and showcase a student's work, while other institutions implement them as a means to aggregate assessment data. However, very few products—open source or commercial—perform both tasks well. Software development organizations and learning communities equally recognize the need to strike a balance between the two sets of needs. Olson, Schroeder, and Wasko (2009) list students, faculty, and institutions as stakeholders for eFolio Minnesota, the eportfolio tool used by the Minnesota State Colleges and Universities (MnSCU). The tool is "designed to support and document interconnections among these three key stakeholders" (Olson, Schroeder, & Wasko, 2009, p. 171). Funded through workforce development initiatives, eFolio Minnesota is a prominent example of industry-education partnerships that focus on users' needs. As a result of this partnership, eFolio is farther along than most tools in supporting diverse uses.

As this chapter encourages avoiding monocultures, it is equally important to avoid a monoculture of eportfolios. Deciding which approach to take with eportfolios—institution-centered or student-centered—is not an either-or situation for a department or institution. Instead, eportfolio products and processes should be used as part of a suite of teaching and learning tools. Tools such as learning management and assessment management systems are often used to collect data for the institution, while eportfolios can provide control for individual students. Helen Barrett (2004) expands a previous version of a helpful table that outlined the differences between ePortfolios and assessment management systems (Barrett & Knezek, 2003, p. 6). The revised table compares each tool's purpose; data structure, types, and storage; who has control of what and how items are displayed; and level of technological competency required. Barrett terms the coordinated use of both a balanced assessment system.

What should be done when more than one ePortfolio "tool" is being used on a campus? We have found that we have been able to support a larger number of instructors and departments by establishing a central clearinghouse, or informational Website, with Web-based tutorials for students and faculty, and narrowing our support of eportfolio growth to two "build-options": a hosted Web-based technology (a version of the software used to support eFolio Minnesota) and HTML templates published to each student's SF State Web space (using Seamonkey, Mozilla's free Web editor). We have also investigated potential systems for campus-wide implementation, laying the groundwork for scaling up to a growing demand.

Mapping ePortfolio Artifacts to Objectives at Different Levels

To begin using eportfolios for either a course or program, it is important to map the products that students create—i.e., eportfolio artifacts— to specific objectives, outcomes, or standards. Course or program objectives describe which knowledge, skills, or attitudes students should be able to show they have mastered. By assigning projects that align directly with these objectives, students know what is expected and instructors know what to evaluate. When mapping artifacts to the objectives, it is also important to think about the level of competency required. For example, asking a nursing student to write down the process for finding a vein and inserting a needle is a lower level of competence than asking that same student to demonstrate that he or she has actually done it (e.g., through a video clip or an observation log written by supervising doctor or nurse in the field). Reflective statements allow students to describe how they feel when performing the skill.

Standards created by outside agencies, such as teacher credential agencies and discipline-specific accreditation bodies, often predetermine what skills and knowledge students need to show. Figure 2 shows how outcomes or objectives at different levels can be aligned, how they are influenced by various drivers, and how electronic portfolios allow students to demonstrate competencies at multiple levels. Instructors can still be creative

with how students use an eportfolio to demonstrate their competencies. Instructors can also add components that the standards often do not require, such as reflective statements, leadership skills, and community-based activities.

Eportfolios provide opportunities to accommodate students' different learning styles and different learning needs. If possible, instructors should give students options regarding how they demonstrate skills and competencies. These options can be related to the format used or the content covered in completing the eportfolio assignment. Examples of different formats to achieve the objective include writing a paper, giving and recording a presentation, or creating a video. Giving options related to content can be as simple as providing four essay questions and asking students to answer one of them, as long as they can show the same skills or knowledge with each one.

Many campuses are shifting away from "checkbox filling" to "intentional and integrated learning." While students must complete all the requirements for a class or program, it is also important for them to know why they are doing it and to make choices about classes or eportfolio assignment topics that move them toward some goal. Asking students to write reflective statements about individual artifacts is one way to get them to think about why they are doing an eportfolio assignment and how it relates to the class, the program, or their life goals. They demonstrate integrated learning by providing eportfolio pieces related to internships, jobs, or other co-curricular work. Reflective statements should demonstrate students' understanding of the links between delivered curriculum, or what the instructor prepares and presents; experienced curriculum, or what the student derives from it; and lived curriculum, or what the student learns throughout his or her life prior to, alongside, and after the coursework (Yancey, 2008).

Throughout the course or program, instructors can involve others in the evaluation process.

Figure 2. Levels of mapping: from student artifacts to department outcomes, institutional goals, and beyond

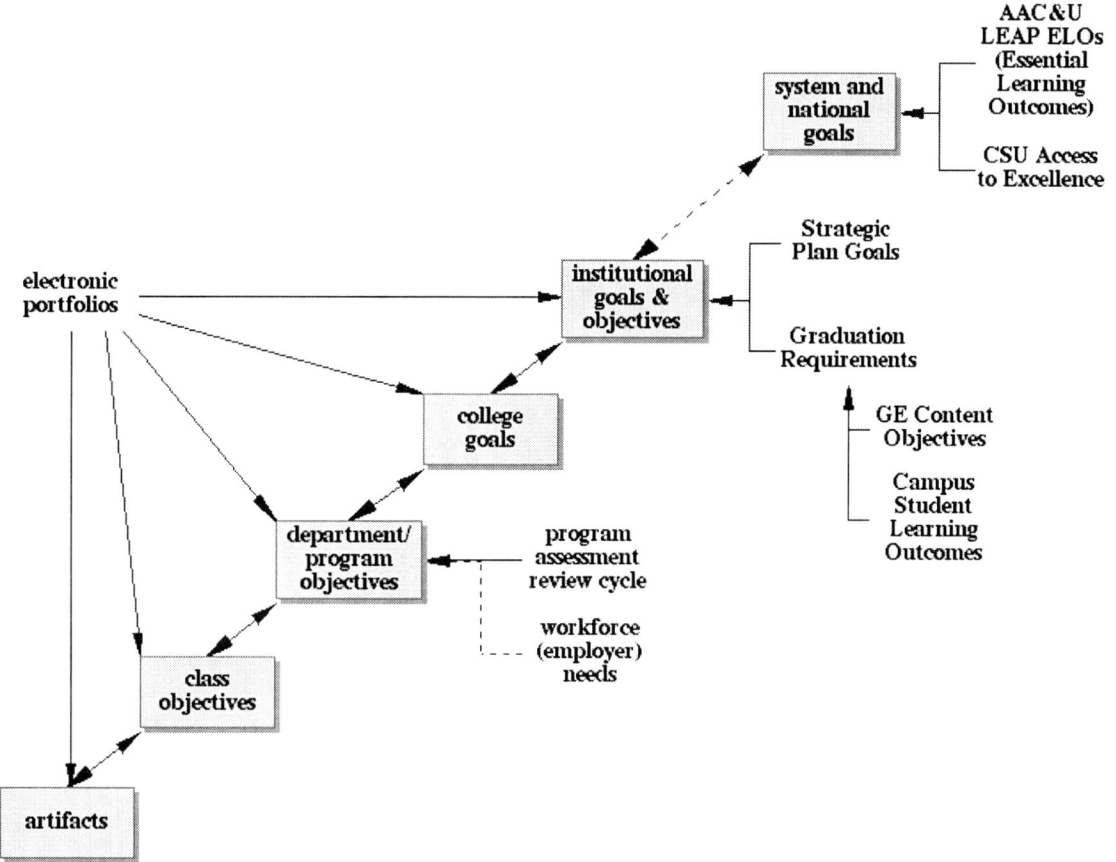

Some use student peer review as a way to help students get feedback before submitting artifacts or reflections for a grade. Other instructors solicit experts' review when a student does co-curricular work, such as a field experience class, internship, or oral presentation. If students use an eportfolio throughout a program, you may construct panels to review final portfolios for completeness, even though the individual artifacts and reflections have already been given grades from the instructors who assigned them. An oral presentation of the portfolio may also be a part of your assessment strategy.

Some programs invite panels of employers from their field to evaluate eportfolios after students have graduated to solicit feedback about the methods and types of evidence used to demonstrate competencies. The evaluation of individual student assignments happens at the course level. However, if assignments are archived in an eportfolio, instructors can review artifacts themselves, the student's reflections about the value or meaning of each artifact, and different instructors' feedback about the student's work. In this way, the instructors and advisors can collectively track a student's growth and development and provide formative guidance about next steps or areas to improve. Departments may also have both formative and summative reviews of a cohort or cluster of student portfolios. The Western As-

Figure 3. Levels of mapping: Life Sciences example

CSU ANYWHERE: Mapping Example

National > Institution > College > Department > Course > Artifact Level Goals

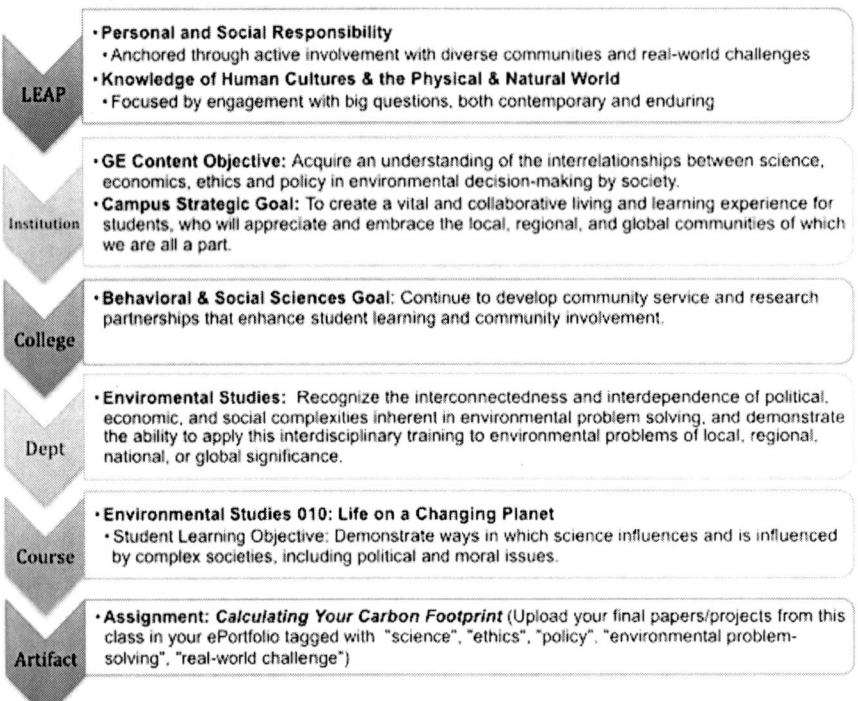

sociation of Schools and Colleges (WASC, 2008) provides guidelines and a rubric for departments interested in using eportfolios to assess program learning outcomes.

Figure 3 shows how eportfolios can be used to map individual student work to the overarching campus goals. Campuses can build on the process from the top down during program review cycles by helping departments align their program objectives with university strategic plan goals and/ or graduation requirements. These graduation requirements often include General Education (GE) content objectives, campus student learning outcomes (SLOs), or both. At the same time, campuses can promote the use of eportfolios to assess students' achievement of program objectives. Academic technology units and faculty development centers can work with departments and instructors from the bottom up to map course objectives to program objectives. Next, staff and faculty-in-residence can work with individual instructors to identify student projects that would generate appropriate artifacts to demonstrate student competencies. When these two approaches meet in the middle, it is then possible to show the connections between student work and institutional goals.

Eportfolios can extend beyond the campus for purposes of transfer and career bridging. The Association of American Colleges and Universities has identified Essential Learning Outcomes (ELOs) that many institutions use to form their own campus-level student learning outcomes. As more institutions adopt outcomes based on common elements, the transfer process may improve for higher education students. Employers have become stakeholders in the electronic portfolio process as well. Some employers, such as some K-12 schools, rely on discipline-based standards that are sometimes referenced in eportfolios, via tags or preset menus. In recognition of the important links between education and industry, workforce development funding helps pay for an electronic portfolio for every citizen of the state of Minnesota as part of the eFolio Minnesota project. As mentioned above, some college and university programs engage local employers in dialogue about what competencies they expect from graduates. The Career Center at Florida State University holds a contest each year in which student eportfolios are reviewed by employers and university administrators to identify high-quality work (Lumsden, 2007, p. 52). This practice builds upon a study commissioned by AAC&U (2008), which included employers' perspectives on the effectiveness of higher education assessment practices. The study participants ranked multiple-choice testing the lowest and authentic assessment strategies—elements typically found in an eportfolio, such as capstone projects and co-curricular work—the highest.

Case Stories: Eportfolio-Based Program Assessments at SF State

Several programs have worked with us to develop eportfolio-based program assessments on this model. Most recently, in Journalism, all students in a capstone course, JOUR 609, were required to complete an electronic portfolio. Eighty-eight students submitted a portfolio, which included published and unpublished work from student publications. In an external direct review process, reviewers concentrated on eight of twelve competencies: News Judgment, Critical Thinking, Cultural Competence, Analytical Competence, Research/Reporting, Visual Competence, Critical Evaluation, and Writing. Of the almost ninety portfolios, a systematic random sample of twenty were chosen to review. The five-member review committee, which consisted of three faculty and two external journalism professionals, reviewed the portfolios. Three members were assigned to assess two competencies, and two members were assigned to assess one competency each. Members assessed the competencies on a scale of 1-5, with 5 being the highest. They marked their assessment on the chart and the data was combined and analyzed for the accreditation report.

The Journalism assessment benefits from the extensive experience of the Masters of Public Health (MPH) program. Since 2005, the Health Education Department has kept an archive of MPH student eportfolios. These eportfolios are used for assessment, development, and presentational purposes. During their MPH program, students use their eFolio sites to archive evidence from their academic classes, practice courses, internships, and culminating experience projects. In 2009, the eportfolios will be shared directly with the Council on Education for Public Health (CEPH) as the accreditation team visits campus.

Professional competencies in Health Education are based upon the standards for the preparation of graduate public health practitioners established by the Society for Public Health Education (SOPHE) and the American Association for Health Education (AAHE).

MPH student eportfolios include:

- A professional mission statement
- Evidence of work across national competencies in public health
- Community-based and professional experience
- Culminating experience report and presentation
- Evidence of leadership skills

The electronic format of these portfolios allows students to archive a wider range of their work, using many different media sources. The MPH eFolios have been designed to support assessment, advising, and a deeper reflection on academic and professional development, ultimately demonstrating core competence in Community Health Education.

These eportfolios are created using the eFolio software, an easy to use, Web-based platform, widely used in the Minnesota State College and University system. Students register online for their eFolios and spend several hours in initial computer-lab training on campus getting familiar with the software. No Web-authoring skills are required: A text editor enables users to manage and update text in a simple-to-use Microsoft Word-like text editor window, as well as "E–Z link" technologies, to make building the portfolio similar to using a word processor. eFolio provides a quick and easy system for uploading images, video, audio, or documents throughout each site, allowing for a personalized and comprehensive portfolio.

The use of eportfolios at a program level is introduced at the first orientation meeting with these goals:

- Provide students with the ability to develop an electronic portfolio demonstrating core competence in community health education through archived evidence (signature assignments, presentations, multimedia work, Web-links etc.) from academic classes, practice courses, and culminating experience projects;
- Develop eportfolios using the portfolio process to "collect, select, reflect, build, publish, link and share" their academic work and their mastery of the responsibilities and competencies required for a master level health education;
- Share their eportfolios with Advisors, Faculty CE Committee members, and par-

ticipate actively in a peer review for both formative and summative assessment of their MPH work;
- Encourage students to showcase the professional, leadership, team, and communication skills that they have gained from the MPH program;
- Support future employment opportunities and utilize eportfolios to showcase skills in public health practice for further academic and professional development and international outreach as public health professionals;
- Use eportfolios to assess the MPH curriculum effectiveness in developing the master level core competencies in community health education.

This department has been working to share student eportfolios in an accreditation review with the Council on Education for Public Health (CEPH-- the Independent agency recognized by the US Department of Education to accredit schools of public health and graduate public health programs.) The visit in the fall of 2009 will represent the first time electronic portfolios will be shared as a part of the review process in the discipline.

Each year, a large poster "quilt" of the graduating cohort is created along with a digital archive of the portfolio sites (Figure 4). A representative eportfolio can be viewed at: http://oscarmacias.efolioworld.com/comps

CONCLUSION

Designing a New Educational Landscape

The institutional culture is perhaps the most critical component in making eportfolios an integral teaching and learning tool. Institutions may answer questions related to technology, assessment, and

Figure 4. Snapshot Poster of SF State Master of Public Health eportfolios (2008 Cohort)

logistics concerning mechanically implementing equipment and personnel. Yet only with "buy-in" at all levels will comprehensive assessment strategies that emphasize knowledge-building and growth over time be possible. Some departments may have a mature and fully developed curriculum tied to portfolio use, while others may be just beginning to consider using portfolios. Tapping into grassroots leadership from those departments with established, comprehensive assessment strategies can be extremely valuable in promoting the concept of eportfolios.

Elements for Successful Planting

Any eportfolio project will need to give attention to *vision, assessment, technology, logistics, and*

culture. We suggest that the most essential element that needs to be planted is that of shifting, re-defining, or adapting the existing *culture of assessment.* Attitudes, values, goals, and practices underlying how disciplines expect students to demonstrate their learning varies radically, from high-stakes testing to observation/demonstration to comprehensive portfolios. Cultivating a common cultural approach to curriculum and assessment has proven to be a significant, ever-present challenge. Building internally on the expertise of your already "portfolio cultured" departments is an important first step. (Health Education, as explained in the previous section, has been such a department at SFSU.) These departments can help to model how changing the culture of assessment can help to:

- Promote project-based learning and assessment
- Balance tensions between institutional assessment and student-centered eportfolios
- Map eportfolio artifacts to objectives at different levels

Encouraging Edu-Diversity

Eportfolios are the embodiment of new, learner-centered teaching methodologies that put the student, and the educational products they produce, at the center of instruction and assessment. When creating an eportfolio, the student, rather than the instructor, is the producer of the educational content, which is represented in various forms of digital media, including webpages, photos, video, sound, and graphics.

True to any university technology-enhanced teaching and learning initiative, an exemplary implementation of eportfolios at a post-secondary institution dedicates appropriate attention and resources to three intersecting areas:

- Educational Best Practices: The initiative demonstrates best teaching and learning practices from an educational planning and assessment perspective; and integrates universal design for learning principles to ensure accessibility for all.
- Student and Faculty Support Systems: The initiative offers comprehensive and tailored pedagogical and technical support for faculty and students as they develop the technical and cognitive skills associated with assigning, creating, or evaluating media-rich eportfolios, including training, resources, consultations, and help desk support.
- Technology Infrastructure: The initiative provides a reliable, scalable, and robust technological solution for creating, hosting, and archiving eportfolios; the system integrates with, and extends, the current campus technological environment.

Addressing these core areas can help to grow a new, more diverse assessment culture. We now have the technology to support the unique, discipline-specific papers and creative projects that students are devising each day. Our institutions can leverage a more transparent "window" into academic achievement to benefit both individuals and institutions. Faculty buy-in is key. Reflective writing and clarity around the choice of artifacts and learning objectives at different levels can guide students toward a more vital record of their academic identity and toward sustaining pride in their achievements. We recommend a flexible approach, not necessarily using only one tool to demonstrate students' competencies, but focusing more on eportfolio processes that encourage students to make connections between curricular and co-curricular work.

REFERENCES

Association of American Colleges and Universities (AAC&U). (2008, January 9). *How should colleges assess and improve student learning? Employers' views on the accountability challenge.* Washington, DC: Association of American Colleges and Universities.

Barrett, H. (2004, July 17). *Differentiating electronic portfolios and online assessment management systems.* Retrieved October 29, 2009, from http://electronicportfolios.com/systems/concerns.html

Barrett, H., & Knezek, D. (2003, April 21-25). e-Portfolios: Issues in assessment, accountability and preservice teacher preparation. In *Proceedings of the American Educational Research Association (AERA) Conference,* Chicago, IL.

Clark, J. E., & Eynon, B. (2009). E-portfolios at 2.0: Surveying the field. *Peer Review, 11*(1), 18-23. Retrieved October 29, 2009, from AAC&U website: http://www.aacu.org/peerreview/pr-wi09/pr-wi09_eportfolios.cfm

Darling-Hammond, L. (2009, November 17). *Lessons from abroad: International standards and assessments.* A webinar presented for Edutopia and the Stanford Center for Opportunity Policy in Education in collaboration with the Council for Chief State School Officers.

Deneen, P. (2009, March 26). *Against monoculture.* Retrieved October 29, 2009, from http://www.frontporchrepublic.com/?p=1739

Edutopia. (2008, February 28). *Why teach with project learning? Providing students with a well-rounded classroom experience.* Retrieved on November 30, 2009, from Edutopia website: http://www.edutopia.org/project-learning-introduction

Gulbahar, Y., & Tinmaz, H. (2006). Implementing project-based learning and e-portfolio assessment in an undergraduate course. *Journal of Research on Technology in Education, 38*(3), 309–327.

Lumsden, J. (2007). Development and implementation of an e-portfolio as a university-wide program. *New Directions for Student Services, 119*, 43–63. doi:10.1002/ss.248

Olson, L., Schroeder, L., & Wasko, P. (2009). Moving eFolio Minnesota to the next generation. In Cambridge, D., Cambridge, B., & Yancey, K. (Eds.), *Electronic portfolios 2.0: Emergent research on implementation and impact* (pp. 165–174). Sterling, VA: Stylus.

Robinson, P. (2009, March 27). *COMPORT: A comparative study of e-portfolio implementation in work-based learning (Final project report).* Bristol, UK: Joint Information Systems Commission.

Siemens, G. (2006). *Knowing knowledge.* Retrieved December 3, 2009, from http://www.elearnspace.org/KnowingKnowledge_LowRes.pdf

The Association of American Colleges and Universities. (2009). *VALUE: Valid Assessment of Learning in Undergraduate Education.* Retrieved October 29, 2009, from AAC&U website: http://www.aacu.org/value/

Thomas, J. W. (2000). *A review of research on project-based learning.* San Rafael, CA: The Autodesk Foundation.

Wardlaw, C. (2006, September). *Mathematics in Hong Kong/China: Improving on being first in PISA.* Paper presented at the 50th Annual Meeting of the Australian Mathematical Society, Sydney, Australia.

Western Association of Schools and Colleges. (2008). *Program learning outcomes.* Retrieved July 24, 2008 from WASC website: http://www.wascsenior.org/findit/files/forms/Program_Learning_Outcome_Rubric__080430_.pdf

Yancey, K. (2008, July). *Outcomes, reflection, electronic portfolios.* Paper presented at the St. Jerome's University Eportfolio Conference, Waterloo, ON, Canada.

Chapter 6
21st Century Teaching and Learning through E–Portfolios:
Potentials and Challenges in Teacher Education

Yi-Ping Huang
University of Maryland Baltimore County, USA

ABSTRACT

Drawing upon the experience of institutionalizing ProcessFolio in a teacher education unit, the author outlines the processes of design, implementation and institutionalization; strategic changes in program, curriculum and assessment; and uses of data and technology to leverage change and increase efficiencies in policymaking, teaching practice, and organizational operations. Through discussions of coherent program-wide and career-wide ePortfolio systems, the author invites teachers and learners to re-examine the potential of eportfolios in realizing collective goals of quality enhancement and to re-envision eportfolios as a framework for reciprocal transformation of the teaching profession and professionals in the 21st Century.

DOI: 10.4018/978-1-4666-0143-7.ch006

GREATER EXPECTATIONS AND THE PROMISES OF EPORTFOLIO IN AN ERA OF ACCOUNTABILITY

The promise of synergistic integration of teaching, learning, assessment and accountability associated with electronic portfolios have led to renewed interest and increased adoption in teacher preparation and education programs in the United States (Elliott, 2003; Huang, 2006). In the context of teaching and learning, eportfolios enable a learner-centered, standards-based, and outcomes-oriented approach for generating, assessing and documenting learning and achievement, in and over time. Rather than being short-term and episodic, a program-wide eportfolio is sustained throughout the teacher education cycle, focusing on cyclical and reciprocal processes that connect theory with practice. In the context of assessment and accreditation, the implementation of a program-wide eportfolio requires defined accountability processes and outcomes at individual, collective and material levels and, hence, facilitates the creation of a "culture of evidence." The demand for systemic commitment to educational excellence through the provision of rigorous processes that generate, assess and use data for quality assurance and enhancement has been a dominant trend in the American teacher education reform agenda. This trend is evident in national accreditation processes and requirements set forth by the National Council for Accreditation of Teacher Education (NCATE) and the Teacher Education Accreditation Council (TEAC) (Cochran-Smith, 2005; Murray, 2005; Wise, 2005).

In the broader context of 21st century education needs and aspirations, coherent career-wide eportfolios, spanning from teacher preparation programs for pre-service teachers to teacher education programs for practicing teachers, potentially transcend traditional barriers faced by the teaching profession. At the individual level, eportfolios democratize learning through deeply personalized engagement and empower practitioners to become both adaptive experts and knowledge creators. If we consider the "process" of creating an eportfolio (often characterized as create, collect, select, reflect and project) as "the proof" of individualized teaching and learning, the eportfolio "product" can be seen as an individualized acknowledgment of competencies and celebration of achievements for the duration of a teacher's career. At the collective level, eportfolios help the establishment of *communities of creators*, extend interactions beyond classrooms to *communities of practice*, and expand teacher research beyond core subjects to include 21st century themes and skills. The continuous support for teachers' professional development, as operationalized through career-wide and standards-based eportfolio development and assessment, helps instill *mutual accountability* and facilitates *reciprocal transformation* between the professionals and the profession in realizing collective goals of quality enhancement.

EDUCATION ACCOUNTABILITY SYSTEM (EAS): PROFILE OF A TEACHER EDUCATION UNIT

The Department of Education at the University of Maryland Baltimore County (UMBC) offers teacher preparation programs for initial licensures and teacher education programs for practicing teachers. These programs are approved by the Maryland State Department of Education (MSDE), accredited by the NCATE, and nationally recognized by the Specialized Professional Associations (SPAs). Central to the accreditation and quality improvement processes are the development, implementation and sustenance of the Education Accountability System (EAS).

The institutionalization of the *EAS* is the result of strategic visions and actions aiming to enhance teaching, learning and collaboration within the P-20 continuum and is reflective of the changing dynamics in policymaking, teaching practice, and organizational operations. The discussion of the

EAS, as operationalized through the ProcessFolio, contextualized by the teacher education unit and its professional community with the following areas of focus: (1) the EAS framework; (2) the *Five-R* processes (re-envisioning, re-organization, re-engineering, realization and renewal) and their impact on organizational culture and infrastructure, on program, curriculum and assessment, and on resources, support, and system renewal; and (3) the potentials and challenges of program-wide and career-wide eportfolio as frameworks for establishment of mutual accountability and reciprocal transformation of the teaching professionals and the teaching profession in the 21st century.

The EAS Framework

Grounded in the theory and practice of capacity and linkage building, the EAS (Figure 1) is a community-based system that actively engages and encourages collaborative interactions among stakeholders of the UMBC teacher education programs, its P-12 Professional Development Schools (PDSs), and the national and state accreditation agencies. The EAS is a dynamic system that integrates teaching, learning, assessment, management and reporting functions, and is delivered through CampusTools HigherEd, software developed by Tk20, Inc. The EAS consists of three integrated production components: Candidate Performance, Program Quality and Unit Operations.

Assessments of candidate performance are conducted through the ProcessFolio (Figure 2) structure of the EAS. ProcessFolio is a program-wide portfolio system that generates and documents both learning processes and learning outcomes. The contents of the ProcessFolios are based on Program Master Plans (PMPs) (Tables 1 and 2) that align programs, curricula, standards, assessments and outcomes for each of the teacher preparation and teacher education programs.

Figure 1. Education Accountability System (EAS)

Education Accountability System (EAS)

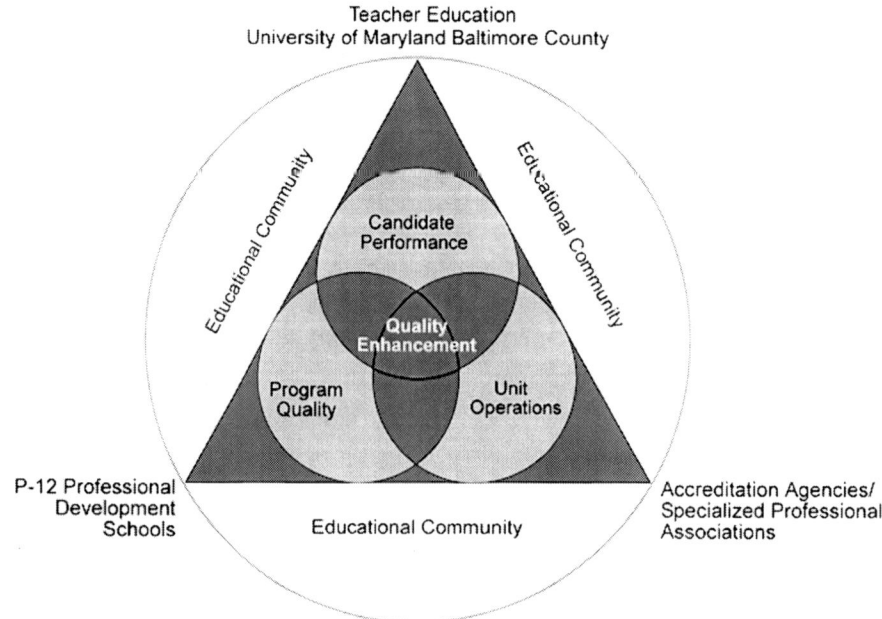

The program-specific PMPs detail performance-based assessments and course-embedded key assignments at each of the four benchmarks (entrance, field experience, clinical practice and program exit). A teacher or degree candidate's ProcessFolio will, thus, include: (1) personal and academic information; (2) course-based key assignments that are assessed by university faculty throughout the program; (3) field and performance-based assessments conducted by the university supervisor, the P-12 mentor teacher and the teacher candidate himself or herself throughout the program; (4) TeachingFolios (Figures 5 and 6) which highlight competencies and achievements during internship/clinical practice and are assessed by the university supervisor, the P-12 mentor teacher, and the teacher candidate himself/herself at program exit; and (5) academic (GPA) and standardized test (PRAXIS I and II) results.

ProcessFolio and the Five-R Processes

ProcessFolio is developed and institutionalized through the Five-R Processes (Figure 3): (1) Re-envisioning; (2) Re-organization; (3) Re-engineering; (4) Realization; and (5) Renewal. Collectively, the Five-R Processes are not once-and-done but, rather, cyclical and ongoing.

The Re-Envisioning Process

The creation of quality control systems and improvement machineries has been the focus of accreditation processes since the introduction of the NCATE standards in 2001, and the TEAC quality principles in 2003. Development, sustenance and enhancement of accountability systems have become some of the most challenging aspects of the accreditation process, as they involve changes

Figure 2. ProcessFolio Education Accountability System

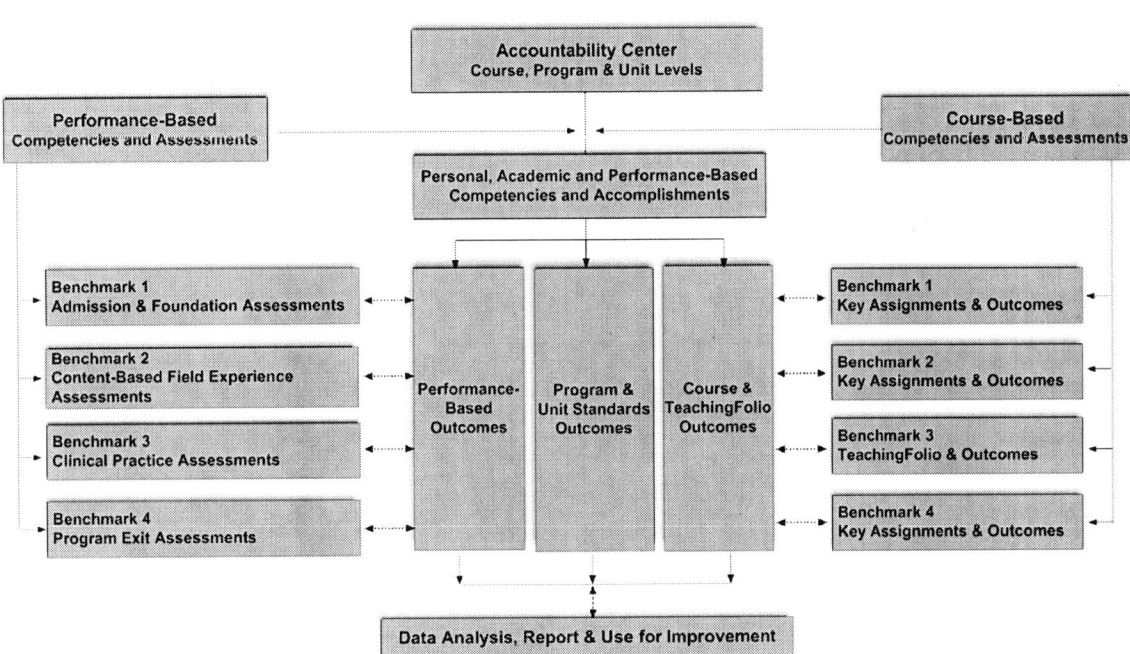

Table 1. Teacher preparation program: ESOL Program Master Plan and ProcessFolio content

	TESOL Standards	Benchmark 1: Admission and Entry-level Course Assessments	Benchmark 2: Level Two Course Assessments & Entry Into Internship	Benchmark 3: Clinical Practice Assessments Phase I and II	Benchmark 4: Program Exit Assessments
1	Licensure Assessment	BA with 3.0+ **GPA** 500 on Verbal **GRE**, (527+ on Praxis I for Certificate) 550+ **TOEFL** for International Students	Passing scores on **Praxis I** (527+ composite score) or 1000 or better on the **GRE** 3.0+ **GPA** on program coursework	3.0+ **GPA** on program coursework	Successful completion of MA course work with better than 3.0 **GPA** Passing scores on **Praxis II** ESOL
2	Assessment of Content Knowledge	**EDUC 625** Proficient (3) (80%+) scores on final examination **LING 694** Proficient score (3) on informant language assessment	**EDUC 644** Proficient (3) (80%+) scores on final examination	**EDUC 792L Teaching-Folio** Proficient scores indicating mastery of Professional Standards on TeachingFolio	**Comprehensive Examination** Proficient assessment (3) on candidate's Comprehensive Examination TeachingFolio Presentation and Review
3	Assessment of Candidate Ability to Plan Instruction	**EDUC 688** Proficient scores (3) on assigned lesson plan projects **EDUC 625** Proficient scores (3) on assigned lesson plan projects	**EDUC 655** Proficient scores (3) on assigned Unit plans	**CPPAs for Phase II** Proficient evaluations of lesson planning from internship mentors and supervisors	**Summative CPPA** Average of 3+ on summative CPPAs for Phase II evaluation
4	Assessment of Student Teaching		**EDUC 636** Proficient (80%+) score on final examination	**Formative CPPAs** Average of 3+ on formative CPPA's for Phase II evaluations	**Summative CPPA** Average of 3+ on summative CPPAs for Phase II evaluation
5	Assessment of Candidates Effect on Student Learning	**EDUC 688** Student journals		**EDUC 792L** Assessments of student writing samples inspired by intern's Phase II assignments	TeachingFolio Presentation and Review Proficient assessment (3)
6	Assessment of Candidates' Philosophy of Teaching	**Entrance Requirement** Statement of Purpose for studying ESOL with application.		**EDUC 792L Teaching-Folio** Proficient statement of philosophy in Teaching-Folio	TeachingFolio Presentation and Review Proficient assessment (3)
7	Additional Assessment that Addresses TESOL Standards				**EDUC 794** Proficient assessment (3) of candidates on projects produced
8	Additional Assessment that Addresses TESOL Standards		**MLL 670** Proficient evaluations (3) on projects produced		

TESOL: Teachers of English to Speakers of Other Languages

Table 2. Teacher Education Program: MAE Program Master Plan and ProcessFolio content

Benchmark	Benchmark Criteria	Goals & Competencies	Key Assignments & Outcomes
Benchmark 1 Admission	• Minimum overall graduate GPA of 3.0 • Candidate advisement interview • Online application via Education Accountability System (EAS via Tk20) • Application to Graduate School • Recommendations	• Certified in a Field of Study • Admission to UMBC	• UMBC and LEA Admission Criteria • Entrance Interview • EAS via Tk20 Application
Benchmark 2 Study of Teaching	• Minimum overall graduate GPA of 3.0 • Continuing Advisement • Study of Teaching Classroom Research Project	• Create a review of literature • Use variety of research methods to improve teaching and professional effectiveness • Formulate research questions • Present study in a written report and orally to colleagues	• **EDUC795 Study of Teaching** Focuses on the examination and interpretation of classroom experience, resulting in the modification of content presentation and classroom practices based on the findings of the teachers' research in their own classrooms.
Benchmark 3 Teacher Leadership	• Minimum overall graduate GPA of 3.0 • Continuing advisement • Teacher Leadership Project for the School or District	• Understand dynamics of teacher leadership • Enhance participant's knowledge of adult learning • Create long-term strategies for mentoring beginning teachers	• **EDUC781 Leadership Research Project** Emphasis is placed on the understanding and importance of teacher leadership in schools. Requires the teacher to assume a leadership role as a mentor, and to conduct a leadership activity in the school or district.
Benchmark 4 Capstone	• Minimum overall graduate GPA of 3.0 • Continuing Advisement • Surveys of the program • Capstone Project	• Generate knowledge and understanding at the classroom level • Establish research question, create data-gathering systems, analyze data and determine conclusions • Communicate teacher research findings	• **EDUC792 The Capstone Seminar** Continues the focus on research and integration of content, and provides the opportunity for participants to demonstrate the synthesis of understandings developed throughout the entire master's program.
Benchmark 5 Post Graduation	• Alumni Survey • Employer Survey • Advisory Council Reviews of Program	• Teacher Perception & Adoption • Teacher Retention & Performance • Impact of Classroom & School-based Research • Impact of Leadership Initiatives • Impact on Student Outcomes	• **Follow-up Survey & Program Self-Study** • Employer Survey

MAE: Master of Arts in Education is a program for in-service teachers.

in culture, policy and practice at individual, collective and material levels.

The re-envisioning process begins with a series of conversations reflecting and reframing accountability with regards to context, content, process, assessment, technology, and resources. These conversations are critical as they provide opportunities to better understand current culture and policy; invite deep reflections on beliefs and practice; and encourage personal investment and ownership. A major outcome of the re-envisioning process is the articulation of common visions and missions. The EAS model (Figure 1), for example, is reflective of a community-based vision that involves IHEs, P-12 schools, and professional organizations at state and national levels. The dynamic model aims to facilitate co-construction of teacher education programs from design through oversight, implementation, and evaluation among the key constituents. The goal is to create authentic learning and assessment opportunities that are connected to real world questions and challenges

Figure 3. The Five-R Processes

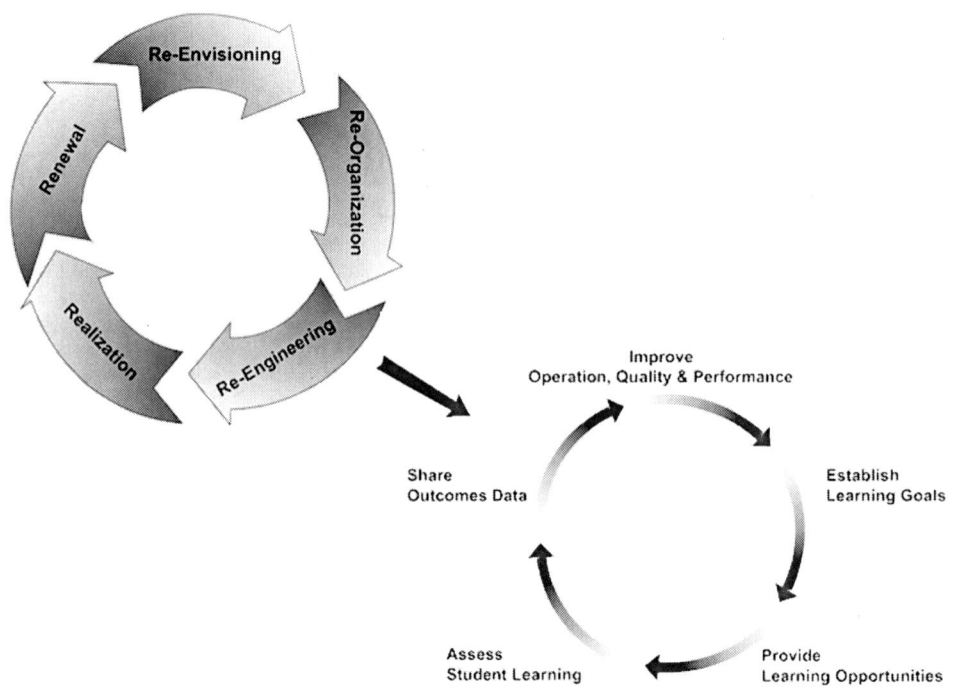

through P-20 collaboration. A second outcome of the re-envisioning process is the articulation of missions in the form of actionable goals and measurable objectives. The Program Master Plans (Tables 1 and 2), for example, specify assessments and expected outcomes at benchmarks for teacher preparation and teacher education programs.

The Re-Organization Process

The re-organization process helps create contacts and conditions that maximize capacity and linkage. Capacity building substantially increases the probability for successful and sustainable interventions. Linkage building enables connection, communication, and transfer of capacities (Spillane & Thompson, 1997; Fullan & Stielgelbauer, 1991; Fullan, 2000). Strategic goals and actions for quality enhancement have thus

been focused on building individual, collective and material capacities, as well as constructing structural, relational, ideological and temporal linkages among the capacities.

One major outcome of this process was the reorganization of the teacher education unit (Figure 4). Structures that existed prior to 2003 are represented by oval-shaped boxes, while structures that were established after 2003 are represented by rectangle-shaped boxes. The newly-instituted structures are program-based committees addressing programmatic and curriculum issues and standards-based committees addressing policies and practices related to national, state and institutional standards and accreditation. The establishment of specialized committees heightens awareness of capacity and needs for change and encourages the building of individual, organizational, and material capacities. The involvement of a critical mass of

Figure 4. UMBC teacher education organization chart

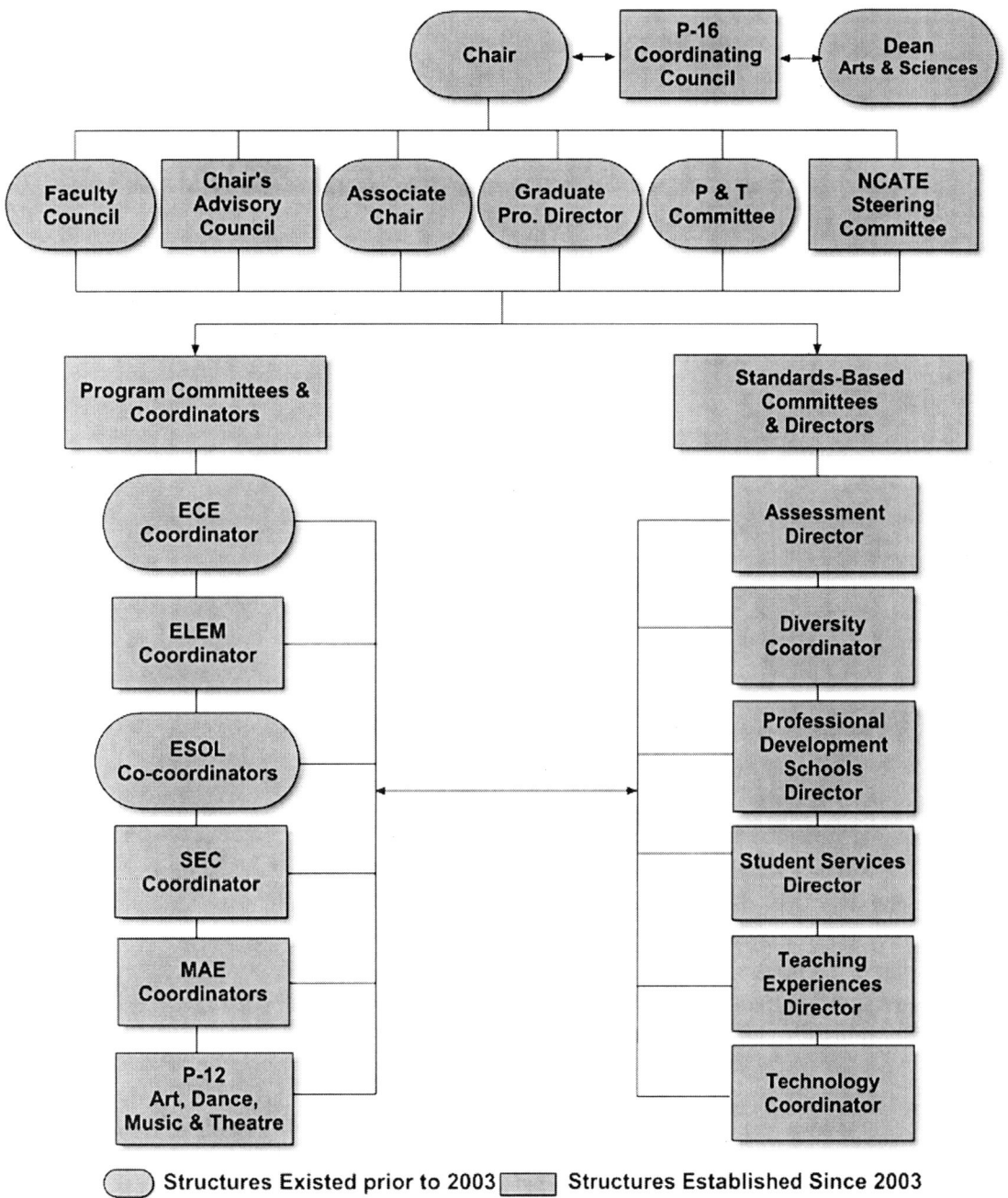

UMBC Teacher Education Organization Chart

Structures Existed prior to 2003 Structures Established Since 2003

ECE: Early Childhood Education Program; ELEM: Elementary Education Program;
SEC: Secondary Education Program; and MAE: Mater of Arts in Education Program.

Figure 5. Internship seminar administrated through the Education Accountability System

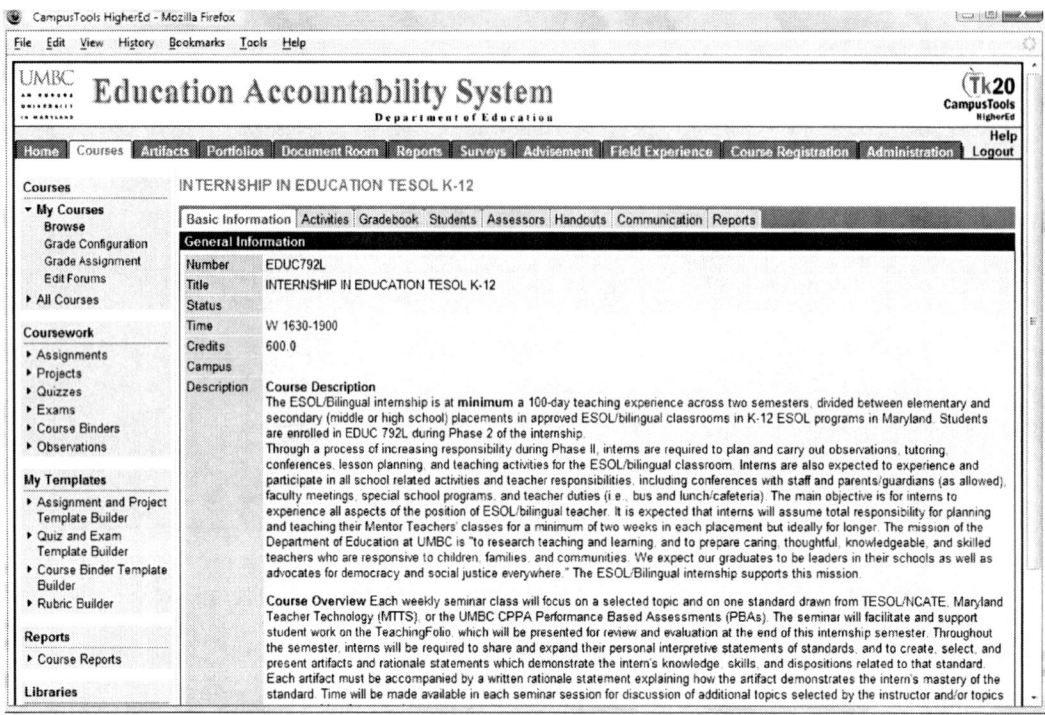

faculty further provides opportunities to create the linkages and ownership necessary for effective and sustained interventions (Huang, 2006). By actively engaging and challenging members of the unit, the re-organizational process facilitates shared governance in creating a new *culture of evidence* with defined charges and processes for each of the committees. Chairs of each of the committees further become champions for the adoption of the new environment of *mutual accountability* through the implementation of the EAS.

TeachingFolio is an eportfolio created during clinical practice/internship. The left portion of the screen shows the eight sections of the ESOL TeachingFolio (Introduction, TESOL Domains/ Standards 1-5, Maryland Teacher Technology Standards, and Curriculum Vitae). The right portion of the screen shows the assessment rubrics used for each of the eight sections.

The Re-Engineering Process

The re-engineering process focuses on the alignment of programs, curricula, standards, instruction and assessment (Figure 3). It demands systematic, program-wide planning and execution of curriculum, instruction and assessment to ensure logical and supportive development, leading to candidate mastery of program standards and outcomes. It demands faculty to reconsider content, instruction, and assessment in the context of individual courses and in relation to other content and professional courses in the program. Consequently, it demands re-negotiation of deeply embedded values and beliefs held by the faculty, expanding and transforming from *course* ownership to *program* ownership and shifting from *creator* and *instructor* to *co-creator* and *facilitator*. Though time-consuming, the transformation is rewarding as capacities and linkages are developed through

Figure 6. TeachingFolio: M.A. Program in English for Speakers of other Languages (ESOL)

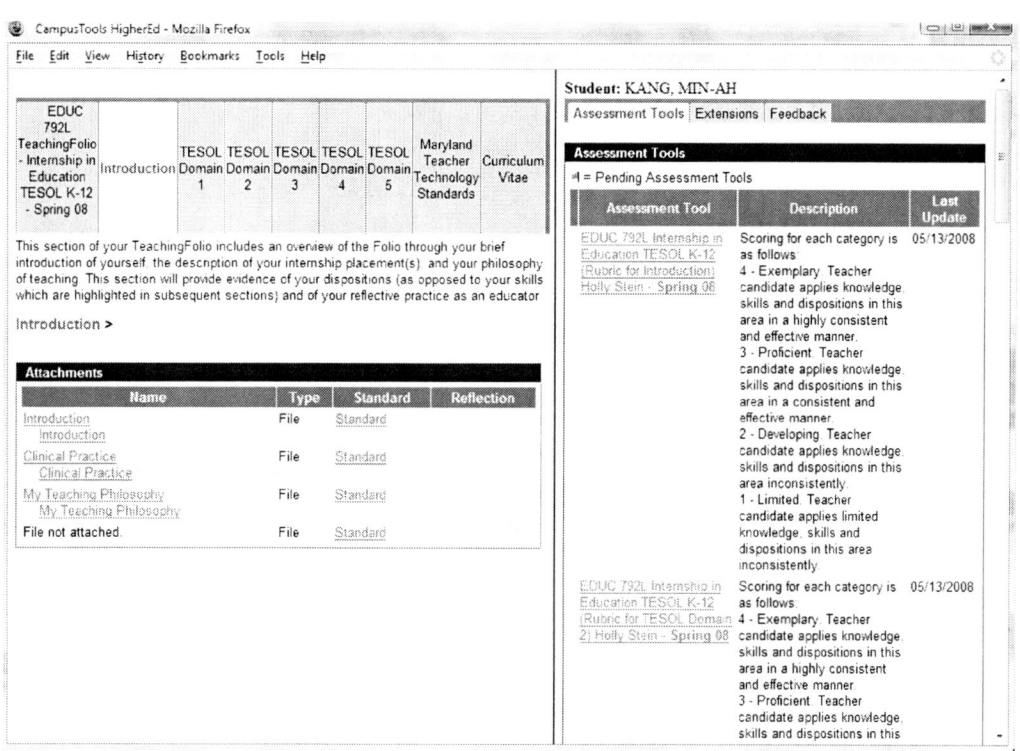

program-specific collaboration and needs-based professional development. Faculty renew their affiliations and contributions in defining content, constructs, strategies, and processes of assessment, and in translating data into actions for quality enhancement.

A major outcome of the re-engineering process was the development of Program Master Plans (Tables 1 and 2) for each of the teacher preparation and education programs. Program committee members work collaboratively in defining benchmark courses at each of the four program benchmarks (entrance, field experience, clinical practice and program exit). Instructors of the benchmark courses are responsible for designing and delivering standards-specific key assignments that are coordinated to demonstrate candidates' competencies and growth in and over time. Table 1 is an example of a Program Master Plan from the ESOL/BL program. The top row indicates

the four benchmarks across the teacher education cycle, while the first column indicates the types of assessment and their alignment to disciplinary standards as defined by the Specialized Professional Associations (SPAs). Each cell lists course identification, key assignments, and proficiency expectations. Results of individual candidates and individual programs can be accessed "live" through the dynamic EAS.

The Program Master Plans have gone through several revisions based on evolving visions, needs, and goals of the faculty and programs, as well as the standards instituted by state and national accrediting agencies. The purposes and goals remain consistent: create a coherent program experience, integrate planning with assessment, streamline data collection, and maximize use of on-demand data for quality enhancements.

The Realization Process

The realization process focuses on development and implementation of the quality control systems and improvement machineries that help realize the goals and objectives of the EAS as defined by the unit. The author and the unit's assessment committee conducted environmental scans with a series of strategic SWOT (strengths, weaknesses, opportunities, and threats) analyses on context, content, process, assessment, technology, and resources. Campus-wide campaigns involving the Provost's office, the Dean's office, the Registrar Office, the Office of Institutional Research, the Office of Information Technology and the Office of the General Counsel were conducted to ensure institution-wide understanding of the integrity of the EAS and its implementation in collaboration with Tk20.

Five modules were designed and implemented by the author and the unit using the functions provided by CampusTools HigherEd. The user information module contains the user's personal, academic and performance information, within which demographic information, registration and transcripts were mined from the institutional Student Information System (SIS) to ensure data consistency and integrity. The assessment modules contain: (1) course-based key assignments delivered through course containers; (2) performance-based assessment delivered through field experience containers; (3) TeachingFolio delivered through portfolio functions; and (4) perceptual and self-reporting surveys administered through the survey functions. The advisement module contains program-specific requirements and benchmark assessments with auditing and annotation functions to track progress. The teaching experience module contains placement information about the candidates, university supervisors, P-12 mentor teachers and the schools/sites. The administration module enables general system and user management, customization through form and database extension builders, as well as generation of queries and reports.

Sustaining comprehensive systems and technology-rich initiatives requires long-term commitment of resources and supportive infrastructures for mutual accountability among the constituents and the institution. Systematic planning with coherent design, development and delivery of professional development and support services is critical to ensuring successful implementation and continual enhancement. A management team was established within the unit's Office of Assessment. On the system side, the team is responsible for developing systems and contents, managing business and operational processes, upgrading software and hardware, conducting data analysis, and compiling assessment and accreditation reports. On the user support side, the team is responsible for providing professional development for faculty, supervisors, and P-12 mentors on content, constructs and processes of assessment and technology use, as well as a wide-variety of user training and support services for candidates, alumni, and other constituents in the education community.

The Renewal Process

The changing policies and practices of assessment and accountability, as embodied in the ways in which schools of education approach curriculum, assessment, and continuous improvement, have been common themes in education conferences and journals. While much energy has been devoted to the development of assessment and accountability systems, limited attention has been paid to issues relating to sustenance and enhancements of such systems and consequential changes in policymaking, teaching practice, and organizational operations in teacher education.

Institutionalization of the EAS demands integrated strategic planning and actions with strong leadership, commitment, collaboration, support, and resources. Sustaining the EAS further requires attention at multiple levels that build capacity and linkage, and requires community-wide commitment and engagement in and over time. The renewal process is, thus, critical to help ensure the cyclical nature of interventions and to sustain the changes made by each of the "R" processes. For example, the re-envisioning process helps articulate community visions and goals. The re-organization process helps establish organizational infrastructures and leadership teams. The re-engineering process helps develop assessment processes and accountability. The realization process helps create technological infrastructures and delivery capabilities. The renewal process helps review progress, manage change expectations and re-energize capacity and linkage for sustained implementation.

The renewal process at the teacher education unit is overseen by the Assessment Committee, which consists of the Director of Assessment, Department Chair, Associate Chair, Graduate Program Director, Director of Professional Development Schools and Program Coordinators from each of the programs. Each member is responsible for communicating and implementing assessment policies and practices within the area(s) he or she represents. The review and renewal process is based on outcomes data, feedback, and experiences gained through implementation. With regards to systems development, the renewal process enables faculty and the management team to refine conceptual designs by further customizing functional and technical requirements and processes. It facilitates the revision of software designs that strengthen architectures and interfaces for enhanced interactions. It also helps strategic planning with realistic budgeting of resources, support and expectations, and informs actions that are responsive to the changing culture and environment with evolving visions, goals and needs.

With regards to quality enhancement, the renewal process facilitates data-driven decision-making. Course-embedded key assignments are evaluated with rubrics by the course instructors and are collectively reviewed by the program coordinators at each of the four benchmarks. University supervisors and the P-12 mentor teachers conduct performance-based assessments using the Clinical Practice Performance Assessment (CPPA) instruments multiple times throughout the 100-day internship. Teacher candidates also conduct self-evaluations using the CPPAs during their internships. Results are shared with teacher candidates at pre/post observation conferences and through the EAS. TeachingFolios are evaluated by a combination of faculty, supervisors and/or mentor teachers. Data are triangulated and compiled each semester by the Director of Assessment and are collectively reviewed by the program committees and the Assessment Committee. Results and recommendations for improvement are presented to the faculty at monthly faculty meetings and at fall and spring faculty retreats.

Data driven decision-making aimed at improving candidate performance, program quality and unit operations is reflected in ongoing changes in organizational culture and infrastructure; in program, curriculum and assessment; and in resources, support and system renewal. At the unit level, the establishment of program-based committees addressing programmatic and curriculum issues and standards-based committees addressing accreditation standards are examples of change aimed at enhancing operational effectiveness. At the program level, the development of PMPs is an example of change leading to revisions of standards-based curriculum and assessments to help ensure that candidates know and are able to demonstrate the knowledge, skills and dispositions that are expected within each program. At the candidate level, results from the CPPAs and TeachingFolios help identify strengths and weaknesses, assisting in candidates' mastery of expected competencies as established by state and national standards.

21ST CENTURY TEACHING AND LEARNING THROUGH EPORTFOLIO: POTENTIALS AND CHALLENGES

The demands of the global economy, culture and polity of the 21st century require a more informed, participatory and active citizenship (Kellner, 2000). This elevates the role and poses new challenges for education in terms of both excellence and equity. While aspirations for producing fully engaged citizens through P-12 education have been articulated through initiatives like the Partnership for 21st Century Skills, with nine states adopting the Framework for 21st Century Learning, the needs and challenges to cultivate new and veteran teachers with the knowledge, skills and dispositions necessary to help all students succeed in 21st century schooling are fundamental and urgent. These challenges will need to be addressed through the creation of a coherent and collaborative *teacher preparation-education continuum* spanning from pre-service teacher training to in-service teacher professional development. To help realize the collective goals of excellence and equity in education, these challenges will also need to be addressed through the creation of a coherent and collaborative *P-20 continuum* among schools and universities.

To better support teaching professionals and better position the teaching profession, Linda Darling-Hammond (2006) cited three critical components in constructing 21st century teacher education: (1) tight coherence and integration among courses and between course work and clinical work; (2) extensive and intensive clinical work linking theory and practice; and (3) new school-university relationships leading to changes in the content of schooling as well as teacher training. A program-wide and standards-based portfolio could potentially transform traditional teacher education models that are often based on passive and disjoined curricula and experiences, achieving coherence. The institutionalization of

the EAS and the ProcessFolio, for example, illustrates systematic planning and strategic changes in program, curriculum and assessment leading to enhancements in program coherence. With regards to collective transformation, a career-wide and standards-based portfolio could potentially bridge the gaps of teacher professional development through genuine interactions among communities of practice. The involvement of P-20 researchers and practitioners in the co-construction of ProcessFolios, for example, facilitates the reciprocal connections of theory and practice, and, hence, the reciprocal transformation of teaching professionals and the profession.

The transformative potential of program-wide and/or career-wide eportfolios depends on the alignment of contents and expectations in P-12 schooling, licensure requirements, and teacher preparation and education programs. The impact of the transformative power on teachers and learners will rely on the creation of blueprints that link local priorities, state standards, and national frameworks. The sustainability of collective transformation will rely on the creation of coherent portfolio/accountability systems connecting policies and resources with leadership and administrative infrastructures to ensure equity and excellence. With continued advancement of the portfolio processes, assessment and technology, a co-constructed and highly individualized documentation of authentic learning processes and outcomes, with both qualitative and quantitative assessment results that are portable across educational levels and transferable among institutions of learning, will one day be possible.

REFERENCES

Anderson, C. (2006). *The long tail: Why the future of business is selling less of more.* New York, NY: Hyperion.

Cochran-Smith, M. (2005). Studying teacher education. *Journal of Teacher Education, 56*(4), 301–306. doi:10.1177/0022487105280116

Cochran-Smith, M. (2005). Teacher accreditation. *Journal of Teacher Education, 56*(4), 299–300. doi:10.1177/0022487105280117

Darling-Hammond, L. (2006). Constructing 21st-century teacher education. *Journal of Teacher Education, 57*(3), 300–314. doi:10.1177/0022487105285962

Elliott, E. (Ed.). (2003). *Assessing education candidate performance: A look at changing practices*. Washington, DC: National Council for Accreditation of Teacher Education.

Huang, Y. (2006). Sustaining ePortfolio: Progress, challenges and changing dynamics in teacher education. In Jafari, A., & Kaufman, C. (Eds.), *Handbook of research on eportfolios* (pp. 2150–2162). Hershey, PA: Idea Group. doi:10.4018/978-1-59140-890-1.ch045

Kellner, D. (2000). New technologies/new literacies: Restructuring education for the new millennium. *Teaching Education, 11*(3), 245–265. doi:10.1080/713698975

Murray, F. (2005). On building a unified system of accreditation in teacher education. *Journal of Teacher Education, 56*(4), 307–317. doi:10.1177/0022487105279842

Naisbitt, J. (2006). *Mind set!: Reset your thinking and see the future*. New York, NY: HarperCollins.

Partnership for 21st Century Skills. (2007). *The intellectual and policy foundations of the 21st century skills framework*. Retrieved March 1, 2009, from http://www.21stcenturyskills.org/route21/images/stories/epapers/skills_foundations_final.pdf

Pink, D. (2006). *A whole new mind: Why right-brainers will rule the future*. New York, NY: Penguin.

Wise, A. (2005). Establishing teaching as a profession. *Journal of Teacher Education, 56*(4), 318–331. doi:10.1177/0022487105279965

Section 2
The Developing World

Chapter 7
EPortfolio Use in Africa

Hédia Mhiri Sellami
University of Tunis, Tunisia

ABSTRACT

This chapter presents a review of eportfolio use in Africa through analysis of some statistics and some case examples. The author proposes a centralized eportfolio center supported by the Ministry of Education in each country.

INTRODUCTION

Portfolios have been used for many years by artists, painters, and architects to present their best achievements. Electronic portfolios have become more popular in the wider community; however, as learning tools, knowledge retention mechanisms, and forms of assessment (Lougheed, 2005). Although ePortfolios are defined differently, the definition by Scott Wilson is useful: "An ePortfolio is a repository of information about a particular learner provided by the learner and by other people and organizations, including products in a range of media that the learner has created or helped to create alongside formal documents from authoritative sources, such as transcripts

of assessed achievement, which the learner has chosen to retain" (Zubizarreta, 2009).

Researchers propose different structures for the ePortfolio. A commonly used structure is proposed by the Association for Supervision and Curriculum Development (Wade, 2005). This structure includes three sub-ePortfolios:

1. The learning sub-portfolio (also known as a "process" or "working" portfolio) shows the student's progress in knowledge acquisition. It may contain works in progress, may track student learning over time, and may be temporary because students move on to either an assessment or presentation portfolio. The creation of this sub-ePortfolio is a reflective exercise designed to promote learning. This type of portfolio is primarily a

DOI: 10.4018/978-1-4666-0143-7.ch007

device for teacher and learner to assess skills, reflect upon one's learning, and establish new learning plans (Barrett, 2005).

2. The assessment sub-portfolio (also known as an "accountability" or evaluation portfolio) supports evaluation by teachers. It provides evidence of learning and of measurable outcomes useful for faculty evaluators. The student writes a brief designed to prove that learning has taken place.

3. The presentation sub-portfolio (also known as a "showcase" or "marketing" portfolio) exhibits the student's best work. It is generally used to illustrate the level of accomplishment that the student has attained. Students often use this portfolio during college applications or for professional employment purposes (Barrett, 2005).

ANALYSIS OF PORTFOLIO USAGE

Problematic Results

To examine the extent of portfolio use in Africa, we consulted google.com with four results that are less illuminating than we had hoped. First, the same experiment using google.com was conducted on August 24, 2008 and November 11, 2009. Although this kind of experiment is not a rigorous one, it points to the range of significance of portfolios in Africa in relation to other places. In Table A1 (Appendix A1), we calculated the ratio of the ePortfolio's occurrence in relation to the population numbers on each continent similarly for both years. The word *ePortfolio* has an importance of 0,00007 in Africa but is three times more important in Europe (0,0002, four times as important in America, and nearly thirty times as important in Australia (0,002). These figures may indicate a gap between Africa and Europe or America in the information and communication technology (ICT) needed for ePortfolios. These ratios do indicate that the importance of the ePortfolio is

much higher in the developed countries than in Africa where it is still nearly absent.

Second, to obtain an accurate estimation of the technology gap we made the same comparison with the pioneers of ePortfolio use, the United States and Canada (Cloutier et al., 2006). The results shown in Table B1 (Appendix B) clearly indicate that while the population in Canada is 0,04 lower than in Africa (Population, 2008), the use of ePortfolios is thirty times more important there (0.02 and 0,00007).

Third, as the word *ePortfolio* is tightly related to the Internet, we looked for the same ratios but with the word *portfolio*, which is more independent from the Internet, because a portfolio can be in paper form. Table C1 (Appendix C) can indicate portfolio use in online and paper forms.

Although the results in Table C1 may lead to the conclusion that the concept of portfolio is more important in Africa (0,02) than in Europe (0,005), a confounding factor was the use of portfolio in contexts other than education. The word portfolio is used in the tourist field and in the financial one. Nearly every African country has portfolios that represent many tourist focuses such as the sea, the Sahara, animals, hotels, and traditional villages. Also, many African countries that benefit from international funds from institutions such as the African Bank and the United Nations have Internet pages dealing with the distribution of these funds. Because of this confounding factor, the same task was repeated by using the two words portfolio and education. Although the results shown in Table D1 (Appendix D) are more logical, many pages contained only the word *education*, so, again, we do not have clear evidence of the range of portfolio use in education in Africa.

Four, in a final attempt, we used the words *ePortfolio*, *portfolio*, and *portfolio education* to try to calculate the ratio of the word *ePortfolio* over the population in some African countries. In Table E1 (Appendix E), the results are inconclusive, because so many sites carried names of an

African country with no relation to the educational or portfolio field.

Useful Results

Examples of Experienced Practitioners

Consulting the maximum number of sites having the word *ePortfolio*, we looked for experiences with eportfolios. Table 1 catalogues some of those experiences.

Much debate over the concept of portfolio took place in Morocco (Elouriach, 2005) and Algeria where UNESCO encouraged its use by pupils and teachers (Pare, 2006). Some countries consider that the introduction of the portfolio is one element of innovation in education, as is the case of Egypt (CFCC, 2007).

CASES

Four cases highlight ePortfolio practices in four African sites. In Tunisia, paper portfolios have been in use in primary school since the beginning of the 21st century. Since the reform of education in 2002, pupils have been asked to collect their different tasks in a portfolio, and the teacher is expected to give them a mark at the end of each term (Edunet, 2008). But since the use of portfolios by secondary school inspectors in Tunisia is a real experiment, we consider it in our first case study (Guide, 2005; Paqset, 2005).

The second case study centers on South Africa where each new student at the University of Pretoria (UP) has to present a portfolio for registration in some master degrees (University of Pretoria, 2008a).

The third case study focuses on the University of South Africa (UNISA), which offers services and facilities to its students, including the portfolio (http://www.unisa.ac.za).

The fourth case study, initiated by collaborative action between the Agence Universitaire de la Francophonie (AUF) and the University of Montreal, is entitled Micro programme intégration pédagogique des TIC. It aims at integrating ICT in many African institutions, including secondary school and university.

First Case Study: CENAFFE of Tunisia

In 2004, the Tunisian Ministry of Education made an executive order requiring that each student-inspector take courses in the National Center CENAFFE, the Centre National de Formation des Formateurs en Éducation (Cenaffe, 2008). The CENAFFE is a Tunisian center ensuring the training of inspectors who are in charge of implementing and controlling courses in Tunisian secondary schools. Student-inspectors must take a two-year course at the end of which they are expected to produce a portfolio in paper format with a CD copy.

The required contents of this portfolio, specified by decree in the Tunisian official journal of October 15, 2004, include:

- a project proposing innovation in the learning process that should be relevant to the student locality,
- copies of student achievement reports made during training inspections,
- a report on collaborative training, and
- a report to describe each course taken in order to specify the benefits drawn and to present suggestions and critiques.

The content of this portfolio is so important that it counts up to 30% in the evaluation process.

The CENAFFE encourages the use of the portfolio to ameliorate the quality of the Tunisian educational system and has some projects like the Paqset Projet d'Amélioration de la Qualité du Système Educatif Tunisien (Paqset, 2005). The result of this project was a guideline to help supervising teachers and inspectors in their work.

Table 1. Websites showing experiences with eportfolios

Country	ePortfolio	Site
Algeria	2 230	http://eduportfolio.org/304 http://eduportfolio.org/614ateacherattheuniversityA/Mira in Bejaia
Egypt	3 230	http://dinaelkassas.wordpress.com/ a teacher at the university of Mina
Morocco	10 900	http://www.lahcenjair.net/index.asp?rub=Portfolio&idrub=2

Tunisia	2 960	http://eduportfolio.org/558 Many examples used by students to realize the work required by the modules of Database or ICT
		Plan of portfolio
		- Les séries TIC Série 1 TIC Série 2 TIC Série 3 TIC
		    - Les séries de BDTD 1
		        TD 2
		        o TD 3
		    • Examens Exam Mars 2006
		        o Exam Sept 2006
		    • Examen Mars 2007
		The answers of the students:
		such as http://eduportfolio.org/600
		http://eduportfolio.org/6913
		http://eduportfolio.org/6859

Benin	1 380	Portfolio of Attenoukon Serge, who teaches at the Faculté de droit et de sciences politiques / Université d'Abomey-Calavi (Bénin)
		Portfolio Anago Didier
		http://eduportfolio.org/632
		Deals with e-learning by describing its principles and giving a set of sites relevant to it
		http://benin.crifpe.ca/anago/mfd/
		    • Projet de recherche
		    • Plateforme e-learning
		    • Site de ressources pédagogique

Burkina Faso	2 080	Portfolio de Atji Abdouramane http://eduportfolio.org/621 He teaches history and geography at a secondary school in Burkina Faso.
Cameroun	723	Teacher at the university of Yaounde in Cameroun http://eduportfolio.org/3661/ Portfolio of Basile Guy Richard Bossoto He teaches mathematics at the University of Marien Ngouabi. http://eduportfolio.org/3363 Portfolio of Martin D. Yemani http://eduportfolio.org/portfolio.php?usager=5486 He teaches computer science at a secondary school. Akoa Mekoale Patrck Didier, http://eduportfolio.org/ 8700 professeur des sciences de la vie et de la terre He teaches biology at a secondary school.
Congo Brazzaville	24	Jean Paul Marie Bissoumounou: http://eduportfolio.org/3362 Portfolio de Guy Bernard Malonga http://eduportfolio.org/3370

continued on following page

Table 1. Continued

Country	ePortfolio	Site
République Démocratique du Congo		Portfolio de Marie Bernatte Tefoue http://eduportfolio.org/8657 She teaches science of pedagogy at Douala in Cameroun. • Portfolio of Hippolyte KITAMBALA DWAN ESSA http://eduportfolio.org/3358 o AUX ETUDIANTS G2-G3 ISP/GOMBE o Aux Etudiants de G1A/IFASIC o Aux Etudiants de G1B/IFASIC o Aux Etudiants de G2A/IFASIC o Aux Etudiants de G2B/IFASIC o Aux Etudiants de L1EMM/IFASIC o Aux Etudiants de L2EMM/IFASIC http://eduportfolio.org/3367 Portfolio of Franck OTETE http://eduportfolio.org/3360 http://eduportfolio.org/8344 Portfolio of Mambuku Marc Umba
Côte d'Ivoire	313	http://eduportfolio.org/639 o Sites web
Gabon	3 530	http://eduportfolio.org/3365: Grégoire Ndolly
Ghana	5 830	Clétus Adohinzin http://eduportfolio.org/8692
Niger	1 680	Portfolio of Kouawo Achille, a researcher in computer science http://eduportfolio.org/638 Portfolio of Mahaman Yahouza, http://eduportfolio.org/3260 He teaches at a secondary school of Niamey.
Togo	1 590	Portfolio de Tété Enyon Guemadji-Gbedemah, A teacher of sociology at the University of Lomé. http://eduportfolio.org/5475
Iles Comore/ Madagascar		Attoumani Mohamed Karim: http://eduportfolio.org/5667 Hasinavalona Lova A Didact'portfolio A teacher of physics in a secondary school http://eduportfolio.org/6992 Portfolio of Jeannot Raveloson http://eduportfolio.org/6998 A teacher at the higher institute of InformationCompétences d'encadrement Compétences technologiques o A portfolio of Jean Christian Andriambahiny, a computer science teacher at the University of Toliara http://eduportfolio.org/6989
Botswana	11100	http://students.kennesaw.edu/~kpatel13/index2.html
South Africa	12200	http://web.up.ac.za/default.asp?ipkCategoryID=740&language=0

It was also proposed as a tool for pedagogical innovation. This project proposes a set of items that should compose a portfolio of educational personnel regardless of the level taught (Paqset, 2005). This was done in partnership with the Tunisian Ministry of Education and also the Tecsult International from Canada (Tecsult, 2008).

Second Case Study: University of Pretoria

The second case study is the University of Pretoria (UP). Students have to present a portfolio if they intend to obtain a Bachelor of Arts in Fine Arts (BA Fine Arts) or a Bachelor of Arts in Information Design (BA Information Design) in the Department of Visual Arts (University of Pretoria, 2008b). Guidelines stipulate that a portfolio containing at least twelve colored postcard-size photographs of examples of work from the last two years be submitted to the Department of Visual Arts. This portfolio may include visual artwork, photographic work, illustrations, designs, images from the student's visual diary, or technical drawings (University of Pretoria, 2008b). The photographs of work should be of an excellent quality, mounted and presented in a bound A4-format. Each work should include a brief description such as the commissioner of the work, mentioning whether it was for school, for a client, or self-commissioned; the idea/concept behind the work; the size and medium (e.g., pencil, oils, pastels) of the work; and the year that the work was completed.

In the same university (UP), the School of Medicine in the Faculty of Health Sciences decided in 2003 to implement an electronic portfolio system that would profile students' progress throughout their six-year study curriculum. As no system could be found that would comply with all the specifications and needs set out by the school, it was decided to develop a customized, homegrown web-based system to accommodate their needs (Scheepers, 2008). The usage of this system was, however, stopped at the end of 2007, due to problems experienced by staff and students in rural areas in South Africa with low bandwidth access. A pilot project on the use of the eportfolio of WebCT Vista was conducted during the first half of 2008.

Third Case Study: University of South Africa

The website of the University of South Africa (UNISA) proposes to its students, under the section "job searching skills," a detailed description of the portfolio and its advantages in the learners' life careers (Port-Unisa, 2008).

The site details the content and the benefits of a portfolio, how it can be a tool to manage a student's career, and how to implement it. The different sections are:

- My career portfolio,
- What is a career portfolio,
- Why do I need a portfolio,
- Why is a career portfolio effective as a career management tool,
- What does the portfolio consist of,
- What is the suggested format for my portfolio,
- What are the benefits of a portfolio, and
- What steps are involved in the portfolio process.

Unfortunately, the university does not offer its students a site to create and to lodge their own ePortfolios (Port-Unisa, 2008).

Fourth Case Study: Edu-Portfolio

The French agency Agence Universitaire de la Francophonie (AUF) (http://www.auf.org) and the University of Montreal began an initiative in some African countries, essentially the sub-Saharan ones, to integrate ICT in the learning process (Portfolio, 2006). It was an opportunity for many African teachers to adopt this concept and to create their own ePortfolio via the site of the University of Montreal, edu-portfolio.com. Table 1 presents examples of these ePortfolios, but there is little consistency across use. The content of the portfolios created in this program varies from those with very elementary level content to those with consistent and original content (edu-portfolio.com/621 or 8344 or 639). Also, many of these teachers have now discontinued their work in the ePortfolio field, even though they have kept on encouraging the use of ICT throughout their courses.

Another African use of the ePortfolio is a personnel initiative at the Institut Supérieur d'Enseignement et de Formation Continue (IS-EFC) of Tunis in Tunisia (Mhiri, 2006). The students at this institute are working people who carry on their studies to improve their administrative hierarchical level. Considering the students' busy work load, the courses at this institute are scheduled on weekends or holidays. Many of the teachers are administratively linked to other universities, so courses are scheduled according to their availability. Because of this pedagogical discontinuity, ePortfolios were proposed with some courses to follow the students' progression while they did required exercises (Mhiri, 2005). For example, in the databases course and a course dealing with information and communication technology (ICT), which are given by the same teacher, the teacher's ePortfolio includes exercises for both courses (Mhiri, 2005). The teacher explains the concept of the ePortfolio to the students who each create an ePortfolio (http://eduportfolio.org/600 or http://eduportfolio.org/6913 or http://eduportfolio.org/6859). The teacher's remarks are presented as comments on each student's ePortfolio.

This small overview of the African use of the ePortfolio shows three types of experiments: initiatives supported by governments or national institutions (Cenaffe, 2008; University of Pretoria, 2008a); initiatives supported by non-African organizations (Karsenti & Williams, 2008; Ynternet, 2008); and initiatives emerging from individuals (Mhiri, 2007a).

CENTRALIZING EPORTFOLIO MANAGEMENT

ePortfolio use is sparse on the African continent due to many factors, such as poor infrastructure in schools and in universities. Computers are not always available (Chéneau-Loquay, 2009), Internet installations are not available in all parts of African countries, and connection quality is often of very low quality. Educational systems in some countries suffer problems that are more urgent than initiating their teachers or learners into the ePortfolio concept. For these countries, we propose, as a first step, the introduction of the paper portfolio to keep up with developed universities where ePortfolio is becoming a basic tool. The ePortfolio has also become a necessity when applying for a job, and it is a component of the lifelong learning process (Bragg, 2006). Experience with paper portfolios will facilitate later switching to the electronic portfolio. Introducing the concept of portfolio in our learning system is an opportunity for our pupils and students to be more active in their learning process and to rethink their knowledge acquisition process.

For other African countries, where Internet infrastructure is more developed, we propose not to follow the scenario used by the developed countries. There is no need to begin by encouraging learners and their teachers to select any tool to create their own ePortfolio (http://www.osportfolio.org/) (Elgg, 2008; Barrett, 2006) and then to discover that those portfolios do not prove competency because there is no control of content and adherence to standards (Cambridge, 2009).

Our proposal is to create, in each country, an ePort_center, a national organization, hierarchically relevant to the Ministry of Education. This center's role is to attribute an ePortfolio to every pupil beginning in primary school (Mhiri, 2007b). This ePortfolio should then follow the learner during his knowledge acquisition process: it is a lifelong ePortfolio. This lifelong ePortfolio should follow its owner from primary school to university and through different jobs until retirement (Figure 1).

We also propose considering a centralized structure for the ePort_center to manage the ePortfolios of different learners. By this configuration, the ePort_center may alleviate management responsibilities of the learning institutions. As building and maintaining ePortfolios is time consuming, we should take advantage of the rich knowledge base collected in each step through which a person evolves to constitute a dynamic ePortfolio. A lifelong ePortfolio should be accessible via Internet with a set of specific privileges depending on the user's profile. To carry out these tasks, the ePort_center should have a concentration of human resources as well as software and hardware resources. In fact, many webmasters should control access to these ePortfolios with each webmaster managing ePortfolios for institutions appointed to that person.

The ePort_center should be equipped with servers connected to the learning institutions. Beginning with the enrollment of a learner in an educational institution, often first a primary school, the associated webmaster offers each student an ePortfolio. Once a learner's ePortfolio is created, his teachers can introduce information relevant to their courses such as comments on and evaluations of tasks.

This ePort_center should regroup programs necessary to its running, such as a system to manage the ePortfolios. It may be a database management system or a more complex system able to grant and revoke privileges to learners and to their teachers at appropriate moments.

The centralization of the ePortfolio's management in one ePort_center for each country is not impossible to achieve if we are convinced that the ePortfolio is an important element in the lifelong learning process. This centralized solution is certainly the most adapted to a lifelong ePortfolio for African countries. It is also adequate whether the strategy is to have an ePortfolio for each school year or for each level in the learning process.

Different experiments throughout the world implicitly indicate that ePortfolio use in a country should be supported by the government to have a maximum chance of success (Europass, 2004; Cloutier et al., 2006). Generally free selection of ePortfolio content and technology leads to problems of incompatibility, incoherence, and lack of interoperability (Vancoillie, 2007). The ideal is that each country should have its own ePortfolio strategy used by all of its learning institutions, as

Figure 1. A centralized ePort_center

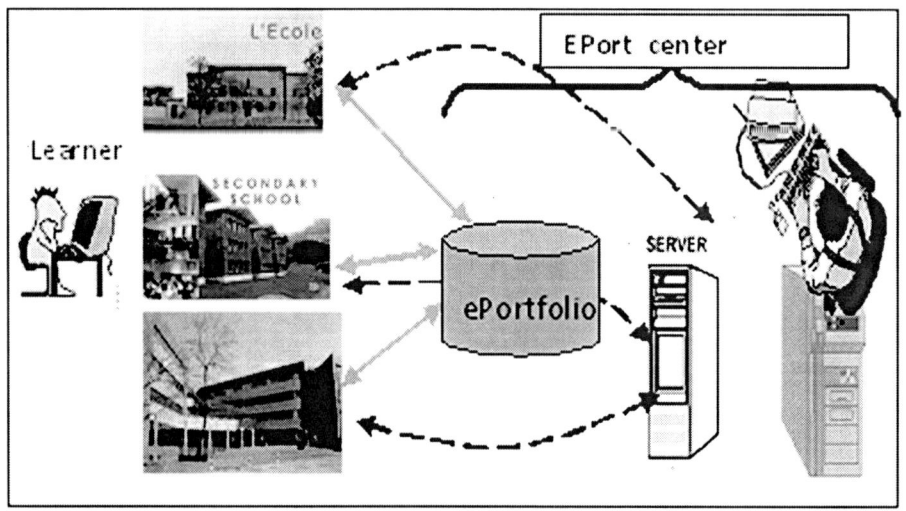

it is the case for some experiments in Australia (McCowan, 2005), in France (Education, 2006), in Canada (Cloutier et al., 2006; BC, 2007), and in the United Kingdom (JISC, 2008). This individual strategy, however, should be synchronized with international standards (IMS, 2007; Harman, 2007) to enable ePortfolio use across nations. This would require an international dialogue, if we accept the hypothesis that each country has its own ePort_center. We may take the example of the Internet where the decisions of the World Wide Consortium are discussed by representatives of each country. Describing and manipulating a learner's competency and knowledge is not less important than describing a URL and the globalization tendency accords to the human competency more and more importance.

The international benefits of a centralized management of the ePortfolio should be preceded by national decisions such as encouraging ePortfolios or even considering ePortfolios compulsory for all pupils (Cloutier et al., 2006; BC, 2007). This requirement may reduce the reluctance of teachers and learners. This centralized solution also supposes that all learning institutions are connected to the ePort_center via Internet so that learners and teachers can handle the ePortfolio wherever they are and at any time. The ePort_center should also federate institutions to a compatible ePortfolio model. For example, all primary schools should use a specific model as they have similar needs; this may certainly facilitate the webmaster task when a learner changes from one institution to another. The centralized practice solves the question of holding the data when changing institutions as it is always located at the ePort_center.

Because the ePort_center is attached to the Ministry of Education and is connected to every teaching institution, the webmaster's tasks are facilitated because he needs to collaborate with the teachers, the students, and the institution's staff to ensure the authenticity of the ePortfolio's content. For example, at the beginning of a school year or a semester, the webmaster must be given a list of the modules for each learning level, a list of teachers for each module so that he can attribute them temporal privileges, a list of tasks that the learners are expected to do, and the deadlines appointed to them. After each deadline, the webmaster may not allow the learner to deposit a new version of his achievement or the teacher to modify his evaluation of the learner's work. A tight collaboration between the webmaster and the different actors in the learner's environment, such as the headmaster and members of the pedagogical team, is very important to attribute the right access privilege to the right person and at the right time.

To ensure effective functioning of the process, the ePort_center has to interface distributed systems and heterogeneous platforms, thus it needs optimal integration and interoperability to be able to integrate functionality from the existing IT environment and its evolution.

THE FUTURE

This paper proposes a lifelong perspective on electronic portfolios. It proposes one ePortfolio per person, the lifelong ePortfolio. It follows the learner from his primary school through the secondary school and the university. To ensure the authenticity of the ePortfolio's content, we propose an ePort_center attached to the Ministry of Education. The ePort_center is responsible for managing the ePortfolio of all learners so it has to interface many institutions with different infrastructures. By adopting an ePort_center, a country may increase the enthusiasm of teachers, students, and decision-makers to invest in ePortfolios.

REFERENCES

Barrett, H. (2006). *Authentic assessment with electronic portfolios using common software and Web 2.0 tools*. Retrieved March, 15, 2009, from http://electronicportfolios.org/web20.html

Barrett, H., & Carney, J. (2005). *Conflicting paradigms and competing purposes in electronic portfolio development.* Retrieved November 30, 2009, from http://electronicportfolios.org/systems/paradigms.html

Bragg, S. M. (2006). *Outsourcing: A guide to selecting the correct business unit, negotiating the contract, maintaining control of the process* (2nd ed.). New York, NY: John Wiley & Sons.

British Colombia (BC). (2007). *Adult graduation diploma program (Adult Dogwood).* Retrieved May, 3, 2008, from http://www.bced.gov.bc.ca/graduation/portfolio/

Cambridge, D. (Ed.). (2009). *E-Portfolios and global diffusion: Solutions for collaborative education.* Hershey, PA: IGI Global.

Cambridge, D., Cambridge, B., & Yancey, K. (2009). *Electronic Portfolios 2.0: Emergent research on implementation and impact.* Sterling, VA: Stylus.

Centre National de Formation des Formateurs (CENAFFE). (2008). *Ministère de l'éducation.* Retrieved March 19, 2009 from http://www.cenaffe.edunet.tn/index.php

CFCC. (2007). *Journées de réflexion sur l'évaluation du français – Egypte.* Retrieved March 3, 2009, from http://www.ambafrance-eg.org/cfcc/IMG/pdf/Message d ouverture R. Adam.pdf

Chéneau-Loquay, A. (2009). Accès aux nouvelles technologies en Afrique et en Asie: TIC et service universel. In L'Harmattan (Ed.), *Cahiers des sciences socials sur les enjeux des technologies de la communication dans les SUD* (4th ed.). Versailles, France: CEA-CNRS. Retrieved March 22, 2010, from books.google.com

Cloutier, M., Fortier, G., & Slade, S. (2006). *Le portfolio numérique, un atout pour le citoyen apprenant. Société de formation à distance des commissions scolaires du Québec (SOFAD) et Cégep@distance. Récupéré le 11 septembre 2009 du site de la SOFAD.* Retrieved from http://www.sofad.qc.ca/pdf/portfolio_numerique.pdf

Education en France. (2006). *Plan en faveur des technologies de l'information appliquées à l'éducation.* Retrieved March 19, 2009, from http://www.education.gouv.fr/cid3949/plan-en-faveur-des-technologies-de-l-information-appliquees-a-l-education.html

Edunet. (2008). *Portail Educatif Tunisien.* Retrieved March 19, 2009, from http://www.edunet.tn

EduPortfolio. (2006). *Portfolio de TIC et Education.* Retrieved March 24, 2009, from http://eduportfolio.org/791

Elgg. (2008). *Powerful, professional social networking.* Retrieved March 5, 2009, from http://elgg.org/

Elouriachi, M. A. (2005). *Le portfolio numérique en classe.* Retrieved March 5, 2009, from http://www.ibnrochd.ma/gallery_files/porfolio_eleve_inspect_oujda.doc

Europass. (2004). *Five documents to make your skills and qualifications clearly and easily understood in Europe.* Retrieved September 19, 2008 from http://europass.cedefop.europa.eu

Harman, K., & Koohang, A. (2007). *Learning objects -Standards, metadata, repositories, and LCMS.* Santa Rosa, CA: Informing Science Institute.

IMS. (2007). *ePortfolio best practice and implementation guide.* Retrieved May, 3, 2007, from http://www.imsglobal.org/ep/epv1p0/imsep_bestv1p0.html

JISC. (2008). *ePortfolio key resources*. Retrieved May 10, 2008, from http://www.jisc.ac.uk/what-wedo/themes/elearning/eportfolios/resources.aspx

Karsenti, T., & Williams, M. (2008). *EduPortfolio*. Retrieved May 5, 2008 from http://www.eduportfolio.org

Lougheed, P., Bogyo, B., Brokenshire, D., & Kumar, V. (2005). Formalizing electronic portfolios in the SPARC ePortfolio tool. In *Proceedings of the Applications of Semantic Web Technologies for E-Learning workshop at the Third International Conference on Knowledge Capture.*

McCowan, C., Harper, W., & Hauville, K. (2005). Student e-Portfolio: The successful implementation of an e-Portfolio across a major Australian university. *Australian Journal of Career Development, 14*(2).

Mhiri, H. (2005). *Cours: Technologie de l'Information et de la communication*. Retrieved March 23, 2009, from http://ut.uvt.rnu.tn/course/category.php?id=12

Mhiri, H. (2005). *Portfolio de Hédia Mhiri Sellami*. Retrieved May 5, 2008, from http://eduportfolio.com/558

Mhiri, H. (2005, July 6). Some difficulties in distance learning in developing countries. In *Proceedings of the IEEE 3rd International Workshop on Technology for Education in Developing Countries*, Kaohsiung, Taiwan.

Mhiri, H. (2007a, May). L'utilisation de l'ePortfolio pour le suivi d'étudiants en formation continue. In *Proceedings of the Congrés de l'Association Internationale de Pédagogie Universitaire*, Montreal, QC, Canada. Retrieved September, 29, 2008, from http://aipu2007.umontreal.ca/appel.php

Mhiri, H. (2007b). One ePortfolio for the life. *In Proceedings of the E-LEARN World Conference on E-Learning in Corporate, Government, Healthcare, and Higher Education.* Retrieved March 20, 2009, from http://www.editlib.org/j/ELEARN/v/2007/n/1

Paqset. (2005). *Professionnalisation des formateurs Tunisiens*. Retrieved August 29, 2009, from http://affinitiz.com/space/professionnalisme/tag/apprentissage

Pare. (2006). *Réforme de l'éducation et innovation Pédagogique en Algérie*. Retrieved March 26, 2009, from http://unesdoc.unesco.org/Ulis/cgi-bin/ulis.pl?catno=158372&set=495A2B23_3_48&gp=1&lin=1

Port-Unisa. (2008). *University of South Africa. Your career portfolio*. Retrieved March 9, 2010, from http://www.unisa.ac.za/default.asp?CMD=ViewContent&ContentID=15162

Scheepers, M. D., Jordan, A. J. J., & Mostert, E. (2008). Analysis of three different models used to acquire three e-learning solutions at the same university. *International Journal of Emerging Technologies in Learning, 3*(1).

Tecsult. (2008). *Tecsult Group*. Retrieved December 12, 2008 from http://www.tecsult.com

University of Pretoria. (2008a). *Information design*. Retrieved March 24, 2009, from http://web.up.ac.za/sitefiles/File/46/1584/ma_infodesign(2).htm

University of Pretoria. (2008b). *Department of Visual Arts: Selection Procedure for BA Fine Arts*. Retrieved March 24, 2010 from http://web.up.ac.za/sitefiles/file/46/1584/selection%20procedure%20FA%202010.doc

VanCoillie, M. (2007, October 16-19). Building Europass CV ePortfolio application profiles. In *Proceedings of the First Human Capital and Social Innovation Technology Summit*, Maastricht, The Netherlands.

Wade, A., Abrami, P., & Sclater, J. (2005). An electronic portfolio to support learning. *Canadian Journal of Learning and Technology, 31*(3). Retrieved November 30, 2009, from http://www.cjlt.ca

Ynternet. (2008). *Communication Libre pour une société Libre*. Retrieved November 12, 2008, from http://www.ynternet.org/ynternet.org

Zubizarreta, J., & Millis, B. J. (2009). *The learning portfolio: Reflective practice for improving student learning* (2nd ed.). New York, NY: John Wiley & Sons.

APPENDIX

Appendix A.

- The arrow "Population's number" gives the number of the population in each continent (Population, 2008).
- The arrow "Population in a Continent/Population in Africa" is the ratio of the number of population in a continent over the number of the African population.
- For each continent, we have the number of occurrences of the word "ePortfolio" given by Google.
- The arrow "Ratio: the word in a continent/word in Africa" gives, for each continent, the ratio of occurrences of the word "ePortfolio" over its occurrence in Africa.
- The arrow "The occurrence of ePortfolio/the number of population" gives the ratio of the occurrence of the word ePortfolio in a continent over the number of its population.

	2008					2009				
Population's number	Africa	Europe	America	Asia	Australia	Africa	Europe	America	Asia	Australia
	917 607 051	734 129 205	902 157 549	3 97 3 31 0 39 2	33 594 581	978 798 199	736 765 100	916 465 689	4 08 3 59 6 53 7	34 958 075
Population in a Continent/ Population in Africa	Africa	Europe	America	Asia	Australia	Africa	Europe	America	Asia	Australia
	1	0,8	0,98	4,3	0,036	1	0.7	0.9	4	0.035
The occurrence of the word ePortfolio	Africa	Europe	America	Asia	Australia	Africa	Europe	America	Asia	Australia
	66 8 00	121 000	300 0 00	39 90 0	59 300	368 00	8150 0	62200	30 30 0	51700
Ratio: the word in a continent / word in Africa	Africa	Europe	America	Asia	Australia	Africa	Europe	America	Asia	Australia
	1	1,8	4,5	0,5	0,88	1	2.21	1.6	0.8 2	1.4
The occurrence of ePortfolio / the number of population	Africa	Europe	America	Asia	Australia	Africa	Europe	America	Asia	Australia
	0,00 007	0,00 02	0,000 3	0,0 00 01	0,002	0.00 003	0.00 01	0.000 06	0.0 00 00 7	0.001

Appendix B.

Town	Canada (2008)	USA (2008)	Canada (2009)	USA (2009)
Number of population	33 091 228	303 350 706	33 504 680	305 651 442
The occurrence of the word ePortfolio	69 200	88 800	162000	183000
Population in a country/Population in Africa	0,04	0,33	0.034	0.31
Ratio: the word in a country/ word in Africa	1	1,3	2.3	2.6
The occurrence of ePortfolio/the number of population	0,002	0,0003	0.004	0.0005

Appendix C.

Portfolio	Africa	Europe	America	Asia	Australia
Google.com	19 600 000	3 680 000	44 500 000	25 200 000	16 300 000
Ratio: the word in a continent/word in Africa		0,18	2,27	1,3	0,83
Number of population	917 607 051	734 129 205	902 157 549	3 973 310 392	33 594 581
The occurrence of ePortfolio/the number of populatio	0,02	0,005	0,04	0,006	0,4

Appendix D.

Portfolio education	Africa	Europe	America	Asia	Australia
Google.com	2 930 000	3 140 000	3 660 000	3 120 000	349 000
Ratio the word in a continent/word in Africa		1,2	1,3	1,05	0,2
Number of population	917 607 051	734 129 205	902 157 549	3 973 310 392	33 594 581
Proportion in the continent	0,003	0,004	0,004	0,0007	0,01

Appendix E.

Country	Population	ePortfolio	Ration:number of the word ePortfolio/ Population in the country	portfolio	Portfolio education
North Africa					
Algeria	33 333 216	2 230	0,00006	2 900 000	1 640 000
Egypte	78887007	3 230	0,00004	207 000	3 640 000
Libya	5 900 754	1 360	0,0002	2 580 000	1 490 000
Morocco	33 757 175	8 910	0,0002	4 380 000	1 720 000
Tunisia	10 175 014	2 960	0,0002	2 790 000	148 000
Sub-Saharian					
Benin	7 862 944	1 380	0,0002	1 980 000	82 700
Burkina Faso	13 902 972	2 080	0,0002	2 130 000	732 000
Burundi	8 691 005	1 950	0,0002	2 150 000	702 000
Cameroun	17 340 702	723	0,00004	1 760 000	968 000
Cap Vert	455294	32	0,0000007	26 800	3 460
Centrafrique	4303356	14	0,000003	20 800	4 430
Congo Brazzaville	3702314	24	0,00006	28 600	33 500
République Démocratique du Congo	62660551	182	0,000002	9 740	13 100
Côte d'Ivoire	17654843	313	0,00001	154 000	671 000
Gabon	1424906	3 530	0,0024	1 940 000	1 120 000
Gambie	1641564	17	0,00001	30 300	9 850
Ghana	22409572	5 830	0,002	5 520 000	137 000
Guinée	9690222	946	0,00005	36 500	9 020
Guinée Bissau	1442029	292	0,0002	10 200	586 000
Guinée Equatoriale	540109	255	0,0004	18 000	580 000
Libéria	3631318	1 380	0,0003	2 330 000	1 440 000
Mali	11956788	861	0,00007	1 770 000	888 000
Mauritanie	3177388	380	0,0001	204 000	854 000
Niger	12525094	1 680	0, 001	2 500 000	1 350 000
Nigeria	131859731	6 540	0,00004	5 390 000	2 200 000
Rwanda	8 648 248	3 080	0,0003	2 240 000	1 400 000
São Tomé & Principe	193 413	5	0,00002	52 400	20 200
Senegal	11 987 121	4 710	0,0003	4 110 000	1 410 000
Sierra Léone	6 005 250	990	0,0001	182 000	1 210 000
Tchad		1 330	0,0001	2 760 000	1 510 000
Togo	5 681 519	1 590	0,00002	2 370 000	1 350 000
Afrique Orientale					

continued on following page

Appendix E. Continued

Country	Population	ePortfolio	Ration:number of the word ePortfolio/ Population in the country	portfolio	Portfolio education
Djibouti	768 900	660	0,0008	1 860 000	607 000
Erythrée	4 786 994	6	0,000001	1 320	1 010
Ethiopie	74 777 981	56	0,0000007	36 600	6 180
Île Maurice	1 248 592	145	0,0001	20 500	10 900
Kenya	34 707 817	5 980	0,0001	6 380 000	156 000
Madagascar	18 595 469	1 550	0,00008	2 760 000	1 010 000
Mayotte (FR)	201 234	98	0,0004	1 850 000	646 000
Ouganda	30 262 610	587	0,0001	4 340 000	117 000
Réunion (FR)	787 584	10	0,0001	9 050	1 300
Seychelles	83 688	927	0,01	1 810 000	545 000
Somalie	8 863 338	177	0,00001	28 000	29 500
Soudan	41 236 378	1 600	0,00005	3 750 000	1 630 000
Tanzanie	37 979 417	597	0,00005	28 800	1 580 000
Afrique Australe					
Angola	13 115 606	1 820	0,001	3 190 000	875 000
Botswana	1 639 833	1 530	0,0009	2 880 000	856 000
Lesotho	2 022 331	3 510	0,001	2 250 000	483 000
Malawi	13 013 926	406	0,00003	1 840 000	394 000
Mozambique	19 686 505	1 010	0,00005	1 640 000	475 000
Namibie	2 044 147	553	0,0002	14 300	62 700
South Africa	44 187 37	28 400	0,006	6 220 000	2 990 000
Swaziland	1 136 334	750	0,0006	767 000	161 000
Zambie	11 502 010	536	0,00004	13 900	416 000
Zimbabwe	12 382 920	1 480	0,0001	1 860 000	747 000

Chapter 8

Can We Do Both? Eportfolios for Student Learning and Assessment:
Lessons Learned at an American University

Candyce Reynolds
Portland State University, USA

Judith Patton
Portland State University, USA

ABSTRACT

Eportfolios in higher education are useful for both student learning and for program assessment. Too often, eportfolios are conceptualized primarily as assessment tools, and this can hinder student learning. This chapter presents a case study of one institution in the United States where both the goals of student learning and assessment are served well through the use of eportfolios.

INTRODUCTION

The use of eportfolios in American universities has proliferated over the last ten years as administrators and educators have discovered the rich opportunities that they provide for both promoting and assessing student learning (e.g., Stefani, Mason, & Pegler, 2007). Through eportfolios, students have the opportunity to make connections and more intentionally develop integrative learning. Assessing actual student work in an eportfolio is also a plus for administrators and faculty in that it provides a more authentic way of measuring

DOI: 10.4018/978-1-4666-0143-7.ch008

student and program success. However, in this perhaps perfect storm, managing the tension between facilitating student learning and providing a structure for assessment is paramount. Too often, institutions of higher education prioritize assessment over student learning, creating assignments and protocols that ease assessment of student work while at the same time ignoring the valuable aspects that creating an eportfolio can provide for students, rendering the eportfolio as merely another assignment.

This chapter focuses on lessons learned in University Studies, Portland State University's four-level interdisciplinary general education program, about the importance of balancing assessment needs with student learning needs.

BACKGROUND: PORTLAND STATE UNIVERSITY

Portland State University is a comprehensive, urban, public institution in Oregon's largest city. Situated at the south end of downtown Portland, the University has almost 30,000 enrolled students and serves a population of over 40,000 in credit or noncredit classes each year, including nearly one-third of the Oregon University System's enrolled graduate students. The urban location of the university provides the impetus for engaging with the community as a key part of the curriculum, and PSU adopted the motto, "Let Knowledge Serve the City" as part of a nationwide project to define public urban institutions. The university re-envisioned itself and engaged in targeted systemic change that touched almost every area of the institution from administration and front line student services to interdisciplinary education and general education. University Studies was adopted as the general education program for the majority of students with the goal of shifting the university to a student-centered learning institution. Because the new general education program

was such a differently structured course delivery system, it was important to design assessment that would align with the new way of thinking about students and about learning and that would also allow the university to feel assured that the program was delivering on its goals. The situation provided a fertile ground for integrating learning goals, student work and assessment in a way that supported each endeavor.

The University Studies Program and Freshman Inquiry Portfolio

University Studies is Portland State University's four-year, interdisciplinary general education program. The program is organized around four goals:

1. inquiry and critical thinking
2. communication
3. the diversity of human experience
4. ethical issues and social responsibility.

Courses taken at all levels of the program are designed to enhance student skill development and learning in these areas. (For a more complete description of the program, see White (1994)or http://www.ous.pdx.edu.) The foundation of the program is a yearlong Freshman Inquiry course designed to address all four goals of the program. This course is organized around interdisciplinary themes. Examples of these themes include: Ways of Knowing, On Democracy, The Work of Art, Sustainability, Design and Society, and Human/Nature. The courses were designed to replace general education social science, science, humanities and writing courses. Students take a five-credit course each quarter for their first year, totaling 15 credits for the three quarters that make up the academic year. It is approximately one third of their credit load for the first year.

Students create electronic portfolios in the interdisciplinary Freshman Inquiry courses. The portfolio serves as a concrete manifestation of the learning goals of the course and student progress towards those goals as well as the general education goals. A yearlong course that is also interdisciplinary is complex and can be confusing. The eportfolios provide a strategy for locating and connecting the various assignments to each other and to the program goals. Paper portfolios were used at the beginning of the program to both enhance student learning and serve as an instrument of program evaluation. Twelve years ago, faculty began the move from paper to electronic based portfolios in order to leverage some of the advantages of the technology.

The electronic portfolio for the Freshman Inquiry course contains work that students have produced throughout the year. It also contains reflections on their progress toward the program's four goals and has linkages to works that demonstrate achievement in those goals. The portfolios are web-based. Students build web pages, which are then stored in controlled-access websites.

BALANCING THE NEED FOR ASSESSMENT WITH THE NEED FOR STUDENT LEARNING

It is easy for assessment to overshadow the learning potential of portfolios. Certainly, using eportfolios for the assessment of individual students, programs and institutions is important (Hamp-Lyons & Condon, 2000; Kahn, 2001). However, it is imperative that faculty conceptualize the eportfolio as a tool to enhance learning and reflection as well (Cambridge & Williams, 1997; Labissiere & Reynolds, 2004). The activities involved in creating an electronic portfolio have the potential to provide rich opportunities for developing students as lifelong reflective learners. In our work with the Freshman Inquiry eportfolios, it is all too easy to give students an assignment to create an eportfolio without offering the supportive pedagogy to aid in student learning. The

following are suggestions to help faculty utilize specific pedagogies to assist students in learning beyond their requirement to create an eportfolio for assessment. We will conclude with a summary chart of these strategies.

Scaffold the Experience

The creation of an eportfolio is a large project. First of all, a student needs to acquire the skills to create one using the available technology, such as saving artifacts in an electronic format, the basic building of a webpage, and the creation of hyperlinks. Beyond technical skills, one also needs to engage in the planning of an eportfolio, thinking strategically about what to include, how to represent oneself with photographs, colors, fonts and other artifacts as well as what should be included in the eportfolio. Building these skills should be logically and sequentially scaffolded into the curriculum rather than seen as an afterthought at the end of the term.

The planning of an eportfolio can be especially challenging. Students must consider what they want to include in their portfolio as well as how to make connections through hyperlinking. Faculty in the program have assigned course mind maps as a way of asking students to reflect upon and represent what they have learned. The maps can then be used to inform eportfolio organization. The potential scaffolding strategies are nearly endless. For portfolio development to be successful, it is important to introduce and foster skills in a progressive manner so that students will both derive maximum learning value from each skill and master the requisite skills needed to construct their eportfolios.

Use Collaborative Learning Activities

Unlike other class assignments, eportfolios help leverage the social aspects of learning. Learning is a dynamic, social activity that is supported by relationships and by community. It is well-documented in educational and psychological literature that collaboration enhances learning (e.g., Rogoff, Turkanis, & Bartlett, 2001). Collaborative learning practices encourage students to work together to enhance their own learning and to maximize the learning of the entire class (Aronson & Patnoe, 1997). The eportfolio process provides regular and ongoing occasions for students to work together.

As creating an eportfolio demands a variety of skills, students can support and provide feedback to each other. For example, some students may have skills in visual representation and others may have skills in writing. Providing class time to collaborate on each other's eportfolios is one way to facilitate this kind of cooperation. Pedagogically, this practice interrupts the common perception of scholarship as a solitary activity and communicates the value of collaboration in learning. Students develop norms of cooperation and collaboration in assuming their roles as scholars.

Teach and Provide Practice in Reflection Skills

Reflection is the centerpiece of the eportfolio. Without reflection regarding the learning that the artifacts in the portfolio represent, the eportfolio is simply a file cabinet. We know that activities that demand reflection, organization, and connection enhance metacognition (e.g., Alexander et al., 1995). Because of its importance, reflective practices need to be directed and frequent to be most effective.

Educators cannot expect students to know how to engage in reflective practice without adequate coaching by the instructor. In other words, reflective skills need to be taught and supported throughout the process. Examples of activities that can support reflective practice include practices such as course-related dialogue journals, periodic classroom assessment techniques (CATs) where the class pauses to reflect on their learning experiences, blog entries, and periodic reflective essays. These activities require students to reflect upon and engage in what they are learning in a variety of ways. For maximum pedagogical value, reflective activities should be prompted and frequent, allowing students to both look back at their experience and project forward to future goals and closing gaps in understandings.

Focus on Growth

Eportfolios provide students with an opportunity to see the progression of their learning. Students can include early work and make comparisons with a more polished assignment. An eportfolio makes the inclusion of such work easy and manageable. A student can simply include a link to early work in his or her reflection on his or her progress. This gives value and meaning to these otherwise discarded tracks of student learning and development.

Through such practices, students can come to appreciate the value of mistakes or failures in shaping their scholarly identities. This technique shifts the focus away from "best work" and allows student to glimpse the relevance of learning from mistakes and failures. Honest self-assessment is critical to academic development.

Leverage the Public Nature of the Eportfolio

While it is important to give students control over what they choose to share in their eportfolios, student learning is further enhanced by the public review of their product, much like a peer review process. During formal eportfolio review sessions, also conducted in small groups, students can celebrate each other's work, pick up tips, and provide feedback to others. Viewing each other's work helps students understand that their work has an audience beyond the professor and builds motivation to create their best work. In addition,

Table 1. Eportfolio pedagogical suggestions

Pedagogical Practice	Examples of Practice
Scaffold the experience. Provide learning opportunities or assignments to facilitate learning the necessary skills needed to create the eportfolio. Don't just assign an eportfolio.	Learning eportfolio software Planning the look of the eportfolio Using Mind Maps to think about organization of eportfolios
Use collaborative learning activities. Encourage collaborative and cooperation in the development of the eportfolio	Provide opportunities for students to share expertise and teach each other Provide opportunities for students to share their ongoing work and give feedback to each other
Teach and provide practice in reflection skills. Provide opportunities for learning to reflect on one's learning through directed prompts	Course-related dialogue journals Periodic classroom assessment techniques (CATS) where the class pauses to reflect on their learning experience Blogs Letters to the professor
Focus on growth. Allow students to explore the progression of learning, fostering honest self-assessment and the role of early work and mistakes	Reflections comparing best work to earlier work Reflecting on what has been learned and how that was achieved Faculty modeling learning from his or her own mistakes
Leverage the public nature of the eportfolio. Make the creation of the eportfolio a public experience	Peer Review Sessions Eportfolio showcases and contests

viewing each other's work establishes consensus about quality and sets norms regarding effective standards and practices. The criterion for excellence becomes visible and meaningful (Table 1).

USING THE EPORTFOLIO FOR ASSESSMENT

Placing the eportfolio at the center of the curriculum allows it to function primarily as a tool to deepen student learning. At the same time, it also becomes a rich portrait of authentic student learning to utilize for program assessment. Over the past 20 years, higher education accreditation boards in the United States have begun to demand that colleges and universities go beyond the traditional indicators of student pass/fail ratios and student evaluations of teaching as a measure of their success. Accreditation boards are asking colleges and universities to utilize actual student works in their assessment of program success. Eportfolios provide faculty and administrators with authentic work samples to assess. In our case, the Freshman Inquiry eportfolio allows program administrators and faculty to assess and understand student progress in the four University Studies goals. Because the eportfolios are integrated into each course curriculum, students are graded on their work in the eportfolio and on the eportfolio itself as part of the class work. Students take the creation of the eportfolio seriously as it is seen as part of their grade in the course.

The faculty created a common end-of-year eportfolio assignment to use for program assessment. The common assignment was also crafted to facilitate student learning, providing multiple opportunities to reflect on their growth in the four goals as well as to make connections between what they have learned inside and outside of the classroom.

The assignment asks students to reframe the goals in their own words. This part of the assignment grew out a faculty practice that showed that the goals were more relevant and portfolios stronger when students claimed the goals as their own. As the goals for the program were written more for faculty and administrators, we have found that students identified personally when they translated the goals into their own language. Students choose work that they believe demonstrates their learning in each goal and write a short reflection explaining those choices. Students are asked to include their research project as part of their work. All other work in the portfolio is selected by the student. We found that the more the design and planning of the eportfolio is left in the students' hands, the more strongly it supports student learning. Each portfolio includes a selection of student work samples in each of the program goal areas. The final part of the eportfolio is a prompted reflection on the year's learning experience. This final reflection essay provides for a more holistic assessment of the student experience in the Freshman Inquiry course as well as allowing students to define their experience as a whole.

Once the students have completed the eportfolios, the program administrators and faculty can begin the process of assessing the program. At the end of the academic year, a sample of eportfolios is randomly selected from each Freshman Inquiry course. After grades have been turned in, University Studies hosts a two to three day eportfolio review process. The program sends out a general call for evaluators across the institution. Faculty, program mentors and graduate students from within and outside of the program can participate. Evaluators are paid a small stipend for their work. Two of the four goals are assessed each year.

The eportfolios are assessed using program level rubrics. Rubrics are an assessment tool that specify and make visible criteria for success. Because the goals and objectives are broadly available, courses align student activities with program outcomes. Again, student learning is at the forefront of using rubrics to assess student progress. These rubrics are public, and faculty share with students what is expected of them and at what level. When students know what to aim for, they are more apt to attain that level of work. Program faculty have developed rubrics for each goal. (They are available at http://www.pdx.edu/unst/university-studies-goals.)

Each review day begins with a rubric calibration. Each evaluator reads the same works sample for the goal of the day and scores it using the program level rubric. The scores are shared and outliers asked for their reasoning on their scoring. Sometimes, the reasoning moves the group to a different understanding of the rubric. Often, the discussion clarifies what evaluators are looking for in the various score levels. Evaluators are asked to use the rubric and also to record any problems with the rubric or ideas that might be incorporated into them. Those notes are collected and used by the program to revise and improve the rubrics.

Once all evaluators have gained an understanding of the meaning and levels of the rubrics, they begin scoring the approximately 250 eportfolios in computer labs. Two evaluators score each eportfolio on the specific goal of that day. If the scores are more than one point apart, a third evaluator then scores the eportfolio. If there continues to be a range in the scores, all three evaluators consult to come up with an appropriate score.

The eportfolio review at the program level is not related to individual faculty, since only approximately five eportfolios are scored per class, but the data does give the faculty team useful information showing how well their team-developed curriculum achieves student learning in relation to the goals of the program. The data is also program level information that demonstrates how well the program is delivering on the student learning goals at the entering student level. Each year, the program publishes an assessment report that contains the results of all the assessment activities at each level of the program including the Freshman Inquiry eportfolio review data. The data also is shared with faculty who teach at each level at an annual fall retreat. In the Freshman Inquiry level, each team is asked to review its data, reflect on what the data means for their curriculum and to report any changes they plan to make in their course design to increase any low scores. Faculty teams have carried out action research projects to see the effect of the changes they make and study what classroom practices make the most difference to student learning. The results of assessment are only meaningful if the program uses that information to make curriculum and teaching strategy changes and to study if those changes actually increase student learning.

CONCLUSION

What we have found is that, yes, you can do both, focusing on student learning and also using the in-class work products for program assessment. When student learning is at the center of curricular design and assessment, higher education transformation is possible. The use of eportfolios is a strategy that allows a reconsideration of classroom practice and of the place of learning at the institution. Assessment of authentic student work shows whether the learning we believe and plan to be the result of a course or program of study is actually taking place. Eportfolios also give students a way to see their learning as it develops, to determine next steps in their learning careers and to reformulate their work for the creation of a resume or application to graduate school. With the design and end product of the eportfolio remaining in student control, students invest in their learning and in the eportfolio creation in ways not seen before. Students and programs benefit from rich student work and assessment practices. The use of eportfolios is the first educational strategy that can be integrated throughout the curriculum and that allows students to see the relevance of their study from course to course and from year to year. Reflective practice in eportfolios helps students develop the ability to self-evaluate and to understand where they are and where they could go.

The developmental transformation of a student can clearly be facilitated if we choose to focus on pedagogical practices in the creation of student eportfolios. When asked what they learned in college, students will not just say, "Well, I wrote a bunch of papers and took a bunch of tests." They will instead be able to identify where and how they learned critical thinking, time management, writing skills, analytical thinking, and a whole host of other important understandings and skills that will help them throughout their personal and work lives. They will then have a toolkit that they will know how to open and use along their life paths.

REFERENCES

Alexander, J. M., Carr, M., & Schwanenflugel, P. J. (1995). Development of metacognition in gifted children: Directions for future research. *Developmental Review*, *15*, 137. doi:10.1006/drev.1995.1001

Aronson, E., & Patnoe, S. (1997). *The jigsaw classroom: Building cooperation in the classroom*. New York, NY: Longman.

Cambridge, B. L., & Williams, A. C. (1997). *Portfolio learning*. Upper Saddle River, NJ: Prentice Hall.

Hamp-Lyons, L., & Condon, W. (2000). *Assessing the portfolio: Principles for practice, theory and research*. Cresskill, NJ: Hampton Press.

Kahn, S. (2001). Conclusion: Recommendations. In Cambridge, B. L. (Ed.), *Electronic portfolios: Emerging practices in student, faculty and institutional learning*. Washington, DC: American Association for Higher Education.

Labissiere, Y., & Reynolds, C. (2004). Using reflective electronic portfolios to enhance student learning. *Creative College Teaching Journal*, *1*(1), 49–61.

Rogoff, B., Goodman Turkanis, C., & Bartlett, L. (Eds.). (2001). *Learning together: Children and adults in a school community.* New York, NY: Oxford University Press.

Stefani, L., Mason, R., & Pegler, C. (2007). *The educational potential of e-portfolios: Supporting personal development and reflective learning.* London, UK: Routledge.

Chapter 9
Electronic Portfolios for Career Exploration

Gabriela Alpírez
Instituto Experimental de la Asunción, Guatemala

ABSTRACT

The author discusses the inclusion of job shadowing as a critical element of an electronic portfolio in the context of an all-girls school in Guatemala. The chapter also describes the reasons behind and the development of electronic portfolios for the School. It concludes that job shadowing and student success in career exploration are related and of particularly benefit to the student if started at an early stage.

INTRODUCTION AND BACKGROUND

Instituto Experimental de la Asunción, founded in 1956 by the Assumption Sisters Order, is an all-girls Catholic school located in Guatemala City, Guatemala. For more than 50 years, their educational project has aimed to shape the intelligence and the heart of every girl so that they will fulfill their vocation and become strong, resilient women.

In accordance with the school's mission, in 2005 the forward-looking school counselors wanted to increase the students' awareness of the importance of exploring and planning their professional careers, as it was recognized by many national and international organizations that women who received a formal education could have a greater impact on the economic, political, and social life of their communities.

To address these new requirements, a "Career Exploration" class was established in 2005 (later in 2008, it became a Module for "My Life Plan Project") the objectives of which were:

- To encourage students to choose a career based on their interests, values, abilities, and talents;

DOI: 10.4018/978-1-4666-0143-7.ch009

- To recognize their talents, abilities, and skills, and publish them on an electronic portfolio;
- To experience the world of work by means of shadowing a professional related to their career choice;
- To promote a healthy and positive self-esteem amongst students.

WHAT WAS DONE

The *American School Counselor Association* (ASCA) had then recently produced in 2004 a set of National Standards for Students "to identify and prioritize the specific attitudes, knowledge and skills that students should be able to demonstrate as a result of participating in a school counseling program." These standards were reviewed by Asunción's counselors, and a subset as follows was considered particularly relevant to the school in relation to student competencies:

Academic Development

- **STANDARD C:** Students will understand the relationship of academics to the world of work and to life at home and in the community.
    - **A:**C1.2 Seek co-curricular and community experiences to enhance the school experience
    - **A:**C1.3 Understand the relationship between learning and work
    - **A:**C1.5 Understand that school success is the preparation to make the transition from student to community member
    - **A:**C1.6 Understand how school success and academic achievement enhance future career and vocational opportunities

Personal /Social Development

- **STANDARD A:** Students will acquire the knowledge, attitudes and interpersonal skills to help them understand and respect self and others.
    - **PS:**A1 Acquire Self-knowledge
    - **PS:**A1.1 Develop positive attitudes toward self as a unique and worthy person
    - **PS:**A1.2 Identify values, attitudes and beliefs
    - **PS:**A1.10 Identify personal strengths and assets

Career Development

- **STANDARD A:** Students will acquire the skills to investigate the world of work in relation to knowledge of self and to make informed career decisions.
    - **C:**A1 Develop Career Awareness
    - **C:**A1.6 Learn how to set goals
    - **C:**A1.7 Understand the importance of planning
    - **C:**A1.8 Pursue and develop competency in areas of interest
    - **C:**A1.9 Develop hobbies and vocational interests
    - **C:**A2 Develop Employment Readiness
    - **C:**A2.6 Learn how to write a résumé
- **STANDARD B:** Students will employ strategies to achieve future career goals with success and satisfaction.
    - **C:**B1 Acquire Career Information
    - **C:**B1.2 Identify personal skills, interests and abilities and relate them to current career choice
    - **C:**B2 Identify Career Goals
    - **C:**B2.5 Maintain a career-planning portfolio
    - **C:**C2 Apply Skills to Achieve Career Goals

○ **C:C2.1** Demonstrate how interests, abilities and achievement relate to achieving personal, social, educational

Together the school counselors, curriculum coordinator, teachers, and technology facilitators then decided that an electronic portfolio would be the best vehicle to introduce a student to their job shadow partner. This means that the person who the student will shadow will know much more about the student's interests, abilities and community involvement before they meet, than they otherwise would have.

"JobShadow.org" (or *JobShadow*) is a coalition of a number of organizations that at the time of writing include:

• Junior Achievement
• America's Promise
• Association for Career and Technical Education
• United States Department of Education
• United States Department of Labor
• Society for Human Resource Management
• AT&T

JobShadow describe their program as "an academically motivating activity designed to give kids the unique opportunity of an up-close look at the world of work and provide the answer to the commonly asked question, 'Why do I have to learn this?' Students across America 'shadow' workplace mentors as they go through a normal day on the job. The program invites students to see firsthand how the skills learned in school relate to the workplace."

With self-efficacy in mind, consider the following statements made by the *JobShadow* initiative in relation to "Junior Achievement" (JA), itself a highly respected organization dedicated to inspiring and preparing young people to succeed in a global economy:

"The local chapter for Junior Achievement, "the world's largest organization dedicated to educating students about workforce readiness, entrepreneurship and financial literacy through experiential, hands-on programs," had an established Job Shadowing program, so partnering with them was a good option."

Recent studies by Junior Achievement stated "Ample anecdotal evidence exists to support the claim that JA students are more prepared to enter the world of work. Students who participate in JA's work-readiness programs demonstrate higher levels of self-efficacy."

According to JA in their *Executive Summary on Work-Readiness Impact of JA Program Participation*, "Key findings demonstrate that JA program participants exhibit statistically significant gains in content, skill development, and self-efficacy relative to work-readiness concepts and tasks" (1), and "Junior Achievement programs provide students with the opportunity to gain the knowledge and skills needed to feel more prepared for the future" (3).

Furthermore, JA asserts in the same document, "Consistently, students report higher levels of career-related self-efficacy after participating in JA programs." (3), and "More than 7 out of 10 high school students (75%) who participated in JA Job Shadow agreed that they now know how to prepare for a future career" (4).

All of these statements underscore the importance of self-efficacy in the individual.

THE EFFECTS OF SELF-EFFICACY

For the reasons mentioned above, we (Asunción) also wanted the electronic portfolio to be a vehicle to increase self-efficacy in our students, as we recognized the following characteristics as exemplified by Bandura's social cognitive theory (Pajares & Schunk, 2001):

[S]elf-efficacy beliefs influence the choices people make and the courses of action they pursue. Individuals tend to engage in tasks about which they feel competent and confident, and avoid those in which they do not.

- The beliefs people have about their capabilities are critical elements of success
- How people behave can often be better predicted by the beliefs they hold about their capabilities
- Efficacy beliefs also help determine how much effort people place on an activity, if they will persevere when confronting obstacles, and how resilient they will be if they face adversity.
- Assessing students' self-beliefs can provide schools with important insights about their pupils 'academic motivation, behavior, and future choices.
- Individuals form their self-efficacy beliefs by interpreting information primarily from four sources: mastery experience, vicarious experience*, social persuasions, and physiological reactions.
- self-efficacy beliefs influence the choices people make and the courses of action they pursue.
- Individuals tend to engage in tasks about which they feel competent and confident and avoid those in which they do not.

*Note that emphasis added for "vicarious experience" because job shadowing is especially recognized by professionals in career development as a vicarious experience, which heavily influences an individual's career choice.

SELF ESTEEM

During 2004, the soap manufacturer Dove had started their "Campaign for Real Beauty," in which they recognized that "Self-Esteem has an effect on every aspect of a person's life. Too many girls develop low self-esteem from hang-ups about looks."

Their research also found that "when girls and women feel positive about themselves and the way they look, they are more likely to engage in life, enjoy social interactions and live up to their full potential" and that "teenage girls can learn to recognize how good they are in what they do, by writing or documenting their thoughts and feelings."

At Asunción, we wanted our students to value their knowledge, skills, talents and academic progress as key elements to professional success, and we wanted them to showcase their achievements, goals, and interest through an electronic portfolio that would incorporate the job shadowing experience as a critical element.

THE FIRST SYSTEMS

Having reviewed several electronic portfolio programs, we opted for an open source system called "*Klahowya*," developed by Amanda Emily, a student from Washington University. The code and the text were in English, but we translated it into the Spanish language and offered students their first electronic portfolio with a fixed menu that included:

Profile:

1. My commitment
2. Motivation and Academic Perception
3. My values
4. Ideal place to work
5. Curriculum Vitae
6. Plans
7. Personal Learning Plan
8. Letters of Reference
9. Community Service
10. School Activities
11. Recognitions

Students liked it and completed their first e-portfolios. However, many had limited or no knowledge of HTML and could not edit their texts or add images, resulting in a product that was not attractive to the reader. Further, *Klahowya* did not have a file system, and students could only upload new files to create new entries or substitute content in existing entries. Viewers could not comment on content or contact the student, and, on the administrative panel, menus could be edited, but passwords were not masked, and users could be eliminated but not modified. Having said that, the system represented a very positive start to the implementation of electronic portfolios at Asunción.

By 2006, we had developed our own system, consisting of a combination of open source and "homegrown" code. With the benefits of functionality that we needed, the system was available in Spanish, used local expertise, and had no software license fee. In subsequent years, we faced the challenge of increased development costs, as the first set of code became obsolete, and also the loss of expert staff necessary to sustain and to scale-up the system.

At this stage, the electronic portfolio was added to the Career Guidance Class in Moodle, our Learning Management System (LMS), and included a set of defined topics with due dates, regular feedback, forum participation, and links to readings or examples of successful implementation of electronic portfolios. We encouraged students to be inspired by local and global movements, such as UNESCO's Manifesto 2000 for a culture of peace and non-violence. Importantly, the few "Portfolio Champions," school counselor, curriculum coordinator, and mentors were involved from the beginning of the program and remain committed.

METRICS

Following the set of Five Rules for implementing electronic portfolios as presented by Chappell and Schermerhorn, we evaluated our program and found that because it was mandatory (students had to complete it for their Career Guidance class), there was little resistance on the part of students. Students were encouraged to learn new computer skills that were helpful for the presentation of their content, and help was available from technology integration facilitators (our personnel in charge of computer labs/technology integration centers).

Using the "Critical Factors for Successful Implementation," (Gathercoal et al., 2002) as a basis for measuring the effectiveness and success of our system, we were able to provide students, teachers, and administration with confidence that the system was performing and providing benefits as intended.

INFLUENCE OF SOCIAL NETWORKS

By the end of 2008, we became very much aware of the frequency and comfort of use by students of social networks, such as High-Five, MySpace, and Facebook.

The Pew Internet Project survey on "Social Networking Websites and Teens" conducted from October 23 to November 19, 2006, found that "more than half (55%) of all online American youths ages 12-17 were using online social networking sites. The survey also found that older teens, particularly girls, were more likely to use these sites. For girls, social networking sites are primarily places to reinforce pre-existing friendships; for boys, the networks also provide opportunities for flirting and making new friends."

The survey went on to describe that "while private messaging within social networks is

Table 1 Refers to the analogous references of Gathercoal et al. (2002).

Critical Factor	Observations
1. Information Services Cooperation	The service was able to support the Internet traffic to and from the webfolio server; The service had problems retrieving passwords, which led to denied access to few students.
2. Administrative Support	Funding was committed to the design, implementation, and evaluation of the electronic portfolio system "Mi Portafolio Académico," to the development of the curriculum.
3. Technology Infrastructure	All participants have Internet Access from home and/or Technology Integration Center
4. Portfolio Culture	Students complete portfolios as "Job Shadow Program requirement", Graduation Requirement "Life Plan Project" Portfolios carry significant weight in determining a student's participation in a Job Shadow program. Multiple teachers/supervisors/mentors read and comment on students' portfolio work.
5. Student Learning-Centered Culture	Students routinely address unstructured problems. Teachers routinely give students assignments in written form.
6. "Implementing Force" and Project Champions	The push for adoption and implementation of electronic portfolios comes mainly from counselors. We need more commitment and stamina to make it work for everyone.
7. Implementation Milestones	An implementation plan exists with reasonable milestones that are measurable and collectively lead to full implementation.
8. Training and Help Resources	Open computer lab assistance is available for students and teachers. Opportunities exist for teacher/mentor training (more are needed, on continued basis) More electronic portfolio documentation needs to be available for teachers/mentors and students.
9. Teacher Commitment	Teams of teachers agree to cast program standards into uniform format, including an artifact-producing activity demonstrating mastery of program standard modules (End-of-year Exposaberes)
10. Competency Based Curriculum	Career Guidance Class follows ASCA standards, and the "Guatemalan Curriculum Nacional Base"
11. Integrated Curriculum Developed by Teams	Team of coordinators, mentors, counselors, and teachers periodically review and revise the content of the curriculum for "Life Project" and "Job Shadow" and are aware of the content of classes making up the entire program. Courses and/or program requirements are designed and sequenced to build student mastery of standards.
12. Feedback Provided by Counselors/Mentors/ Teachers using the Electronic Portfolio	Mentors, classmates, and business partner from Job Shadow Project present feedback to students. Students value the feedback.

common, 84% of young social networkers also regularly post messages on friends' pages - or on their "walls," as they're commonly known" (Irvine, 2007).

Findings from the 2006 survey include the following statistics that are relevant to our school:

- "55% of online teens use social networks and 55% have created online profiles; older girls predominate."

- "55% of online teens have created a personal profile online, and 55% have used social networking sites like MySpace or Facebook."

- "66% of teens who have created a profile say that their profile is not visible to all internet users. They limit access to their profiles."

- "48% of teens visit social networking web-sites daily or more often; 26% visit once a day, 22% visit several times a day."
- "Older girls ages 15-17 are more likely to have used social networking sites and created online profiles."
- "70% of older girls have used an online social network compared with 54% of older boys."
- "70% of older girls have created an online profile, while only 57% of older boys have done so.".

As a result of the survey, it became clear that we needed to introduce at least some elements of social network capabilities to our system. After reviewing a number of open source solutions, we decided to add ELGG, a social networking system licensed under the terms of the GNU General Public License v2, to our design as it provided a solid framework, was free to download and use, had Spanish language capability, and could be recoded if needed.

Students' first impressions were very favorable; the frequency of visits, posting on walls, selection of members, and upload of documents and images all increased substantially. Students agreed that the electronic portfolio felt more up-to-date, dynamic, and friendly.

Correspondingly, increased levels of security were implemented. For example, only those who received a system-generated link could have access to it and could send messages directly to students through their school accounts without revealing their email addresses. This functionality was particularly important when students needed to share their electronic portfolio with their job shadowing partner, mentor, and counselor.

FUTURE WORK

We are facing issues regarding the file navigation system and storage space, as students are interested in adding podcasts, movies, and music files to their electronic portfolios. To address concerns raised by this necessary enhancement, we are currently looking at Google Apps, as the school already relies on Gmail for the students' electronic mail accounts, and also at the Mahara electronic portfolio system, since it is already integrated with Moodle, our LMS.

Our students should be able to use a variety of different formats to showcase their talents, abilities, and skills and to have the choice to transfer it to another system without any challenges: one portfolio for their professional career that starts at school and continues beyond with them.

In the future, we would like students to use our system "*Mi Portafolio Académico*" when providing information to other electronic portfolio systems such as the National Association of Student Councils (NASC) Student Leaders Program Application "Building Your Portfolio." As with NASC, a number of associations are requesting students provide printed versions of their portfolios. We see this as counter-intuitive and would like to develop our system such that it can provide different views on the content of the existing electronic portfolios that would nonetheless conform to the requirements of these other associations, especially in the context of displaying their desired menu system that often unique to each association. In the meantime, in the case of NASC, we will encourage students to apply (for certification as a student leader) but will request on their behalf that an electronic version be acceptable in lieu of a printed version.

CONCLUSION

By starting to use electronic portfolios at an earlier age, students are better equipped to make more informed choices in terms of the direction they would like to take their careers.

Electronic portfolios let students showcase and present evidence of their own self-realization and, by creating a portfolio prior to meeting with their job shadowing partner, the partner is then better informed of the students' capabilities, which has the benefit of positively reinforcing and enriching the job shadowing experience.

Students will get to know themselves through their accomplishments and talents. In this regard, we have shown that students will develop a strong sense of self-efficacy and will persevere when faced with challenges.

REFERENCES

American School Counselor Association. (2004). *ASCA national standards for students.* Alexandria, VA: Author.

Dove. (n. d.). *Campaign for real beauty.* Retrieved August 7, 2007, from http://www.campaignfor-realbeauty.com.au/self-esteem-fund/why-it-matters.asp

Gathercoal, P., Love, D., Bryde, B., & McKean, G. (2002). *On implementing Web-based electronic portfolios.* Retrieved March 6, 2006, from EDUCAUSE website: http://net.educause.edu/ir/library/pdf/eqm0224.pdf

Irvine, M. (2007, January 8). Survey illuminates teen social networks. *USA Today.* Retrieved from http://www.usatoday.com/tech/news/2007-01-08-teen-networks_x.htm

Ittelson, G. L. (2005, July). *An overview of e-portfolios.* Retrieved January 14, 2008, from EDUCAUSE website: http://net.educause.edu/ir/library/pdf/ELI3001.pdf

Junior Achievement of Middle America. (2009). *Executive summary: Work-readiness impact of JA program participation.* Retrieved January 10, 2010, from http://jamidamerica.org/docs/rf/ExecutiveSummary-Work-ReadinessImpactof-JAProgramParticipation.pdf

Junior Achievement of Middle America. (n. d.). *About.* Retrieved January 14, 2005, from http://www.ja.org/about/about.shtml

Lenhart, M., & Madden, M. (2007). *55% of online teens use social networks and 55% have created online profiles; older girls predominate.* Retrieved August 1, 2007, from Pew Internet website: http://www.pewinternet.org/Reports/2007/Social-Networking-Websites-and-Teens/Data-Memo/Findings.aspx

Manifesto. (2000). *The 6 key points.* Retrieved January 14, 2006, from Unesco website: http://www3.unesco.org/manifesto2000/

Pajares, P., & Schunk, D. H. (2001). *Self-beliefs and school success: Self-efficacy, self concept, and school achievement.* Retrieved October 19, 2010, from Emory University website: http://www.des.emory.edu/mfp/PajaresSchunk2001.html

Portafolio Academico Geatec. (2008). *Mi portafolio.* Retrieved from http://www.geatec.net/portafolio2009/

Portafolio-Asuncion. (n. d.). *Portafolio- Klahowya.* Retrieved January 8, 2010, from http://web.asuncion.edu.gt/portfolio/index.php

Wilder, M. V. (n.d.). *Klahowya student portfolio solution.* Retrieved February 2005, from Sourceforge website: http://sourceforge.net/projects/klahowya2/

Chapter 10

ePortfolios:
From Business School to Business Office

Eleanor J. Flanigan
Montclair State University, USA

ABSTRACT

This chapter highlights the types of portfolios most frequently used in the business world or in preparation for entering a career. It shows that content in each area can be cumulative or separate. It will describe ideas for the types of artifacts to compile along with how to format them effectively and digitize them creatively. Compiling a digital portfolio is a strong contribution to a student's learning path as well as providing a business professional with a means of collecting and preserving valuable projects. Continual reflection upon their work provides individuals with more confidence in their own worth as they embark upon their professional careers or justify their desires for advancement.

INTRODUCTION

Developing an innovative and original electronic business portfolio is one of the most effective tools that could be used by either the business professional or the student entering the business community. It constitutes a lasting comprehensive experience for both groups. Continual reflection upon their work arms students and business people alike with more confidence in their own

competence and worth as they embark on their professional careers or justify their desires for advancement.

Unless people are unusually reflective and deliberately trace their intellectual and professional growth, most go with the flow of daily living and work needs. Many are not consciously aware of the paths that lead them from one level of knowledge or from one career to another. Whereas professionals keep pace with new requirements placed

DOI: 10.4018/978-1-4666-0143-7.ch010

upon them, most students move ahead according to the required collegiate curriculums. Students take the prescribed courses as directed without much reflection on their cumulative knowledge or recognition of the connection between these courses. Both groups, however, accumulate valuable experiences along their paths, sometimes forgetting how they actually got to some pinnacle of experience. Important anecdotes or incidents are tucked away in memory but are not documented otherwise.

Professional and business people are certainly aware of keeping their resumes up to date, although they may not do this until some employment crisis forces them to reflect and report on their accomplishments. Annual job assessment reviews often prompt scrambling through the papers or memories of the prior year to compile a report for the desired salary raise or promotion.

Similar to this situation, students find that as graduation approaches and career opportunities present themselves, preparing comprehensive resumes requires them to sum up their achievements and experiences. This is usually an onerous task. Rather than waiting until the end of the program, it may increase the students' ability to comprehend the path of learning if they had to collect and preserve their work in a creative accumulative project, reflecting and assessing during the process.

Developing a creative portfolio can also help to guide writing a creative resume. Overall declarations of competence or experience in resumes are strengthened by providing concrete examples of these competencies and skills attained. Statements on the resume can be linked to the portfolio artifacts to show specific examples of projects or supporting documents for claims made by the interviewee. This is "show and tell" brought to life by the creator of a digital portfolio who not only proclaims that he/she knows about technological advances but can put them into practice, using

them for creative enhancement of the traditionally static resume.

This chapter will confine itself to the types of portfolios most frequently used in the business world or in preparation for entering a career, showing that content in each can be cumulative or separate. It will describe ideas for the types of artifacts to compile along with how to format them effectively and digitize them creatively. It will give answers to "Why create a portfolio?", "Who should have one?", "What should be in it?", and "How are portfolios created?"

Portfolio Overview

Although comparatively innovative in business settings, structured portfolios are not new to many other disciplines. Their uses range, depending on their purpose and their intended audiences. Whereas self-reflective portfolios serve as journals or organizers of activities and experiences, academic portfolios show student learning and progress or the development of skills. Professional portfolios are used in career determination or assessment of accomplishments as well as serving as demonstrations to validate claims of professional development.

Some portfolios consist of one's own work while others, such as teachers' portfolios, incorporate the tasks they developed for their students along with evaluations, exemplary projects, or external and internal assessments.

Another definition of portfolios is common in the financial world. There, a portfolio is a collection of monetary assets reflected in stocks, bonds, real estate, and personal possessions. Reallocating and shifting these assets for optimal return is the task of financial analysis. Borrowing from this description of an asset portfolio, another way of summing up one's assets is by evaluating a collection of one's personal achievements. These assets are perhaps more precious than mere monetary accumulations. It takes a lifetime of work to acquire educational, professional, and personal assets. Enhancing this theme of portfolios as a collection of assets, Poore (2001) considers a person's business career as a portfolio of well-chosen investments.

ePortfolios

ePortfolios, also known as electronic portfolios or digital portfolios, are collections of digitized artifacts used to validate claims made by the creator. These artifacts are in a creative variety of formats: text documents, Web pages, presentations, research papers, assessment instruments, original projects, artifacts of academic or external teamwork, documentation of internships, performance videos, certificates of achievement, spreadsheets, databases, digital images, and multimedia demonstrations. Another term for the process of organizing artifacts for use in portfolios is cataloging relevant material.

These digital portfolios serve the business student population as well as business professionals, encouraging them to look critically at their work and analyze it objectively. Using the concrete examples of their achievements and growth, portfolio developers create technologically creative resumes with the portfolio artifacts to support statements of proficiency in their chosen fields.

Thus, a general portfolio is a demonstration of skills and abilities, containing evidence of growth and competence. Portfolios can be learning tools, job search tools, and career growth tools. The purpose of the portfolio to some degree dictates the artifacts collected as well as the format of the design. The ePortfolio goes one step further in that the artifacts within it are digitized. This process thus allows original documents to be preserved and assures the integrity of precious historical materials which highlight achievement or serve as snapshots of a discrete period in a person's career development.

TYPES OF ePORTFOLIOS FOR ASSESSMENT, JOB SEARCHES, AND INTERVIEWS

Learning and Assessment Portfolio

Students create portfolios as part of classwork for assessment or for tracking their growth during their academic careers. While collecting the artifacts of learning, students realize that they have concrete evidence to support their perceptions of their own development. Their belief in their own growth is given support by looking objectively at the increasing complexity of their projects. Their self-assessment is substantiated by recognizing how their knowledge base changed comparing the artifacts from the beginning of their studies with the more sophisticated projects done toward the end of their academic years.

This reflection on one's work prompts another important area that of developing the ability to be objective when assessing both the quality and/or quantity of materials used in the portfolio. Nicholson (2004) considers self-reflection as "the first step in knowledge construction" (p. 322). With encouragement from a teacher/mentor, the students have a chance to reflect upon their progress, do remedial work, and plan their paths for continued growth.

Students also find portfolios invaluable when pursuing internships or employment at the conclusion of their program. Learning portfolios preserve artifacts that later can become part of career portfolios. Thus, the initial portfolio done as a student provides a base or example for any future portfolio development. At many points in a work career, the employee frequently pursues further skills or education in a full degree program, a certification, or even a workshop. It is important that these achievements be documented to demonstrate growth or achievement to the employer. So the portfolio is the constant base ready to receive and preserve new artifacts.

Initial Job Inquiry Portfolio

In advertisements for employment, the candidate is often directed to send documents such as resumes or supporting material electronically. If the initial inquiry is made online, a small portfolio of work examples could be submitted along with an electronic resume as an e-mail attachment. The content of the portfolio would consist primarily of text documents including a resume and several work examples or a few highly compressed images. The portfolio creator must be aware that sending this type of portfolio has restrictions in that there are a variety of e-mail systems on the receiving end, some of which limit the size of attachments.

An alternative to actually sending the resume, text documents, or supporting images would be to compose a resume and cover letter with internal hyperlinks directing the reader to a web-based portfolio. This type of portfolio can also take the form of an expanded web resume or be an extensive multimedia web-based presentation. This different strategy means that the original portfolio need not be restricted in size. In these cases, the portfolio is web-based and simply linked from the job application materials.

The introductory portfolio differs in structure from a comprehensive portfolio in the amount of material available. The introductory portfolio might also be an electronic document tailored for each job application or initial inquiry, showing just the type of experience, skill, or education that best pertains to each company or position being sought. Thus the creator would pick and choose among the various artifacts in order to focus on the needs expressed by the employer or interviewer. This more personal, focused approach would show depth of preparation as well as forcing the prospective employee to focus on addressing the specific requirements of the job proposed.

Interview Presentation Portfolio

This portfolio should also be tailored to the particular needs of the company or the position sought, perhaps using the mission statement of the specific company as the base for comparison with the job-seeker's competencies. Since the purpose of this portfolio is to add to the smaller introductory portfolio, it should include more materials since size is not as great a limitation. Graphically, this portfolio should follow the rules of good visual communication for presentations, being aware of appropriate colors or formatting. This type of portfolio lends itself to including slide presentations or multimedia projects.

This portfolio should fit on a CD, with several copies available. When taken to a job interview, the applicant can present the portfolio during the interview session. A copy can then be left with the interviewer to accompany their application materials following the interview.

Career Growth Portfolio

Once hired, the employee should continue to collect artifacts and include them into portfolios to demonstrate the work performed and growth achieved in skills and responsibilities. This type of portfolio is very helpful in yearly performance reviews and for applications for promotion. As Williams et al. (2004) states, "the portfolio should be designed to transition" (p. 2) with the employee. Quality artifacts should increase as the years on the job increase.

For the busy employee, it is easy to forget one's achievements in the previous year or from one assessment to the next. Since one project usually piles on another or several projects overlap, the employee tends to try to keep up with the crisis on hand. What is lost in the active flux of the working day is the time to reflect or to actively stop to preserve any final projects. Much is lost if the history of a project is not categorized and analyzed. These processes allow greater efficiencies in that they can be applied to similar projects and roadblocks can be avoided.

However, in the crush of work, what is needed is constant awareness that the preservation of artifacts serves several purposes. Not only can the efficiencies mentioned above be utilized but also preservation of projects and achievements can add weight to an employee's description of activities required for job assessment, request for promotion, or avoidance of being part of a reduction in force in the company.

An ePortfolio would provide strong evidence of successful projects. For example, by having digitized testimonial letters from clients, the employee could show expertise in customer relations. A video clip of the company's manufacturing branch in another country would remind the employee's managers of the exhaustive work done or the extensive business trip taken and the valuable contributions the employee has made. Once the ePortfolio is compiled with digitized proof of successful work, the employee can present this at the annual review in an organized and professional manner. The ePortfolio is a somewhat objective piece that could be largely self-explanatory while viewed by both employee and manager.

As an example of the concept of transition during one's career, the field of teacher education has been at the forefront for the past decade encouraging portfolio development. Wilcox and Tomei (1999) address developing portfolios to fit three growth phases of a professional career in education: teacher as learner, teacher as expert, and, finally, teacher as scholar. These phases are direct reflections of the portfolios of many professional educators.

This type of portfolio could fit on a CD or, if it includes video or other multimedia, could be distributed on DVD. If there is a yearly review, the parameters of the review should dictate the main content of this type of portfolio. The employee would choose artifacts focusing on more recent achievements and would not include irrelevant or outdated material.

When the phase of teacher as learner is active, artifacts of the ePortfolio can be a mix of certification acknowledgment and creative curricular planning as well as incorporating student involvement. Video clips of classroom activities provide strong channels of communication and assessment for the novice teacher and his/her mentor.

An ePortfolio from the phase of teacher as expert would show one's growth and sophistication. Artifacts from this phase would include curricular innovation and classroom activities as well as generative sharing of techniques with novice teachers.

Many activities and artifacts from the phase of teacher as scholar would be captured well by an ePortfolio as here the growth expands both laterally and vertically. Digitizing professional papers as well as video clips of presentations or testimonial documents may serve multiple purposes. Here, the roles of teacher-expert and teacher-scholar can be documented to help in assessing the valuable contributions made to the academic field.

PORTFOLIO ARTIFACTS

A simple rule of thumb is to save everything that relates to work, professional growth, and achievement. It is vital to organize storage methods and to digitize artifacts as soon as possible. Artifacts may be digitized by scanning or photographing them with a digital camera. Once the materials are digitized, it becomes less important to store artifacts in paper form. It is important to create at least one backup of the original digital materials.

The purpose of the portfolio will determine which of the artifacts is placed into the digital document when it is time to create the digital portfolio. For example, a career portfolio would contain the documentation enumerated in Table 1.

Table 1. Career portfolio artifacts

Personal Information	Evidence of personal interests, mentors, role models, personality inventory or assessments
Educational Credentials	Evidence of education history, thesis or other major papers or research, examples of coursework products
Career Achievements	Evidence of work history, career plan, references, inventory of career accomplishments
Communication Competencies	Evidence of communication skills, technical skills, certifications, speaking, diversity skills, teamwork
Professional Activities	Examples of publication, presentations
Recognition	Evidence of academic honors, workplace achievement or recognition, promotions

Table 2. Interview presentation portfolio artifacts

Statement of Career Goals	Statement of how their skills and competencies will enhance the mission of the company
Academic Achievements	Transcripts, relevant courses taken, honors, awards, internships
Evidence of Competencies	Skill-based projects, reports, papers, relevant team activities, original computer- based cases
Exterior Assessment	References, academic commendations, club or group affiliations, leadership roles, community service, volunteer work

Students may find the suggestions in Table 2 for documents helpful in preparing their portfolios for the interview presentation portfolio.

The sample of careers and the relevant portfolio artifacts listed in Table 3 may be helpful to those preparing for new job interviews, for annual reviews, or for promotion requests.

PORTFOLIO PRODUCTION TIPS

Digitizing documents and objects for archiving is different than scanning or photographing for presentation. For archiving, the highest quality file possible should be created. It should be the highest resolution in RGB color mode at the largest scale the hard drive, digital camera, or scanner can handle.

Table 3. Career-appropriate artifacts

Graphic Artists	Professional graphics, artwork, commercial projects, freelance work, gallery showing, private commissions
Sales and Marketing Personnel	Presentations, reports on client success, service awards, promotion paths, recognitions
Office Personnel	Creative documents, relevant projects, recommendations, management reviews
Information Systems Workers	Multimedia or sophisticated technical projects, proof of certifications, images of systems projects, commendations
Help Desk Personnel	Commendations from clients, technical manuals, performance reviews

If the original document becomes lost or disintegrates through aging, this technique of using the maximum settings creates the best possible digital representation of the document. Using the highest settings allows for creating additional smaller files, optimized for portfolio presentation.

Creative Digitizing

Digital documents that are originals should be copied and stored at least twice. Full-size original digital files should be kept on fixed media or in the cloud. The archivist should be alert to several situations relating to present and future technologies. Digital files should be in standard formats. Proprietary or native application formats may not stand the test of time. Files should also be saved in a standard format such as TIFF for images or RTF for text documents with formatting. The original files are best saved uncompressed. Once the files are sized and prepared for a portfolio, then they can be compressed.

Physical artifacts should also be documented. Good, high-resolution digital pictures of the objects should be taken and backed up. It is sometimes worth the time and cost to get a professional to create quality images as artifacts. If a non-professional chooses to take digital pictures, the photos should be shot in a large format with the highest resolution the camera allows. Natural or bright artificial lighting is necessary to illuminate the object in order to separate it from the background.

Tape or digital audio and video media may be used in portfolios. Since analog tape media degrades in the duplication process, the tape that is closest to the original edit should be kept and backed up digitally. When preparing files for a portfolio, the file size may be reduced or compressed, but the best quality digital copy of the original serves as backup.

Digital Portfolio Formats

Portfolios can be constructed using a variety of media, including popular office applications programs as well as portfolio software and Web-based platforms.

Text-Based Portfolio Formats

Among many other programs available, text-based digital portfolios can be easily created with Microsoft Word, PowerPoint, and Adobe Acrobat, commonly used programs with a multitude of features. These popular software programs are very efficient, especially for the novice to use when creating a portfolio. For example, presentations created with PowerPoint's attractive and color-coordinated templates provide the backdrop for appropriate content enhanced with animations, video clips, or voice integration. Once created, an abstract of the full presentation can introduce the topic. If the observer wishes to view the entire slide set, it is available within the ePortfolio.

Viewing files created with Adobe Acrobat requires a free plug-in, but this is rarely a limitation since the Acrobat Reader is a business standard and can be installed on virtually all computers. This program particularly makes the collection of creative artifacts possible as it allows for a combination of text, graphics, video, Web projects, and interactive displays to be integrated into an easily accessible electronic format. Since Portable Document Format (PDF) files are transportable across all platforms, they are readable by both sender and receiver.

Another key criterion for software selection, according to Barrett (2004), should be its capability to allow hypertext links between stated goals and outcomes and the artifacts. Each of these programs has sophisticated hypertext features which provide flexibility in portfolio design while still maintaining coherence when relating one section to another. In the example given with the PowerPoint presentation, the ePortfolio creator would provide a hyperlink within the introduction to allow immediate access to the entire slide set if desired.

Hyperlinking is also useful within the testimonial letters. For example, one slide in the presentation could contain thumbnail images of several letters. The captions under each letter could then be formatted as hyperlinks to allow the observer to see the full sheet testimonial. Another example of effective use of hyperlinks is in the table of contents. When observing the ePortfolio, the hyperlinks provide opportunity to move randomly throughout the material.

Portfolio Software

There are several software programs which specialize in areas crucial to portfolio creation. Among these include Extensis Portfolio, Cumulus Canto, and Epsilen Portfolios. The underlying goal of each of these programs is digital asset management (DAM), which is the underpinning of portfolios. DAM is an enabling technology and solution to creating, archiving, managing, and finally using the collected artifacts or assets.

There are two key benefits to using ePortfolio-specific programs. First, they provide the structure needed to create portfolios efficiently. Second, they catalog the digitized assets or artifacts using metadata, which is data about the data describing the artifact. This description standardizes the naming and filing of each artifact, thus enabling the portfolio creator to find appropriate material when creating different portfolios needed during various levels of a professional career.

Web-Based Portfolio Formats

The three software programs mentioned, Extensis Portfolio, Cumulus Canto, and Epsilen Portfolios, are also Web-based. Their features vary, but secure server storage is common to all three. Along with storage, the most desirable features in Web-based software should include the structure needed to create and archive artifacts, create personal Web pages, provide suggestions for Web design, and offer well-designed templates. Helpful features should also guide the user through the steps needed for distribution of the portfolio, burning to CDs or DVDs, creating QuickTime movies, developing slide shows, and e-mailing.

Although some Web-based ePortfolio programs are available through subscription, others are completely free to academic users, both students and educational professionals. One such program is Epsilen, which has many sophisticated academic topics and is continually expanding its features in the free portfolio creation section.

Another Web-based portfolio collection and storage area is available through a feature in Blackboard, a widely used educational course management system. (Many course management systems now include ePortfolio functionality.) The Blackboard Content System includes the ability not only to store artifacts but also to manage the portfolio by allowing the creator to control its availability to external users and to check that the links to items within the portfolio maintain their validity.

Constructing and implementing Web-based portfolios successfully involves more than just collecting artifacts and distributing an attractive and useful portfolio for career purposes. Academic use during a student's development may aid in greater reflection on the scholastic path the student is on. Counselors can enhance their interaction with students by tapping into students' portfolios for advisement. Course work and assignments could be checked and commented on by instructors with further suggestions for improvement. Due to the ability to store securely on institutional servers, students and teachers could develop a more collaborative association.

ePortfolio software needs to support the use of portfolios for multiple purposes. A webfolio, according to Gathercoal, Love, Bryde, and McKean (2002), is more than simply a traditional portfolio digitized. Since the portfolio could be made available to external viewers, it could be made an integral part of a curriculum. Serving several purposes, it could be used by students as a "working portfolio generating artifacts only they can view, a developmental portfolio they share with faculty, and a showcase portfolio they share with the world" (Gathercoal, Love, Bryde, & McKean, 2002, p. 31). Although these purposes sum up concisely the goals of having a portfolio and suggest the use of artifacts for personal or public scrutiny, Batson suggests that ePortfolios should primarily be used as learning portfolios, "emphasizing ...ownership of their own work" rather than using them as assessment manager (Batson, 2007). Batson criticizes the mixing of learning portfolios with other types, among them showcase portfolios or advisement portfolios as well as assessment portfolios. EPortfolio systems need to allow students to create multiple portfolio versions to address these different purposes.

Using the Web as a storage medium and then manipulating artifacts to fit appropriately into a variety of portfolios as the need arises permits portfolio creators to be more adaptive and flexible. The base portfolio, perhaps created during student years and stored on the Web, could become a lifelong touchstone for professional and career advancement. Other versions could be created for specific contexts and purposes.

One objection to using proprietary servers for Web-based portfolios is the temporary storage available. In most institutions, once a student graduates, their course management system account is closed, thus cutting off access to the portfolio materials stored there. Thus, using a subscription-based or free service is preferable once a student has left the academic server environment.

Multimedia Use: Pros and Cons

Some career documentation is most effectively delivered via multimedia or motion media, such as audio, video, or animation. This type of docu-

mentation is usually not appropriate for inclusion in an email attachment due to file size.

With multimedia, the important consideration is the software or plug-ins that are required on the user's computer in order to view the multimedia files in the sender's portfolio. If the end user computer lacks the programs needed, then the multimedia portfolio files cannot be viewed. If users get an error, they may stop viewing the portfolio altogether. Therefore, the decision to include multimedia should be based on analyzing the delivery method. Using Web-based servers is a viable option for portfolios containing relevant multimedia artifacts. Using multimedia effectively within a portfolio enhances it as it requires not only the contents of the creative artifact but also the technical ability to create it and then to publish it. This is an area where the creator gets to achieve a three-part goal. Not only can he or she document relevant achievements to prove professional competence, but he or she can also prove technical competence and do this creatively.

To avoid problems, preview the portfolio on the broadest possible range of computers, operating systems, and installations. Multimedia in non-standard formats is safest when used in presentations made directly from a laptop or computer during an interview, guaranteeing that there will be no problems with plug-ins or missing software. The user should be particularly careful to confirm and restore any hyperlinks used.

CONCLUSION

Compiling the digital portfolio is a strong contribution to a student's learning path as well as providing a business professional with a means of collecting and preserving valuable projects. It serves not only as an archive for precious material that may otherwise be lost over the years but also serves as an organizing principle, according to Campbell (2004). Learning theory reminds us that people remember what they do and what they produce instead of what others have done for them. So portfolios provide a memory jog with a record of quantitative and qualitative growth over time.

For academic use and supporting student learning, portfolios capture a moment in time when students were acquiring the skills and competencies needed for their careers. However, having had the experience of creating a portfolio, the student-turned-professional can build upon it and add to it during his or her business career. The reflections made when collecting and archiving projects allow students to make cohesive connections between concepts learned in various courses. Both during its creation and when the portfolio is completed, the student is able to connect the knowledge dots to see how one experience led to the other.

The portfolio provides concrete evidence of learning, improvement, and success. It serves as a snapshot of knowledge-growth and experiences attained. Overall, it serves as proof to claims of skills and competencies for potential employers and provides students with concrete evidence of some of their achievements.

For business personnel, the portfolio also serves the purpose of memory-jogging for assessment. It captures significant documents, projects, images, video clips, reports, recommendations, testimonials, presentations, and programs. Prior to developing a formal portfolio, these artifacts are often misplaced physically as well as forgotten at just the time when the employee needs all the support possible to shore up a request for promotion or to keep a job.

Often, the employee's artifacts lead to a significantly enhanced conversation with the assessing manager as they both review and rehash the projects from the previous year. These assessment interviews often evolve into deeper project assessment and reviewing of the employee's corporate experiences. Keeping relevant artifacts also shows the employee his or her growth within the company as the projects assigned become more complex. The employee could keep several intact portfolios,

labeled with specific years, along with separate artifacts from all of the time periods. The intact portfolio acts as a snapshot of a discrete period of time and serves as a comparison to later years. Keeping the artifacts all available separately, preferably on an accessible Web server, allows an employee to select the most relevant examples of competence or achievement when creating separate portfolios.

Although these are but a few uses for ePortfolios within either an academic or business setting, the creator becomes more adept as he/she grows professionally. The brain may be the best "server" for storing memories, but using technology such as ePortfolios allows the creator to share his/her achievements with a wide audience.

REFERENCES

Amirian, S., & Flanigan, E. (2006). *Create your digital portfolio: The fast track to career success.* Indianapolis, IN: JIST.

Barrett, H. (2004). *Standards-based electronic portfolio handbook for assessment and evaluation.* Retrieved March 1, 2009, from http://electronic-portfolios.com/handbook/index.html

Batson, T. (2007). The ePortfolio hijacked. *Campus Technology.* Retrieved March 1, 2009, from http://campustechnology.com/articles/2007/12/the-eportfolio-hijacked.aspx

Campbell, D., Cignetti, P., Melenyer, B., Nettles, D., & Wyman, R. (2004). *How to develop a professional portfolio.* Boston, MA: Pearson Education.

Canto. (n. d.). *Cumulus.* Retrieved August 28, 2008, from http://www.canto.com

Epsilen. (n. d.). *Portfolios.* Retrieved July 30, 2008, from http://www.epsilen.com

Extensis. (n. d.). *Portfolios.* Retrieved August 25, 2008, from http://www.extensis.com

Gathercoal, P., Love, D., Bryde, B., & McKean, G. (2002). On implementing Web-based electronic portfolios. *EDUCAUSE Quarterly, 25*(2), 29–37.

Nicholson, B. (2004). Course portfolio. In Galbraith, M. (Ed.), *Adult learning methods: A guide for effective instruction* (pp. 321–340). Malabar, FL: Krieger.

Poore, C. (2001). *Building your career portfolio.* Clifton Park, NY: Thomson Delmar Learning.

Wilcox, B., & Tomei, L. (1999). *Professional portfolios for teachers.* Norwood, MA: Christopher-Gordon.

Williams, A., & Hall, K. (2004). *Creating your career portfolio: At a glance guide.* Upper Saddle River, NJ: Prentice Hall.

Section 3
Australasia

Chapter 11
Current ePortfolio Practice in Australia

Gillian Hallam
Queensland University of Technology, Australia

Wendy Harper
Queensland University of Technology, Australia

Lynn McAllister
Queensland University of Technology, Australia

ABSTRACT

This chapter provides an overview of ePortfolio practice in Australia where a national research project has successfully documented ePortfolio practice in Australian higher education, and a parallel study has investigated emergent practice in the vocational education and training (VET) sector. It examines the policy context for ePortfolio activity in Australia, introduces the Australian ePortfolio Project and then presents a review of the research findings. This chapter discusses how ePortfolios offer the potential to be a meaningful medium for convergence and integration of education and training. This is done in order to support innovation and productivity, ensuring ongoing national economic development and growth.

INTRODUCTION

Specific drivers for an ePortfolio approach to learning and teaching in the Australian education system include the need to understand the future employment skills requirements; the need to overcome current and emerging skills shortages; and the need to focus on retraining and up-skilling the workforce to address factors that may lead to skills obsolescence, under-employment or even unemployment. In order to support innovation and productivity to ensure ongoing national economic development and growth, the current policy environment of the Australian Federal Government seeks to enhance the quality of education, encourage widened access to education opportunities, and stimulate integration between vocational education and training and higher education. There is evidence of strong interest across the different education sectors, with a growing awareness that ePortfolios have the potential to establish some degree of cohesion between the

DOI: 10.4018/978-1-4666-0143-7.ch011

different elements of education and employment, increasing the quality of learning and the value of education outcomes.

The higher education sector in Australia currently comprises 39 universities, of which 37 are public institutions and two are private. The federal government has the primary responsibility for the public funding of universities, although, administratively, the majority of institutions have been established under state and territory legislation (Department of Education, Employment and Workplace Relations DEEWR, 2010a). Accordingly, regulation and governance is spread across the federal government, the state and territory governments and the institutions themselves. In 2008, the number of university students in Australia exceeded one million (1,066,100). The study mode ratio is roughly 70% full-time to 30% part-time. 63% of enrolled students are aged under 25 years, 55% are female and 17.5% are international students (Australian Bureau of Statistics ABS, 2010).

In Australia, a national research project has successfully documented the state of play in ePortfolio practice in Australian higher education, while a parallel study has investigated emergent practice in the vocational education and training (VET) sector. This chapter provides an overview of ePortfolio practice in Australia. It examines the policy context for ePortfolio activity in Australia, introduces the Australian ePortfolio Project and then presents a review of the research findings.

THE POLICY CONTEXT FOR EPORTFOLIO ACTIVITY IN AUSTRALIA

Higher education policy is set against the background of the broader education policy. Following the federal election in Australia in November 2007, the new Department of Education, Employment and Workplace Relations (DEEWR) established a Review of Australian Higher Education (the Brad-

ley Review). The terms of reference for the review panel included the need to report on the sector's "fitness for purpose in meeting the needs of the Australian community and economy" (DEEWR, 2008a), as well as the options for ongoing reform. The issues of national productivity, participation in the labour market and the ability to respond to the needs of industry were topical, specifically in the context of positioning of higher education within the broader tertiary education sector in order to achieve a more integrated relationship with vocational education and training. In 2009, the Federal Government responded to the recommendations of the Bradley Review by proposing a reform agenda that promised to "transform the scale, potential and quality of the nation's universities and open the doors to higher education to a new generation of Australians" (DEEWR, 2009).

One of the critical aspects of current government policy is to consider the relationship between education and employment given the present focus on the skills shortage in Australia. The significance of policy drivers for ePortfolio practice in Europe and the UK should be considered in the Australian context. The Australian education community is committed to the goals of the Bologna Process, which encourages greater consistency and portability of qualifications within and across different education systems. The Bologna Process aims to facilitate communication and movement between European education institutions. An Australian Government discussion paper released in 2006 argued that there is a danger of Australia losing European enrollments if such a system were to become the international norm without Australia as a party (Department of Education, Science and Training DEST, 2006). Australia's role as a major education provider in the Asia-Pacific region was also a factor to consider. The importance of student mobility, which can be supported through formal documentation such as the Diploma Supplement (http://www.aei.gov.au/AEI/GovernmentActivities/DiplomaSupplement/default.htm) as well as through the personalized records of learning outcomes, is therefore highly relevant to the ePortfolio debate.

The Australian Flexible Learning Network has a keen focus on ePortfolio implementation in the Vocational Education and Training (VET) sector, acknowledging the importance of cross-sector engagement. Authors of the background paper to the national symposium on ePortfolios in the VET sector held in June 2008 underscored the importance of policy development to address the general development and management of ePortfolio services; the portability of information about qualifications and competencies; recognition of prior learning; the management and provision of secure and verifiable personal information and privacy (education.au, 2008a).

The federal Digital Education Revolution policy has been described as aiming to create "sustainable and meaningful change to teaching and learning in Australian schools that will prepare students for further education, training, jobs of the future and to live and work in a digital world" (DEEWR, 2008b). The debate about online access and the use of digital resources continues in Australia with the proposed rollout of a National Broadband Network (NBN, 2010) that promises to open up fast and reliable access to the Internet for most Australians. If ePortfolios were to be embedded in learning and teaching in schools, there would be raised expectations of and familiarity with the ePortfolio process by the time the student reached the higher education sector. Among the new funding commitments is one to support "collaboration with states and territories and Deans of Education to ensure new and continuing teachers have access to training in the use of ICT that enables them to enrich student learning" (DEEWR, 2008b), thus promoting the use of ePortfolios in teacher education and professional development.

In 2010, the Tertiary Education Quality and Standards Agency (TEQSA) was established with the goal of ensuring "renewed emphasis on learning and teaching quality as the bedrock of the Australian higher education system" (DEEWR, 2009, p. 15), building on the quality assurance activities undertaken by the Australian Universities Quality Agency (AUQA, 2010). The National Vocational Education and Training (VET) Regulator has been established in this role for the VET sector (2010). There is a possibility of a merger of the two agencies in 2013. There is the potential for ePortfolios to provide crucial support for the evidencing of teaching excellence across the higher education sectors.

The recent Australia 2020 Summit identified education as a key theme in the national "productivity agenda." One of the ways in which Australia can become more productive is by equipping Australians "with the capacity to contribute and innovate through an education and training system that leads the world in excellence and inclusion" (Australian Government, 2008, p. 10). The need to develop strong connections through "collaborations in education, business and innovation" (Australian Government, 2008, p. 10) has been recognized as an important aspect of the process. The Australia 2020 report also indicates the need to widen participation in higher education in order to meet the employability skills requirements. The report specifically indicates the vision to build "life learning centres" for working age career needs and to support full participation in the digital economy (Australian Government, 2008, p. 12). The need for ongoing skills development is also part of the need to address the critical problem of a skills shortage and has seen further manifestations in training programs such as the Productivity Places Program (DEEWR, 2010b).

In recent years, there has been a growing interest in "employability skills." While Australia currently has no government policy to mandate the formal recording or reporting of employability skills, strategies have been in place in the VET sector to incorporate employability skills into the National Training Packages, with consideration given to the options for assessing and reporting on the individual's acquisition of skills. In 2006,

DEST commissioned the Allen Consulting Group to examine the issues associated with recording and reporting of employability skills with the goal of developing a better understanding on the part of learners, trainers and employers (Allen Consulting Group, 2006). One of the key recommendations in the report to DEST was that learners should be encouraged to develop their own portfolios of employability skills.

Learners would consequently be better informed about the range of employability skills needed for specific jobs, as well as about where and how to develop the skills through work and study. It is argued that they would, as a result, be better prepared for job interviews. Transition into and through training courses in single or multiple institutions, with the ability to support the recognition of prior learning (RPL), may be managed more easily (education.au, 2008a). It has been noted that some Australian employers favor an ePortfolio approach as it gives a more informed picture of the job candidate than is possible through a traditional resumé. Nevertheless, employers tend to have their own perspective on ePortfolio, which means that the demands of the employer are not always commensurate with the educational goals of individual development and empowerment (Ward, 2008).

The interest in foundation and generic skills has continued to grow. Skills Australia (2010a) has stressed the importance of transferable skills that enable unemployed and underemployed workers to enter the labor market or to access further training. The potential of "individual learning plans" has been highlighted as a strategy to manage diversity and individual needs (Skills Australia, 2010b). Skills Australia has initiated a consultation process to support reforms that will enable the VET sector to become more responsive and to provide learners with greater choice and better pathways. This will require learners to have a good understanding of their skills and knowledge so that they are able to exercise these in the current labor market. This is aligned with

a move for employers to understand workforce development strategies, career planning and the personal learning plans developed by students, as for example in South Australia where students have the opportunity to bring together formal school subjects, vocational training and community learning to meet the requirements of the South Australian Certificate of Education (SACE). This internationally recognized certificate helps students transition to work, training and further study (SACE Board of South Australia, 2010).

Similar themes have emerged in the interface between the higher education and employment sectors. Industry groups and professional bodies have advocated the need for universities to offer courses that more adequately meet current industry and market place needs, especially within the area of graduate attributes or generic capabilities. In 2000, the Department of Education, Training and Youth Affairs (DETYA) commissioned a study of employers' satisfaction with university graduates. Findings revealed that employers believed that as many as 75% of Australian university graduates were not suited to the jobs for which they applied (AC Nielsen Research Services, 2000). Employers indicated that the apparent lack of preparedness is not in the technical areas but in the "generic" capabilities of oral and written communication, interpersonal dealings, critical thinking, problem-solving and ethics training.

In 2007, the Business, Industry and Higher Education Collaboration Council (BIHECC) was asked to undertake research into the development, teaching, assessment and reporting of graduate employability skills. The study acknowledged (Precision Consultancy, 2007) that employability skills were developed by university students through curriculum and course design, work placements such as fieldwork and internships, exposure to professional settings, advice and guidance by university careers services, and opportunities offered by part-time employment, volunteer work and community participation. ePortfolios have potential to support reporting of employability skills development.

The political agenda arguably has reached a position where a mature ePortfolio environment could play a significant role in bringing the tertiary education, vocational education and employment sectors to develop linkages and to attain a useful and potentially highly rewarding synergy. Through the Australian ePortfolio Project, the Australian Learning and Teaching Council (ALTC) has provided an opportunity to raise awareness of the potential of ePortfolios for university students.

THE AUSTRALIAN EPORTFOLIO PROJECT

In April 2007, the Australian Learning and Teaching Council (ALTC) (formerly known as the Carrick Institute for Learning and Teaching in Higher Education) issued a research brief to commission a study to develop a deeper understanding of ePortfolio practice in Australian universities (Carrick Institute, 2007).

The ALTC advised that the proposal for a "national portfolio assessment scheme" was influenced by the concept of the Higher Education Progress File in the United Kingdom (UK), which should consist of two elements: "a transcript recording student achievement... and a means by which students can monitor, build and reflect upon their personal development" (Dearing, 1997; Quality Assurance Agency in Higher Education QAA, 2001). As part of the higher education reform process in Australia, a discussion paper had been developed to consider how the sector could achieve higher levels of quality in learning, teaching and scholarship. Attention was paid to the need for student-centered curriculum structures, with the Business Higher Education Round Table (BHERT) supporting the concept of a portfolio to support both student mobility and lifelong learning.

The commissioned ePortfolio research project (http://www.eportfoliopractice.qut.edu.au) was granted to a multi-institutional team with Queensland University of Technology (QUT) as lead agency, and also included the University of Melbourne, the University of Wollongong and the University of New England. The project examined the range of approaches to ePortfolio engagement current at that time in Australian higher education. The Australian National Diploma Supplement project ran concurrently (http://www.aei.gov.au/ AEI/GovernmentActivities/DiplomaSupplement/ default.htm).

The involvement of the University of Melbourne and the University of New England in both the Australian ePortfolio Project and the National Diploma Supplement project ensured a close interplay between the investigations into the two dimensions of institutional academic information and individual learning.

The goals of the Australian ePortfolio Project (AeP) were to develop a clearer understanding of the types of ePortfolios being used in Australian universities, particularly the different models of practice (e.g., institution-wide, or faculty/school wide), the purposes for which they are used and the audiences for the ePortfolios, together with the type of tools and programs utilized. The project developed three questionnaires that targeted personnel in the learning and teaching, academic management and human resources areas. They were piloted and made available as online questionnaires, accessible for three weeks in November 2007. Most universities submitted multiple responses, with seven universities responding to all three survey instruments. The project also developed separate surveys that were developed for new university students who may be encountering an ePortfolio for the first time and for students and graduates who had been using ePortfolios for some time. Researchers also held focus groups and semi-structured interviews during the data collection phase of the project.

Table 1. AeP 2007/2010 survey responses

Responses	No. valid responses Nov 2007	No of universities 2007	Valid responses Sept 2010	No of university respondants 2010	No of VET sector respondants 2010
Learning and Teaching survey	73	34	65	34	24
Management survey	28	23	19	12	5
Human Resources survey	12	11	9	4	3
Total	113		94		

The Australian ePortfolio Project extended over a twelve-month period, with the final report released in October 2008 (Hallam, Harper, Mc-Cowan, Hauville, McAllister, & Creagh, 2008). The AeP report presented, for the first time, a comprehensive national snapshot of ePortfolio use in the Australian higher education sector. A supplementary study was undertaken in 2010, to update the data collected by the AeP project team in the initial audit. The goal of this "postscript to AeP" (AePPS) project was to refresh the picture of ePortfolio practice in Australia by collecting new data to identify and map the use of ePortfolios in adult learning, encompassing the higher education and VET sectors (Hallam, Harper, McAllister, Hauville, & Creagh, 2010). The project presented these updated findings at the ePortfolios Australia Conference 2010 (EAC2010) (Australian Flexible Learning Framework, 2010a).

The Current Picture of ePortfolio Practice in Australia

The Australian ePortfolio Project audit of national practice was undertaken in late 2007, while student surveys and interviews were conducted during the first semester of the 2008 academic year. The data therefore presented a picture of the state of play at that particular time. The theme of ePortfolios in education is, however, highly dynamic: The Australian ePortfolio Project had in itself increased the awareness of ePortfolios in general and had also encouraged some academic staff to consider

the possibility of introducing new projects at their own institutions. The AeP PS Survey in 2010 served to update the picture, as well as to extend the reach of the research into the VET sector.

For the purposes of presenting the findings from the audit, this chapter will detail the data collected in the Learning and Teaching survey, which focuses on the experiences and, in some cases, the plans of academic staff and educational developers working with students in the area of ePortfolio practice. The subjects of the Management survey were those involved in university governance, policy and administration. The Human Resources survey focused on the use of ePortfolios by academic and professional staff at an institution.

The research findings outline the different understandings of the concept of "ePortfolio," the extent of ePortfolio practice in Australian universities at the time of the study, the types of ePortfolio technology used in different settings, and the diverse ways ePortfolios were being used in the academic programs. Beyond these specific practice issues, the project sought to determine which staff or areas of the university held responsibility for project implementation and for the policy and strategy for ePortfolio activity. The study also considered the impact of ePortfolio use on students and staff and the extent to which there had been any formal evaluation of the different projects.

UNDERSTANDINGS OF "EPORTFOLIO"

The opening question in the national audit asked respondents to briefly describe, in their own words, their understanding of the term "ePortfolio." The most frequently reported understandings of ePortfolios in the responses to the Learning and Teaching survey in 2007 considered ePortfolios either collections or tools for learning and reflection or as providing evidence of learning and development for a purpose. In 2010, respondents added a strong sense of holistic student development, noting the spectrum of "intra- and extra-curricular learning" documented to demonstrate development. Reflection was noted as an important dimension to support the individual's "learning journey." The ePortfolio was recognized as a digital tool that accommodated diverse file formats (text, image, video and audio), with the flexibility to tailor the content for different purposes and different audiences.

Respondents from the VET sector (2010 AeP PS) also stressed the idea of ePortfolio as an electronic collection of evidence to support learning and development. In addition, there was a stronger understanding of the functional role of ePortfolios, as highlighted by the terms "CV" (curriculum vitae), "resumé," "RPL" (recognition of prior learning) and "employment" from this group of respondents.

The understandings of respondents to the Management survey in 2007 were exemplified by the concept of a collection used for assessment, for managing learning, and for demonstration of learning and personal achievement. These comments illustrate a more employability-related conception of ePortfolios: the definitions refer to the idea of the ePortfolio as a repository and the recording of activities that relate to the students' development of skills with a focus on work. In 2010, the institutional managers expressed the importance of access and sharing the ePortfolio across a range of purposes. Managers in the VET sector were cognizant of the pragmatic role that ePortfolios could play in the assessment of competencies and RPL.

Respondents to the 2007 Human Resources survey also spoke of ePortfolios as collections but with emphasis on personal development, career progression and career planning, or, in essence, the development of skills over a period of time. The respondents in 2010 commonly referred to ePortfolios as supporting the integration of learning, assessment, achievements and reflection, within a digital or online environment.

The respondents to the 2010 AeP PS survey seemed to have had a keener and, indeed, more consistent understanding of the concept of ePortfolios, compared to the earlier AeP survey. It was noted that some respondents drew on "formal" definitions which were promulgated within their institutional documents, indicating that ePortfolio practice was more mature than it was in 2007. It could be argued that respondents felt that they were in a more informed position than earlier, with a number making reference either directly or indirectly to the AeP report (Hallam et al., 2008).

In the 2007 survey, the highest response rates to the question of purpose of use were received for the use of ePortfolios by students to collect evidence of learning with a strong response for reflecting on learning. There was a strong correlation between the two dimensions: when ePortfolios were used for collecting evidence of learning, it was highly likely that there would also be the need to reflect on learning. However, the common pattern was that ePortfolios were used in multiple ways. In 2010, the two principal uses of ePortfolios were collecting examples of evidence of learning and summative assessment, with the reported use of ePortfolios to help students reflect on their learning falling in the later survey responses. It is interesting that there was an increase in the use of ePortfolios for summative assessment, while the use for formative assessment remained constant.

The use of ePortfolios for summative assessment was important for both VET (17%) and higher education (18%).

One quarter of respondents from the VET sector reported that the principal use of ePortfolios was to collect evidence of learning, e.g., for the purposes of recognition of prior learning, compared with 17% of respondents in higher education. Nevertheless, respondents underscored the diversity of practice, stressing that there was a wide range of use of ePortfolios across the institution.

It was clear that the academic or teaching staff continued to play a key role in reviewing or assessing the ePortfolios, but, significantly, there had been an increase in peer review amongst students. Where there was student or peer review, there was always further assessment by teachers. Where there was review by external specialists, the process was frequently accompanied by student peer review.

Findings from both the 2007 and 2010 surveys underscored the need for support from academic and teaching staff, with time allocated in the course for students to work on their ePortfolios.

The Type of ePortfolio Technology Used

There was one survey question addressing the technology used to support an ePortfolio. In 2007, there was considerable diversity of practice even within individual institutions. The Learning Management System (LMS) or Virtual Learning Environment (VLE) was the most common option, but there was an even distribution of alternative technologies, e.g., student webpages, paper-based systems, and blogs and wikis. Specific platforms mentioned were LMS/VLE systems, such as Blackboard, WebCT and Vista; open source platforms, such as Sakai (formerly OSP), CareerHub, Mahara and WordPress; and home-grown platforms. More generically, HTML programs such as Dreamweaver or MS FrontPage, or office tools, such as

PowerPoint and Word, were also utilized. There was emerging interest in the Web 2.0 tools, such as blogs and wikis, YouTube, Flickr and MySpace.

In 2010, there was a higher level of consistency in the use of ePortfolios. The current data show a significant increase in the use of specific ePortfolio software platforms as presented in Table 2.

A range of wiki and blog platforms were also being utilized, e.g., Wetpaint, Mediawiki, WordPress, along with the wiki tools as a component of an LMS. Web 2.0 tools such as Google Sites and Flickr were used to manage audio files and digital photos. One respondent reported using industry portals that were required for students to demonstrate the attainment of the relevant professional standards.

Responsibilities for ePortfolio Practice

A series of questions was presented to consider the areas of responsibility for ePortfolio practice in adult education, with three particular questions relating to ePortfolio implementation, policy and strategic direction.

ePortfolio Implementation

In 2007, the teaching unit or the faculty was most commonly responsible for the implementation of an ePortfolio. In the 2010 survey it was evident this trend for a distributed model of implementation had continued, but, in addition to the continuing role of the department or school, centralized services had become more active, with information technology services and teaching and learning support (including eLearning services) highlighted.

There was considerable joint activity in individual institutions. ITS, for example, would be working with teachers and educators as well as with teaching and learning support services in the implementation process. Where careers and employment services were involved, ITS, eLearn-

Table 2. ePortfolio software reported in use 2010

ePortfolio software	Number
PebblePad	15
Mahara	12
Chalk & Wire	3
Vumi	2
Adobe ePortfolios	2
Desire2Learn	1
Digication	1
Sakai	1
Skillsbook	1
Custom built	3

ing services and the teaching unit would also be partners in the activities. In the VET sector, the primary players were ITS and the teaching units, while in universities, the teaching units, faculty and ITS were the main proponents. Some of the comments stressed the energy and drive of individual teaching staff.

ePortfolio Policy

In 2007, there were few instances of formal ePortfolio policies in Australian universities. Policy work was likely to be driven by teaching and learning support services. In 2010, the leading role was played by teaching and learning support services, as had been anticipated, sometimes in conjunction with information technology services. The key player in academic institutions tended to be the Deputy Vice Chancellor or Pro Vice Chancellor responsible for teaching and learning. In the VET sector, the manager of the RTO was likely to manage the policy issues. A number of VET respondents reported that there were, as yet, no policies or that the policy arena was still embryonic.

ePortfolio Strategy

In both 2007 and 2010, teaching and learning support services were primarily responsible for driving the strategic direction of ePortfolio practice in the individual institutions. In 2010, a more centralized approach to strategic issues had emerged, with less responsibility lying with the faculty, although they were acknowledged to play a role in some institutions. While enterprising teaching staff were identified as leading the way in some institutions, the engagement would not necessarily translate into any cohesive strategy for the whole organization. Careers and employment services had a lower profile than reported in the earlier survey. Some respondents from the VET sector commented on the absence of any specific ePortfolio strategic direction within their institutions.

The Drivers for and Barriers to ePortfolio Implementation

Respondents were asked about the drivers or factors that had contributed to the implementation of an ePortfolio project, rating each on a 4-point Likert scale of "very important," "important," "not very important" or "not applicable".

In 2007, the most important factors were reflective learning and discipline-specific/professional skills requirements. While these two factors remained significant in 2010, the role of the practicum or work placement now ranked more highly. As in the earlier findings, improved transparency of learning outcomes and improved assessment were considered "important" rather than "very important," while comparatively little weight was given to entry into courses/programs as a driver. In their comments, respondents noted that employability, external professional accreditation and graduate attributes policy also played a role.

There was a marked difference between the use of ePortfolios in "professional education" and in "vocational training." Higher education respondents determined that the most important driver was reflective learning, closely followed by professional skills and the practicum. Respondents from the VET sector, however, gave greatest weight to RPL, integrative learning and the practicum, highlighting a more pragmatic approach to adult learning.

For teachers, the themes that emerged as barriers included time, lack of academic interest, resistance to eLearning initiatives, reluctance to engage in reflective practices and competing priorities. Interestingly, learners themselves were generally not perceived as presenting any barriers. Institutional factors such as staff time, funding, technology infrastructure and change management were more of a concern. Respondents from the VET sector identified highly pragmatic issues that impacted the students' ability to make progress with ePortfolios. In the higher education area, respondents suggested that the absence of strategic direction, resulting in a lack of cohesion in eLearning, and competing demands for technological solutions across the institution contributed to the difficulties.

The most widely perceived factors for success were effective planning and project management, particularly in terms of coordination across the different stakeholder groups. Cross-institutional collaboration, influential champions and enthusiastic, passionate and excited staff - also described as "dedicated, hardworking and stubborn" – were also important, along with some external drivers such as national professional standards, the Tertiary Education Quality and Standards Agency (TEQSA), Australian University Quality Agency (AUQA), Australian Curriculum, Assessment and Reporting Authority (ACARA), industry skills councils and formal professional accreditation bodies.

The Evaluation of ePortfolio Use

Overall, there was limited evidence of formal evaluation of ePortfolio practice. It was very clear in 2007 that there were few or no evaluation activities. By 2010, there was evidence that some evaluation work had been undertaken, through a range of approaches including classroom evaluations, student surveys, final years audits, assessment review, academics' reflections and reports on ePortfolio pilot activities.

At a more formal level, three respondents reported that they had published articles and research reports, and one respondent indicated that he or she was currently completing a Ph.D in the area. Some of the progress in these areas between 2007 and 2010 may have been a result of the AeP Project and associated symposia encouraging staff to adopt an evidence-based approach to their teaching.

ePortfolios in Vocational Education and Training in Australia

The Australian federal government has recognized the potential value of ePortfolios in supporting the Employability Skills Framework by providing funding for an ePortfolio initiative (DETA, 2007). In 2004, DEST contracted education. au, the Australian ICT agency for education, to develop and trial a national ePortfolio tool that could be used for the recognition and recording of employability skills (Curyer, Leeson, Mason, & Williams, 2007). In 2005, a beta-release called My e-Portfolio was developed for MyFuture, the federal government's career information service. Trials were conducted using a small sample of secondary schools, institutes of Technical and Further Education (TAFE) and tertiary institutions. While this ePortfolio project remains a work in progress and is not publicly available, it provides an opportunity for further national development (Curyer et al., 2007).

The Australian Flexible Learning Framework released a report in April 2007 that documented the current issues and developments associated with ePortfolios, particularly in the Australian vocational education and training (VET) sector (Curyer et al., 2007). The report presented five specific use cases for ePortfolios within VET:

- Transition into the VET sector
- Learning within the VET sector
- Transition from the VET sector to further education or work
- Managing a VET workforce
- Transition into self-employment.

The report considered the specific issues of functionality and ePortfolio services, along with the business rules, policy areas and technical standards that would be required for the effective implementation of ePortfolios (Leeson, 2008).

In the background paper on ePortfolios in the VET sector, education.au (2008a) has listed a range of issues that need to be considered by the various stakeholders. Of relevance to the policy context of the higher education sector and, indeed, across the education and employment sectors, are:

- **Policy issues:** These include those related to general development and management of ePortfolio services, portability of information about qualifications and competencies, recognition of prior learning and the management and provision of secure

and verifiable personal information and privacy.

- **Standards and specification to enable interoperability and portability.** Portability is the ability to transfer an ePortfolio from one place to another without having to recreate the e-portfolio in another system. Portability can be achieved if there is interoperability (that is, the ability of one system to talk to another). Portability and interoperability increase the longevity of ePortfolios. At a system level, a framework of common standards and specifications will be required to facilitate portability from institution to institution or across states.

- **Service-oriented approach to e-portfolios (JISC e-portfolio Reference Model):** This approach allows the aggregation of services from a number of providers. Key issues for discussion include how this service can be provided and managed, what collaborative structures are required and where it is best placed.

- **Future proofing ePortfolios:** Implementers will need to consider how ePortfolio services might need to interact with other applications and services. Some might be other e-portfolio services while others could relate to services supporting ePortfolio activities. In short, ePortfolio standards will need to be addressed within an organization's infrastructure to include authentication and authorization services, digital rights management, persistent identifiers and so forth.

The research work into ePortfolio practice in the VET sector undertaken by education.au culminated in a national symposium held in June 2008.

Stakeholders in the ePortfolio arena, including policy and decision makers, were invited to the national symposium to discuss key strategic issues and directions. Draft recommendations drawn from the symposium discussions were released, presenting a series of ideas that cluster around five key themes:

- Ownership and purpose
- Interoperability
- Shared understandings
- Training and user/teacher support
- Resourcing

(education.au, 2008b)

More recently, the Australian Flexible Learning Network has published a national strategic plan for VET sector, the VET E-portfolio Roadmap (Australian Flexible Learning Framework, 2009a). The Roadmap aims to assist in the development of a standards-based approach to ePortfolios and is supported by guidance documentation that considers the issues of ownership, privacy, verification, access control and security for ePortfolios (Australian Flexible Learning Framework, 2009b). The business activity is supported by the E-portfolios Reference Group (ERG), which acts as the cross-sector stakeholder group by providing advice and support to the E-portfolios Business Manager (Australian Flexible Learning Framework, 2010b).

There has also been an environmental scan of the use of ePortfolios in the context of RPL (Australian Flexible Learning Framework, 2009c). It is argued that ePortfolios can productively support the various components of RPL practice and therefore benefit RPL candidates, in particular those individuals who are geographically isolated or who live in different time zones from their assessors, by:

- Utilizing templates to structure the presentation of RPL evidence and tags to organize and find artifacts, which helps streamline the assessment process
- Reducing the need for paper-based, hard copy evidence and limiting excessive evidence collection

- Developing and strengthening information and communication technology (ICT) or digital literacy skills.

(Australian Flexible Learning Framework, 2009c, p. 1)

The framework also links aspects of e-assessment to ePortfolios through research into the use of digital technologies in assessment (Australian Flexible Learning Framework, 2010c). While there was an increase in the use of ePortfolios as an assessment tool, there were some ongoing concerns about the authenticity of the evidence presented by learners and about the validity of the assessment tasks undertaken.

A number of funded initiatives have encouraged further engagement with ePortfolio practice, including a series of ePortfolio implementation trials (Australian Flexible Learning Framework, 2010d, 2010e). The trials have the specific goals of:

- Increasing the efficiency of the learning process – through the better flow, use, re-use and exchange of information to improve communication and collaboration
- Enhancing the learning experience – through either individual learning plans, personal/career/workforce development planning, or continuous professional development.

The VET National Data Strategy also proposes the introduction of a "unique student identifier" for VET (VET National Data Strategy Action Group, 2010). A unique student number could be allocated to all learners to "track students as they progress through education and training (and to) further support a seamless schooling, VET and higher education experience for students" (p. 1), thereby enabling more widespread ePortfolio use.

Many of the issues considered in the VET sector are naturally pertinent to ePortfolio practice within the higher education sector and across the different education and employment sectors in

Australia. The VET e-Portfolios Showcase and the ePortfolios Australia Conference 2010 (EAC 2010) (Australian Flexible Learning Framework, 2010a) have played an important role in linking the strategic directions with practice in education. Cross sectoral engagement and collaboration, involving the schools sector, the VET sector, the higher education sector and employers and the professions, as well as with the policy makers, can help ensure there are indeed common aims and shared understandings, with appropriate policies and strategies, to effectively contribute to the achievement of the federal government's education and productivity goals.

Examples of ePortfolio Practice in Australia

Both the 2007 and 2010 ePortfolio surveys asked about the scope of ePortfolio use. For example, use could be unit- or subject-based as opposed to institution-wide, and undergraduates, postgraduates, and/or research students might use ePortfolios. The following two examples illustrate the current picture of ePortfolio use in Australia. These implementations represent the diversity of ePortfolio activity currently seen in Australia. The 2010 AeP PS survey revealed there had been an increase in the use of ePortfolios in the university-wide context and a sustained level of practice at the course-wide level, compared to the earlier evidence of greater use at the subject- or unit-specific level. It was evident at the ePortfolios Australia Conference in 2010 that conversations around the implementation of ePortfolios across the Australian education sectors had matured considerably since 2007. The examples presented in the following section are the Queensland University of Technology Student ePortfolio Program and the Curtin University iPortfolio.

The QUT Student ePortfolio was Australia's first institution-wide, purpose built ePortfolio application. It was developed in 2000-2001 and released across the institution in 2003. The QUT ePortfolio program exemplifies the maturation process of ePortfolio application in a university-wide setting. The Curtin University implementation represents current widespread activity across Australian universities that are exploring the different possibilities for ePortfolio applications both in terms of available software and across different discipline areas to support a diverse range of learning and teaching goals in order to achieve enhanced learning and teaching outcomes.

QUT Student ePortfolio

The Queensland University of Technology (QUT) Student ePortfolio Program is premised on the belief that critical reflection is central to ePortfolio learning and to enhancing the learning outcomes for all students, regardless of background, as it draws on the individual learning experience. The program guides students to reflect meaningfully on the diverse range of learning experiences, both at university and in the broader environment. Through critical reflective practice, students develop the ability to recognize and understand their knowledge and skills development and to plan for future learning experiences as a lifelong and life-wide pursuit. They make connections between their university learning, their broader life experiences, and their professional and career goals and aspirations. The program is integral to the QUT learning experience. Feedback from current students, alumni, academics and employers suggests that taking an ePortfolio approach to learning has a positive and sustained impact on the formal learning, lifelong learning and future professional development of QUT graduates.

Planning for the QUT Student ePortfolio Program commenced in 2001 when the Deputy Vice Chancellor (Teaching, Information and Learning Support), Professor Tom Cochrane, returned from a symposium at Harvard University with a desire to provide students with greater evidence of their achievements than could be presented in an academic transcript. The "project" approach of the early days viewed the ePortfolio as a product or electronic tool. However, with a strong collaborative approach and scholarly framework underpinning the development of the ePortfolio, the emphasis quickly expanded to include the ePortfolio as being a pedagogy and process for learning and teaching. Accompanying this change was a shift of focus in ePortfolio from a "tool" to a "program" that encompasses a holistic framework to support academic staff and students. The QUT Student ePortfolio Program encompasses: 1) the ePortfolio tool; 2) policy directions; 3) a flexible mixed-mode model of engagement; 4) support from the team that consists of technical and learning staff; 5) online and print resources; and 6) workshops and training.

The initiative resulted from the collaborative work of the Division of Technology, Information and Learning Support and the Careers and Employment Office. Central to the design of the student ePortfolio was the development of the Employability Skill Set, derived from both QUT and industry-identified graduate attributes, and developed in consultation with every QUT faculty. The schema includes life-wide perspectives on academic, work, community and personal achievements. Through ongoing development, the graduate attributes have been mapped to a range of schema for professional standards, e.g., education, nursing, business, law and engineering.

The Student ePortfolio Program has been very successful. It expanded from an initial pilot in September 2003 with a small group of library science students to a full release to all QUT students in June 2004. Between 2004 and 2009, the number of students initiating an ePortfolio in a unit of study has increased steadily from 495 in 2004 to over 5,000 in 2009, with more than 40,000 ePortfolios still active. Through the management, reflection and articulation of artefacts and experiences, students take responsibility for their own learning and are able to make connections between learning at the university and their future careers.

Over the past seven years, there has been progressive take-up of ePortfolio practice across the different faculties and schools at QUT. In 2011, more than 40,000 QUT students had developed their own ePortfolios. The Student ePortfolio is used across all faculties at QUT to support academics' learning and teaching goals and to enhance the student experience. The Faculty of Education has embedded the ePortfolio Program across the Bachelor of Education degree. Students are actively involved in a range of reflective practice assessments designed to enhance the practica across the degree. In undergraduate coursework units, there is a range of activities carried out in nursing and midwifery – to support clinical placements and competency attainment; human movement studies, creative industries, psychology, business, law, accounting, management, – to support career planning and professional identity; and in built environment and engineering – supporting work-integrated learning activities.

At the postgraduate course work level, there is a whole-of-course approach to the student ePortfolio in nursing and midwifery, paramedics, social work and library and information science, where students engage in ePortfolio learning to evidence professional standards and competencies, develop professional identity, and manage clinical placements. The School of Business encourages students to use the ePortfolio on a voluntary basis to develop their career perspective by making links between university study and the workplace. The School offers formal support and leadership recognition to students undertaking this Business Advantage option. During 2009, the QUT Student ePortfolio was redeveloped to support Professional Staff and is currently used to underpin career progression and professional development at QUT.

Both academics and students have access to a range of support resources and strategies, including video and animated resources, print and online resources, lecture style and hands-on sessions and contextualized resources developed in collaboration with the QUT Strategic Initiatives Team. Resource development is ongoing and based on user feedback.

Curtin University iPortfolio

During 2007-2009, Curtin undertook a university-wide curriculum review (Curriculum 2010 known as C2010) that concluded that graduate employability should be a key driver of learning and teaching at Curtin (Oliver, 2008). Central to assuring graduate employability is the mapping, assessing and evaluating of graduate capabilities (or attributes) (Oliver, 2010). These processes were developed extensively at Curtin during the C2010 initiative. However, finding ways to evaluate student achievement of the capabilities was a challenge, and the idea of an ePortfolio system that could offer this facility was very attractive. In September 2008, an Academic Board forum was held to gather information from students and staff at Curtin to inform the implementation of such an ePortfolio system. Over 100 participants were asked to give feedback on a range of questions such as: *Why might we want an ePortfolio? What is its purpose? Should it be used for formal credit and accrediting supplementary achievements? Who should be able to view it?* (Oliver, Jones, & Ferns, 2010).

As a result of this consultation process, research was undertaken to capture evidence of student use of mobile devices and social networking applications, and this evidence informed the design and delivery of a new ePortfolio system (Oliver & Nikoletatos, 2009). Central to its focus was Curtin's graduate attributes and the triple-i curriculum (Oliver et al., 2010) which communicates Curtin's goal to produce graduates who are industry-ready, intercultural and interdisciplinary. For this reason, the new system is called iPortfolio.

The iPortfolio was developed during 2009 by Curtin's Office of Assessment Teaching and Learning (OATL) and Curtin IT Services (CITS)

with guidance from the iPortfolio Working Party. The iPortfolio was piloted with both students and staff from August to December 2009. Feedback during this phase was largely positive and has informed continuing development of the system. It was fully implemented in 2010, meaning that any staff or student could access the system by creating an account. By the end of 2010, some 16,000 accounts had been created (from a potential user base of about 40,000 students and 3,500 staff). There are two features in the iPortfolio which are particularly innovative. First, users can rate their own and peers' achievement of Curtin's graduate attributes and the triple-i curriculum using an online five star rating system underpinned by the Dreyfus and Dreyfus novice to expert categories (Dreyfus, 2004). These data can be captured system-wide to feed into course and program review processes. Secondly, all evidence and reflection in the iPortfolio can be tagged using the graduate attribute and triple-i curriculum tags. A free iPhone app (iPortfolio Mobile) enables users to capture evidence of learning "as it happens" (for example, beyond the classroom and in work placements) and upload the tagged evidence (text, audio, video) directly to their iPortfolio.

Future enhancements include the potential incorporation of mechanisms such as holistic rubrics to enable the capture of standards of achievement of the graduate attributes as well as learner access to self-managing learning tools. For example, in the future, it is possible that through the iPortfolio, students will be able to access a map of their degree program curriculum, as well as employer and graduate feedback on the importance of the capabilities and attributes that count most for early professional success.

Framework of Information Standards for ePortfolio Practice

Regardless of geographical location, learner mobility within and between education, training and employment sectors, set alongside the concepts of lifelong learning and the global education market, are significant drivers for the requirement to move beyond static repositories to ensure ePortfolio data is secure, accessible and able to be exported and imported across different systems and services. ePortfolio specifications are the focus of work being undertaken by IMS Global Learning Consortium and the JISC Centre for Educational Technology Interoperability Standards (CETIS) in the United Kingdom. Meanwhile, the emerging Web 2.0 technologies and services bring new perspectives to the standards-driven approach to portability and interoperability. Researchers are arguing that social networking initiatives like MySpace and Facebook encompass, and may even threaten to subsume, aspects of the ePortfolio concept.

Croger Associates (2007), in the report published by the Australian Information and Communications Technology in Education Committee, highlighted the importance of collaboration in the education and training sectors, nationally and internationally. A meeting at the Australian ePortfolio Symposium in February 2008 brought together a group of nationally and internationally recognized experts, broadly representing the various areas of education government. Australia, through DEEWR, is already a party in the international eFramework for Education and Research project, working with JISC in the UK, the SURF Foundation in the Netherlands and the New Zealand Ministry of Education, which means that there is a strong foundation for technical interoperability within and across the education sectors.

The standards expert group operates as an example of a community of practice that has been collaboratively developing the vocabularies and ontologies that support a shared language to underpin the relationships and mapping of ePortfolio practice across the different sectors and contexts. By participating in the IMS ePortfolio standards initiative (IMS Global Learning Consortium, 2008), the working group progresses the dialogue about formal ePortfolio specifications, open standards and dynamic and evolving web

services. To avoid reinventing the wheel and to encourage innovation, the working group provides an opportunity for ICT managers and policy makers to review and evaluate implementation issues around IMS standards to facilitate the exchange of information and data across institutional, sectoral and jurisdictional boundaries.

CONCLUSION

In Australia, as in other regions of the world, an individual student's journey from school to work is no longer a linear path from school to training to university. There is increasing evidence of the multiple avenues of transition within and between vocational education and training and higher education. Work is concurrent with study, and the former divide between vocational and professional learning has become blurred. Student mobility sees them move not only between the sectors but also across institutions or even across faculties within the same institution. With a clearer focus on the potential of ePortfolios to record and assess employability skills in vocational arenas, it is essential that students are not only provided with the opportunity to continue their ePortfolio practice if they move from a TAFE into a university, or to ensure that ePortfolio work undertaken at university will be portable if they move into a vocational program, but that they can also migrate between institutions and between programs. As greater emphasis is placed on the value of congruency between the different government policy arenas, ePortfolios offer the potential to be a meaningful medium for convergence and integration of education and training. Importantly, a sound and coherent national infrastructure is required to achieve the desired goals. Indeed, the issues of education, training and lifelong learning cannot be isolated from the issue of equitable access to broadband services in Australia.

Many early adopters of ePortfolio practice in Australia have recognized the potential of the ePortfolio process, when it is embedded in learning and teaching activities, to help students move beyond the state of knowing *what* they have learned to consider *how* they have learned. By reflecting on their own learning and achievement, learners are encouraged to plan for their personal, academic and career development. Currently, ePortfolio practitioners in higher education are eager to break away from their sense of isolation and work collaboratively across disciplines and institutions to further their knowledge and understanding. Compared with more mature ePortfolio contexts, such as the UK, USA and the Netherlands, where there are close links between research and practice, Australia is in the early stages of the ePortfolio journey. There is scope to develop communities of practice in these countries that will provide valuable channels of communication between educators with shared interests and ideas and that will encourage scholarship and research. It is hoped that the higher education sector can work collaboratively to foster scholarship and research of the impact of ePortfolios on learning outcomes within and beyond university and college activities, especially to investigate how ePortfolios might be used to achieve transformation in key areas of educational and workforce policy.

If the education sectors are to effectively fulfill their roles in producing a skilled workforce which, through continuous learning, career progression and coherent employability strategies, will play a significant role in the future community and economic success of Australia, then the potential of ePortfolios to bring together educational technologies and quality learning processes and to provide evidence of individual achievement and employability skills should not be ignored. Policies and strategies at both the sectoral and institutional levels can help ensure that advantage is taken of the opportunities for connectivity and cohesion in the fragmented world of eLearning, flexible delivery, social networking and mobile technologies.

REFERENCES

AC Nielsen Research Services. (2000). *Employer satisfaction with graduate skills: Research report.* Retrieved November 23, 2010, from http://www.dest.gov.au/archive/highered/eippubs/eip99-7/eip99_7pdf.pdf

Allen Consulting Group. (2006). *Assessment and reporting of employability skills in training packages.* Retrieved November 23, 2010, from http://www.dest.gov.au/NR/rdonlyres/D77220DC-78AB-42C6-86A6-2FA61BE1A69D/12778/Assessment_and_Reporting_Employability_Skills_3103.pdf

Australian Bureau of Statistics (ABS). (2010). Higher education. In *Yearbook Australia 2010.* Retrieved November 23, 2010, from http://www.abs.gov.au/AUSSTATS/abs@.nsf/Lookup/6751D1E2E91DF21ECA25773700169C93?opendocument

Australian Flexible Learning Framework. (2009a). *The VET e-portfolios roadmap: A strategic roadmap for e-portfolios to support lifelong learning.* Retrieved November 23, 2010, from http://www.flexiblelearning.net.au/files/Managing_Learner-Information_FINAL.pdf http://www.flexiblelearning.net.au/files/VETePortfolioRoadmap_web.pdf

Australian Flexible Learning Framework. (2009b). *Managing learner information: Important considerations when implementing e-portfolios in VET.* Retrieved November 23, 2010, from http://www.flexiblelearning.net.au/files/Managing_Learner-Information_FINAL.pdf

Australian Flexible Learning Framework. (2009c). *E-portfolios for RPL assessment key findings on current engagement in the VET sector.* Retrieved November 23, 2010 from http://www.flexiblelearning.net.au/files/E-portfolios_for_RPL_Assessment_Final_190309.pdf

Australian Flexible Learning Framework. (2010a, November 3-4). *ePortfolios Australia Conference (EAC2010)*. Melbourne, Australia. Retrieved November 23, 2010, from http://www.flexiblelearning.net.au/content/e-portfolios-australia

Australian Flexible Learning Framework. (2010b). *E-portfolios reference group*. Retrieved November 23, 2010, from http://www.flexiblelearning.net.au/content/e-portfolios-reference-group-erg

Australian Flexible Learning Framework. (2010c). *E-assessment and the AQTF: Bridging the divide between practitioners and auditors*. Retrieved November 23, 2010, from http://www.flexiblelearning.net.au/files/Eassessment_AQTF_final.pdf

Australian Flexible Learning Framework. (2010d). *E-portfolio implementation trials*. Retrieved November 23, 2010, from http://www.flexiblelearning.net.au/content/e-portfolios-funding

Australian Flexible Learning Framework. (2010e). *2009 e-portfolio implementation trials*. Retrieved November 23, 2010, from http://www.flexible-learning.net.au/content/2009EIT

Australian Government. (2008). *Australia 2020 summit: Initial summit report*. Retrieved November 23, 2010, from http://www.australia2020.gov.au/docs/2020_Summit_initial_report.pdf

Australian Universities Quality Agency (AUQA). (2010). *Home page*. Retrieved November 23, 2010, from http://www.auqa.edu.au/

Business and Higher Education Round Table (BHERT). (2001). *The critical importance of lifelong learning (BHERT Position Paper No. 4)*. Sydney, Australia: Author.

Carrick Institute for Learning and Teaching in Higher Education. (2007). *Research brief: e-portfolios for university students*. Retrieved March 21, 2008, from http://www.carrickinstitute.edu.au/carrick/webdav/site/carricksite/users/siteadmin/public/grants_priority_eportfolios_research-brief_april2007.pdf

Croger Associates Pty Ltd. (2007). *Research report: Interoperability standards across the Australian education and training sector*. Retrieved November 23, 2010, from http://www.aictec.edu.au/aictec/webdav/site/standardssite/shared/Interoperability%20Standards%20Report.pdf

Curyer, S., Leeson, J., Mason, J., & Williams, A. (2007). *Developing eportfolios for VET: Policy issues and interoperability*. Retrieved November 23, 2010, from http://e-standards.flexiblelearning.net.au/docs/vet-eportfolio-report-v1-0.doc

Dearing, R. (1997). *National Committee of Inquiry into higher education*. Retrieved November 23, 2010, from http://www.leeds.ac.uk/educol/ncihe/

Department of Education. Training and the Arts (DETA). (2007). *ICT pedagogical license*. Retrieved November 23, 2010, from http://education.qld.gov.au/smartclassrooms/strategy/tsdev_pd-licence.html

Department of Education. Employment and Workplace Relations (DEEWR). (2008a). *Review of Australian higher education*. Retrieved November 23, 2010, from http://www.deewr.gov.au/highereducation/review/pages/reviewofaustralianhighereducationreport.aspx

Department of Education. Employment and Workplace Relations (DEEWR). (2009). *Transforming Australia's higher education system*. Retrieved November 23, 2010, from http://www.deewr.gov.au/HigherEducation/Pages/TransformingAustraliasHESystem.aspx

Department of Education. Employment and Workplace Relations (DEEWR). (2010a). *Overview*. Retrieved November 23, 2010, from http://www.deewr.gov.au/HigherEducation/Pages/Overview.aspx/

Department of Education. Employment and Workplace Relations (DEEWR). (2010b). *Productivity places program.* Retrieved November 23, 2010, from http://www.deewr.gov.au/Skills/Programs/SkillTraining/ProductivityPlaces/Pages/default.aspx

Department of Education Employment and Workplace Relations (DEEWR). (2008b). *Digital education revolution: Overview.* Retrieved November 23, 2010, from http://www.digitaleducationrevolution.gov.au/about.htm

Department of Education, Science and Training. (DEST). (2006). *Bologna process and Australia: Next steps.* Retrieved November 23, 2010, from http://www.dest.gov.au/sectors/higher_education/publications_resources/profiles/bologna_process_and_australia.htm

Dreyfus, S. E. (2004). The five-stage model of adult skill acquisition. *Bulletin of Science, Technology & Society, 24*(3), 177–181. doi:10.1177/0270467604264992

education.au. (2008a). *National symposium on e-portfolios: Background paper.* Retrieved November 23, 2010, from http://educationau.edu.au/jahia/webdav/site/myjahiasite/shared/papers/eportfolio_background_paper.pdf

education.au. (2008b). *E-portfolio symposium: Draft recommendations.* Retrieved July 20, 2008, from http://educationau.edu.au/jahia/Jahia/pid/637

Goody, A., & von Konsky, B. (2010). *Giving life to teaching portfolios.* Retrieved February 9, 2011, from http://www.flexiblelearning.net.au/files/EAC2010_Abstracts_eBook_20101109.pdf

Hallam, G., Harper, W., Hauville, K., McAllister, L., & Creagh, T. (2008). *ePortfolio use by university students in Australia: Informing excellence in policy and practice.* Retrieved November 23, 2010, from http://www.eportfoliopractice.qut.edu.au/docs/Aep_Final_Report/AeP_Report_ebook.pdf

Hallam, G., Harper, W., McAllister, L., Hauville, K., & Creagh, T. (2010). *ePortfolio use by university students: Informing excellence in policy and practice. Supplementary report.* Retrieved November 23, 2010, from http://www.eportfoliopractice.qut.edu.au/survey/index.jsp

IMS Global Learning Consortium Inc. (2008). *IMS global consortium.* Retrieved February 22, 2008, from http://www.imsglobal.org/ep/index.html

Leeson, J. (2008). *ePortfolios: Policy issues and interoperability.* Retrieved November 23, 2010, from http://www.avetra.org.au/AVETRA%20WORK%2011.04.08/CS3.2%20-%20Jerry%20Leeson.pdf

National Broadband Network (NBN). (2010). *Home page.* Retrieved November 23, 2010 from http://www.nbn.gov.au/

Oliver, B. (2008, July). *Graduate employability as a standard of success in teaching and learning.* Paper presented at the Australian Universities Quality Forum, Canberra, Australia.

Oliver, B. (2010). *Teaching fellowship: Benchmarking partnerships for graduate employability.* Sydney, Australia: Australian Learning and Teaching Council.

Oliver, B., Jones, S., & Ferns, S. (2010). *Curriculum 2010 final report.* Perth, Australia: Curtin University.

Oliver, B., & Nikoletatos, P. (2009). *Building engaging physical and virtual learning spaces: A case study of a collaborative approach.* Paper presented at the Same Places, Different Spaces Ascilite Conference, Auckland, New Zealand. Retrieved from http://www.ascilite.org.au/conferences/auckland09/procs/oliver.pdf

Precision Consultancy. (2007). *Graduate employ-ability skills: Prepared for the business, industry and higher education collaboration council.* Retrieved November 23, 2010, from http://www. dest.gov.au/NR/rdonlyres/E58EFDBE-BA83-430E-A541-2E91BCB59DF1/20214/Graduate-EmployabilitySkillsFINALREPORT1.pdf

Quality Assurance Agency in Higher Education (QAA). (2001). *Guidelines for HE progress files.* Retrieved November 23, 2010, from http://www. qaa.ac.uk/academicinfrastructure/progressFiles/guidelines/progfile2001.asp

SACE Board of South Australia. (2010). *Personal learning plan.* Retrieved November 23, 2010, from http://www.saceboard.sa.edu.au/newsace/plp.php

Skills Australia. (2010a). *Australian workforce futures: A national workforce development strategy.* Retrieved November 23, 2010, from http://www.skillsaustralia.gov.au/publications. shtml#workforce-futures

Skills Australia. (2010b). *Creating a future direction for Australian vocational education and training.* Retrieved November 23, 2010, from http://www.skillsaustralia.gov.au/publications. shtml#yoursay

VET National Data Strategy Action Group. (2010). *A unique student identifier for Australia's vocational education and training system: A consultation paper about introduction a USI in VET.* Retrieved November 23, 2010, from http://www. training.com.au/Documents/Unique+Student+Identifier+consultation+paper-+July+2010.pdf

von Konsky, B., & Comfort, J. (2010). *The iPortfolio: A tool for work integrated learning for health promotion students* Retrieved February 9, 2011, from http://www.flexiblelearning.net.au/files/EAC2010_Abstracts_eBook_20101109.pdf

Ward, R. (2008). *E-Portfolio practice in higher education: (something of) the UK experience.* Paper presented at the Australian ePortfolio Symposium, Brisbane, Australia. Retrieved November 23, 2010, from http://www.eportfoliopractice. qut.edu.au/docs/AeP_presentations_web/AeP_Ward_7Feb08.pdf

Chapter 12
ePortfolios for Higher Education:
A Hong Kong Perspective

Dean Fisher
City University of Hong Kong

Yingjun Chen
City University of Hong Kong

Hok Ling Cheung
City University of Hong Kong

Yin Fan Chan
City University of Hong Kong

Valerie Pickard
City University of Hong Kong

Man Chun Wong
City University of Hong Kong

ABSTRACT

This chapter describes the current situation regarding eportfolios in the government-funded universities of Hong Kong with particular focus on the authors' local institution, City University of Hong Kong. Despite some attempts at collaboration, there is as yet no unified approach across the universities regarding the use of eportfolios for learning, self-development or career preparation. Major challenges to achieving an eportfolio culture identified in the chapter are multiple perceptions of what eportfolios are; difficulties with teacher and student motivation; a lack of planned pedagogical support; varied and rapidly changing eportfolio enabling technologies; and the lack of consistent funding. Solutions explored include institutional commitment, multi-level collaboration, continuous research, training and support, and comprehensive promotion. Finally, the authors outline possible future directions for the eportfolio movement in Hong Kong.

INTRODUCTION

Portfolios for learning, self-development, and career preparation facilitated and enhanced by computing and Internet technologies have taken hold particularly in the West; the use of ePortfolios is now gaining momentum in some Asia Pacific regions. This article discusses the issues of and solutions to ePortfolio adoption in the Hong Kong higher education context. It provides an example of a bottom-up approach, working towards an institution-wide adoption of ePortfolios at City

DOI: 10.4018/978-1-4666-0143-7.ch012

University of Hong Kong (CityU), one of the eight government-funded universities. Reference will also be made to practices in other Hong Kong universities.

BACKGROUND

Three initiatives in 2005 influenced the current status of ePortfolios in Hong Kong. First, at CityU, the Office of Education Development and General Education (EDGE, formerly known as the Education Development Office, EDO) and the English Language Centre (ELC) collaborated to research, develop, and integrate ePortfolios into language courses.

Secondly, the broader Hong Kong educational context changed in significant ways. The University Grants Committee (UGC) issued a directive to all local universities in Hong Kong to adopt outcomes-based approaches to teaching and learning. In addition, the then Education and Manpower Bureau published a report to drive the implementation of a new academic structure, seen as an opportunity for both universities and secondary schools to review their curricula. The new 3-3-4 system reduces senior secondary education by a year and expands university education from three to four years, thus aligning its system with those of mainland China and the US.

The new structure was expected to open the way for secondary schools to broaden and diversify their curricula, to encourage students to keep records of their learning achievements in Student Learning Profiles, and to encourage participation in other learning experiences as a way of developing the whole person.

At the tertiary level, the curriculum was expanded from three to four years, and a new suite of general education courses were designed and piloted to enhance and broaden students' learning experiences and perspectives. The ensuing discussion among and within the universities has been keen as reflected in both public symposiums and internal activities about questions such as:

- How should we define graduate outcomes/ attributes?
- In what ways should the curriculum change to enable students to accomplish these outcomes?
- What evidence is needed to assess the accomplishments?
- What support and resources are required to assist students with the transition from, first, secondary school to university and, later, from university to the workplace?
- How can educational technology help with these emerging needs?

Thirdly, a joint-universities project on Student English Language ePortfolios acquired funding to develop a web-based learning and/or exit ePortfolio project. Thus, all eight English language centers from the government-funded universities started to investigate the technology and pedagogy of ePortfolios. Although regular meetings and sharing sessions were conducted, universities selected different applications or even custom made their own ePortfolio platforms. In addition, varied approaches and contrasting ideas about the content and structure of the language ePortfolios emerged. When all of the universities finally reached consensus, however, a common language ePortfolio template was designed. Nevertheless, the funding was withdrawn. Since then, in an ad hoc approach to ePortfolio research and development, universities continue to investigate and use ePortfolios with alternative sources of funding.

Meanwhile, other academic and administrative units in the respective universities, some unrelated to the English language project, were beginning to understand the relevance and benefits of ePortfolios for learning, development, and employment. A small number of investigative projects started emerging from bottom-up/grassroots enthusiasts.

The current project is an extension of two former projects: the "English Language Portfolio" that started in 2005 and the subsequent "Electronic Learning Portfolio" that began in 2007. These two projects not only helped reveal the vast potential of ePortfolios for teaching and learning enhancement but also identified the necessary support services and critical pedagogical considerations for encouraging user adoption. At City University, "ePortfolios for All: A Roadmap for Success (2009-2011)" is the third phase of a Teaching Development Grant-funded project co-organized mainly by EDGE and the ELC with co-investigators and participating teachers from diverse disciplines: Biology and Chemistry, Electronic Engineering, Information Systems, Building Science and Technology, Public and Social Administration, English, and Applied Social Studies. The Mainland and External Affairs Office and the Alumni Office also joined the collaboration and promoted the use of ePortfolios to non-local students. The aims of the current project are to further explore the value, uses, and impact of ePortfolios for learning, development, and eventual employability and to lay the foundations for an institution-wide ePortfolio culture. The project uses a three-pronged approach:

1. The creation of a "Roadmap for University Success" in the form of a graduate ePortfolio template and an ePortfolio repository (http://www.cityu.edu.hk/edge/eportfolio/template/roadmap/)
2. The design and provision of ePortfolio workshops, seminars, and competitions
3. The provision of support services and resources for both students and teachers to develop and use ePortfolios

Using an action research approach, the project collects data and feedback from different stakeholders at various stages to learn about the impact of ePortfolios and to improve the above strategies and services.

ISSUES AND CHALLENGES

Perception

As other writers have noted (e.g., Gibson, 2006; Barrett & Knezek, 2003; Grant, 2005; Greller, 2007), a major challenge to achieving an ePortfolio culture is the confusion caused by widely differing definitions and perceptions of the nature and functions of ePortfolios. ePortfolios are not only different things to different people, but they can also be different things to the same person as perspectives and purposes change. It thus becomes more difficult to make progress towards a common goal if all the players have a different goal in mind. Adding to this confusion, *Asia's World City* (as Hong Kong markets itself), in its attempts to build up tertiary institutions as centers of international excellence, simultaneously looks for best practice examples *towards* and attracts teaching and administrative staff *from* Europe, the UK, the USA, Canada, and Australia.

From our perspective in Hong Kong, each of these countries seems to be responding to its own driving forces (e.g., the promotion of citizen mobility in Europe or the need for transparency through standards in the USA), so they place differing emphases on what Attwell et al. (2007) identify as the three broad approaches to ePortfolios: "the use of e-portfolios as an assessment tool, the use of e-portfolios as a tool for professional or career development planning (CDP), and a wider understanding of e-portfolios as a tool for active learning" (p. 29). An inter-institutional discussion of ePortfolios organized by CityU in September 2010 revealed that all three approaches are currently being adopted in Hong Kong.

In our experience at CityU, when the type, purpose, and audience of the portfolio have not been clearly defined by the instructor, classroom participants are frustrated. For example, in both formal and anecdotal feedback, students, unaware that they would need to create separate portfolios for job applications, have expressed doubts that employers would look at their learning portfolios. Additional confusion arises in reconciling a) ePortfolios for learning and ePortfolios for assessment, b) ePortfolios as a product versus ePortfolios as a process, c) the need for just one or multiple ePortfolios, and d) university ownership of ePortfolios versus student ownership.

Multiple and misunderstood definitions of ePortfolios have caused frustration at City University. Barrett and Carney (2005) have described the problems arising from conflicting paradigms and purposes of ePortfolios when they are used as both assessment and learning tools. This tension is expressed by a frustrated ELC teacher at City University who, after a rather heated debate, wrote:

I found it difficult to make sense of the discussion when we were talking about the ePortfolio from too many different perspectives. I was under the impression when we started that we were talking about the ePortfolio as a pedagogical tool. But then I soon realized that we were not. Many colleagues were talking (about) the Written Language ePortfolio, the Spoken Language ePortfolio, or the FE1 ePortfolio. So we were actually talking about the different ePortfolio requirements of different courses, and how the requirements were not reasonable.

Changing conditions, including moves from single unit to whole institution adoption, inclusion of social networking, and emerging pedagogies influence ease of adoption. Identifying different take-up models for institutionalization, Lambert and Corrin (2007) distinguish between 'academic integration via the curriculum' and integration 'prompted' by central departments such as the Careers Services or Learning Development Centres. At least three Hong Kong universities are moving toward university-wide approaches with two Hong Kong universities promoting ePortfolios as a tool for whole-person development and a means to showcase transferable skills for future employers. Considering the problems of differing perception, this move from a more course/department-based or organic approach to planned institutional adoption (Wong, Wong, & Cheung, 2006) is fraught with potential pitfalls. Also, shifts in social networking and changes in pedagogy include expectation that the ePortfolio will allow for collaboration and comment.

The aim of our project is to develop an ePortfolio culture which will encompass both the academic/course-based, self-learning approach and the support/personal development/professional approach. All stakeholders need to see that ePortfolios can be used for different purposes and that individuals are likely to develop either more than one portfolio or one portfolio with multiple views. These portfolios will be influenced by changing demands from institutions and employers and by changing technology, such as mobile networking. We discuss later in this chapter ways in which we can collaborate to clarify definitions and perceptions to work toward a Hong Kong-wide ePortfolio culture.

Motivation

In their recent presentation to the Hong Kong Association of Self Access Learning and Development (HASALD) entitled *Learner Autonomy and the Role of Technology* Miller and Hafner (2010) described how their students responded with gusto to their academic literacy project in which they researched a topic and presented their findings in a BBC style YouTube documentary. Because this enthusiasm presents a very different picture from a lackluster reception of ePortfolios, we need to generate motivation for comparable student energy around ePortfolios.

The project team has learned that teacher attitude is central to students' impressions about ePortfolios. The critical point of leverage, therefore, is convincing the teachers of the value of ePortfolios rather than the students. The cause/effect systems diagram below describes a reinforcing cycle: positive beliefs affect motivation positively and so more highly-motivated students achieve better academic results, which is likely to reinforce a teacher's belief in the usefulness of ePortfolios for learning. Similarly, negative beliefs create a negative reinforcing cycle. A positive or negative cycle can be tipped towards the opposite direction by the variables listed on the right-hand side of the diagram. The less user-friendly the technology, for example, the less favorable teachers and students are likely to feel towards the ePortfolio, and vice versa (Figure 1).

Encountering significant student resistance to ePortfolios in the first phase of the project (Cheung et al., 2009), we have adopted strategies in response to this challenge. Unfortunately, though, none of the attendees at our inter-institutional ePortfolio meeting were able to report a keen uptake of ePortfolios in their institutions. Similarly, Henrich et al. (2007) report that most colleagues in the Institute of Sciences and Technology at Massey University, New Zealand:

are not aware of the benefits of portfolios for lifelong learning for our students and hardly any employer would explicitly ask for a portfolio. What is missing is the reinforcement of the message from academics, professional bodies and industry in general to create an environment for changing the mindset of the students (p. 661).

Indeed, within our project, we have begun to focus more on transferable skills and graduate or employment portfolios in order to appeal to our students' strong sense of extrinsic motivation.

Pedagogy

Adoption of ePortfolios for learning must be accompanied by ePortfolio integration at different levels of the curriculum. In Hong Kong the secondary education system is currently undergoing a major restructure with the new curriculum giving schools and teachers a greater say in their pedago-

Figure 1. Teacher/student motivation cycle

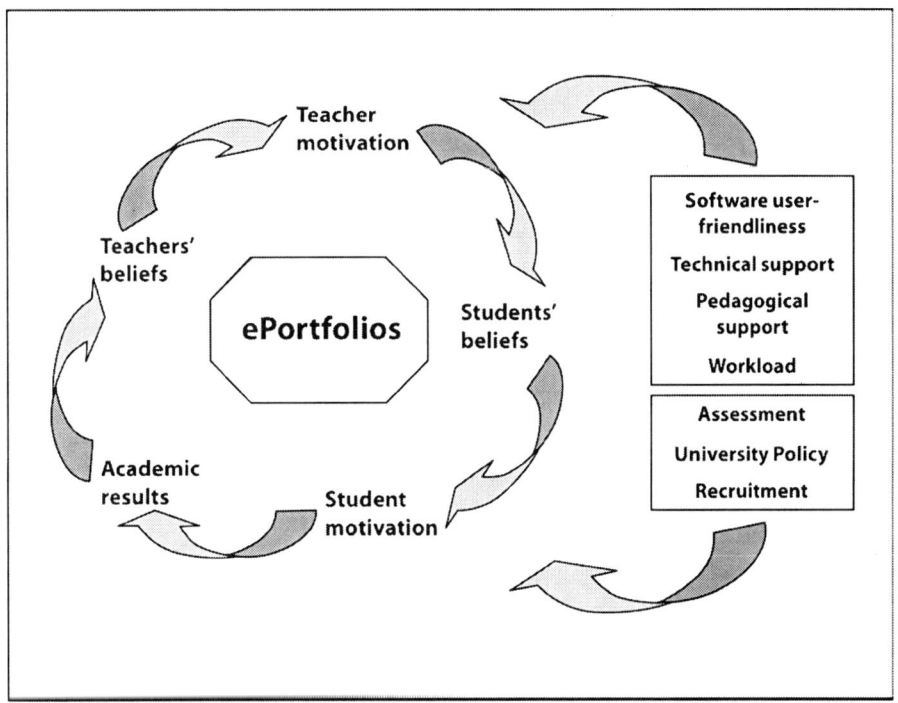

Figure 2. Critical issues to consider when planning ePortfolio integration in courses

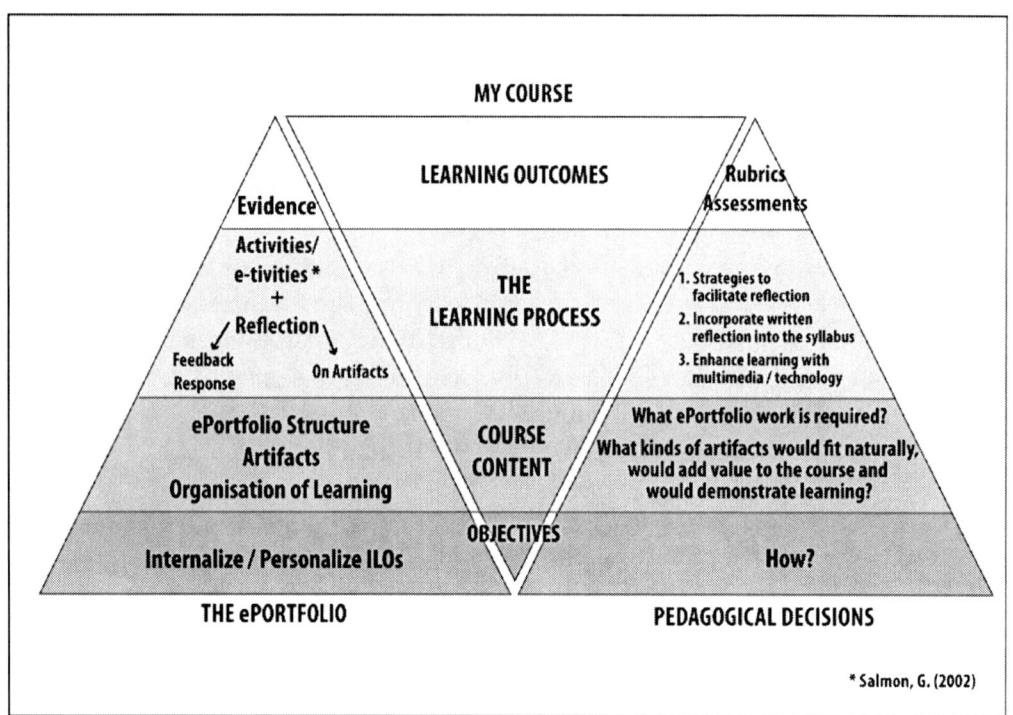

gies and with greater emphasis on student self-management, independent thought, and reflection. EPortfolios may become part of this learning process, but pedagogies must be in place first. This fundamental shift to new modes of learning with different objectives will take some time at both secondary and university levels. Chen et al. (2005) refer to this shift in perception as 'efolio thinking.' EPortfolios have also been described as a pedagogical process or an 'approach' to teaching and learning.

To adopt the ePortfolio as a learning tool, teachers must adapt the curriculum and modify their teaching approach. Salmon (2005) warns that 'Changing the way thousands of teachers teach...is a most demanding endeavour that cannot be achieved by learning technologies alone.' Pedagogical support must accompany ePortfolio adoption as a way to enhance learning. At a university the size of CityU, with over one thousand

teaching staff members, providing support is challenging but necessary.

Even in the English Language Centre, where paper-based portfolios have been the norm for a number of years, resistance to their replacement by electronic portfolios has arisen for a number of reasons. They include fear and frustration about technology; need for clear explanations of ePortfolio use beyond a single course; need for initiation into viewing ePortfolios as process rather than merely product; need for establishing procedures for feedback, response, and reflection; and fear about an increase in student and teacher workload.

Figure 2 highlights major questions about pedagogy that need answers for the successful integration of ePortfolios at the course level.

- How might the ePortfolio help learners engage with the course-intended learning outcomes and course content?

- How should the portfolio be structured to facilitate the learning process?
- What particular artifacts, both required and optional, might demonstrate achievement of the course outcomes?
- How might individual and collaborative reflection be incorporated into the syllabus?
- How might the ePortfolio facilitate assessment for learning?
- How is the ePortfolio work assessed, and what kinds of rubrics are needed?
- In summary, how does the ePortfolio support, become integral to, and add value to the course?

Technology

Technological challenges can depend on the definition of the ePortfolio. Eportfolios can range from a simple reflective blog to a lifelong collection of artifacts stored and presented in a complex system incorporating a large repository with intelligent search feature (Figure 3). Technology needs to support the purpose of the ePortfolio rather than the ePortfolio supporting the format and capacity of the technology.

Both teachers and students can become de-motivated as technology platforms continually change. The lack of agreed universal standards allowing portability from one platform to another and from one university to another (Treuer & Jensen, 2003), compounded by the lack of consistent university policies regarding the integration of ePortfolio tools within the wider Learning Management System, has hampered use at CityU. Within the span of five years, we have piloted and used a number of different portfolio platforms and technologies. Figure 4 illustrates our various attempts.

Meanwhile, other Hong Kong universities have had similar experiences. Responding to constraints such as limited budgets and training requirements, two universities have developed home-grown systems tailor-made to the specific needs of their students and the institution, while others have used the less easily customizable built-in function of an LMS such as the Blackboard Portfolio or Mahara, an open source e-portfolio system.

The rapidly evolving technology highlighted the need for us to come up with our own evaluation criteria. Using a heuristic approach, we devised our own evaluation matrix shown in Figure 5. A detailed explanation of the matrix rubric can be found in Zhou et al. (2010). However, within less than twelve months, we have observed changes in the demands we make of the tools: we are now placing a greater emphasis on the ability to search for documents within a repository, the need to show different views of the same artifacts, and the need for a much greater degree of collaboration within the portfolios.

Funding

The pace and extent of ePortfolio research, piloting, and implementation at Hong Kong's eight government-funded universities have so far depended almost entirely on grants awarded by the University Grants Committee. Such funding, however, has been intermittent and sporadic.

Funding for the inter-university English language webfolio is a case in point. Research about ePortfolios is complicated by a constantly evolving technology and diverse educational settings and agendas. The UGC withdrew funding from the inter-university English language webfolio project in 2008 because its desire to rationalize a language showcase portfolio for Hong Kong employers was at odds with the project investigators' more immediate desire to research and implement ePortfolios to enhance the language learning skills of students in their own particular institutions. The project appeared to lack cohesion as the different university language centers employed different platforms and focused on the uses and purposes for the ePortfolio most appropriate to their own individual contexts.

Figure 3. Diverse ePortfolio technologies

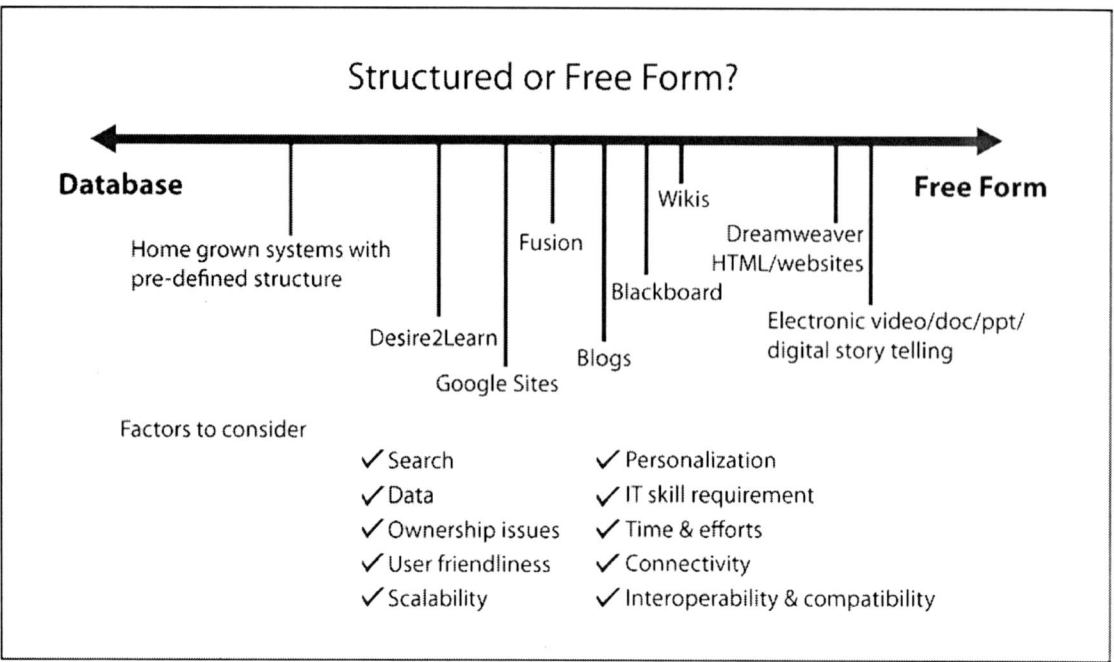

Since then, a few universities have maintained momentum in their ePortfolio research, development, and implementation by receiving funds internally from Teaching Development Grants (TDG). Some institutions, however, including CityU, face an end to funding for their ePortfolio projects, evoking concern for the long term. In other institutions, projects have ground to a halt through a lack of funding and little commitment from senior management.

The process of ePortfolio research and development is slow and involves many different challenges at the levels of technology, the learners, the teachers, faculty, and the institution. Without the funding of university teaching and learning centers to investigate how ePortfolios enhance learning, the drive to implement ePortfolios will come from technology rather than pedagogy, prioritizing what is possible technically over what is desirable educationally.

SOLUTIONS AND RECOMMENDATIONS

Institutional Commitment

Most ePortfolio development in Hong Kong higher education happens from the bottom up with faculty members and/or academic support staff who recognize the ePortfolio trend and the potential value of technological innovation for education. Carr (2001) asserts that grass-roots enthusiasts can trigger innovation and its practical application. As ePortfolio innovation in Hong Kong has up to now relied heavily on limited, time bound resources and funding, the momentum towards adoption and greater diffusion requires institutional commitment. So far, institutional commitment at CityU remains at the level of promotion. With no strategy to institutionalize ePortfolios, support from the top needs to accompany bottom-up initiatives to maximize benefits.

Figure 4. The chronology of CityU's ePortfolio technologies

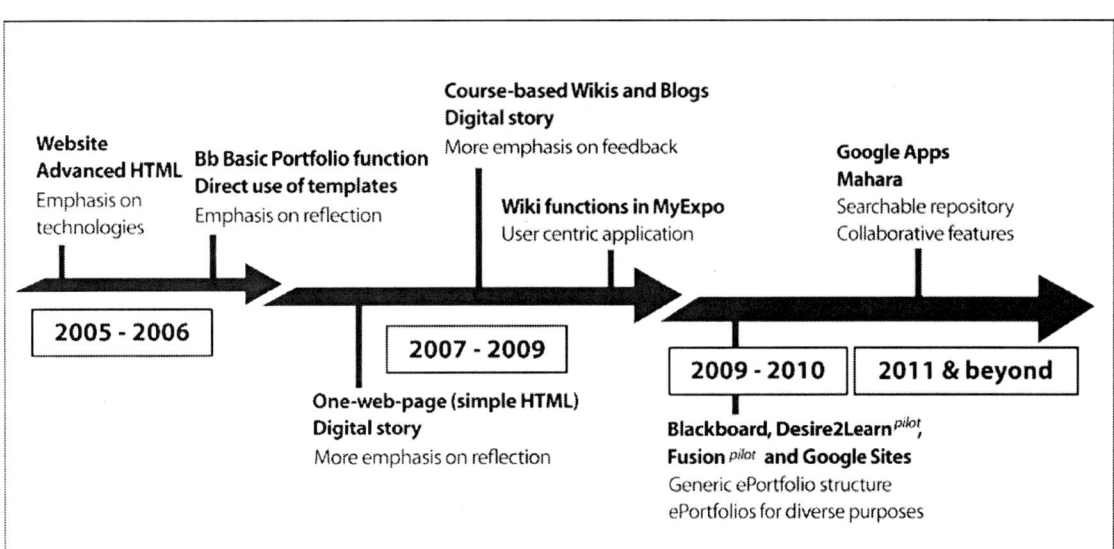

Figure 5. Platform evaluation matrix

	Bb Blackboard	campus Fusion	Google	Desire2Learn	Note:
Content Construction	✓	✓	✓	✓	✓ means good performance;
Content Management	△	✓	△	✓	△ means average performance;
Personalization & Aesthetics Control	△	✗	✓	✓	✗ means poor performance or function is not available
Interaction & Networking	△	✓	✓	△	
System Integration	✓	✓	✗	△	
Assessment	✗	✗	✗	✓	
Reports	✗	✗	△	✓	
Cost	△	△	✓	△	* Zhou et al. (2010)

Most ePortfolio projects in Hong Kong, however, struggle to gain commitment and practical support at the senior management level. For example, one university operates a "centrally developed application" that uses a common system to provide information on non-academic activities and requires its students to create "student development portfolios." Funding for that application, however, extended only until 2011 with no future university plan in place. Institution-wide ePortfolio adoption would require providing technology, building collaboration, supporting staff, doing research, providing training and support, and highlighting adoption and promotion.

Collaboration

Multi-level collaboration is one of the most important factors for successful institution-wide implementation of ePortfolios. Through collaboration, different perspectives are brought into the picture, making it easier to construct a common definition of ePortfolios. Collaboration with different parties also brings academic and technical expertise to the project, helping address various pedagogical issues. In addition, collaboration motivates ePortfolio developers in an indirect way. In our experience, when ePortfolios are used in different areas, for different purposes, and with different people, developers see the potential value of ePortfolios and are therefore more motivated to develop their own.

Collaboration Inside Universities

Collaboration takes place at multiple levels: within, across, and outside universities. Within universities, collaboration can be between administrative and academic support units, faculties, academic departments, and individual teachers. The CityU ePortfolio project began in 2005 as collaboration between two very different departments. While EDGE was able to take advantage of its networks to reach across the whole university and to provide most of the technical support, team members from the ELC offered a practical perspective on pedagogy. In addition, initial implementation of ePortfolios was carried out in ELC language courses, where a large number of students are enrolled every year. The fact that both departments bring different expertise to the project makes the collaboration more effective.

Most projects in other universities in Hong Kong also started with interdepartmental collaboration. For example, in one university, the Centre for English and Additional Languages (CEAL) began an ePortfolio project in 2007, with technical support from the Information Technology Services Centre (ITSC). In 2010, this project continued with further collaboration from the Teaching and Learning Centre (TLC). In another university, the ePortfolio project involves several departments: the Student Affairs Office (SAO), the ITSC, and the Centre of Learning Enhancement and Research. In a third university, the SAO and the ELC, having worked independently on self-development and language portfolios respectively, feel the need to bring together their expertise.

While getting the administrative and academic support units on board is an effective approach in the initial stages, ongoing collaboration with academic departments is essential to involve more teachers and students. At CityU, we have identified the importance of integrating ePortfolios as seamlessly as possible into course structures to add value and depth to the learning experience, to constructively align ePortfolio use with learning outcomes, and to convince students of the value of the ePortfolio as a tool for learning. These courses can be either academic or co-curricular, e.g., exchange programs, student ambassador schemes, etc. The university where CEAL works in collaboration with ITSC and TLC has integrated ePortfolios into CEAL's co-curricular courses to record evidence of students' independent learning activities.

Collaboration is important as it also makes sharing expertise possible. While our project team provides training and support in ePortfolio construction, faculty teachers offer insight into how ePortfolios can facilitate teaching and learning at the course level. One of our strategies to enhance collaboration has been to invite faculty teaching staff as project co-investigators. This strategy not only expands the scale of the project, but also helps to positively influence teachers who have not used ePortfolios in their teaching.

Collaboration across Universities

Collaboration among projects across universities that share common aims and visions offers significant possibilities. Collaborations might include: 1) creating a Hong Kong universities' ePortfolio website that shares resources and experience and provides mutual support; 2) organizing joint university activities such as ePortfolio competitions, training workshops, and sharing seminars; 3) building a joint university ePortfolio repository where students' ePortfolios are accessible for employers' review and consideration; and 4) initiating collaboration on research. These approaches all aim to create an ePortfolio community in Hong Kong to share expertise, expand influence, and motivate outsiders. Genuine interest in such collaboration was expressed by all attendees of the inter-institutional discussion held by CityU in September 2010.

Collaboration Outside Universities

The purposes of collaboration with external parties, in addition to obtaining sponsorship, are to understand outsiders' views in order to inform the development of our project and to motivate ePortfolio developers by making an impact outside universities.

Distinguished CityU alumni and successful people from various industries have been invited as role models to create their Showcase ePortfolios. This collaboration not only enables successful people to use ePortfolios as a tool for celebrating their achievements but also enables them to share with students their journeys to success. In addition, we also work with the public to obtain mutual support. For instance, our media partners, Headline Jobs, have assisted the research project by distributing questionnaires to employers. In return, we help promote their activities that are relevant to our students in our workshops. The sponsorship gained from other collaborators has enabled us to run annual ePortfolio competitions and to buy gifts for those who participate in the research project as a token of gratitude.

Challenges to effective collaboration lie in identifying common perceptions of ePortfolios at different levels of the university and identifying common interests of stakeholders beyond the university. Some of the above approaches have proved to be effective, while others await trial, but one certainty is that collaborative effort over a substantial amount of time is a critical factor for the success of an institution-wide implementation of ePortfolios.

Research

Research findings have helped us focus the direction of the project and have enabled us to communicate the role of ePortfolios in teaching, learning, and employment more effectively to students and teachers. This first-hand information helps create a more motivated and positive ePortfolio community in the University.

Data are currently being collected about the effectiveness of our training and support, ePortfolio developers' perceptions of the generic structure and the current recommended platform (Google Sites) of our ePortfolio, ways that ePortfolios enhance learning and encourage reflection, and employers' views of ePortfolios as an employment tool.

Questionnaires are administrated after workshops to collect participants' feedback and to inform us about areas for improvement. Another round of questionnaires is distributed several weeks after a workshop to investigate developers' experiences of adopting the generic structure and using Google Sites to create their ePortfolios.

This year, with the help of our media partners, we conducted an online survey and face-to-face interviews with local employers to seek their opinions regarding ePortfolios and to identify their company's performance management practices. Employers' opinions are important, because preliminary research results suggest that students see the most value in ePortfolios designed for job applications. By understanding what local employers look for when recruiting fresh graduates and their company's performance management practices, we can improve the generic ePortfolio structure design and can provide final year students with effective guidance in workshops.

Our preliminary research results (Appendix A, Table A1) show that the development of ePortfolios can help students develop a set of skills and attributes that employers are looking for. A promising correlation exists between the attributes and skills valued by employers and the skills and strategies students think they have developed through the creation of ePortfolios.

Because sought-after attitudes and skills may be developed in the process of creating ePortfolios, the primary value of ePortfolios for employment purposes lies in the process of creating them rather than in the end product. This realization echoes Leece's (2005) statement that "the creation of an end product is not as significant as the process of self-awareness developed through the reflective learning aspect of creating the portfolio" (p. 77). We also note a seemingly untapped po-

tential for students to "stand out from the crowd" given the reported willingness by some employers to use ePortfolios as part of the selection process.

Apart from the above research areas, we have tested different platforms to find one that can best suit our needs. In the last few years, we have evaluated four e-learning tools in eight areas of functionality: content construction, content management, personalization and aesthetic control, interaction and networking, assessment of teaching and learning, reporting, system integration, and cost (Zhou et al. 2009). Although an "ideal" platform may not exist, we see research in this area as important, because it not only addresses the technical issues, but it also provides some solutions to pedagogical concerns.

Training and Support

If collaboration is the catalyst, training and support are the conditions necessary for a positive chemical reaction. At CityU, we deliver workshops, provide online guides, and recommend a generic structure to train and support ePortfolio developers.

Figure 6. ePortfolios and employability: Three research questions

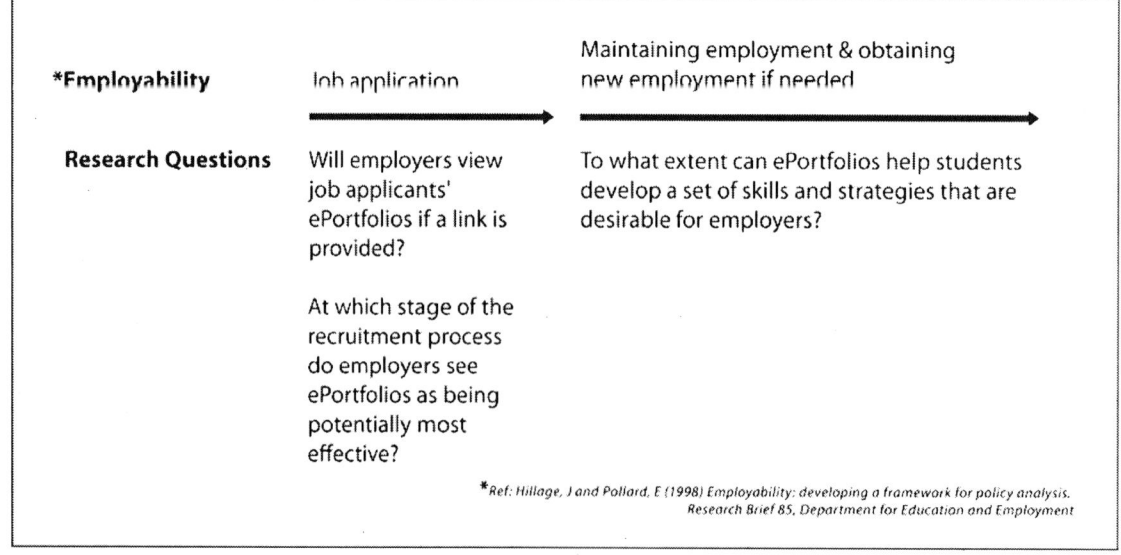

Workshops

Most universities in Hong Kong report providing workshops to introduce ePortfolio concepts and features and to teach necessary technical skills for creating ePortfolios. At CityU, a range of workshops address conceptual information, technical skills, and generic skills such as setting goals and reflecting and presenting oneself to help students develop their ePortfolio content. Apart from those requested by collaborating teachers and departments, open workshops for learning, employment, and teacher development are also offered, usually at the beginning of every semester.

Post-workshop support is also provided at CityU. Consultation sessions are scheduled before competitions or by individual request. Hotline assistance is available during working hours, and email enquiries are also handled by the team.

Online Support

In the inter-institutional discussion held in September 2010, one teacher correctly pointed out that students seem to be good at technical skills but mainly for social purposes. When trying to use technical skills for academic purposes, they too often fall short. Therefore, sufficient technical support that students can access anytime is crucial. Online guides continue to be created for this purpose. At CityU, an online repository of ePortfolio resources, animated guides, and screen capture user guides have been created and promoted through the project website (http://www.cityu.edu.hk/edge/eportfolio/). For students who have missed workshops, a learning ePortfolio course site (http://www.cityu.edu.hk/edge/eportfolio/) helps them learn the concepts and skills on their own time. We also have a series of course sites that introduce ePortfolios for employment, exchange experiences, teaching, and performance appraisal. These course sites are designed to reflect the structure of each workshop, with all teaching materials and activities accessible online.

Generic Structure

Our preliminary research results show that students find content selection and artifact organization challenging as they start an ePortfolio. Students often do not have a clear purpose or target audience in mind and are therefore unable to align the content accordingly. Moreover, the use of different headings in an ePortfolio can lead to inconsistent interpretations and create confusion for viewers. Seldin (1991), Zubizarreta (2004), Lorenzo and Ittelson (2005), and Nikirk (2008) report further problems in ePortfolio development: As context affects the purpose of an ePortfolio, which in turn affects the content required, problems can arise regarding ownership, motivation, and, more importantly, the transferability of skills and strategies for the ongoing, lifelong development of ePortfolios. Consequently, having a core structure with essential common elements across all types of ePortfolios as a guide provides necessary structure but also freedom to customize ePortfolios for different purposes and requirements. One immediate and effective way to address initial problems is to provide ePortfolio developers with a generic structure.

The generic structure at CityU contains four sections: Profile, Summary, Showcase, and Qualifications (PSSQ). The Profile section presents basic information about the ePortfolio developer and helps construct his or her self-identity. The Summary section outlines the theme and purposes of the ePortfolio and highlights the developer's major accomplishments. Developers reflect on their overall experience and accomplishments, identify strengths and weaknesses, and make an action plan to achieve future goals.

The Showcase section is the essence of an ePortfolio. It contains the developer's actual work to support the claims made in the Summary section. Recently, we have incorporated a learning log mechanism into the Showcase section of a learning ePortfolio template. The learning log is a repository that collects artifacts in six categories: academic studies, language learning, exchange programs, internship/work experience, community service, and other co/extra-curricular activities. Students can adopt the categories that work for them. The learning log reveals student development and effort made over a period of time. Students are reminded to select the most representative work for showcasing. In the final Qualifications section, developers present objective and official evidence of their competencies and achievements.

This PSSQ structure provides an immediately accessible scaffold to alleviate certain problems and concerns caused by the diversity of portfolio types, content structures, and requirements. The generic structure (Figure 7) makes portfolios specific, strategic, and manageable. This structure may consequently lead to a decreasing demand for training and support resources.

A common concern about adhering to a recommended structure, however, is over-reliance on the structure at the expense of expressing one's personality and creativity. In addition, too much structure may become an obstacle for experienced ePortfolio developers. To address these concerns, students are reminded that they can easily customize the PSSQ structure to express their individuality. We expect developers to rely heavily on the generic structure in the earlier stages but to move beyond the structure through further customization to meet individual purposes later on.

Training and support are always on the agenda of ePortfolio projects. But finding the best way to deliver the most effective training and provide the most comprehensive support can be a long-term endeavor requiring ample research, experimentation, and reflection.

Promotion

No launch of a new concept or implementation of a new tool can survive without a certain amount of effort to promote it. We continue to communicate the benefits of the ePortfolio as an effective teaching and learning tool to people inside and outside the University. Every year,

Figure 7. Recommended generic ePortfolio structure

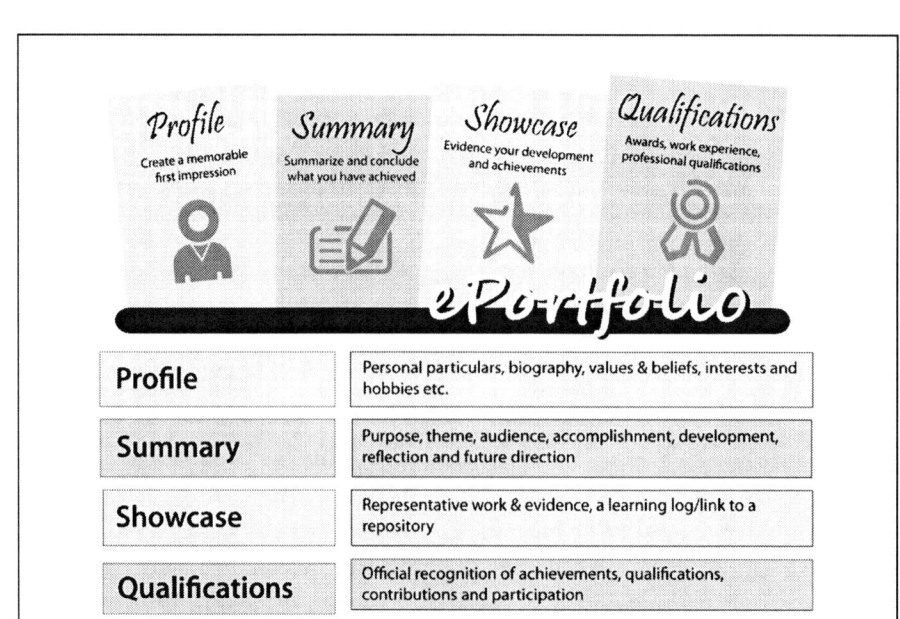

ePortfolio competitions are held to encourage more students and teachers to create portfolios. In addition, publicity materials, including posters, flyers, leaflets, and booklets, are produced and distributed throughout the University. Sharing sessions are organized inside the University and across institutions to facilitate collaboration and expand influence. Websites, user guides, online courses, and trendy videos are created to provide support and arouse interest. Such efforts are meant to contribute towards the establishment of a university-wide ePortfolio culture.

FUTURE DIRECTION

Our current issues and evolving solutions point to our future direction. In CityU in particular, we hope that increased institutional commitment will facilitate a push towards a university-wide ePortfolio culture through the provision of effective training and support services underpinned by extensive collaboration and research.

Institutional Commitment

The use of ePortfolios to promote learning already features in CityU's five-year strategic plan for 2010-2015. With this in mind, the CityU ePortfolio project team is currently working on a proposal for possible institutional implementation to be submitted to senior management. We see ePortfolios as playing an integral role in the university's Outcomes Based Approach. The use of templates, for example, helps raise awareness of graduate outcomes.

Other future visions for large scale adoption involve centrality of ePortfolios in general education, in programs, and in evaluation of courses and teachers. Eportfolios could be integrated into General Education core courses for all first year students. Going beyond the course level, we would like to see program level adoption of ePortfolios.

Further proposals envisage the use of ePortfolios for course evaluation and quality assurance. We are also preparing teachers for the possible introduction of ePortfolios for peer review, collaboration, and performance appraisal.

Collaboration and Research

Research continues to be an essential part of our vision and practice. We are presently conducting research with faculty on the impact, experience, pedagogy, and technology of ePortfolios. We will continue our collaboration with local employers to investigate the effects of ePortfolio development on employability and track possible changes in attitudes towards ePortfolios for employment. Although we have initial research on this question, our data can be more convincing by adding to the number of employer respondents.

Through our ePortfolio Commons, utilizing a number of social networking platforms, we will continue to share experience and research with colleagues from other local and/or overseas universities. Such local collaboration could be pivotal considering the disparate nature of the research and development of ePortfolios in Hong Kong.

Training and Support Services

We aim to expand our collection of sample ePortfolios, especially those which have been developed for specific purposes. We intend to develop further training materials, such as online course sites, to help users with both the technical and conceptual aspects of ePortfolio development. We will produce a handbook for teachers in an effort to encourage them and to convince them of the value of ePortfolios for learning, development, and employment. Simultaneously, we will keep proposing ePortfolios as an integral part of the University e-learning agenda.

CONCLUSION

Over the past few years, all eight government-funded universities in Hong Kong have been piloting different types of ePortfolios for different purposes. However, the piloting and use of ePortfolios have been rather fragmented. Pockets of activity exist, and, even within the same institution, these pockets are not necessarily connected. Similar complex challenges are being faced by all eight universities. Motivation and stakeholder 'buy-in' at the levels of practice and policy remain key concerns. The educational institutions in Hong Kong, and indeed all over the world, are still grappling with the ways in which e-learning affects the process and dynamics of learning. The ePortfolio, however, is not simply another e-tool or a learning application in the way to which we are accustomed. It adds more layers to the learning process by emphasizing learning management and self-development. This requires a paradigm shift in the way e-learning, learning in general, and instruction are perceived, but this critical shift in mindset needs time to evolve. These issues are further complicated by contextual coloring. Different contexts determine different purposes, but varied purposes cause confusion about the fundamental nature of ePortfolios, which consequently blurs the way forward. Despite the lack of a clear roadmap, this paper has proposed several solutions and possible paths forward for Hong Kong higher education as it incorporates ePortfolios into its research and practice.

ACKNOWLEDGMENT

We would like to thank the following teachers and staff members for their valuable input into this article during an ePortfolio inter-institutional discussion held in September 2010 at City University of Hong Kong: From Chinese University of Hong Kong, Paul Lam, Carol Chiu, Chris Zhang, Eric Chan, Max Cheung, Frank Leung, Alex Li, Shelly Lire, Sammi Poon, Sam Tong, Samuel Yung, Phebe Lee, and Ricky Tai; from the Hong Kong Polytechnic University, Dorinda Fung, May Yeung, Doris Lee, Peter Duffy, Juliana Chau, and Peggy Lui; from the Hong Kong Institute of Education, May Chan, Ronnie Shroff, Mike Chui, and Elson Szeto; from Hong Kong Baptist University, Stewart Chu and Rosa Tang; from the University of Hong Kong, Cecilia Chan, and from Lingnan University, Preet Hiradhar.

REFERENCES

Attwell, G., Chrzaszcz, A., Hilzensauer, W., Hornung-Prähauser, V., & Pallister, J. (2007). *Grab your future with an e-portfolio – Study on new qualifications and skills needed by teachers and career counselors to empower young learners with the e-portfolio concept and tools – Summary report.* Retrieved October 14, 2010, from http://www.mosep.org/study

Barrett, H. (2000). *Electronic teaching portfolios: multimedia skills + portfolio development = professional power.* Retrieved September 20, 2010, from http://electronicportfolios.com/portfolios/site2000.html

Barrett, H., & Carney, J. (2005). *Conflicting paradigms and competing purposes in electronic portfolio development.* Retrieved October 14, 2010, from http://pdfcast.org/pdf/conflicting-paradigms-and-competing-purposes-in-electronic-portfolio-development

Barrett, H., & Knezek, D. (2003). *E-Portfolios: Issues in assessment, accountability and preservice teacher preparation.* Retrieved October 14, 2010, from http://electronicportfolios.com/portfolios/AERA2003.pdf

Carr, V. H., Jr. (2001). *Technology adoption and diffusion.* Retrieved October 3, 2010, from http://www.au.af.mil/au/awc/awcgate/innovation/adoptiondiffusion.htm

Chen, H. L., Cannon, D., Gabrio, J., Leifer, L., Toye, G., & Bailey, T. (2005). Using Wikis and weblogs to support reflective learning in an introductory engineering design course. In *Proceedings of the American Society for Engineering Education Annual Conference & Exposition*, Stanford, CA.

Cheung, H. L., Fisher, D., Pickard, V., & Chan, Y. F. (2009). *Scaffolding student learning: Integrating ePortfolios into the university experience.* Paper presented at the Improving University Teaching International Conference, Burnaby, BC, Canada.

Emmett, D. J. (2003). *E-portfolios at QUT: Providing the potential for competitive advantage and a motivating learner-centred environment.* Paper presented at the OLT Excellence: Making the Connections Conference, Brisbane, Australia.

Grant, S. (2005). *Clear e-portfolio definitions: A prerequisite for effective interoperability.* Paper presented at the ePortfolio Conference, Cambridge, UK.

Greller, W. (2007). A sample e-portfolio service model for higher education In Griffiths, D., Koper, R., & Liber, O. (Eds.), *Service oriented approaches and lifelong competence development infrastructures* (pp. 68–74). Manchester, UK: TENC.

Hafner, C. A., & Miller, L. (2010). *Learner Autonomy and the role of technology.* Seminar presented at the Hong Kong Association of Self-Access and Learner Development, Hong Kong.

Heinrich, E., Bhattacharya, M., & Rayudu, R. (2007). Preparation for lifelong learning using ePortfolios. *European Journal of Engineering Education*, *32*(6), 653–663. doi:10.1080/03043790701520602

Leece, R. (2005). The role of eportfolios in graduate recruitment. *Australian Journal of Career Development*, *14*(2), 72–79.

Lorenzo, G., & Ittelson, J. (2005). *An overview of e-portfolios.* Washington, DC: EDUCAUSE Learning Initiative. Retrieved October 6, 2010, from http://www.educause.edu/LibraryDetailPage/666?ID=ELI3001

Nikirk, M. (2008). Digital portfolios. *Tech Directions*, *68*(5), 13–15.

Salmon, G. (2002). *E-tivities: a key to active online learning.* London, UK: Routledge.

Salmon, G. (2005). Flying not flapping: a strategic framework for e-learning and pedagogical innovation in higher education institutions. *ALT-J: Research in Learning Technology*, *13*(3), 201–218. doi:10.1080/09687760500376439

Seldin, P. (1991). *The teaching portfolio: A practical guide to improved performance and promotion- tenure decisions.* Bolton, MA: Anker.

Treuer, P., & Jenson, J. D. (2003). Electronic portfolios need standards to thrive. *EDUCAUSE Quarterly*, *26*(2), 34–42.

Wong, Y. W., Wong, S. K., & Cheung, H. L. (2006). *Adoption of e-learning: From organic to planned.* Paper presented at the International Conference on Improving University Teaching, Dunedin, New Zealand.

Zhou, M., Cheung, H. L., & Wong, M. C. Chan. Y. F., & Pickard, V. (2010, January). *An evaluation of electronic portfolio platforms in higher education.* Paper presented at the e-CASE & e-Tech Conference, Macau, China.

Zubizarreta, J. (2004). *The learning portfolio: Reflective practice for improving student learning.* Bolton, MA: Anker.

ADDITIONAL READING

Albert, K. (2006). *An e-Portfolio model for learning, assessment, and employment in teacher education at West Chester University of Pennsylvania* (Unpublished doctoral dissertation). University of Delaware, Newark, DE.

Attwell, G. (2007). *Personal learning environments - the future of eLearning?* Retrieved October 14, 2010, from http://www.elearningeuropa.info/files/media/media11561.pdf

Avraamidou, L., & Zembal-Saul, C. (2006). Exploring the influence of web-based portfolio development on learning to teach elementary science. *AACE Journal, 14*(2), 178–205.

Barrett, H., & Wilkerson, J. (2004). *Conflicting paradigms in electronic portfolio approaches.* Retrieved October 14, 2010, from http://electronicportfolios.com/systems/paradigms.html

Batson, T. (2005). The current state of electronic portfolios in higher education. *Educause Connect.* Retrieved October 14, 2010, from http://www.educause.edu/Resources/TheCurrentStateofE-Portfoliosin/158784

Buzzetto-More, N., & Alade, A. (2008). The Pentagonal e-portfolio model for selecting, adopting, building, and implementing and e-portfolio. *Journal of Information Technology Education Innovations in Practice, 7, 45–70.*

Cambridge, D. (2010). *E-Portfolios for lifelong learning and assessment. San Francisco, CA: Jossey Bass. Cambridge, D., Cambridge, B., & Yancey, K. (2009). Electronic Portfolios 2.0: Emergent research on implementation and impact.* Sterling, VA: Stylus.

Cheung, H. L., Williams, F., & Chan, Y. F. (2007). *Promoting active and reflective learning through ePortfolios: Difficulties and challenges.* Paper presented at the Improving University Teaching International Conference, Jaén, Spain.

Cohn, E. R., & Hibbitts, J. B. (2004). Beyond the electronic portfolio: A lifetime personal web space. *Educause Quarterly, 27*(4). Retrieved October 14, 2010, from http://www.educause.edu/apps/eq/eqm04/eqm0441.asp?bhcp=1

Cotterill, S., McDonald, T., Drummond, P., & Hammond, G. (2004). *Design, implementation and evaluation of a 'generic' ePortfolio: the Newcastle experience.* Paper presented at the ePortfolio Conference, La Rochelle, France.

Gross, R. (1991). *Peak learning: How to create your own lifelong education program for personal enjoyment and professional success.* New York, NY: Tarcher/Putnam.

Jafari, A. (2004). The 'sticky' ePortfolio system: Tackling challenges and identifying attributes. *EDUCAUSE Review,* 38–48.

Kilbane, C. R., & Milman, N. B. (2003). *The digital teaching portfolio handbook: A how-to guide for educators.* Boston, MA: Allyn & Bacon.

Kinnard, J. (2006). *From crayons to cyberspace: Creating a professional teaching portfolio.* Florence, KY: Wadsworth.

Lambert, S. R., & Corrin, L. E. (1007). Moving towards a university-wide implementation of an ePortfolio tool. *Australian Journal of Educational Technology, 23*(1), 1-16.

MacDonald, L., Liu, P., Lowell, K., Tsai, H., & Lohr, L. (2004). Graduate student perspectives on the development of electronic portfolios. *Tech Trends Washington, 48*(3), 52–55.

Ravet, S. (2007). *Position paper on ePortfolio - For and ePortfolio enabled architecture.* Retrieved October 14, 2010, from http://www.eife-l.org/publications/eportfolio/documentation/positionpaper

Reardon, R. C., Lumsden, J. A., & Meyer, K. E. (2005). Developing an e-portfolio program: Providing a comprehensive tool for student development, reflection, and integration. *NASPA Journal, 42*(3), 368–380.

Ring, G., Weaver, B., & Jones, J. H. Jr. (2008). Electronic portfolios: engaged students create multimedia-rich artifacts. *Journal of the Research Center for Educational Technology, 4*(2), 103–114.

Smith, K., & Tillema, H. H. (2001). Long term influences of portfolios on professional development. *Scandinavian Journal of Educational Research, 45*(2), 183–203. doi:10.1080/00313830120052750

Smith, K., & Tillema, H. H. (2003). Clarifying different types of portfolio use. *Assessment & Evaluation in Higher Education, 28*(6), 625–648. doi:10.1080/0260293032000130252

Song, K., Scordias, M., Huang, C., & Hoagland, C. (2004). Implementing e-portfolios in a university: An enterprise solution. In *Proceedings of the Society for Information Technology and Teacher Education Conference*, Atlanta, GA.

Strivens, J. (2007). A survey of e-pdp and e-portfolio practice in UK higher education. *The Higher Education Academy*, 1-24.

Ward, C., & Moser, C. (2008). E-portfolios as a hiring too: Do employers really care? *EDUCAUSE Quarterly*, (4): 13–14.

Wolf, K. (1999). *Leading the professional portfolio process for change*. Arlington Heights, IL: Skylight Professional Development.

APPENDIX

Appendix A.

Table A1. Results of the ePortfolio developers' post-experience & employer surveys

Number of Respondents: 34	Strongly Agree	Agree	Neutral	Disagree	Strongly Disagree
Goal Setting & Action Planning					
"Creating ePortfolios helps me set clear goals and plan accordingly"?	16.7%	57.6%	22.7%	0.0%	3.0%
Within your company, for appraising your staff, how important is setting goals and planning accordingly?	32.4%	55.9%	11.8%	0.0%	0.0%
Identify Strengths & Weaknesses					
"Creating ePortfolios helps me recognize my strengths and weaknesses"?	26.5%	52.9%	20.6%	0.0%	0.0%
Within your company, for appraising your staff, how important is recognizing one's strengths and weaknesses?	41.2%	41.2%	11.8%	5.9%	0.0%
Record Accomplishments					
"Creating ePortfolios helps me record accomplishments"?	16.7%	62.1%	18.2%	1.5%	1.5%
Within your company, for appraising your staff, how important is recording one's accomplishments?	20.6%	55.9%	17.6%	5.9%	0.0%
Provide Evidence for Performance Claims					
"Creating ePortfolios helps me provide evidence for performance claims"?	15.2%	65.2%	16.7%	1.5%	1.5%
Within your company, for appraising your staff, how important is providing evidence for performance claims?	32.4%	44.1%	20.6%	2.9%	0.0%
Establish a Positive Image					
To what extent do you agree with the statement "Creating ePortfolios helps me establish a positive image of myself"?	20.6%	64.7%	14.7%	0.0%	0.0%
Within your company, for appraising your staff, how important is establishing a positive image of oneself?	14.7%	50.0%	14.7%	17.6%	2.9%

Appendix B.

Some Useful University ePortfolio Websites

A Showcase of Award-Winning ePortfolios (The Hong Kong Polytechnic University)
http://www.polyu.edu.hk/sao/publications/emagazine/issue120/specialaward/
Diagnostic Digital Portfolio (Alverno College)
http://ddp.alverno.edu/
e-Portfolios at Penn State: A Space for Reflection and Growth (Penn State University)
http://portfolio.psu.edu/
Selecting Your Portfolio Structure (University of Wisconsin-Superior)
http://www.uwsuper.edu/teachingtools/chalk/portfoliostructure.cfm
Student Portfolio (Queensland University of Technology)
http://www.studenteportfolio.qut.edu.au/

Chapter 13
Faculty Teaching Beliefs, ePortfolios, and Web 2.0 at the Crossroads

Gary Brown
Portland State University, USA

YoonJung Cho
Oklahoma State University, USA

Ashley Ater-Kranov
ABET, USA

ABSTRACT

The research on faculty teaching beliefs and teaching strategies reported in this study suggests that, without comprehensive new approaches for faculty preparation, faculty in higher education are unlikely to capitalize on the potential eportfolios present and the world of Web 2.0 requires. Without deep rethinking of teaching and learning in a technology enriched and increasingly complex global context, educators are unlikely to promote the kind of learning eportfolios represent, learning that is necessary in a world of increasing challenges and opportunities.

INTRODUCTION

The advent of open knowledge and open source and the ubiquity of the phenomenon identified as Web 2.0, as evidenced by the phenomenal growth of Facebook, Google, and hundreds of other open and social Internet applications, have ramifications for education. Many educators are speculating on the implications of Web 2.0 for the future of

education (Grush, 2008) while others argue that it *is* the future (Hargadon, 2008). Whether the impact is imminent or upon us, as Batson (2008) observes, "designing anything in Web 2.0 requires new thinking" (2008, p. 2).

At the same time, educators have been slow to understand that it is how we implement a technology, not the technology itself, that most influences learning. Yet research that focuses on discreet implementation variables rather than the technologies themselves are only incrementally

DOI: 10.4018/978-1-4666-0143-7.ch013

gaining purchase in the literature and perhaps even less so in practice. It is in this context of technology, in the thinking that guides teaching practice, that the study reported here was conducted. In particular, and in collaboration with the Inter/National Coalition for Electronic Portfolio Research, the study reported here is focused on ePortfolios as a nexus application—nexus in that ePortfolios can be used as either an application for traditional or teacher-centered assessment management, or they can be used as a Web 2.0 learner or learning-centered generative, social, and integrating application. How ePortfolios are being and will be used depends in large measure on the teaching beliefs that guide their implementation and the quality of learning that follows. It is that range of application and the variation in the understanding of ePortfolios that make it a valuable lens for examining the relationship between faculty teaching beliefs, teaching practice, and educational innovations.

THEORETICAL FRAMEWORK

Faculty Teaching Beliefs

Faculty members often report that they have not previously taken the opportunity to reflect on and identify their own teaching beliefs in terms of how students learn and how their teaching strategies influence student learning. Although faculty beliefs exist in an implicit form without being articulated or verbalized, these implicit beliefs play an integral role in guiding many aspects of teaching practice (Ajzen, 1985; Pajares, 1992). Pajares (1992) notes that beliefs play a significant role in determining how people perceive, interpret, and organize information. They become a basis for teacher behaviors and actions in the classroom (Trigwell & Prosser, 1999). A substantial body of research indicates that an effective way to change teaching practices is to help teachers make their implicit beliefs explicit

(Ajzen, 1985; Pajares, 1992; Brookfield, 1995; Kane, Sandretto, & Heath, 2002). It is therefore critical to help faculty develop awareness of their own teaching beliefs, and an important way to promote that awareness is to sharpen the ways teaching beliefs are assessed (Nottis, Feuerstein, Murray, & Adams, 2000; Van der Schaaf, Stokking, & Verloop, 2008). However, measures of faculty beliefs are primarily found in research on K-12 or pre-service teachers (Trigwell & Prosser, 2004). Furthermore, those measures tend toward a dualistic approach that distinguishes generally between traditional teacher-centered beliefs and learner-centered beliefs. Some existing measures of teacher beliefs attempt to isolate more progressive constructivist approaches to teaching but do not differentiate social from individual theories of constructivism. In order to meet the challenges implicit in a Web 2.0 social networking-rich environment, teachers must embrace the theory of social constructivism and the principles of collaborative learning (Bruffee, 1995) and learning communities (Lave & Wenger, 1991) that have presaged and deepened the theory and develop new strategies for expanding the principles (Batson, 2008; Grush, 2008).

Theories of learning loosely inform the current notions of teaching and learner-centered practice, and it is common to point to behaviorism as it may outline traditional or teacher-centered practice. Behaviorism was a predominant learning theory in the 1960's and relies heavily on an understanding of learning that is measurable and driven by a complex interaction of incentives. To the extent that those incentives are provided by external agencies that shape learning behaviors, it understandable that the provisioning of those incentives by a controlling agent—a teacher for instance—has led to an association between behaviorism and teacher-centered practice. Ongoing research built upon key aspects of behaviorism as cognitivism emerged, which allows for an understanding of critical learning gains that may not be observable. Cognitivism has been followed by constructivism, which reflects a deepening understanding in the individual's agency in and responsibility for learning. The newer theories of social constructivism and connectivism are both emerging and gaining credence as evidence of the social nature of learning has become irrefutable. That recognition generally underpins the learner-centered concept, an acknowledgement or belief that to construct one's own understanding, a learner needs to actively engage or create that understanding. A close reading of educational research reveals that each new theory does not counter old theories so much as it subsumes, expands, and extends them. That understanding further surfaces the problematic tendency of rendering teaching-beliefs into two simple camps—teacher and learner.

As theories of learning and knowledge become increasingly sophisticated, it follows that teachers' beliefs about learning and knowledge have remained elusive (Kane, Sundretto, & Health, 2002). Few studies examine teachers' epistemological beliefs, particularly in higher education settings and relative to technology mediated teaching. Though recent efforts to enhance the quality of student learning increasingly reflect enthusiasm for the affordances of technology integration, the constructivist theories from which much of the enthusiasm springs have been hard to document in teaching practice (Danielson, 1996; Fosnot, 1996; Richardson, 1997; Haney & McArthur, 2002).

An initial review of the literature necessary to develop the survey instrument used in this study focused on differences among three categories of teaching beliefs associated with three essential underlying learning theories. Researchers developed the survey to refine the existing categories—*teacher-centered and learner-centered*—and to add a third category—*learning-centered*—in order to discern some key aspects of social-constructivism and connectivism. The first two categories were drawn to some extent from Trigwell's and Prosser's (2004) previous work. That work delineates the distinction between teaching

and learning-centered models and the extension of practices associated with those beliefs. In that work, Trigwell and Prosser do much to distinguish the teacher-centered model of transmission of information from learner-centered beliefs that uphold more active learning strategies. The third categorical distinction added in this study draws on principles outlined in the descriptions of learning in Web 2.0 and connectivism in Downes (2005) and Siemens (2004). Siemens, in particular, articulates a new theory of connectivism that extends principles of social constructivism by underscoring the distinction that not only is learning influenced by interaction, but also that interaction itself is learning. At this end of the emerging continuum where learning-centered social constructivism yields to connectivism, individuals necessarily assume greater responsibility and agency for their own learning; or, from an instructional vantage, student agency is characterized by the extent that the allocation of learning control is designed into curricula (Jackson, 2003; Pruyn, 1996). Student agency, as rendered in the learning-centered construct of the survey, represents an emerging understanding of learning as it is playing out on the open read/write web or in learning-centered ePortfolios that are sometimes referred to as personal ePortfolios or personal learning environments (PLE). The earlier distinction made by Bruffee (1995) between cooperative learning and collaborative learning informed the distinction reflected in the survey developed for this study. In Bruffee's work, cooperative learning is when students work together to search for and identify a previously established right answer. In contrast, when students work together to develop their own creative and unique answers or solutions in an ill-structured domain, that work is characterized as collaborative learning.

In simple terms, the three categories can be explained as (a) teaching-centered in which the faculty member determines what is to be learned and how that learning is to be measured; (b) learner-centered, in which the faculty member determines what is to be learned but encourages student agency to engage more fully in the process of determining answers or solutions as well as affording some leeway as to how evidence of that work might be presented; and (c) learning-centered, in which the faculty member allocates increased agency for learners to have some determination in not only how the work will be represented, but also in determining what it is that is necessary to learn. Finally, in learning-centered practice, it is presumed that students will collaborate, employ peer review, and a larger network of people and resources to inform their learning process.

This study reports first on the development and validation of an instrument designed to measure faculty teaching beliefs and expand the constructs of that measurement in accord with the implications of Web 2.0 and the attendant emergence of social networking as they relate to higher education. Secondly, this study reports the results of that survey in order to further understand the complex relationship between faculty teaching beliefs, practice, and their understanding of the potential of an important new technology.

The survey has been designed, finally, to promote faculty awareness of their teaching assumptions in ways that may ultimately help improve teaching practice and student learning.

Hypothesis

The study forwards three hypotheses: two related to establishing a valid instrument and one focused on the results that that instrument might evince:

HO¹ Teaching-centered, learner-centered, and learning-centered beliefs represent distinct teaching belief constructs.

HO² Faculty teaching beliefs are not singular; individual faculty may hold two or more beliefs simultaneously.

HO³ Faculty teaching beliefs will correlate with different perceptions of the utility of ePortfolios, and, more precisely, teacher-centered beliefs will find less utility for ePortfolios than will learner- and learning-centered beliefs.

METHOD

Participants

A total of 153 faculty members from various disciplines at a large northwestern university participated in this study. They were contacted by email and asked to complete an online survey. The overall response rate was 30.6%, with 57.5% male and 41.2% female faculty responding. Participants had the following breakdown by rank: assistant professor was 43.6%, associate professor 24.8%, and full professor 31.6%.

Measures

Faculty Teaching Belief Survey

The Faculty Teaching Beliefs Inventory was developed and validated by a research team to assess teacher-centered, learner-centered, and learning-centered beliefs. The survey instrument included questions relative to four categories of teaching (curriculum, instruction, assignment/activities, and assessment). A total of 23 items were created and participants were asked to rate them on a 7-point Likert scale with 1 being "strongly disagree" and with 7 being "strongly agree." Descriptive Statistics and reliabilities of each subscale are displayed in Table 2.

To determine the construct validity of the instrument, a factor analysis was performed with the principal-axis factoring extraction method and oblimin rotation. Eigenvalues greater than 1 were used as a main criterion for a factor structure. A scree plot was also examined to decide the number of factors.

Faculty Perceptions and Values of the Use of ePortfolio

Open-ended questions were included in the survey to identify faculty awareness, understanding and perceived value of student ePortfolios. Issues investigated included the potential utility and impact of ePortfolios on student learning and faculty teaching, possible challenges and need for technical and instructional support.

RESULTS AND DISCUSSION

A key qualifying finding was that only 12.5% of respondents reported experience with ePortfolios. Alternately, 87.5% reported they had no direct experience. So, the majority of the responses in this study represent perceptions based on the general description of an ePortfolio provided at the beginning of the survey and what respondents may have heard or read from other sources. We aimed to investigate how faculty understands and perceives how e-Portfolios might be used as a tool for student learning and faculty teaching and what exactly this pedagogical application entails.

The hypothesis (HO[1]) that teaching-centered, learner-centered, and learning-centered beliefs represent distinct teaching belief constructs was supported. The three-factor structure, displayed in Table 1, demonstrates reliable subscales (all items loaded on each factor are included). A factor loading cutoff criteria of .35 was used. Loadings for each factor ranged from .36 to .90, and most exceeded .50. The three factors accounted for a total of 39.82% of the item variance. The factor loadings for each subscale are displayed in Table 1.

Indeed, teaching beliefs as defined by groupings of questions based upon learning theory and teaching practice literature do represent discrete and coherent concepts, and the practices antici-

pated can be reliably associated with those concepts.

We provide reliabilities of subscales and example items.

- Teacher-centered beliefs (α=.93)
  - "Giving lectures is important because they model subject matter expertise."
  - "Tests should have clear and correct answers."
- Learner-centered beliefs (α=.89)
  - "My role is to provide opportunities for students to discover key concepts."
  - "It is important to help students reflect upon their thinking and learning processes."
- Learning-centered beliefs (α=.90)
  - "I encourage students to work together to solve authentic problems that students help identify."
  - "It is important to collaborate with students in planning the course."

The hypothesis (HO[2]) that faculty teaching beliefs are not singular but blend according to the individual faculty and the perceived context of their teaching was also supported. Categorically exclusive beliefs reflected only 34% of faculty members who responded to the survey. In contrast, 66% of faculty members scored high on more than two categories of teaching beliefs, demonstrating that they hold blended beliefs. 11% of faculty fell into the blended categories of teacher-centered beliefs and learner-centered beliefs, indicating that learner-centered faculty sometimes incorporate teacher-centered beliefs. There were 23% of faculty who belong to the blended category of learner- and learning-centered beliefs. 5% of faculty scored high both on teacher- and learning-centered beliefs. 14.5% of faculty showed high scores on all of the three categories of teaching beliefs and 12.5% of faculty scored low on all of the three categories.

Table 1. Factor analysis results of faculty teaching beliefs

	Item # (Factor#)	F1 (Teacher- centered)	F2 (Learner- centered)	F3 (Learning- centered)
Giving lectures is important, because they model subject matter expertise.	7 (F1)	.723	.074	-.154
I focus primarily on information students will need to pass the exams.	15 (F1)	.701	-.096	-.005
Tests should have clear and correct answers.	16 (F1)	.691	-.098	.042
I base student grades primarily on quizzes and tests.	19 (F1)	.690	-.118	-.224
I use a textbook to plan my course.	2 (F1)	.519	.071	.110
It is important to present basic knowledge to students.	1 (F1)	.502	.216	-.011
Teachers should know the answers to any questions that students ask.	10 (F1)	.493	-.132	.044
I encourage students to constantly check their own understanding while they are studying.	22 (F2)	.086	.631	-.020
When evaluating students, it is important to consider multiple examples of student work.	12 (F2)	-.035	.619	.063
It is important to help students reflect upon their thinking and learning processes.	8 (F2)	-.035	.618	-.042
Effective teachers consider students' prior knowledge or experience.	21 (F2)	.107	.577	.002
I provide opportunities for students to discuss their development of under-standing of concepts.	11 (F2)	-.058	.554	.218
My role is to provide opportunities for students to discover key concepts.	6 (F2)	-.030	.542	-.010
I use difficult problems to prompt student debate.	23 (F2)	-.057	.433	-.029
I use thematic units to organize my teaching.	4 (F2)	.006	.368	.063
Instruction should be flexible to accommodate students' individual needs.	18 (F2)	-.025	.357	.006
Many of my assignments require students to work in groups to arrive at answers and solutions.	13 (F3)	.061	-.072	.894
I grade students' teamwork skills.	24 (F3)	.158	-.042	.680
My course activities usually require students to work individually.	17 (F3)	.337	.172	-.641
I encourage students to work together to solve authentic problems that students help identify.	3 (F3)	.123	.271	.614
I provide opportunities for my students to critique each others' work.	9 (F3)	-.139	.249	.558
It is important to collaborate with students in planning the course.	5 (F3)	-.101	.077	.494
I value students' self assessment about learning.	14 (F3)	-.026	.228	.420
Eigenvalue		2.80	4.89	1.47
% of Variance Explained		12.15%	21.27%	6.40%

Though most *responses* in this study were learner-centered, responses are not synonymous with respondents (Table 2). The most frequent distribution of faculty who held an exclusive set of beliefs, that is their responses that fell into a single category, were teacher-centered (18%, see Figure 1). Faculty who were exclusively learner-centered accounted for 9%. Finally, 7% of faculty survey respondents were purely learning-centered.

The finding that individual faculty members' responses sometimes included two or even three categories is consistent with the models of learning theory underpinning the questions. As noted, the evolution of learning theories is not marked by sharp breaks but reflects a gradually deepening

Table 2. Descriptive statistics and reliabilities of faculty teaching beliefs

N=153	Teacher-Centered	Learner-Centered	Learning-Centered
Mean	2.89	4.10	3.33
Median	2.86	4.11	3.29
Mode	3.14	4.33	3.00
Std. Deviation	.80	.52	.68
Reliability (# of items)	.93 (7)	.89 (9)	.90 (7)

Figure 1. Distribution of teaching beliefs by category

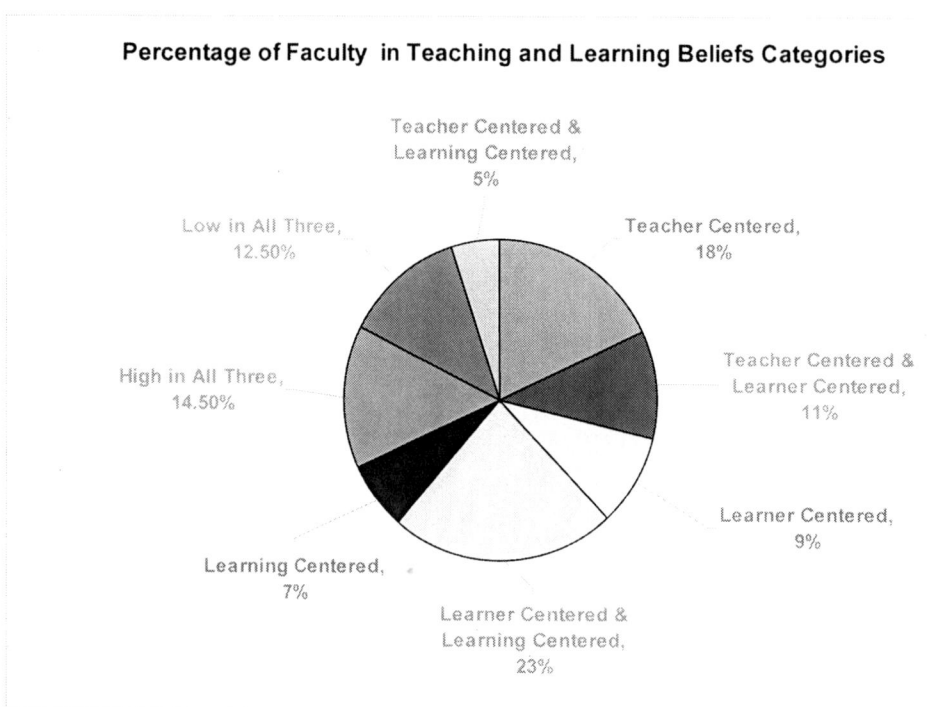

Percentage of Faculty in Teaching and Learning Beliefs Categories

understanding about how people learn. One theory does not fully supplant a preceding theory, but also subsumes elements of it. Figure 1 shows the full distribution of faculty teaching beliefs.

The hypothesis (HO³) that faculty teaching beliefs will correlate with different perceptions of the utility of ePortfolios, and, more precisely, teacher-centered beliefs will find less utility for ePortfolios than will learner- and learning-centered beliefs was also supported.

Student Learning

Table 3 shows responses from faculty from the open-ended question about the perceived utility of ePortfolios for improving student learning. Some faculty report that ePortfolios should be useful for helping students collect and showcase their learning, while some faculty anticipate the value of ePortfolios for helping students review, assess, and reflect upon their learning progress. More specifically, some faculty recognized the value that ePortfolios can be used to encourage

Table 3. Summary of faculty perceptions of ePortfolio impact on student learning

Collecting a student's work	Student responsibility for his own learning
Organizing learning	Building community
Showcasing academic learning	Encouraging students to use metacognitive skills
Integrating university coursework	Increasing use of multimedia
Integrating course projects as a coherent whole	Improving relationship between faculty and students
Integrating academic and non-academic work	Allowing students to work together
Communication between students and instructor	Providing model for future students
A more convenient, more accessible way of using paper-based portfolios	Identifying students' strengths and weaknesses
A greater variety of learning exhibits	Lifelong learning
Useful for review	Showcase for careers
Student self-assessment	Helping students consider a broader audience
Increasing student reflection	Peer assessment
Tracking learning growth	Don't see the value
Setting personal goals	

students to be self-regulated learners by being more responsible for their own learning, identifying their strengths and weaknesses, setting their own personal goals, monitoring their learning growth, and using metacognitive skills. Furthermore, some faculty stressed the social aspect of learning that can be enhanced by using ePortfolios because ePortfolios allow collaboration, consideration of a broader audience, building community, and improving the relationship between faculty and students. At the same time, there were faculties who see no learning value for using ePortfolios at all.

As the Tables 4 through 9 indicate that teacher-centered beliefs do not correlate well with perceptions of the positive utility of an ePortfolio for student learning, faculty use, and overall perceived challenges, as predicted, learner- and learning-centered beliefs tend to view ePortfolio potential more positively.

Specifically, teacher-centered beliefs correlate inversely with the value of documenting growth over time and sharing information across the term (Tables 4 and 5). Teacher-centered beliefs anticipate greater complexity of planning required

of ePortfolios and require training (Tables 5 and 6). Teacher-centered beliefs are likely to have no existing familiarity with ePortfolios (Table 8).

Learner-centered beliefs correlate positively and significantly with the value of tracking and supporting learning growth over time (Table 4), increased use of multimedia (Table 4), and the value of sharing information across a term (Table 5).

Learning-centered beliefs correlate with the value of documenting growth over time (Table 4), and sharing (Table 5) and even more significantly with building community (Table 4). Learning-centered beliefs are more likely to have familiarity with ePortfolios (Table 8) and are inversely correlated with perceived need for training (Table 7).

Finally, faculty members who are less familiar with ePortfolios are more likely to perceive high degrees of challenges in relation to the use of ePortfolios (Table 6).

Faculty Teaching

Faculty who hold learner-centered beliefs are more likely to see the value of using ePortfolios,

Table 4. Correlation between faculty teaching beliefs and the perceived potential impacts of ePortfolio use on student learning

Impact on Student Learning	Teacher-centered	Learner-centered	Learning-centered
Tracking learning growth	-.23	.31*	.21
Building community	.06	.03	.31*
Increasing use of multimedia	.04	.32*	.21

Note. *$p<.05$.

Table 5. Correlation between faculty teaching beliefs and the perceived potential impacts of ePortfolio use on faculty teaching

Impact on Faculty Teaching	Teacher-centered	Learner-centered	Learning-centered
Sharing knowledge across semester	-.13	.32*	.28
Making course planning more complex	-.30*	.20	.20

Note. *$p<.05$.

Table 6. Correlation between faculty teaching beliefs and the perceived potential challenges of ePortfolio use

	Teacher-centered	Learner-centered	Learning-centered
Perceived challenges	.02	.25	.03

Note. *$p<.05$.

because they believe that ePortfolios help them share knowledge across the semester. Teacher-centered faculty beliefs hold that the use of ePortfolios simplifies course planning (Table 5).

Perceived Challenges

Table 6 shows the relationship between faculty teaching beliefs and perceived challenges that they may face in using ePortfolios. Interestingly, faculty teaching beliefs do not appear to affect perceived challenges regarding ePortfolio use, suggesting that faculty recognize ePortfolio-related challenges regardless of their teaching beliefs.

Need for Support Systems

Teacher-centered faculty beliefs correlate with strong need for support in order for the faculty to value using ePortfolios, notable in contrast to inverse correlations in reported need for training for faculty who hold learner- and learning-centered beliefs.

Familiarity with ePortfolio

Learning-centered beliefs were positively correlated with faculty familiarity with ePortfolios, whereas teacher-centered beliefs were negatively related with ePortfolio familiarity.

Faculty with more knowledge of and familiarity with ePortfolios saw more value in using

Table 7. Correlation between faculty teaching beliefs and the need for support systems

Need for Support System	Teacher-centered	Learner-centered	Learning-centered
Support system "Training on the value"	.35*	-.05	-.14

Note. *p<.05.

Table 8. Correlation between faculty teaching beliefs and ePortfolio familiarity

Familiarity	Teacher-centered	Learner-centered	Learning-centered
ePortfolio familiarity	-.30**	.16	.37*

Note. *p<.05, **p<.01.

Table 9. Correlation between faculty familiarity with ePortfolios and their perceptions of ePortfolios

	ePortfolio Familiarity
Impact on Student Learning	.32*
Impact on Faculty Teaching	.35*
Perceived Challenges	-.41**

Note. *p<.05, **p<.01.

ePortfolios and perceived a lesser degree of challenges.

Finally, analysis revealed that there were no significant differences based on faculty rank, teaching experience, discipline, or gender.

IMPLICATIONS AND CONCLUSION

The key limitation of this study is familiar to survey research. It is reasonable to assume that the 30.6% response rate may reflect a potential response bias, and, in particular, a bias more likely to reflect teaching beliefs that are disproportionately learner- and learning-centered. That bias is further suggested by the finding that the majority of faculty who responded to this survey that represented a singular belief were teacher-centered. Furthermore, though teacher-centered faculties are less likely to be familiar with ePortfolios, they nonetheless responded to the survey.

It therefore seems reasonable to suppose that faculty not disposed to responding to an online survey about a new technology are even less likely to be familiar with ePortfolios and are even more likely to be teacher-centered. That conjecture, if true, has disconcerting implications, suggesting that a great majority of educators may be by disposition woefully unprepared for the expanding availability and use of Web 2.0 applications and social networking.

The validation of the instrument that recognizes individual faculty members are generally not singular in their beliefs, however, provides confirmation that a sophisticated understanding of the constellation of learning theories resists reduction. Learning is context dependent, and the fact that most faculty hold beliefs that are similarly protean is a valuable and useful attribute if teachers are to be responsive to the various and dynamic needs of their students. Though they may be unprepared now, there is evidence in this finding that, as the context of education continues to change, so, too, might one's beliefs and teaching practice. In that sense, the addition of the learning-centered construct in this study is particularly important. First, the open-source educational Web 2.0 environment requires new ways to think about teaching and learning. That thinking, as Trigwell's and Prosser's (1999) work confirms, is essential if teaching practice and student learning is to follow. Moreover, the finding that learning-centered beliefs correlate significantly with beliefs that value sharing over a term, learning growth over time, and the building of community is important to the Web 2.0 world and the new political context in which higher education is encountering increasing scrutiny. As Batson (2008) argues, "higher education for centuries has worked within a closed world where educators could design physical spaces and learning sequences (the curriculum) based on predictable circumstances." He adds, however, that in a Web 2.0 world, "we find ourselves talking about 'learning spaces' instead of 'classrooms.' With that noun shift, we've let the genie out of the lamp" (2008, pp. 3-4).

The finding that teacher-centered beliefs correlate inversely with the value of documenting growth over time and sharing knowledge across the term is particularly disconcerting in the context of the changing educational cyberscape. "Lifelong learning" is a ubiquitous and critical outcome routinely claimed in institutional mission statements as well as in most accreditors' requirements. Lifelong learning is, by definition, learning growth over time. Successful achievement of that outcome is contingent upon educational practices that promote learning beyond the silo of the single class, a requirement, further, that requires a community of educators *learning* in concert with accreditors and the employers who will hire graduates of educational programs. Moreover, students are increasingly enrolling in courses at multiple institutions (swirling) and stopping and resuming their education as life circumstances permit. Recognition and accommodation of the patterns of non-traditional learners and their various and individual learning goals is hardly well-served by traditional, teacher-centered practices that not only fail to recognize the new context of learning but even constrain students' preparation for emerging challenges.

At the core of the teaching-centered belief, however, is the critical finding that those beliefs are held by those who perceive a greater complexity and subsequent need for training and planning in order to use ePortfolios effectively. In that correlation is a clear implication that teacher-centered faculty or those who hold those beliefs, regardless of faculty rank, discipline, or gender, are themselves learners, unlike learning-centered faculty, who expect direct instruction not only in the technology but in the rationale for deploying innovation in new ways. It is probably not a coincidence that they are also less likely to be familiar with ePortfolios. No one has told them that ePortfolios and the new learning ecology they represent is something they need to be aware of and familiar with. This combination of findings of faculty who are unfamiliar or reluctant to use ePortfolios because of barriers and the limited numbers of those who possessed both the learner- and learning- centered beliefs associated with the effective deployment of ePortfolios underscores the need for creative leadership in finding ways to provide faculty with encouragement and support for recognizing and responding to the challenges of the new context in which education now finds itself. Adopting and effectively implementing learner- and learning-centered ePortfolios, personal learning environments, and other Web 2.0 applications is one strategy for fulfilling institutional goals of improving the richness of the undergraduate experience. But it will require building a new community of learners—students, faculty, administration, and accreditors—if education is to promote and sustain a learning and assessment culture that engages students with the generative, authentic learning opportunities the world of Web 2.0 requires.

REFERENCES

Ajzen, I. (1985). From intentions to actions: A theory of planned behavior. In Kuhl, J., & Beckmann, J. (Eds.), *Action control: From cognition to behavior* (pp. 11–39). Berlin, Germany: Springer-Verlag. doi:10.1007/978-3-642-69746-3_2

Batson, T. (2008). Is Web 2.0 designed for education? In *Campus Technology.* Retrieved. March 5, 2008, from http://www.campustechnology.com/article.aspx?aid=59341

Brookfield, S. (1995). *Becoming a critically reflective teacher.* San Francisco, CA: Jossey Bass.

Bruffee, K. A. (1995). Sharing our toys: Cooperative learning versus collaborative learning. *Change, 27*(1), 12–18. doi:10.1080/00091383.1995.9937722

Danielson, C. (1996). *Enhancing professional practice: A framework for teaching.* Alexandria, VA: Association for Supervision and Curriculum.

Downes, S. (2006). Learning networks and connective knowledge (Discussion Paper No. 92). In *Proceedings of the Instructional Technology Forum.* Retrieved March 5, 2008, from http://it.coe.uga.edu/itforum/paper92/paper92.html

Fosnot, C. T. (1996). Constructivism: A psychological theory of learning. In Fosnot, C. T. (Ed.), *Constructivism: Theory, perspectives, and practice* (pp. 8–33). New York, NY: Teacher College Press.

Grush, M. (2008). The future of Web 2.0. In *Campus Technology.* Retrieved February 27, 2008, from http://www.campustechnology.com/articles/58872_1/

Haney, J. J., & McArthur, J. (2002). Four case studies of prospective science teachers' beliefs concerning constructivist teaching practice. *Science Education, 86*(6), 783–802. doi:10.1002/sce.10038

Hargadon, S. (2008). *Web 2.0 is the future of education.* Retrieved March 4, 2008, from http://www.stevehargadon.com/2008/03/web-20-is-future-of-education.html

Jackson, B. (2003). Education reform as if student agency mattered academic microcultures and student identity. *Phi Delta Kappan, •••,* 84.

Kane, R., Sandretto, S., & Heath, C. (2002). Telling half the story: A critical review of research on the teaching beliefs of university academics. *Review of Educational Research, 72*(2), 177–228. doi:10.3102/00346543072002177

Lave, J., & Wenger, E. (1991). *Situated learning: Legitimate peripheral participation.* Cambridge, UK: Cambridge University Press.

Pajares, M. F. (1992). Teachers' beliefs and educational research: Cleaning up a messy construct. *Review of Educational Research, 62,* 307–332.

Pruyn, M. (1996). *The social construction of critical student agency in one adult literacy classroom* (Unpublished doctoral dissertation). University of California Los Angeles, Los Angeles, CA.

Richardson, V. (1996). The role of attitudes and beliefs in learning to teach. In Sikula, J. (Ed.), *Handbook of research on teacher education* (pp. 102–119). New York, NY: Macmillan.

Siemens, G. (2004). *Connectivism: A learning theory for the digital age.* Retrieved March 4, 2008, from http://www.elearnspace.org/Articles/connectivism.htm

Trigwell, K., & Prosser, M. (1999). Relations between teachers' approaches to teaching and students' approaches to learning. *Higher Education, 37*(1). doi:10.1023/A:1003548313194

Trigwell, K., & Prosser, M. (2004). Development and use of the approaches to teaching inventory. *Educational Psychology Review, 16*(4).

Chapter 14
Ideal Design and Content of Support Systems for Electronic Teaching Portfolios

Royce Robertson
Walden University, USA

ABSTRACT

It is in the best interest of the institution to design a predictable, sustainable system for improving faculty technology skills in pursuit of creating defensible electronic teaching portfolios for use in the tenure and promotion process. This chapter aims to define the electronic teaching portfolio and describe some conditions to satisfy before implementing a support system. Furthermore, the chapter describes the design and content of an ideal support system that is feasible to implement given that the institution is willing to commit necessary resources.

INTRODUCTION

As technology permeates every aspect of higher education (Goodyear, 1998; Green, 1994, 1997, 2003; NCES, 1997; Otieno, 2001), institutions will need to prepare for its integration into even the most sacred of rituals: promotion and tenure. Administration, campus offices, and faculty groups will need to assess the technological and cultural landscapes (Strudler, 2002) of the institution in order to design systems to support faculty members desiring to create electronic portfolios used for promotion and tenure (Johnson, 2003). These Electronic Teaching Portfolios can take many creative and innovative forms (Barrett, 2004; Seldin, 1997); however, their creation can extend the capacity of the typical repertoire of information technology support (Tomes & Higgison, 1998; Starrett, 2004). It is in the best interest of the institution to design a predictable, sustainable system

DOI: 10.4018/978-1-4666-0143-7.ch014

(Hartman & Truman-Davis, 2001; Strudler, 2002; Wetzel & Strudler, 2005) for improving faculty technology skills in pursuit of creating defensible Electronic Teaching Portfolios (Arreola, 1995). This chapter aims to define the Electronic Teaching Portfolio and to describe some conditions to satisfy before implementing a support system. Furthermore, the chapter describes the design and content of an ideal support system that is feasible to implement, given that the institution is willing to commit necessary resources.

BACKGROUND INFORMATION

ETP Definition

The definition of the Electronic Teaching Portfolio is based on Seldin's (1997, p. 2) definition as a "factual description of a professor's teaching strengths and accomplishments, which collectively suggests the scope and quality of the professor's teaching performance." The following core principles should be used to assist faculty in the development of an Electronic Teaching Portfolio:

1. There should not be one specified template for all faculty members to use; however, there should be learning materials and consultation available to assist faculty in designing a structure for the Electronic Teaching Portfolio that is consistent with the institution's policies and general best practices (AACTE, 1992; Carnegie Foundation, 1989; Moses, 1986; Soder, 1990).
2. A list of potential artifacts (Table 1) for scholarship, teaching, and service should be provided to all participants, and learning materials should be developed illustrating how such artifacts could be achieved technologically (Arreola, 1995; Avalos, 2004; Braskamp, & Ory, 2002; Edgerton, Hutchings, & Quinlan, 1991; Eisen, 1996; O'Neil & Wright, 1993; Rodriguez-Farrar,

1995; Seldin, 1993, 1995, 2000; Shore et al., 1986; Tucker, 1996; United States Department of Education, 2002; University of Western Australia, 2003; Zubizarreta, 1994; Zubizarreta, 2004).

3. A custom electronic portfolio system should be used, as opposed to a common system (Barrett, 2004). Faculty members should be encouraged to develop public web pages for general information and to place personal and professional information within secure password-protected and/or invitation-only systems.
4. The Electronic Teaching Portfolio should be meant to support and extend the existing promotion and tenure documentation at the institution, not to duplicate it.
5. In an ideal environment, individual Electronic Teaching Portfolios should be compiled and used as artifacts in department and institutional portfolios. The ideal conceptual framework for the development of an Electronic Teaching Portfolio at the institution should bear similarity to Love, McKean, and Gathercoal's (2004) maturity model for eportfolio development. This type of developmental model is reflective of more growth-oriented, teaching-centered promotion and tenure systems.

Program Rationale

The rationale for an electronic teaching portfolio as part of the tenure and promotion process is as follows:

1. There are a significant number of tenure-track faculty members at the institution that will require a tenure decision in the next five to six years. A system must be developed for those faculty members to learn about the institution and its tenure policies and processes and to be exposed to a system that assists in their technological development as

well as their development in documenting their own work.

2. If faculty retirement trends mirror the number of faculty seeking tenure, there will need to be accommodations for membership changes. With tenure being a five to six year process, some tenure track faculty members may be required to alter their review committee membership based on retirements and turnover. There needs to be a venue for retiring faculty to provide feedback that can be transferred to the tenure candidate and new committee members assuming the vacated positions.

3. If there is currently no system within the institution for harvesting the collective knowledge and accomplishment of the faculty body as a whole, then one should be considered. An Electronic Teaching Portfolio system would be the foundation for a system that is designed to illustrate collective teaching excellence as a matter of institutional accomplishment, accreditation, and the public trust.

Assumptions

In order to have faculty members successfully build Electronic Teaching Portfolios (ETP) for promotion and tenure, there should be three distinct themes for the Electronic Teaching Portfolio support system:

1. Materials and resources should be available for faculty to study and learn at their own pace through multiple modes of delivery.

2. Technology skill development and Electronic Teaching Portfolio development should not be treated as mutually exclusive concepts; there are many shared skills.

3. Veteran, tenured faculty members should be willing to serve as mentors, assisting with the reflection and self-study consistent with the first six years of the professoriate (Acker,

2003; Ovington, Diamantes, Roby, & Ryan, 2003).

The development of this program should connect to the institutional mission in the following ways:

1. If the institution values excellence in teaching and scholarship as a creative endeavor, then it should embrace the notion that the development of an Electronic Teaching Portfolio is a creative and technologically progressive method of documenting such excellence.

2. If the institution has a vision of student-centered teaching where learners are engaged in preparation for gratifying careers, then the expansion of this paradigm to include faculty members as learners enables the Electronic Teaching Portfolio to be a conduit for organizing and communicating that growth.

Program Goals

The goals of the support system should be as follows:

1. The support system should be designed to assist faculty members in the development of an Electronic Teaching Portfolio that is defensible for both content and design.

2. The support system should be designed to teach faculty members the technological skills necessary to develop an Electronic Teaching Portfolio; therefore, the faculty member will acquire technological skills that can be transferred to other areas of the professoriate.

3. The support system should be designed to assist faculty members in understanding and applying skills involved in portfolio assessment, which include identifying relevant artifacts (Table 1), establishing content

and design, and providing a platform for reflection.

4. The support system should be designed to supplement, not supplant, the existing promotion and tenure process at the institution.

Audience Considerations

The Electronic Teaching Portfolio review process should be multi-faceted and developmental in nature. Overall, there are three audiences that will provide annual feedback to the faculty member. At the highest level, institutional administration, including the President, Vice Presidents, Provosts, Deans, and other administrators may have access to the Electronic Teaching Portfolio, providing feedback necessary to the development of the faculty member. Departmentally, a promotion and tenure committee should exist to review the faculty member's portfolio for content and design and provide feedback on developmental

progress, identifying specific and global areas of accomplishment and growth. In accordance with the institution's promotion and tenure recommendations, in cases where tenured faculty members are not available, other faculty members may be solicited for participation on the committee in order to provide feedback on the nature of the faculty member's artifacts. Finally, the individual, through personal assessment and reflection, becomes an audience of one's self (Barrett, 2000; Centra, 1979; Zubizarreta, 2004). An integration of administrative feedback, student evaluation results, the institutionally-defined promotion and tenure committee, all other artifacts, and the reflection of the individual provide a platform for the individual to establish and chart growth. Also, a rubric should be developed and used as the primary assessment instrument in the process (American Association of State Colleges and Universities, 1999; Dyrud, 2000; Seldin, 1997).

Table 1. Example artifacts for teaching, scholarship, and service

Teaching	Scholarship	Service
• teaching philosophy, including the individual's aims, objectives, and classroom practices • description of the faculty member's teaching load • undergraduate and graduate course syllabi • samples of feedback from peers and supervisors • summations of student evaluations • samples of teacher-made instructional materials and assessments • samples of student work evaluated by the faculty member • examples of technology integration • descriptions of independent studies, supervised research, or supervised teaching • awards and distinctions of teaching excellence • directorship or membership on graduate committees • laboratory directorships • advisory roles • evolutions of their teaching approach • reflection through introspection, self-assessment, and self evaluation	• authoring articles, books, and chapters of books and journals • lead or associate editorship of books and national or state journals • manuscript and book reviewer roles for major publishers • papers and speeches, including presentations and speeches for national, state, and local conferences and meetings • outreach to other institutions of higher education and public elementary and high schools • authorship and administration of research grants • rejected submissions or applications	• consultation with institutional partners and stakeholders • chairing or being a member of university, school or college, or area or program committees • chairing or participating in faculty search committees • being a member of the faculty senate • professional participation, especially in international or national organizations • acting as an elected officer on a regional or national committee • workshops, including organizing, teaching, attending or evaluating them as an artifact of service • consultation including workshop delivery, program design, or program evaluation

PROGRAM DESIGN

The following program design is based on existing literature, institutional documents, survey of tenured and untenured faculty, external surveys to educational technology and promotion and tenure experts, and interviews of potential participants. Four revision cycles produced the following program design, which is included in the dissertation: *Institutional Support Systems Necessary for Teacher Education Unit Faculty Members to Create Electronic Portfolios for Promotion and Tenure* (Robertson, 2006).

Software Considerations

The electronic portfolio software should possess the following characteristics:

1. The tool should be a custom electronic portfolio. This allows for the systemic benefits of a database system, including document security, permission-based access, cataloged organization of files, and date- and time-stamped reflections.
2. The tool should also include common tool qualities such as web page construction and public web page display.
3. The tool should support multiple file types for sound, video, text, images, and other common file types that could be used as artifacts. This should include the ability to attach, embed, or link to other media.
4. The tool should have a reflection component that is functionally similar to an electronic journal where writings could be attached to portfolio categories, attached artifacts, or associated with comments provided in the feedback of the portfolio.
5. The tool should have assessment instruments, such as checklists and rubrics, built into the system, allowing unit faculty and reviewers to score the completed work within the portfolio itself.

6. Portfolio owners should have the ability to create multiple portfolios, connect multiple artifacts to multiple portfolios, and use multiples rubrics to assess multiple areas of each portfolio.
7. The tool should possess technological underpinnings that are universally-applicable, borne of modern programming standards, and conform to the highest security and data integrity standards.

Support, Integration, and Sustainability

In order for this type of initiative to succeed and have an impact on new generations of faculty members, various campus offices will need to be collectively responsible for various aspects of the Electronic Teaching Portfolio.

Academic Affairs Office, specifically, the Provost: should be responsible for directing the development of the program in the arenas of promotion and tenure policies (in conjunction with faculty senates and subcommittees), promotion and tenure decisions, budgets for software contracts and Electronic Teaching Portfolio Consultants.

Institution Faculty Support (Teaching Centers): should be responsible for offering opportunities to develop the reflective and pedagogical skills of the participant faculty.

Information Technology Services (ITS) Department: in concert with the Electronic Teaching Portfolio Consultants and the Teaching Center staff, should be responsible for teaching the skills necessary to document, digitize, and develop many of the technology-based artifacts.

Electronic Teaching Portfolio Consultants: in concert with the Information Technology Services Department and Teaching Center staff, should be responsible for teaching the mechanics of the electronic portfolio system and illustrating connections between technology, pedagogy, and the promotion and tenure process.

Faculty Members: should be responsible for designing the Electronic Teaching Portfolio, developing its content and design, documenting their work using technology, displaying their work in a cohesive manner, and reflecting on aspects of their work.

Department Chair: should be responsible for overseeing the work of the proposed promotion and tenure committee, consulting with all parties involved, and providing constructive feedback to the faculty member.

Software vendor: should be responsible for providing documentation of the product, ensuring continuous server uptime, and communicating with the institutional contacts regarding all changes and alterations to the system.

Reviewers: including but not limited to the promotion and tenure committee, should be responsible for guiding the unit faculty through the promotion and tenure process as well as providing both global and specific feedback relating to the triad of teaching, scholarship, and service.

ETP Work Group: should serve as a conduit for new faculty members to connect with support personnel and develop relationships. Partnering departments should identify appropriate representatives to participate in the ETP Work Group. Those representatives should meet regularly to identify efficiencies and overlaps with other campus processes, organize human and technological resources, deliver and evaluate results of self-assessments to faculty members, design learning plans for faculty members, communicate with faculty members and the institution in general, and plan and deliver workshop sessions.

ETP Support Directory: intended to connect portfolio owners with institution staff mem-

bers or other faculty members who possess specific knowledge and skills in the area of the ETP or the promotion and tenure process.

Policy Revisions

Prior to implementation, the following institutional tasks should be accomplished. These tasks are based on the writing of Carole Barone and the National Learning Infrastructure Initiative (2001), and represent the institutional transformation that should occur for a support system of this magnitude to be successful:

1. Gaining the support of administrative bodies, including the President's Cabinet, would illustrate the courage and commitment to developing faculty members who can document their teaching performance substantively, technologically, and reflectively.

2. Policies and by-laws at the institutional and departmental level would need to be amended to consistently reflect the context and culture of this new generation of documenting performance for tenure-track faculty members. Currently, many policies are specific to paper-based systems.

3. Financial resources would need to be allocated for equipment, time, subscriptions, and incentive to be part of this new community of academicians cooperating creatively with each other to pioneer this program.

4. Instructional materials and a sample portfolio, potentially known as the "electronic portfolio curriculum," will need to be developed. This curriculum will need to address the potential capacity of the support system and use creative delivery methods to communicate core knowledge and skills to the participants.

5. A promotion and tenure rubric will need to be constructed, added to the portfolio contents, and used as a vehicle of providing consistent feedback amongst and between

reviewers. This rubric would ideally be developed for implementation by a subcommittee of the faculty senate in conjunction with the Academic Affairs Office, Deans and Department Chairs, and the academic department's proposed or existing promotion and tenure committees.

6. A list of potential artifacts that address teaching, scholarship, and service should be compiled and presented. The list should be presented to the proper faculty committees for endorsement.

Eligibility

Assuming the faculty member joins the institution as a new faculty member with less than three prior years of transfer toward tenure or promotion, the following Electronic Teaching Portfolio program would be available to them.

To adequately accommodate the current faculty demographic, the following program considerations should be made:

1. The program is voluntary; however, financial and technological incentives should be offered to faculty, mentors, and other support specialists.
2. New faculty who are untenured should be offered first opportunity to participate. Based on turnover estimations for the subsequent six years, the support system could be scaled according to those estimates (given all new faculty who could participate).
3. Given a six-year promotion and tenure cycle, two-year cohort groups could be used for new faculty members. For example, if the support system launched in the fall of 2007, then all new faculty members in the 2007-2008 and 2008-2009 academic years would be part of Cohort 1. This staggering of cohorts and years would allow Cohort 1 Year 1 faculty members to share experiences

and technological skills with others in Cohort 1 Year 2 and so on. The program should be designed to emphasize, but not be solely limited to, connections between Year 1 and 2, 3 and 4, and 5 and 6 of the first six years of the professoriate.

4. An external incentive should be added to a process that already has significant intrinsic incentives. A number of one-time bonuses (of varying dollar amounts based on the estimated enrollment) could be awarded to the faculty members who complete all workshop sessions (or show equivalent competence), build an ETP, and commit ten hours to helping other new faculty members to learn the software and the promotion and tenure process.

Conceptual Stages and Timeline

Three types of years exist in this program. Technological skill development, reflection on teaching, and peer review occur in all years.

Designing Years: characterized by new learning, mapping, and planning the components of the Electronic Teaching Portfolio. Year 1 is a designing year.

Developing Years: characterized by application of learning and construction of many of the artifacts and templates that will house the artifacts with the Electronic Teaching Portfolio. Years 2, 3, 4, and 5 are developing years.

Displaying Years: characterized by demonstration of learning, fine-tuning and organizing, and preparing the Electronic Teaching Portfolio for its fullest scrutiny. Year 6 is a displaying year.

The first year of a given faculty cohort should engage in the following tasks that are consistent with a designing year.

All content and learning materials should be provided in a central electronic location, perhaps the institutional course management system (i.e., Blackboard). Faculty could also be given the book, *Balancing Acts: The Scholarship of Teaching and Learning in Academic Careers*. In the first year as a faculty member, faculty members should be expected to use the materials to learn about the institutional people and processes with less emphasis on technological skills. These learning modules will include:

- Institutional Mission
- Faculty Demographics and Responsibilities
- The Characterization of The Teaching Scholar
- Promotion and Tenure Policies
- Understanding the Promotion and Tenure Rubric
- Role and Function of the Council of Teacher Education
- Documenting Faculty Performance with Artifacts
- Elements of Reflection
- Using the Electronic Portfolio to Weave a Tapestry of Excellence and Growth
- Electronic Teaching Portfolio Design Components

Note: All of these modules would be available for the faculty members to study and learn at their own pace as soon as all Human Resources employment requirements are satisfied. Faculty members should be involved in a minimum of three mandatory face-to-face meetings during the first year.

The first and second meetings are with their promotion and tenure committee and the Chair of their department, respectively. The purpose of these meetings would be to discuss the promotion and tenure processes and to align expectations between the individual, administration (Deans or Chairs), and the Committee.

The third meeting would be with an Electronic Teaching Portfolio consultant who would assist the new faculty member in planning the Electronic Teaching Portfolio. At this time, the faculty member should also complete a technology skill survey, comparable (but not identical) to the Mankato Scale Survey or the Bellingham Public Schools derivation. Using such a skill-based assessment will enhance the Electronic Teaching Portfolio consultant's ability to create a program that minimizes redundancy of learning, maximizes time commitment, and provides solid overlap with any institutional plans for faculty technology skill development programming.

Two specific areas of importance should be addressed: initial design ideas for the Electronic Teaching Portfolio and the types of technology that could be used to document teaching performance. For example, the faculty member may want to videotape himself or herself teaching a specific concept or method in chemistry or audiotape a voice lesson with future music educators. The purpose of the activities in the first year is to document and design; therefore, the actual footage may not be digitized or edited until future years.

As with each year of the cohort cycle, it is highly recommended that the faculty member will also be engaged in reflection. The expectation could be that the faculty member would write specifically about the teaching performances that were documented technologically and also write frequently about what he or she is experiencing as a new faculty member engaging in teaching, scholarship, and service. This process could be stimulated by having the faculty member engage in and write about participation in, for example, a Reflective Practice group, which already exists at many institutions that have teaching centers.

Faculty members should receive feedback via face-to-face meetings and the Electronic Teaching Portfolio. At many institutions, a document resembling an annual faculty report is the vehicle for faculty to report teaching, scholarship, and service accomplishments to the Chair, Dean, Provost, and other administrators. Ideally, feedback from the annual report is distilled into an annual reappointment letter from some member of the administration, highlighting student evaluation feedback and the contents of the annual report. For better or worse, the annual report document and the annual reappointment letters rarely reference each other between and across multiple years. Without quality content, thoughtful design, and reflection weaving and connecting one annual report to another, there is little opportunity for a faculty member to demonstrate proficiency as a continuous process. In the worst case scenario, multiple annual reports and annual appointment letters are self-contained and unrelated to previous and future iterations. Ideally, the annual report would be translated into Electronic Teaching Portfolio "objects" in a manner that catalogs the work of the faculty member over time in a cohesive, interwoven display of organized artifacts connected by reflective writings.

Throughout the course of the first year and every subsequent year, there should also be regularly scheduled Electronic Teaching Portfolio support sessions provided for faculty members and their cohorts to learn skills specific to the electronic portfolio tools. The documentation necessary to learn these skills should also be provided in the centralized, online venue described in the previous section. The topics for the sessions could include:

- Logging Onto the ETP System
- Changing Account Settings and Information
- Adding New Reviewers
- Creating New Portfolios at the Individual and Course Level
- Adding Portfolio Sections
- Uploading Artifacts
- Linking to Online Artifacts
- Translating the Annual Faculty Report into ETP Objects
- Nesting Multiple Artifacts as an Object
- Converting Documents to PDF and HTML

- Using Portfolio Scoring Tools
- Adding Reflections

Note: This documentation should be built and provided through a partnership with the Electronic Teaching Portfolio Consultants, the vendor, and the Information Technology Services Department. The technology skill development tutorials designed for the third through fifth years should also be offered annually in various formats.

The second year of a given faculty cohort, a developing year, should engage in the following tasks. First, the major purpose of the second year is to continue the design process. The notion of design, in this instance, includes designing the Electronic Teaching Portfolio and documenting the design of the faculty member's courses and general outlook toward his or her practice. The design of the Electronic Teaching Portfolio, through scheduled meetings with the Electronic Teaching Portfolio consultant and his or her mentor, should be articulated using concept maps, flowcharts, and other graphical organizers to visually describe the organization of the electronic portfolio.

Second, faculty members should continue to receive informal feedback from committee members. Ideally, this feedback would be provided after the end of the second year. The feedback should be framed according to the promotion and tenure Electronic Teaching Portfolio rubric, which should be developed by the institution. Considering that the review process should be as consistent as possible, the following list of sessions should be added for ETP Reviewers to learn the mechanics of reviewing:

- Logging Onto the ETP System as a Reviewer
- The Committee Member
- Managing Portfolios
- Navigating Portfolios
- Assessing the Portfolio

Third, faculty members should continue to practice the act of reflection, writing about their development in the areas of teaching, scholarship, and service. Through consultation with the mentor and the committee, the faculty member should begin to define and write a teaching philosophy or professional statement. This document should be originally crafted in Microsoft Word; however, it would be converted to HTML or PDF as part of the technology skill development component of the program. Reflective methods may also be exercised through personal journaling in the reflection component of the electronic portfolio software, by engaging in and writing about participation in, for example, a Reflective Practice group, or by working with new faculty members who are in different cohorts. The campus teaching (faculty support) center should work in conjunction with the Electronic Teaching Portfolio consultant to deliver faculty development sessions designed to introduce new unit faculty to the electronic portfolio system while providing veteran unit faculty with a platform for reflection.

Finally, the second year serves as the beginning of a rotation of technology skills development focusing on faculty productivity and continuing the practice of documenting teaching practice.

To support the faculty member's individually-paced learning, the following learning objects should be created for use during the second year and beyond:

- Analyzing Student Evaluation Comments Using Technology
- Importing and Editing Digital Video
- Exporting and Displaying Digital Video
- Converting Documents to HTML and PDF
- Inserting Comments into Microsoft Office Documents
- Using Inspiration and Microsoft Word to Make Graphical Organizers
- Visualizing and Articulating Electronic Portfolio Design

- Building an Electronic Portfolio from a Conceptual Design
- Writing a Teaching Philosophy or Professional Statement

Note: The faculty member should again complete the Mankato-Bellingham Skill Survey in order to measure technological skill development and prioritize technology skill development needs for the third year.

The third, fourth, and fifth years of a given faculty cohort are developing years. The faculty member should engage in the following tasks, extending the activities of the second year that will now be spread out over a three-year period. First, the faculty member should again complete the Mankato-Bellingham Skill Survey in order to measure technological skill improvements and prioritize technology skill development needs for the three-year period. This survey, in combination with personal consultation, should be used to create an individualized three-year technology skill development program for the faculty member. All instructional resources from previous years will be available to the faculty member, as well as new instructional materials focusing on the development of the Electronic Teaching Portfolio.

Second, technology skill development during this three-year period should reflect the development, construction, and organization of the content and design of the Electronic Teaching Portfolio.

All previous instructional materials should be provided and reused. However, the following new instructional materials would be developed for the third through fifth year participants:

- Analyzing and Publishing Long Term Trends in Student Evaluations Using Technology
- Segmenting Multiple Digital Videos to Illustrate Trends in Teaching
- Enhancing Digital Video with Inserted Comments

- Using Digital Audio and Photos to Illustrate Teaching Performance
- Organizing and Cataloging Multiple HTML and PDF Documents
- Using Graphical Organizers to Illustrate Professional Trends
- Developing a Cohesive Electronic Portfolio
- Adding Multiple Artifacts to the Portfolio
- Reflecting on and Revising a Teaching Philosophy or Professional Statement

Third, during the three years of development, reflection is focused on group interactions and identifying changes in practice. The three years of developing could include mentoring of new faculty. New faculty member cohorts should have the opportunity to receive feedback and listen to the struggles and successes of experienced cohorts of this program. Designed according to the protocols of Reflective Practice, this process is beneficial for the new cohorts in learning the process of developing an Electronic Teaching Portfolio as well as allowing the experienced cohort to reflect on ways to devise improvements for the Electronic Teaching Portfolio and the support system in general.

Fourth, the faculty member will engage in many hours of construction of the Electronic Teaching Portfolio. This will include uploading and organizing artifacts in conjunction with the annual reports and appointment letters, creating new sections of the portfolio design to reflect changes in teaching behavior, connecting artifacts and objects through previous reflections, making design decisions related to the look and feel of the portfolio, annually self-rating the portfolio using the institutional rubric, and inviting reviewers to provide input using narrative and rubric-based feedback.

The sixth year of a given faculty cohort, a displaying year, should engage in the following tasks. First, as construction of the portfolio design is completed and content is added, the faculty member would prepare for displaying the portfolio. The schedule of meetings to display the portfolio and how feedback is received from the promotion and tenure committee would correspond to the normal schedule for promotion and tenure defense process at the institution. Secondly, the notion of reflection and feedback would be facilitated through the use of an institutionally-defined promotion and tenure rubric. Reviewers would be invited to comment on the portfolio for a final visit before the portfolio is defended and the promotion and tenure committee renders a decision. Prior to completion of the program, the faculty member would complete a final survey including added questions about the services provided in the support system.

The Display Interview

The evaluation of the Electronic Teaching Portfolio should be culminated with an interview of the candidate, using the ETP as one component to illustrate fitness for promotion and/or tenure. The quality of the responses would be measured according to the ETP rubric. The following questions could be asked:

1. Describe the process you used to develop this ETP.
2. What did you intentionally and unintentionally learn about yourself through this process?
3. What is your approach of the professoriate and how is it illustrated in the ETP?
4. How do you demonstrate excellence in teaching, and how is it illustrated in the ETP?
5. How do you demonstrate scholarship, and how is it illustrated in the ETP?
6. How do you demonstrate service, and how is it illustrated in the ETP?
7. How does your work connect to the overall mission of the department and institution?
8. Describe and evaluate the technological process you employed to create this ETP.

9. What other commitments support your growth as a teaching scholar?

10. How do your current commitments relate to your future commitments as a faculty member?

Program Evaluation

This type of systemic institutional change will require an evaluation model that performs three functions.

1. It must illuminate the impact of the Electronic Teaching Portfolio on the promotion and tenure process at the institution.

2. The evaluation must also provide the institution with feedback on the impact of the support system.

3. The evaluation must also provide insight into the improvement of faculty technology skills as a result of participating in the program design

Considering the design of the program, a holistic approach is necessary to extract the practices and dispositions of the faculty and support providers. The ideal approach would involve participant-oriented elements with influence from the expertise-oriented elements, including interviews, surveys, and observations by laypersons and specialists. Since objective benchmarks will not be created to measure the success of the programs, it is ultimately important to observe what is occurring with the faculty who participate in the program, inquire as to what issues are evolving regarding support, and begin to explain the phenomena that are influencing the next evolution of the program. It would also benefit the program and stakeholders if an external expert in Electronic Teaching Portfolio programs observed the operations of the program in an ad hoc individual manner in order to add dimension to the evaluation.

REFERENCES

Acker, S. (2003). Overcoming obstacles to authentic eportfolio assessment. *Campus Technology.* Retrieved January 23, 2005, from http://www.campus-technology.com/print.asp?ID=10788

American Association of Colleges of Teacher Education. (1992). *RATE V. Teaching teachers: Facts and figures.* Washington, DC: American Association of Colleges of Teacher Education.

American Association of State Colleges and Universities. (1999). *Facing change: building faculty of the future.* Washington, DC: American Association of State Colleges and Universities.

Arreola, R. (1995). *Developing a comprehensive faculty evaluation system: A guidebook for college faculty and administrators on designing and operating a comprehensive faculty evaluation system.* Bolton, MA: Anker.

Avalos, M. (2004). *Promotion and tenure portfolios.* Phoenix, AZ: Office of Research and Faculty Development, Arizona State University – West Campus.

Barone, C. (2001). Conditions for transformation: Infrastructure is not the issue. *EDUCAUSE Review, 2001,* 40–47.

Barrett, H. (2004). *Electronic portfolio handbook* (4th ed.). Retrieved January 23, 2005, from http://www.electronicportfolios.com/handbook/index.html

Carnegie Foundation. (1989). *The condition of the professoriate: Attitudes and trends, 1989.* Princeton, NJ: Author.

Edgerton, R., Hutchings, P., & Quinlan, K. (1991). *The teaching portfolio: Capturing the scholarship in teaching.* Washington, DC: American Association of Higher Education.

Eisen, J. (1996). *Creating a teaching portfolio: The SCRIPT model.* Tampa, FL: Center for Teaching Enhancement, University of South Florida.

Goodyear, P. (1998). New technology in higher education: Understanding the innovation process. In *Proceedings of the Integrating Information and Communication Technology in Higher Education (BITE) Meeting,* Maastricht, The Netherlands. Retrieved January 23, 2005, from http://www. lancs.ac.uk/staff/erapmg

Green, C. (1994). *Campus computing report.* Encino, CA: EDUCAUSE. Retrieved January 23, 2005, from http://www.campuscomputing. net/pdf/1994-CCP.pdf

Green, C. (1997). *Campus computing report.* Encino, CA: EDUCAUSE. Retrieved January 23, 2005, from http://www.campuscomputing. net/pdf/1997-CCP.pdf

Green, C. (2003). *Campus computing report.* Encino, CA: EDUCAUSE. Retrieved January 23, 2005, from http://www.campuscomputing. net/pdf/2003-CCP.pdf

Johnson, D. (2003). A planning and assessment model for developing effective CMS support. *Online Journal of Distance Learning Administration, 7*(1), 1–9.

Katz, R. (1999). Competitive strategies for higher education in the information age. In R. Katz (Ed.), *Dancing with the Devil: Information technology and the new competition in higher education.* San Francisco, CA: Jossey-Bass.

Moses, I. (1986). Promotion of academic staff: Reward and incentive. *Higher Education, 15*(1-2), 135–149. doi:10.1007/BF00138097

National Center for Educational Statistics. (1997). *United States Department of Education.* Retrieved on January 12, 2005, from http://nces.ed.gov

O'Neil, M., & Wright, W. (1993). *Recording teaching accomplishment: A Dalhousie guide to the teaching dossier.* Halifax, NS: Office of Instructional Development and Technology, Dalhousie University.

Otieno, D. (2001). *Faculty perceptions of the impact of information technology on tenure and promotion decisions at technologically advanced institutions of higher education: Comparing perceptions of faculty at a teaching university to those of faculty at a research University in the state of New Jersey* (Unpublished doctoral dissertation). New Jersey Institute of Technology, Newark, NJ.

Ovington, J., Diamantes, T., Roby, D., & Ryan, C. (2003). An analysis of prevailing myths regarding tenure and promotion. *Education, 123*(3), 635–637.

Robertson, R. (2006). *Institutional support systems necessary for teacher education unit faculty members to create electronic portfolios for promotion and tenure* (Unpublished doctoral dissertation). Argosy University, Sarasota, FL.

Rodriguez-Farrar, H. (1995). *Teaching portfolio handbook.* Providence, RI: Center for the Advancement of College Teaching, Brown University.

Seldin, P. (1993). *Successful use of teaching portfolios.* Bolton, MA: Anker.

Seldin, P. (1997). *The teaching portfolio: A practical guide to improved performance and promotion/tenure decisions.* Bolton, MA: Anker.

Seldin, P. (2000). Teaching portfolio's: A positive appraisal. *Academe, 86*(1), 36–44. doi:10.2307/40252334

Shore, M., et al. (1986). *The teaching dossier.* Montreal, QC, Canada: Canadian Association of University Teachers.

Soder, R. (1990). The rhetoric of teacher professionalization. In J. I. Goodlad, R. Soder, & K. A. Sirotnik (Eds.), *The moral dimension of teaching* (pp. 35–86). San Francisco, CA: Jossey-Bass.

Starett, D. (2004). Reward and conquer. *Campus Technology, 1*(1), 42–46.

Strudler, N. (2002). *Faculty development.* Retrieved April 4, 2005, from http://www.pt3.org/stories/faculty.html

Tomes, N., & Higgison, C. (1998). *Exploiting the network for teaching and learning in Scottish higher education: Teaching and learning in the Scottish metropolitan area networks.* Edinburg, UK: Scottish Higher Education Funding Council.

Tucker, A. (1996). *Chairing the academic department: Leadership among peers.* New York, NY: Greenwood.

United States Department of Education. (2002). *E-portfolios: Kick it up a notch, taking professional portfolios from black-and-white to 3D color.* Retrieved April 4, 2005, from http://www.pt3.org/stories/eportfolio.html

University of Western Australia. (2003). *Guidelines for preparing a teaching portfolio.* Crawley, WA, Australia: Evaluation and Teaching Unit.

Wetzel, K., & Strudler, N. (2005). The diffusion of electronic portfolios in teacher education: Next steps and recommendations for accomplished users. *Journal of Research on Technology in Education, 38*(2), 231–243.

Zubizarreta, J. (1994). Teaching portfolios and the beginning teacher. *Phi Delta Kappan, 76*(4), 323–326.

Chapter 15
Challenges and Opportunities in Developing Language E-Portfolios

Yu-Fen Yang
National Yunlin University of Science and Technology, Taiwan

Hui-Chin Yeh
National Yunlin University of Science and Technology, Taiwan

ABSTRACT

Eportfolios have been widely used for different purposes in education for years. However, specific issues regarding the use of language eportfolios are unaddressed. This chapter first discusses the definitions, purposes, and advantages of eportfolios. It then describes the challenges of implementing eportfolios in higher education in Taiwan. Finally, it presents the design of an online language portfolio developed to provide possible alternatives or "opportunities" for the use of language eportfolios in educational settings. The design has three primary goals: reducing students' cognitive load, raising students' reflection on language learning, and fostering social interaction through peer assessment. In order to reduce students' cognitive load, auto-generated keywords alleviate students' workload. Auto-generated concept maps allow students to construct summaries while reading texts. The portfolio also provides students with opportunities to monitor and reflect on their learning process by playing crossword puzzles and writing feedback regarding assigned learning tasks. Students are allowed to post their texts anonymously in order to freely and honestly interact and construct meaningful learning with peers.

1. INTRODUCTION

Over the past decade, e-portfolios have been widely used for different purposes in education, especially in monitoring students' learning processes (Kankaanranta, Barrett, & Hartnell-Young, 2001; Niguidula, 1993), assessing their learning progress, and strengthening their employability after college graduation (Smith & Tillema,

DOI: 10.4018/978-1-4666-0143-7.ch015

2003). Specific issues regarding the use of language e-portfolios, however, are unaddressed: these include whether students could upload and organize their documents in the language e-portfolio without incentives, whether students could consistently reflect on their performances to maximize their learning outcomes, and whether the language e-portfolio will increase students' cognitive load. Because of the unaddressed issues, language educators and system developers have troubles designing language e-portfolios that can reach their maximum beneficial effects on students' learning. The definitions, purposes, and advantages of e-portfolios described here provide readers with background for the further discussion of challenges in developing online language portfolios. The language e-portfolio developed in this study in bridging the gap between the existing portfolios and students' needs addresses reducing students' cognitive load, raising students' reflection on language learning, and facilitating peer assessment through social interaction.

1.1 Definitions, Purposes, and Advantages of E-Portfolios

With the development of advanced technology and the Internet, the use of e-portfolios has extended to realms of teaching, learning, and assessment. Chang (2009) defines an e-portfolio as "the storage of authentic and multiple evidences, representing the demonstration and reflection of personal learning process and the result within a period of time" (p. 391). That is, an e-portfolio collects students' learning processes to illustrate their learning journey over time and to document their achievements (Bulter, 2006). E-portfolios also allow students to upload numerous multimedia file types such as texts, photographs, observations, and evaluations from instructors, and records of students' reflective thinking processes (Lorenzo & Ittelson, 2005; Bulter, 2006). E-potfolios are a useful learning tool for students to manage their learning experiences in virtual contexts.

Students' active participation and reflection on their own learning through e-portfolios (Barrett and Knezek, 2003) enhance their learning and prepare them to become autonomous learners. To enhance students' learning, some e-portfolios consist of three distinct but related learning modules: showcase, assessment, and process. The showcase module in the e-portfolio indicates that the system records students' accomplishments during their life-long learning experience (Lankes, 1998) and prepares students for the competitive job market. Students' presentation of creations, assignments, and certificates can positively influence potential employers. The assessment module refers to students' collection, organization, and evaluation of their relevant learning products to demonstrate the achievements of their learning goals (Biggs, 1996). This module enables teachers and students to monitor and assess the learning process. The process module presents students' learning experiences, including through log files and statistics that illustrate the strategies students employ to accomplish their goals (Meyer, Abrami, Wade, Aslan, & Deault, 2010).

2. E-PORTFOLIOS IN TAIWAN

E-portfolio has been rapidly expanding in Taiwanese universities since its introduction in 2007 (Lai, 2009). More than 80% of universities in Taiwan have implemented e-portfolios on campus, because e-portfolios record students' learning processes and add extra value for students to seek jobs by showcasing their progress.

2.1 Promotion of E-Portfolios by the Ministry of Education (MOE) in Taiwan

As e-portfolios can demonstrate students' learning achievements and illuminate their competences, the Ministry of Education (MOE) in Taiwan has promoted e-portfolios in higher education by launching a series of activities and competitions in developing e-portfolios. For example, an e-portfolio competition regarding university students' job-hunting was held by the MOE in 2008, and three workshops for developing the e-portfolio also took place in the same year.

The integration of e-portfolios into university courses, nevertheless, remains underdeveloped. Most Taiwanese students use e-portfolios only when they are asked to upload and organize assignments by school authorities. As a result, e-portfolios serve merely as showcases, which undervalue students' learning process and progress. Chuang (2010) pointed out that "several studies have warned against the tendency of turning portfolios into mere containers of artifacts with limited in-depth reflective practice" (p. 212). This container model limits meaningful and systematic means of using e-portfolios to enhance students' learning.

2.2 Challenges of Utilizing E-Portfolios in Taiwanese Universities

Taiwanese universities face five major challenges in developing and utilizing e-portfolios. First, e-portfolios seldom record students' online social interactions or behaviors in the system, hence losing track of their learning process, learning progress, and peer interaction. Barbera (2009) indicated that not only individual tasks but also collaborative works could take place in students' e-portfolio. Very few e-portfolios have established learning communities for students to view peers' e-portfolios and provide comments (Barbera, 2009). Moreover, students' records are lost in the current models, and the influence of these current models on students' online interaction and learning modes affects their adoption of new strategies to set goals, organize incoming information, and evaluate what they have learned.

Second, current e-portfolios in Taiwan do not offer students cognitive support when they are collecting and organizing information. Students have few ways to recognize which information to store in their e-portfolios and how to organize and make personal connections among the collected information in a meaningful way. Without scaffoldings implemented in the system, the collected information can become fragmented and disconnected (Barbera, 2009). For example, students may encounter difficulties in identifying their learning goals in e-portfolios since goal setting can be a complicated process in terms of specificity, closeness in time, and difficulty or challenge, all of which affect students' learning motivations, affective reactions, and attentions (Bandura & Schunk, 1981; Zimmerman & Kitsantas, 1997; Zimmerman, 2000).

Third, the integration of e-portfolios into university courses may diminish further if critical uses are missing. Challis (2005) indicated that it was difficult to discover substantive material about the actual use of e-portfolios in the higher education sector in a mature and systematic way. Carney (2005) claims that "electronic portfolios show promise for enhancing learning, but if we fail to critically evaluate our uses of the device, we may find that they will go the way of Papert's Logo turtles and become yet another educational fad—an innovation poorly understood and often implemented in ways contrary to its theoretical underpinnings" (p. 4).

Fourth, the use of e-portfolios may increase students' cognitive load (Smith & Tillema, 2003). Chang, Tseng, Yueh, & Lin (2010) agreed that if students' documents or data were not systematically organized, students' learning may be disrupted. Zeichner and Wray (2001) concluded similarly: "Despite the current popularity of teaching portfolios, there have been very few systematic studies of the nature and consequences of their use for either assessment or development purposes" (p. 615).

Finally, traditional e-portfolios are teacher-centered and lack individualization. Brusilovsky (2004) concluded that students utilized the same materials and online learning system without personalized support. Since most e-portfolios are designed under the "one size fits all" (Vovides, Sanchez-Alonso, Mitropoulou, & Nickmans, 2007, p. 67) principle, they tend to neglect individual student's language proficiency levels and interests. It is difficult to meet all students' individual needs when they are instructed at the same materials.

3. OPPORTUNITIES IN DEVELOPING AN ONLINE LANGUAGE PORTFOLIO

This study endeavors to develop a student-centered online language portfolio to address the challenges described above. Objectives include (1) reducing students' cognitive load, (2) raising students' reflection on language learning, and (3) fostering social interaction through peer assessment. Figure 1 shows how these three aspects are embedded in the architecture of the current language e-portfolio.

3.1 Reducing Students' Cognitive Load

Cognitive load is defined as the mental burden which imposes cognitive capacity on the process of information construction (Sweller, 1998). The demands of the cognitive load are often increased in college students' reading comprehension processes (Antonenko & Niederhauser, 2010), which require students to integrate the essential information in each paragraph of a text into overall concepts by decoding word meaning, generating predictions, and discriminating important and less important information (Afflerbach, 1990; Antonenko & Niederhauser, 2010). To reduce Taiwanese college students' cognitive load as they learn English as a Foreign Language (EFL) and considering that they must read English academic texts to obtain domain knowledge in specialized realms (Kong, 1996), the language e-portfolio developed in this study provides three handy tools

for better ways to learn: vocabulary filter, main idea and keyword extractor, and auto-generated concept map.

Vocabulary Filter

In comprehending academic texts, EFL college students have to master the breadth and depth of vocabulary knowledge (Anderson & Freebody, 1981; Haynes & Baker, 1993; Mehrpour & Rahimi, 2010; Qian, 2002). The vocabulary breadth is defined as the vocabulary size or the numbers of words that a student should know in order to comprehend the text (Qian, 1999; Nation, 2001). With the limited vocabulary size, EFL college students often encounter reading difficulties which impede their comprehension of English academic texts (Mehrpour & Rahimi, 2010).

The depth of the vocabulary refers to the knowledge which helps students understand the multiple meanings of a word in different contexts, including the pronunciation, spelling, meaning, register, frequency, collocations, syntactic properties, and knowledge of the synonymy, antonyms, and hyponymy (Chapelle, 1998; Qian, 1999; Laufer, 1997). Laufer (1997) and Qian (1999) believed that compared to the vocabulary size, the depth of the vocabulary could pave the way for students to achieve better reading comprehension. In Nitsch's study (1977), students who knew the meaning of the vocabulary in various contexts were found to have better comprehension when reading novel texts.

Computer-assisted vocabulary instruction supports students in learning to use strategies or supportive materials, such as online dictionaries or grammar books (Lyman-Hager, Davis, Burnett, & Chennault, 1993; Reinking & Schreiner, 1985). To support students and reduce their cognitive load in selecting essential words in reading texts, the automatic vocabulary filter developed in this study helps students eliminate the less important vocabulary and provides students with a wordlist to choose from for their own vocabulary database.

Figure 1 The architecture of the language e-portfolio

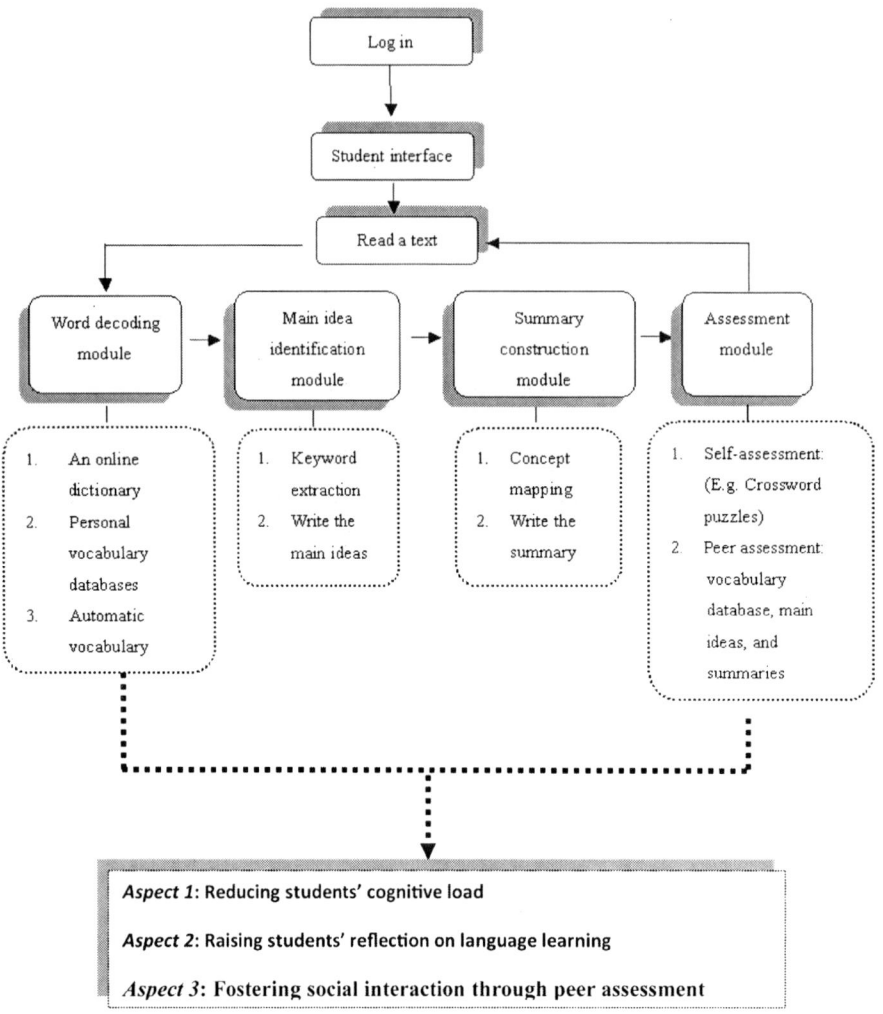

The vocabulary filter reduces the effect of split attention and redundancy on students' vocabulary learning by condensing the amount of vocabulary of an academic text and generating a vocabulary list for students to establish their vocabulary database. The filtering procedures begin with "PDF Vocabulary Extractor" to extract the English vocabulary from an academic text (Figure 2). The second step reduces the inflectional or derivational words of the irregular verbs and plural nouns to their root by *Porter Stemming* software. The third step removes stop or function words, such as *I*, *you*, and *are*. The fourth step of the filtering procedure identifies the difficulty of the vocabulary according to the Common European Framework of Reference (CEFR) – a reference to determine students' proficiency level in foreign language learning. After the system undergoes the four filtering procedures, words in an academic text, in one example, can be reduced from 1100 to 66 words. Then, students can select the 66 words from a vocabulary list for their personal vocabulary database (Figure 3). By clicking on each word, students can listen to the pronunciation. Students can also select the 66 words based on their language proficiency as the difficulty level of the vocabulary is identified. After they have established their vocabulary database, the learned

Figure 2. The procedure of vocabulary filter

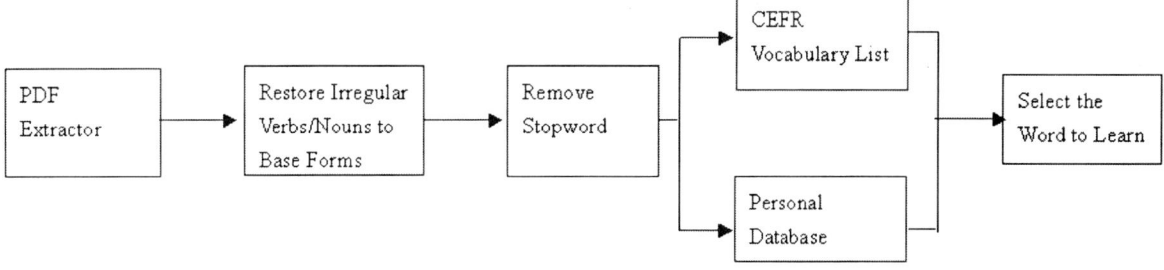

Figure 3. The refined vocabulary list

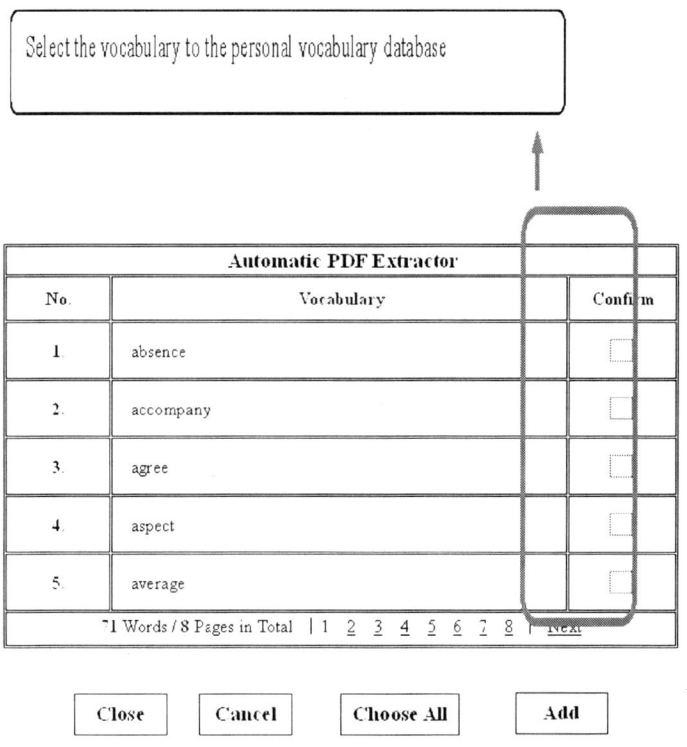

vocabulary is excluded from the vocabulary list of the next academic texts which students read in order to reduce students' cognitive load in vocabulary selection.

Main Idea and Keyword Extractor

Identifying the main idea in a text is a complicated and active meaning construction process in which students read many statements and integrate the statements into a central idea (Anderson, Hiebert, Scott, & Wilkinson, 1985). Determining main ideas is central to successful reading comprehension, because main ideas facilitate efficient and critical reading. (Broek, Lynch, Naslund, Ievers-Landis, & Verduin, 2003; Dishner & Readene, 1973; Williams, 1988). Without the ability to construct main ideas, students will have difficulties with other reading skills, such as outlining, summarizing, and organizing texts (Dishner & Readence, 1973; Steve, 1986).

To scaffold students' recognition and construction of main ideas, keywords are identified as high-frequency words that most authors use to organize ideas and compose their texts (Afflerbach, 1990; Barki, Rivard, & Talbot, 1988; Chen, Kishuk, Wei, & Chen, 2008; Jacobowitz, 1990; Weideman & Strümpfer, 2004). Dishner and Readence (1973) pointed out that recognizing the keywords in a sentence or a paragraph was a prerequisite skill for main idea construction. The relationship between the keywords and the main idea construction was verified by Chen et. al. (2008). Each keyword contains one central idea in a sentence or a passage. There must be some relationships among the keywords. For example, a passage related to greenhouse effect might list the keywords carbon dioxide or water vapor, which both represent causes of the greenhouse effect. The frequency of word occurrence in a text is a criterion for being a keyword, as authors are inclined to employ the same essential words to express their concepts in a sentence or a paragraph. Finally, Chen et. al. (2008) believed that the "distance" between keywords in a sentence could be used to evaluate the relative strengths between keywords (p. 1011). They claimed that keywords found close to each other often had a deeper relationship.

Given the importance of keywords in main idea construction, scholars have contrived systems to help readers identify keywords and the relationships between keywords (e.g., Brossard & Shanahan, 2006; Chen, et. al., 2008; Salton & McGill, 1983; Su & Wang, 2010; Tseng, Chang, Rundgren, & Rundgren, 2010). Most previous systems were developed to extract the keywords by calculating the frequency of the word occurrence in a text and to identify the relative strengths between keywords based on the distance or the co-occurrence of the keywords within a sentence (Chen, et. al., 2008; Tseng, et. al., 2010). Those

researchers believe that the keywords, which have the same frequency of occurrence or are close together within a sentence or a paragraph, are going to have stronger relational strengths. To ensure the frequency of the keyword occurrence, Chen et al. (2008) proposed a normalization process to extract keywords, including keyword clearing, acronym mapping, and suffix stripping. Keyword clearing refers to the removal of symbols, such as dashes, hyphens, and spaces, to avoid the extraction of the synonymous words spelled in different formats, such as *web-based* or *web based*. Suffix stripping removes the suffixes of words, such as *-ed, -ing*, and *-s*. A data base of the acronyms was finally constructed to help the system recognize the original meanings of acronyms in texts.

To reduce the EFL students' cognitive overload resulting from the split attention effect, identifying the main ideas with keywords helps students recall essential information in texts. Hence the current online language portfolio developed a "Main Idea and Keyword Extractor" (Figure 4) located in the "Paragraph" section. By clicking the "Keyword" button on the right hand side, the system can automatically generate a keyword list for students (Figure 5). The keywords are displayed in a chart board according to the frequency of the word occurrence in a text. In addition, the higher the word ranks, the more frequently it occurs in the text. Students are thus able to compose the main idea in paragraphs with the assistance of the keyword list. The keyword list not only alleviates students' cognitive load but also automatically serves as a scaffold in students' language learning.

Auto-Generated Concept Map

A concept map is a scaffold that helps students organize and represent knowledge through nodes that refer to concepts and through links that represent associations between concepts (Novak, 1998; Plotnick, 1997). The use of the concept map has gained increasing interest in various domains, such as curriculum design (Soyibo,

Figure 4. Main idea and keyword extractor

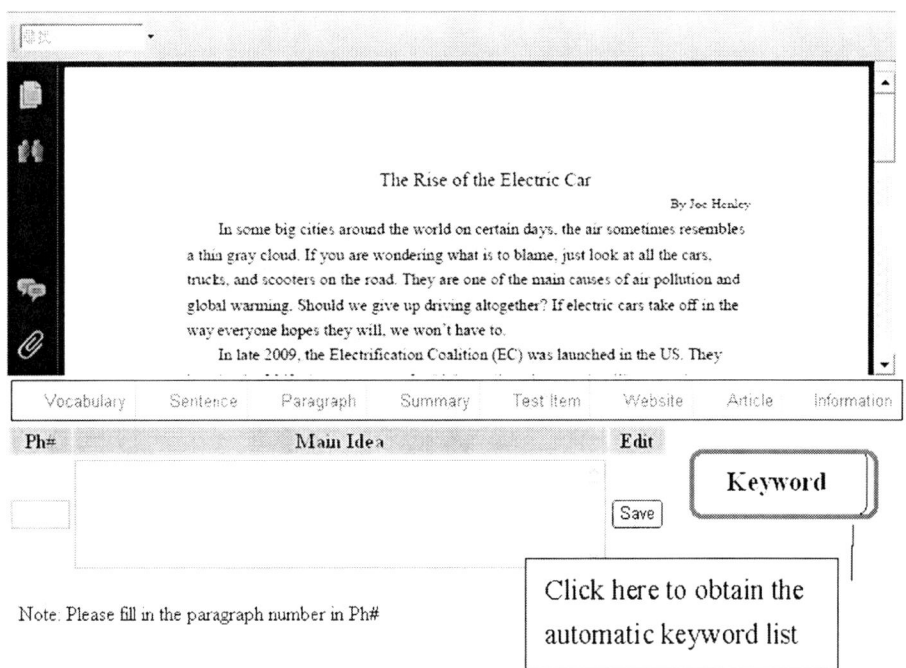

Figure 5. The auto-generated keyword list

1995), assessment (Chang, 2007, Su & Wang, 2010; Tseng, Sue, Su, Weng, & Tsai, 2007), and particularly reading instruction (Cheng, Kinshuk, Wei, & Chen, 2008; Tseng et al., 2010). In reading instruction, the concept map is regarded as an effective tool to reduce readers' cognitive load in processing information and organizing ideas in texts (O'Donnell, Dansereau, & Hall, 2002; Papanikolaou, Grigoriadou, Magoulas, & Kornilakis, 2002). By removing the syntactic and lexical ambiguities, the concept map helps students solve the problem of the attention division and empowers them to efficiently retain and retrieve the essential information in texts (Payne & Reader, 2006). The transferring of the main ideas in each paragraph into a graphical format also aids students in explicitly recognizing the flows or organization of the reading texts (Grey, 1999).

The building of concept maps, however, remains a challenging task for most college students. Chang, Sung and Chen (2001) examined effects of two different concept map models – the

No.	Keyword
1	electric
2	oil
3	energy
4	world
5	major
6	air
7	government
8	american
9	tax
10	make

Close

construct-by-self model and the construct-by-scaffold model. In the construct-by-self model, students develop concept maps without assistance from others, while in the construct-by-scaffold model skeletal expert maps, hints and feedback are provided. The findings indicated that students who received the scaffolds outperformed the students who constructed the concept maps by themselves.

The auto-generated concept map in the current online language portfolio is based on the construct-by-scaffold model. To offer students scaffolds in summarization, for example, the language portfolio displays key words from the text in a graphic figure by a simple click in the "Summary" section (Figure 6). Students can click on the "Concept Map" button to obtain the auto-generated concept map (Figure 7) before they start writing the summary. As each node in the figure represents main ideas applicable for summarization, writing a summary may not be a painstaking task for students anymore.

3.2 Increasing Students' Reflection on Language Learning

In addition to having lower cognitive loads, students need opportunities to reflect on their reading comprehension process (Graves & Levin, 1989). Graves and Levin's findings indicated that students who received explicit instruction and did self-reflection outperformed students who received only explicit instruction in recalling and identifying main ideas.

Although previous studies developed many systems to help students extract keywords to grasp main ideas, little research has examined the effects of vocabulary filtering and automatic keyword extraction in helping students construct main ideas and summaries. Previous systems did not help students recognize and reflect on their own reading process. As a result, school administrators and reading teachers could not identify how students used these implementations in reading and whether the implementations were really helpful to students.

To assist students in reflecting on their reading processes and to enable teachers to monitor their students' reading process, the current language portfolio has two modules, Self-Assessment and Critical Reflection.

Self-Assessment

Learning vocabulary is a basic language skill for EFL students. Gu and Johnson (1996) divided vocabulary learning strategies into four dimen-

Figure 6. The concept map button in "Summary"

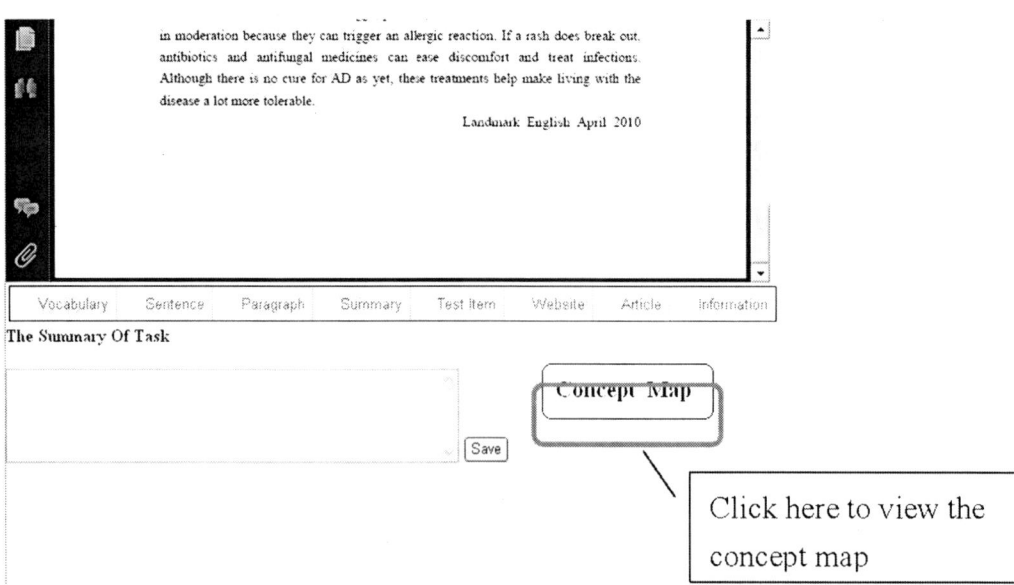

sions: metacognitive, cognitive, memory, and activation strategies. By using metacognitive strategies, students identify essential words in texts and clarify word meanings. Cognitive strategies involve the use of dictionaries, note-taking, and activating personal background knowledge or linguistic clues to guess word meanings. Memory strategies that help students retain vocabulary are building word lists and finding associations between words. Activation strategies are methods by which students can use the learned vocabulary to write a sentence.

In self-assessment modules, students use activation strategies to reflect on their language learning. Students can evaluate their knowledge of vocabulary by filling out crossword puzzles and by comparing their own main ideas and summaries with peers.

(A) Crossword Puzzle

Online crossword puzzles allow students to assess their own vocabulary knowledge to integrate and evaluate what they have learned. When students

Figure 7. The auto-generated concept map

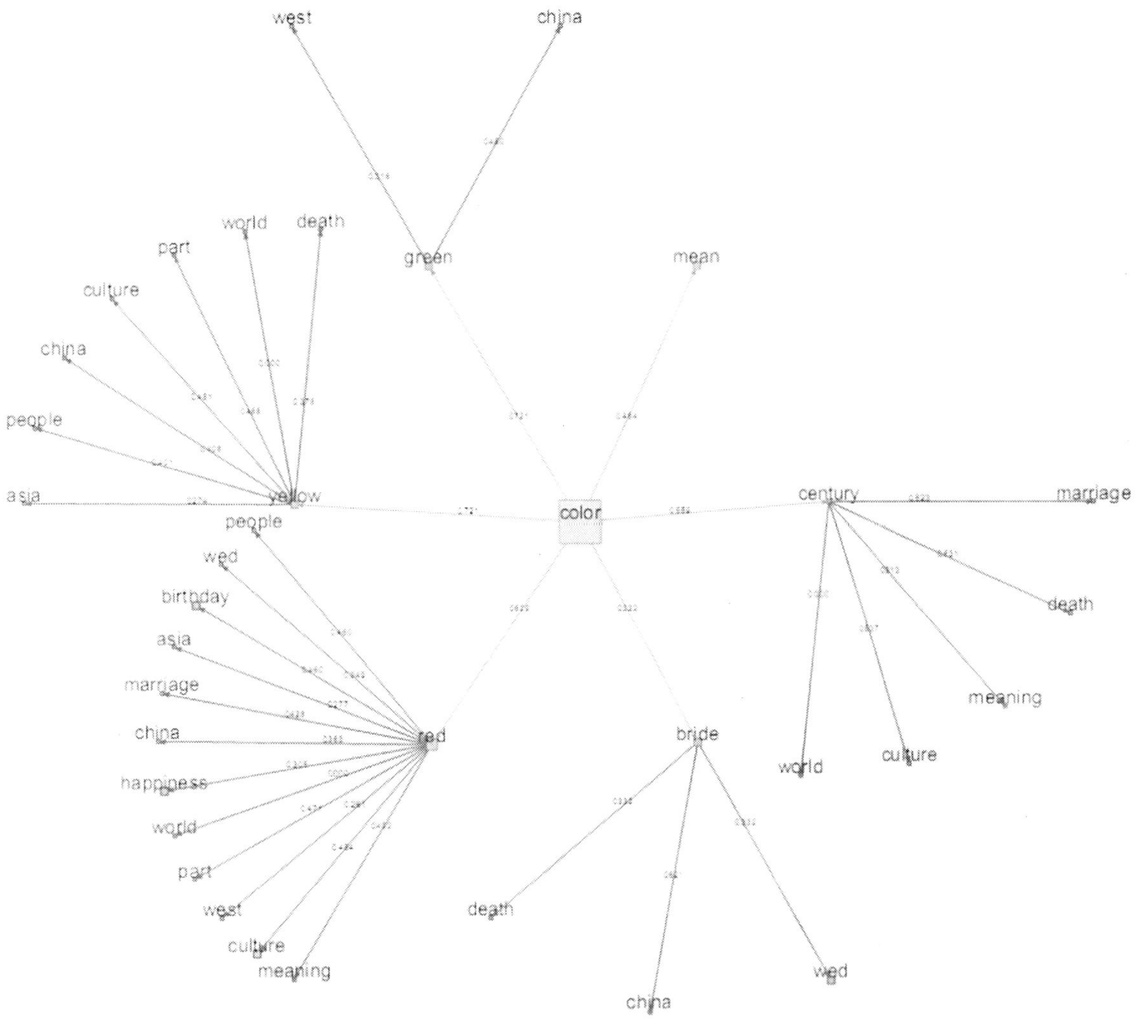

enter the crossword puzzle section in the language portfolio, they can set up "Time," "Game Complicacy," and "Type" (Figure 8). Personalized control over the crossword puzzle provokes students' reflective thinking. By deciding how long the game will last, how complicated the puzzle will be, and which word classification will be played in the puzzle, students need to reflect on their own language proficiency level first.

The puzzle begins by a click of the "Take Quiz!! button (Figure 9). The test items are generated by the system from students' own organization of words. That is, the vocabulary is derived from students' personalized vocabulary databases in the language portfolio. In addition, Chinese definitions are provided as clues to assist students in completing the puzzle. After students work through the individualized crossword puzzle, they can recognize their own strengths and weaknesses in vocabulary learning.

Figure 8. Personalized control over the crossword puzzle

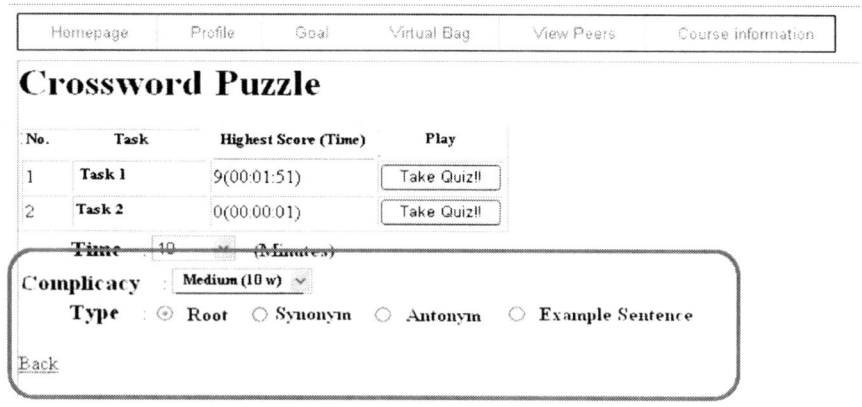

Figure 9. Self-assessment: the crossword puzzle

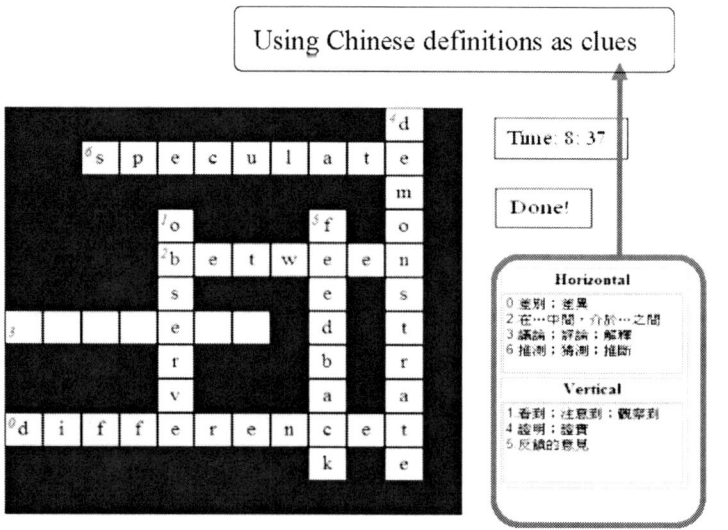

(B) Comparing Main Ideas and Summaries with Peers

Encouraging students to compare their own main ideas with their peers is another way to increase students' reflection on language learning. A "View Peers' Portfolios" section supports students to reflect critically. The current language portfolio randomly selects portfolios from 10 peers for each student to view and compare. When students click on the "Virtual Bag" link on a peer's portfolio, the portfolio automatically directs them to view peers' work on main ideas and summaries (Figures 10 and 11). Students can also "collect" peers' main ideas and summaries as references by clicking on the floppy disk icon.

When students get involved in viewing and comparing peers' main ideas and summaries, or even making the decision of saving peers' work for later reference, they are already reflecting on their language learning. Through these comparisons, they think about the differences, assisting students in monitoring their own comprehension process.

Critical Reflection

The "Trace Results" and "Reflection Prompts" functions guide students to reflect on their language learning process. The "Trace Results" comprehensively records students' actions automatically. Students' strengths and weaknesses in language learning can then easily be observed through these log files.

While the "Trace Results" function guides students to observe their learning process, it is vital for students to write their reflections in order to engage themselves in a deeper reflecting process. Papadopoulos, Demetriadis, Stamelos, and Tsoukalas (2010) stress that students who write reflections cultivate their analyzing and evaluating skills.

In the language portfolio, the "Reflection Prompts" function accompanies major learning activities. These prompt questions are randomly selected by the portfolio from its database. When students finish organizing vocabulary, or writing main ideas and summaries, the reflection prompts pop out to ask students to write their reflections. With the "Reflection Prompts" function, students

Figure 10. Peers' portfolios selected by the language portfolio

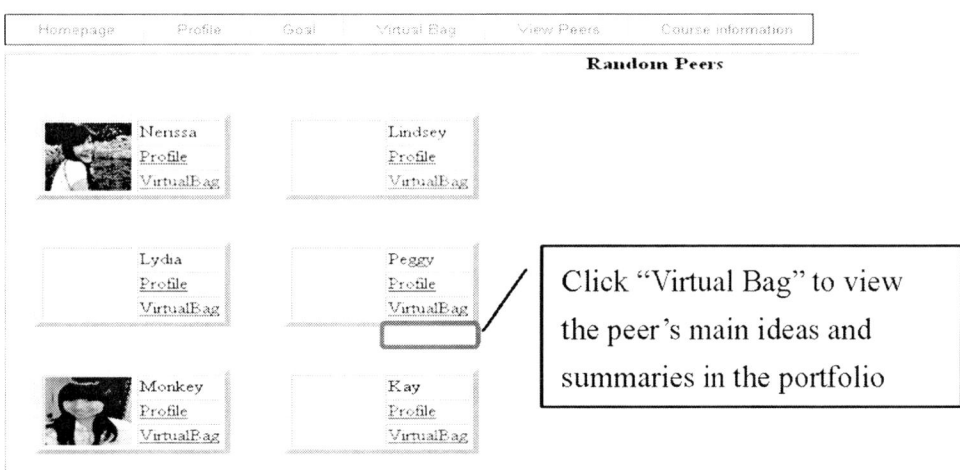

Figure 11. The main idea written by a peer

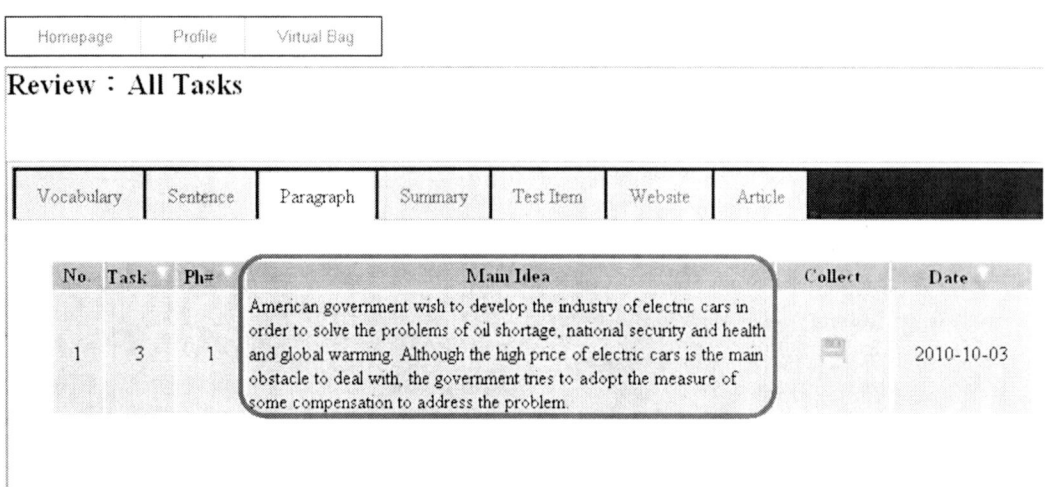

develop the ability to critically reflect on their language learning.

3.3 Fostering Social Interaction Through Peer Assessment

Students need ample opportunities for social interaction during language learning. One of the effective social interactions in learning is peer assessment, a method in which students observe, assess, and provide feedback to peers' work (Topping, Smith, Swanson & Elliot, 2000; Van den Berg, Admiraal, & Pilot, 2006). Peer feedback has several advantages. First, peer assessment provides students with an autonomous and participative learning environment which increases students' learning motivation (Brown, 1998). For example, Lin, Liu and Yuan (2001), who studied students' perceptions about peer assessment, found that students achieved better academic performance and were highly motivated by peer assessment. Stefani (1994) stated that 85% of the students in his study preferred peer coaching over traditional assessment. Second, Paulus (1999) found that students received more individualized and immediate feedback from peers than from teachers. Olson's

(1990) investigation of the effectiveness of the peer coaching on writing showed that students who engaged in peer coaching wrote better final drafts than students who received teacher feedback only. Third, providing feedback, prompting questions, and discussing with peers, students develop metacognitive skills regarding monitoring and evaluating (Liu & Tsai, 2005; Topping, 1998). Through the process of discussion with peers, students are further stimulated to engage in reflective thinking on their learning behaviors or performance (Falchikov, 1995).

Even though many studies have pointed out the positive effects of peer coaching on language learning, this approach still encounters many challenges in the classroom. For example, students often express lack of trust during peer assessment. Nelson and Carson (1998) found that while students regarded peer feedback as helpful in understanding their learning problems, students also complained about peer feedback that was unconstructive and unfocused. Because most students remained dubious about their peers' capability and competence to perform assessment competently, they were more inclined to value feedback from teachers (Brindley & Scoffield, 1998). In addition, ethical problems might also arise in peer coaching (Brew, 1999). Carson and Nelson (1996) stated that in order not to hurt their friends' feelings, students avoided negative criticism of peers' work and gave no conflicting feedback. To solve the problems, the online language portfolio adapted anonymity from the computer-supported collaborative (CSCL) learning environment and developed functions that could increase the quality of peer coaching.

Privacy Setting in the Online Language Portfolio

In an online peer assessment environment where they can choose to be anonymous, students can feel safe in honestly expressing their criticisms of peers' work (MacLeod, 1999). The language portfolio privacy setting allows students to respond spontaneously (DiGiovanni & Nagaswami, 2001; Topping, 1998).

In the "Paragraph," "Summary," and "Test Item" sections, students can check the correctness of their peers' work. To foster active social interaction and promote meaningful learning in each learning process, students can set their own privacy limits. If they wish to remain anonymous when assessing and leaving comments on peers' works, they can simply click on the "Be Anonymous" button in the account settings.

4. CONCLUSION

A range of challenges faces e-portfolio use in Taiwanese universities. The challenges include the lack of records of students' online behaviors, a deficient cognitive framework to support students in language learning, the need to change teaching approaches, an increase in students' cognitive load, and insufficient individualization for students' language learning. An online language portfolio was developed to meet these challenges.

The online language portfolio presented in this study has three objectives: (1) reducing students'

cognitive load, (2) raising students' reflection on language learning, and (3) fostering social interaction through peer assessment. In reducing students' cognitive load, implemented functions such as "Vocabulary Filter," "Main Idea and Keyword Extractor," and "Auto-generated Concept Map" are aids in the online language portfolio. Two learning modules, "Self-assessment" and "Critical Reflection," enable students to increase their reflection ability through self-assessing and critically reflecting on their language learning process. To foster social interaction through peer assessment, students can choose anonymity when interacting and constructing meaningful learning with peers freely and honestly.

Future developments can focus more on how teachers scaffold students in the online language portfolio. By allowing teachers to monitor and document the conversations between students, teachers could provide guidance to students (DiGiovanni & Nagaswami, 2001). The guidance may include assigning texts that are of appropriate language proficiency level to students, facilitating teaching activities and formal assessments, and providing expert suggestions and feedback to students. With guidance from teachers, students are better able to keep their language learning on the right track.

REFERENCES

Afflerbach, P. P. (1990). The influence of prior knowledge on expert readers' main idea construction strategies. *Reading Research Quarterly*, *25*(1), 31–46. doi:10.2307/747986

Anderson, R. C., & Freebody, P. (1981). Vocabulary knowledge. In Guthrie, J. T. (Ed.), *Comprehension and teaching: Research reviews* (pp. 77–117). Newark, DE: International Reading Association.

Anderson, R. C., Hiebert, E. H., Scott, J. A., & Wilkinson, I. A. G. (1985). *Becoming a nation of readers*. Washington, DC: National Institute of Education.

Antonenko, P. D., & Niederhauser, D. S. (2010). The influence of leads on cognitive load and learning in a hypertext environment. *Computers in Human Behavior, 28*, 140–150. doi:10.1016/j.chb.2009.10.014

Ayres, P., & Sweller, J. (2005). The split-attention principle in multimedia learning. In Mayer, R. E. (Ed.), *The Cambridge Handbook of Multimedia Learning* (pp. 135–146). New York: Cambridge University Press.

Bandura, A., & Schunk, D. H. (1981). Cultivating competence, self-efficacy, and intrinsic interest through proximal self-motivation. *Journal of Personality and Social Psychology, 41*, 586–598. doi:10.1037/0022-3514.41.3.586

Barbera, E. (2009). Mutual feedback in e-portfolio assessment: an approach to the netfolio system. *British Journal of Educational Technology, 40*(2), 342–357. doi:10.1111/j.1467-8535.2007.00803.x

Barki, H., Rivard, S., & Talbot, J. (1988). An information systems keyword classification scheme. *Management Information Systems Quarterly, 12*, 299–322. doi:10.2307/248855

Barrett, H., & Knezek, D. (2003). *E-portfolios: Issues in assessment, accountability and preservice teacher preparation*. Paper presented at the Annual Conference of the American Educational Research Association, Chicago, IL.

Biggs, J. (1996). Enhancing Teaching through Constructive Alignment. Higher Education. *The International Journal of Higher Education and Educational Planning, 32*(3), 347–364.

Brew, A. (1999). Towards autonomous assessment: using self-assessment and peer assessment. In Brown, S., & Glasner, A. (Eds.), *Assessment matters in higher education*. Buckingham: Open University Press.

Brindley, C., & Scoffield, S. (1998). Peer Assessment in Undergraduate Programmes. *Teaching in Higher Education, 3*(1), 79–90. doi:10.1080/1356215980030106

Broek, P. V. D., Lynch, J. S., Naslund, J., Ievers-Landis, C. E., & Verduin, K. (2003). The development of comprehension of main ideas in narratives: Evidence from the selection of titles. *Journal of Educational Psychology, 95*, 707–718. doi:10.1037/0022-0663.95.4.707

Brossard, D., & Shanahan, J. (2006). Do they know what they read? Building scientific literacy measurement based on science media coverage. *Science Communication, 28*(1), 47–63. doi:10.1177/1075547006291345

Brown, S. (1998). *Peer Assessment in Practice*. Birmingham: SEDA.

Brusilovsky, P. (2004). Knowledge tree: A distributed architecture for adaptive e-learning. *In Proceedings from the World Wide Web conference 2004* (pp. 104-113).

Butler, P. (2006). *A Review of the Literature on Portfolios and Electronic Portfolios* (Literature Review). Palmerston North, New Zealand: eCDF ePortfolio Project, Massey University College of Education Licensed under the Creative Commons.

Carney, J. (2005). *What kind of electronic portfolio research do we need?* Paper presented at the annual meeting of the Society for Information Technology and Teacher Education.

Carson, J., & Nelson, G. (1996). Chinese students' perceptions of ESL peer response group interaction. *Journal of Second Language Writing, 5*, 1–19. doi:10.1016/S1060-3743(96)90012-0

Challis, D. (2005). Towards the mature ePortfolio: Some implications for higher education. *Canadian Journal of Learning and Technology, 31*(3). Retrieved November 2, 2010, from: http://www.cjlt.ca/index.php/cjlt/article/viewArticle/93/87.

Chang, C.-C. (2009). Self-evaluated effects of web-based portfolio assessment system for various student motivation levels. *Journal of Educational Computing Research, 41*(4), 391–405. doi:10.2190/EC.41.4.a

Chang, C.-C., Tseng, K.-H., Yueh, H.-P., & Lin, W.-C. (2010). (in press). Consideration factors and adoption of type, tabulation and framework for creating E-portfolios. *Computers & Education.*

Chang, K.-E., Sung, Y.-T., & Chen, S.-F. (2001). Learning through computer-based concept mapping with scaffolding aid. *Journal of Computer Assisted Learning, 17*(1), 21–33. doi:10.1046/j.1365-2729.2001.00156.x

Chang, S.-N. (2007). Externalizing students' mental models through concept maps. *Journal of Biological Education, 41*(3), 107–112. doi:10.1080/00219266.2007.9656078

Chapelle, C. (1998). Construct definition and validity inquiry in SLA research. In Bachman, L. F., & Cohen, A. D. (Eds.), *Interfaces between second language acquisition and language testing research* (pp. 32–70). Cambridge, England: Cambridge University Press.

Chen, N.-S., Kinshuk, Wei, C.-W., & Chen, H.-J. (2008). Mining e-Learning domain concept map from academic articles. *Computers & Education, 50*, 1009–2001. doi:10.1016/j.compedu.2006.10.001

Chuang, H.-H. (2010). Weblog-based electronic portfolios for student teachers in Taiwan. *Educational Technology Research and Development, 58*, 211–227. doi:10.1007/s11423-008-9098-1

DiGiovanni, E., & Nagaswami, G. (2001). Online peer review: An alternative to face-to-face? *EFL Journal, 55*(3), 263–272.

Dishner, E. K., & Readence, J. E. (1973). *A systematic procedure for teaching main idea.* Paper presented at the Annual Meeting of the National Reading Conference.

Evans, S., & Green, C. (2007). Why EAP is necessary: A survey of Hong Kong tertiary students. *Journal of English for Academic Purposes, 6*, 3–17. doi:10.1016/j.jeap.2006.11.005

Falchikov, N. (1995). Peer feedback marking: Developing peer assessment. *Innovations in Education and Training International, 32*(2), 175–187. doi:10.1080/1355800950320212

Graves, A. W., & Levin, J. R. (1989). Comparison of monitoring and mnemonic text-processing strategies in learning disabled students. *Learning Disability Quarterly, 12*, 232–236. doi:10.2307/1510693

Grey, D. (1999). Knowledge mapping: a practical overview. Retrieved September 14, 2009, from: http://www.impactalliance.org/file_download.php?location¼S_U&filename¼10383546681Knowledge_Mapping.htm.

Gu, Y., & Johnson, R. K. (1996). Vocabulary learning strategies and language learning outcomes. *Language Learning, 46*(4), 643–679. doi:10.1111/j.1467-1770.1996.tb01355.x

Haynes, M., & Baker, I. (1993). American and Chinese readers learning from lexical familiarizations in English text. In Huckin, T., Haynes, M., & Coady, J. (Eds.), *Second language reading and vocabulary learning* (pp. 130–152). Norwood, NJ: Ablex.

Jacobowitz, T. (1990). A metacognitive strategy for constructing the main idea of text. *Journal of Reading, 33*(6), 620–624.

Kankaanranta, M., Barrett, H. C., & Hartnell-Young, E. (2001). Exploring the use of electronic portfolios in international contexts. In *Proceedings of world conference on ducational multimedia. Hypermedia and telecommunications* (pp. 874–876). Norfolk, VA: AACE.

Kong, H.-C. (1996). Teaching college English: From ESL to ESP. *Studies in English Language and Literature*, *1*, 40–45.

Lai, L.-C. (2009). E-portfolio. Retrieved October 7, 2010, from: http://www.digitimes.com.tw/tw/dt/n/shwnws.asp?CnlID=10&id=0000138304_9A128D2F1YLGAJ3OZJG9N.

Lankes, A. M. D. (1998). Portfolios: A new wave in assessment. *T.H.E. Journal*, *25*(9), 18.

Laufer, B. (1997). The lexical plight in second language reading: Words you don't know, words you think you know, and words you can't guess. In Coady, J., & Huckin, T. (Eds.), *Second language vocabulary acquisition: A rationale for pedagogy* (pp. 20–34). New York: Cambridge University Press.

Lin, S. S.-J., Liu, E. Z.-F., & Yuan, S.-M. (2001). Web-based peer assessment: feedback for students with various thinking-styles. *Journal of Computer Assisted Learning*, *17*, 420–432. doi:10.1046/j.0266-4909.2001.00198.x

Liu, C.-C., & Tsai, C.-M. (2005). Peer assessment through web-based knowledge acquisition: tools to support conceptual awareness. *Innovations in Education and Teaching International*, *42*, 43–59. doi:10.1080/14703290500048838

Lorenzo, G., & Ittelson, J. (2005). *An overview of e-portfolios*. Educause Learning Initiative, ELI Paper, 1-28. Retrieved October 11, 2010, from: http://www.educause.edu/ir/library/pdf/ELI3001.pdf.

Lyman-Hager, M., Davis, J. N., Burnett, J., & Chennault, R. (1993). Une Vie de Boy:Interactive reading in French. In F. L. Borchardt & E.M.T. Johnson (Eds.), *Proceedings of CALICO 1993 Annual Symposium on Assessment* (pp. 93-97). Durham, NC: Duke University.

MacLeod, L. (1999). Computer-aided peer review of writing. *Business Communication Quarterly*, *62*(3), 87–94. doi:10.1177/108056999906200309

Mehrpour, S., & Rahimi, M. (2010). The impact of general and specific vocabulary knowledge on reading and listening comprehension: A case of Iranian EFL learners. *System*, *38*(2), 292–300. doi:10.1016/j.system.2010.01.004

Meyer, E., Abrami, P. C., Wade, C. A., Aslan, O., & Deault, L. (2010). Improving literacy and meta-cognition with electronic portfolios: Teaching and learning with ePEARL. *Computers & Education*, *55*, 84–91. doi:10.1016/j.compedu.2009.12.005

Nation, P. (2001). *Learning vocabulary in another language*. Cambridge: Cambridge University Press.

Nelson, G., & Carson, J. (1998). ESL students' perceptions of effectiveness in peer response groups. *Journal of Second Language Writing*, *7*(2), 113–131. doi:10.1016/S1060-3743(98)90010-8

Niguidula, D. (1993). The Digital Portfolio. A Richer Picture of Student Performance. Coalition of Essential Schools. Retrieved October 7, 2010, from: http://www.essentialschools.org.

Nitsch, K. E. (1977). *Structuring decontextualizedforms of knowledge. Unpublished doctoral disser- tation*. Vanderbilt University.

Novak, J. D. (1998). *Learning, creating, and using knowledge: concept maps as facilitative tools in schools and corporations*. Mawah, NJ: Lawrence Erlbaum and Associates.

O'Donnell, A. M., Dansereau, D. F., & Hall, R. H. (2002). Knowledge maps as scaffolds for cognitive processing. *Educational Psychology Review, 14*(1), 71–86. doi:10.1023/A:1013132527007

Olson, V. L. B. (1990). The revising process of sixth-grade writers with and without peer feedback. *The Journal of Educational Research, 84,* 22–29.

Papadopoulos, P. M., Demetriadis, S. N., Stamelos, I. G., & Tsoukalas, I. A. (2010). The value of writing-to-learn when using question prompts to support web-based learning in ill-structured domains. *Educational Technology Research and Development,* 1–20.

Papanikolaou, K. A., Grigoriadou, M., Magoulas, G. D., & Kornilakis, H. (2002). Towards new forms of knowledge communication: The adaptive dimension of a web-based learning environment. *Computers & Education, 39,* 333–360. doi:10.1016/S0360-1315(02)00067-2

Paulus, T. M. (1999). The effect of peer and teacher feedback on student writing. *Journal of Second Language Writing, 8*(3), 256–289. doi:10.1016/S1060-3743(99)80117-9

Payne, S. J., & Reader, W. R. (2006). Constructing structure maps of multiple on-line texts. *International Journal of Human-Computer Studies, 64,* 461–474. doi:10.1016/j.ijhcs.2005.09.003

Plotnick, E. (1997). *Concept mapping: a graphical system for understanding the relationship between concepts: an ERIC digest.* New York: ERIC Clearinghouse on Information and Technology.

Qian, D.-D. (1999). Assessing the roles of depth and breadth of vocabulary knowledge in reading comprehension. *Canadian Modern Language Review, 56,* 282–308. doi:10.3138/cmlr.56.2.282

Qian, D.-D. (2002). Investigating the relationship between vocabulary knowledge and academic reading performance: an assessment perspective. *Language Learning, 52,* 513–536. doi:10.1111/1467-9922.00193

Reinking, D., & Schreiner, R. (1985). The effects of computer-mediated text on measures of reading comprehension and reading behavior. *Reading Research Quarterly, 20,* 536–551. doi:10.2307/747941

Salton, G., & McGill, M. J. (1983). *Introduction to Modern Information Retrieval.* New York: McGraw-Hill.

Schmitt, N. (1997). Vocabulary learning strategies. In Schmitt, N., & McCarthy, M. (Eds.), *Vocabulary: description, acquisition and pedagogy* (pp. 199–228). Cambridge: Cambridge University Press.

Smith, K., & Tillema, H. (2003). Clarifying different types of portfolio use. *Assessment & Evaluation in Higher Education, 28*(6), 625–648. doi:10.1080/0260293032000130252

Soyibo, K. (1995). Using concept maps to analyze text book presentations of respiration. *The American Biology Teacher, 57*(6), 344–351.

Spector-Cohen, E., Kirschner, M., & Wexler, C. (2001). Designing EAP reading courses at the university level. *English for Specific Purposes, 20,* 367–386. doi:10.1016/S0889-4906(00)00019-3

Stefani, L. A. J. (1994). Peer, self and tutor assessment: relative reliabilities. *Studies in Higher Education, 19*(1), 69–75. doi:10.1080/03075079412331382153

Steve, R. J. (1986). *The effects of strategy training on the identification of the main idea of expository passages.* Center for Research on Elementary and Middle Schools, 4.

Su, C.-Y., & Wang, T.-I. (2010). Construction and analysis of educational assessments using knowledge maps with weight appraisal of concepts. *Computers & Education, 55*, 1300–1311. doi:10.1016/j.compedu.2010.05.027

Sweller, J. (1988). Cognitive load during problem solving: Effects on learning. *Cognitive Science, 12*, 257–285. doi:10.1207/s15516709cog1202_4

Topping, K., Smith, F. F., Swanson, I., & Elliot, A. (2000). Formative peer assessment of academic writing between postgraduate students. *Assessment & Evaluation in Higher Education, 25*(2), 149–169. doi:10.1080/713611428

Topping, K. J. (1998). Peer assessment between students in colleges and universities. *Review of Educational Research, 68*, 249–276.

Tseng, S.-S., Sue, P.-C., Su, J.-M., Weng, J.-F., & Tsai, W.-N. (2007). A new approach for constructing the concept map. *Computers & Education, 49*, 691–707. doi:10.1016/j.compedu.2005.11.020

Tseng, Y.-H., Chang, C.-Y., Rundgren, C. S.-N., & Rudgren, C.-J. (2010). Mining concept maps from news stories for measuring civic scientific literacy in media. *Computers & Education, 55*, 165–177. doi:10.1016/j.compedu.2010.01.002

Van den Berg, I., Admiraal, W., & Pilot, A. (2006). Design principles and outcomes of peer assessment in higher education. *Studies in Higher Education, 31*(3), 341–356. doi:10.1080/03075070600680836

Vovides, Y., Sanchez-Alonso, S., Mitropoulou, V., & Nickmans, G. (2007). The use of e-learning course management systems to support learning strategies and to improve self-regulated learning. *Educational Research Review,* (2): 64–74. doi:10.1016/j.edurev.2007.02.004

Weideman, H., & Strümpfer, C. (2004). The Effect of Search Engine Keyword Choice and Demographic Features on Internet Searching Success. *Information Technology and Libraries,* 56-65.

Williams, J. P. (1988). Identifying main ideas: A basic aspect of reading comprehension. *Topics in Language Disorders, 8*, 1–13. doi:10.1097/00011363-198806000-00003

Zeichner, K., & Wray, S. (2001). The teaching portfolio in us teacher education programs: What we know and what we need to know. *Teaching and Teacher Education, 17*, 613–621. doi:10.1016/S0742-051X(01)00017-8

Zimmerman, B. J. (2000). Attaining self-regulation: A social cognitive perspective. In Boekaerts, M., Pintrich, P. R., & Zeidner, M. (Eds.), *Handbook of Self-regulation* (pp. 13–39). San Diego, CA: Academic Press.

Zimmerman, B. J., & Kitsantas, A. (1997). Developmental phases in self-regulation: Shifting from process to outcome goals. *Journal of Educational Psychology, 89*, 29–36. doi:10.1037/0022-0663.89.1.29

Compilation of References

AC Nielsen Research Services. (2000). *Employer satisfaction with graduate skills: Research report*. Retrieved November 23, 2010, from http://www.dest.gov.au/archive/highered/eippubs/eip99-7/eip99_7pdf.pdf

Acker, S. (2003). Overcoming obstacles to authentic eportfolio assessment. *Campus Technology*. Retrieved January 23, 2005, from http://www.campus-technology.com/print.asp?ID=10788

Afflerbach, P. P. (1990). The influence of prior knowledge on expert readers' main idea construction strategies. *Reading Research Quarterly*, *25*(1), 31–46. doi:10.2307/747986

Ajzen, I. (1985). From intentions to actions: A theory of planned behavior. In Kuhl, J., & Beckmann, J. (Eds.), *Action control: From cognition to behavior* (pp. 11–39). Berlin, Germany: Springer-Verlag. doi:10.1007/978-3-642-69746-3_2

Alexander, J. M., Carr, M., & Schwanenflugel, P. J. (1995). Development of metacognition in gifted children: Directions for future research. *Developmental Review*, *15*, 137. doi:10.1006/drev.1995.1001

Allen Consulting Group. (2006). *Assessment and reporting of employability skills in training packages*. Retrieved November 23, 2010, from http://www.dest.gov.au/NR/rdonlyres/D77220DC-78AB-42C6-86A6-2FA61BE1A69D/12778/Assessment_and_Reporting_Employability_Skills_3103.pdf

Altrichter, H., Posch, P., & Somekh, B. (1993). *Teachers investigate their work*. London, UK: Routledge.

American Association of Colleges of Teacher Education. (1992). *RATE V. Teaching teachers: Facts and figures*. Washington, DC: American Association of Colleges of Teacher Education.

American Association of State Colleges and Universities. (1999). *Facing change: building faculty of the future*. Washington, DC: American Association of State Colleges and Universities.

American School Counselor Association. (2004). *ASCA national standards for students*. Alexandria, VA: Author.

Amirian, S., & Flanigan, E. (2006). *Create your digital portfolio: The fast track to career success*. Indianapolis, IN: JIST.

Anderson, C. (2006). *The long tail: Why the future of business is selling less of more*. New York, NY: Hyperion.

Anderson, R. C., & Freebody, P. (1981). Vocabulary knowledge. In Guthrie, J. T. (Ed.), *Comprehension and teaching: Research reviews* (pp. 77–117). Newark, DE: International Reading Association.

Anderson, R. C., Hiebert, E. H., Scott, J. A., & Wilkinson, I. A. G. (1985). *Becoming a nation of readers*. Washington, DC: National Institute of Education.

Antonenko, P. D., & Niederhauser, D. S. (2010). The influence of leads on cognitive load and learning in a hypertext environment. *Computers in Human Behavior*, *28*, 140–150. doi:10.1016/j.chb.2009.10.014

Aronson, E., & Patnoe, S. (1997). *The jigsaw classroom: Building cooperation in the classroom*. New York, NY: Longman.

Arreola, R. (1995). *Developing a comprehensive faculty evaluation system: A guidebook for college faculty and administrators on designing and operating a comprehensive faculty evaluation system.* Bolton, MA: Anker.

Association of American Colleges and Universities (AAC&U). (2008, January 9). *How should colleges assess and improve student learning? Employers' views on the accountability challenge.* Washington, DC: Association of American Colleges and Universities.

Attwell, G., Chrzaszcz, A., Hilzensauer, W., Hornung-Prähauser, V., & Pallister, J. (2007). *Grab your future with an e-portfolio – Study on new qualifications and skills needed by teachers and career counselors to empower young learners with the e-portfolio concept and tools – Summary report.* Retrieved October 14, 2010, from http://www.mosep.org/study

Australian Bureau of Statistics (ABS). (2010). Higher education. In *Yearbook Australia 2010.* Retrieved November 23, 2010, from http://www.abs.gov.au/AUSSTATS/abs@.nsf/Lookup/6751D1E2E91DF21ECA257737001 69C93?opendocument

Australian Flexible Learning Framework. (2009a). *The VET e-portfolios roadmap: A strategic roadmap for e-portfolios to support lifelong learning.* Retrieved November 23, 2010, from http://www.flexiblelearning. net.au/files/Managing_Learner-Information_FINAL.pdf http://www.flexiblelearning.net.au/files/VETePortfolio-Roadmap_web.pdf

Australian Flexible Learning Framework. (2009b). *Managing learner information: Important considerations when implementing e-portfolios in VET.* Retrieved November 23, 2010, from http://www.flexiblelearning.net.au/files/Managing_Learner-Information_FINAL.pdf

Australian Flexible Learning Framework. (2009c). *E-portfolios for RPL assessment key findings on current engagement in the VET sector.* Retrieved November23, 2010 from http://www.flexiblelearning.net.au/files/E-portfolios_for_RPL_Assessment_Final_190309.pdf

Australian Flexible Learning Framework. (2010a, November 3-4). *ePortfolios Australia Conference (EAC2010).* Melbourne, Australia. Retrieved November 23, 2010, from http://www.flexiblelearning.net.au/content/e-portfolios-australia

Australian Flexible Learning Framework. (2010b). *E-portfolios reference group.* Retrieved November 23, 2010, from http://www.flexiblelearning.net.au/content/e-portfolios-reference-group-erg

Australian Flexible Learning Framework. (2010c). *E-assessment and the AQTF: Bridging the divide between practitioners and auditors.* Retrieved November 23, 2010, from http://www.flexiblelearning.net.au/files/Eassessment_AQTF_final.pdf

Australian Flexible Learning Framework. (2010d). *E-portfolio implementation trials.* Retrieved November 23, 2010, from http://www.flexiblelearning.net.au/content/e-portfolios-funding

Australian Flexible Learning Framework. (2010e). *2009 e-portfolio implementation trials.* Retrieved November 23, 2010, from http://www.flexiblelearning.net.au/content/2009EIT

Australian Government. (2008). *Australia 2020 summit: Initial summit report.* Retrieved November 23, 2010, from http://www.australia2020.gov.au/docs/2020_Summit_initial_report.pdf

Australian Universities Quality Agency (AUQA). (2010). *Home page.* Retrieved November 23, 2010, from http://www.auqa.edu.au/

Avalos, M. (2004). *Promotion and tenure portfolios.* Phoenix, AZ: Office of Research and Faculty Development, Arizona State University – West Campus.

Ayersman, D. (1995). Effects of knowledge representation format and hypermedia instruction on metacognitive accuracy. *Computers in Human Behavior, 11*(3-4), 533–555. doi:10.1016/0747-5632(95)80016-2

Ayres, P., & Sweller, J. (2005). The split-attention principle in multimedia learning. In Mayer, R. E. (Ed.), *The Cambridge handbook of multimedia learning* (pp. 135–146). New York, NY: Cambridge University Press.

Balaban, I., & Bubas, G. (2009). Evaluating an eportfolio system: The case of a hybrid university course. In *Proceedings of the ICL Conference: The Challenges of Lifelong Learning*, Villach, Austria (pp. 638-643).

Balaban, I., & Kisasondi, T. (2009). A lightweight ep-ortfolio artifact integrity method. In *Proceedings of the ICL Conference: The Challenges of Lifelong Learning*, Villach, Austria (pp. 681-686).

Balaban, I., Divjak, B., & Kopic, M. (2010). Emerging issues in using eportfolio. In *Proceedings of the I-Learning Forum*, London, UK.

Balaban, I. (2010). First steps in using eportfolio in a university course. In Landeta Etxeberria, A. (Ed.), *E-learning new tendencies and innovation didactic activities* (pp. 155–164). Madrid, Spain: CEF.

Bandura, A., & Schunk, D. H. (1981). Cultivating competence, self-efficacy, and intrinsic interest through proximal self-motivation. *Journal of Personality and Social Psychology, 41*, 586–598. doi:10.1037/0022-3514.41.3.586

Barbera, E. (2009). Mutual feedback in e-portfolio assessment: an approach to the netfolio system. *British Journal of Educational Technology, 40*(2), 342–357. doi:10.1111/j.1467-8535.2007.00803.x

Barki, H., Rivard, S., & Talbot, J. (1988). An information systems keyword classification scheme. *Management Information Systems Quarterly, 12*, 299–322. doi:10.2307/248855

Barone, C. (2001). Conditions for transformation: Infrastructure is not the issue. *EDUCAUSE Review, 2001*, 40–47.

Barrett, H. (2000). *Electronic teaching portfolios: multimedia skills + portfolio development = professional power*. Retrieved September 20, 2010, from http://electronicportfolios.com/portfolios/site2000.html

Barrett, H. (2004). *Electronic portfolio handbook* (4th ed.). Retrieved January 23, 2005, from http://www.electronicportfolios.com/handbook/index.html

Barrett, H. (2004). *Standards-based electronic portfolio handbook for assessment and evaluation*. Retrieved March 1, 2009, from http://electronicportfolios.com/handbook/index.html

Barrett, H. (2004, July 17). *Differentiating electronic portfolios and online assessment management systems*. Retrieved October 29, 2009, from http://electronicportfolios.com/systems/concerns.html

Barrett, H. (2006). *Authentic assessment with electronic portfolios using common software and Web 2.0 tools*. Retrieved March, 15, 2009, from http://electronicportfolios.org/web20.html

Barrett, H., & Carney, J. (2005). *Conflicting paradigms and competing purposes in electronic portfolio development*. Retrieved November 30, 2009, from http://electronicportfolios.org/systems/paradigms.html

Barrett, H., & Carney, J. (2005). *Conflicting paradigms and competing purposes in electronic portfolio development*. Retrieved October 14, 2010, from http://pdfcast.org/pdf/conflicting-paradigms-and-competing-purposes-in-electronic-portfolio-development

Barrett, H., & Knezek, D. (2003). *E-portfolios: Issues in assessment, accountability and preservice teacher preparation*. Paper presented at the Annual Conference of the American Educational Research Association, Chicago, IL.

Barrett, H., & Knezek, D. (2003, April 21-25). e-Portfolios: Issues in assessment, accountability and preservice teacher preparation. In *Proceedings of the American Educational Research Association (AERA) Conference*, Chicago, IL.

Batson, T. (2007). The ePortfolio hijacked. *Campus Technology*. Retrieved March 1, 2009, from http://campustechnology.com/articles/2007/12/the-eportfolio-hijacked.aspx

Batson, T. (2008). Is Web 2.0 designed for education? In *Campus Technology*. Retrieved. March 5, 2008, from http://www.campustechnology.com/article.aspx?aid=59341

Belanoff, P., & Dickson, M. (1991). *Portfolios: Process and product. Portsmouth, NH: Boynton/Cook, Heinemann. Bolton, G. (2005). Reflective practice: Writing and professional development* (2nd ed.). Thousand Oaks, CA: Sage.

Bertrand, Y. (1995). *Contemporary theories and practice in education*. Madison, WI: Magna.

Biggs, J. (1996). Enhancing teaching through constructive alignment. *Higher Education: The International Journal of Higher Education and Educational Planning, 32*(3), 347–364. doi:10.1007/BF00138871

Boud, D. (2006). Foreword. In Bryan, C., & Clegg, K. (Eds.), *Innovative assessment in higher education*. London, UK: Routledge.

Boud, D., & Falchikov, N. (Eds.). (2007). *Rethinking assessment in higher education*. London, UK: Routledge.

Boud, D., Keogh, R., & Walker, D. (Eds.). (1985). *Reflection: turning experience into learning*. London, UK: Kogan Page.

Bragg, S. M. (2006). *Outsourcing: A guide to selecting the correct business unit, negotiating the contract, maintaining control of the process* (2nd ed.). New York, NY: John Wiley & Sons.

Bräuer, G. (2005). *Analyse der Portfolio-Arbeit im Projekt "Neue Wege in die Ausbildung"* (unpublished project report). Mannheim, Germany: BVJ/perpetuum novile.

Bräuer, G. (2007a). Portfolios in der Lehrerausbildung als Grundlage für eine neue Lernkultur in der Schule. In M. Gläser-Zikuda & T. Hascher (Eds.), *Lernprozesse dokumentieren, reflektieren und beurteilen* (45-62). Bad Helbrunn, Germany: Klinkhardt.

Bräuer, G. (2007b). *Lernplattform und Portfolio* (Arbeitsmaterial, Projekt Scriptorium). Retrieved January 12, 2011, from http://www.scriptorium-project.org/claroline/claroline/document/document.php

Bräuer, G. (2009). Reflecting the practice of foreign language learning in portfolios. *German as a Foreign Language*. Retrieved January 1, 2012, from http://www.gfl-journal.de

Bräuer, G. (1998). *Schreibend lernen: Grundlagen einer theoretischen und praktischen Schreibpädagogik*. Innsbruck, Austria: Studienverlag.

Bräuer, G. (2003). *Schreiben als reflexive Praxis: Tagebuch, Arbeitsjournal, Portfolio* (2nd ed.). Freiburg, Germany: Fillibach.

Bräuer, G. (2006a). Keine verordneten Hochglanz-Portfolios, bitte! Die Korruption einer schönen Idee? In Brunner, I., Häcker, T., & Winter, F. (Eds.), *Das Handbuch Portfolioarbeit. Konzepte, Anregungen, Erfahrungen aus Schule und Lehrerbildung* (pp. 257–261). Seelze-Velber, Germany: Kallmeyer.

Bräuer, G. (2006b). Eine andere Schreibkultur für die Schule bereits im Studium erleben. *Journal für LehrerInnenbildung, 3*(6), 8–13.

Bräuer, G., Keller, M., & Winter, F. (Eds.). (2012). *Portfolio macht Schule. Unterrichts- und Schulentwicklung mit Portfolio*. Seelze-Velber, Germany: Klett-Kallmeyer.

Brew, A. (1999). Towards autonomous assessment: using self-assessment and peer assessment. In Brown, S., & Glasner, A. (Eds.), *Assessment matters in higher education*. Buckingham, UK: Open University Press.

Brindley, C., & Scoffield, S. (1998). Peer assessment in undergraduate programmes. *Teaching in Higher Education, 3*(1), 79–90. doi:10.1080/1356215980030106

British Colombia (BC). (2007). *Adult graduation diploma program (Adult Dogwood)*. Retrieved May, 3, 2008, from http://www.bced.gov.bc.ca/graduation/portfolio/

Broek, P. V. D., Lynch, J. S., Naslund, J., Ievers-Landis, C. E., & Verduin, K. (2003). The development of comprehension of main ideas in narratives: Evidence from the selection of titles. *Journal of Educational Psychology, 95*, 707–718. doi:10.1037/0022-0663.95.4.707

Brookfield, S. (1995). *Becoming a critically reflective teacher*. San Francisco, CA: Jossey Bass.

Brooks, J. G., & Brooks, M. G. (1993). *In search of understanding: The case for a constructivist classroom*. Alexandria, VA: Association for Supervision and Curriculum Development.

Brossard, D., & Shanahan, J. (2006). Do they know what they read? Building scientific literacy measurement based on science media coverage. *Science Communication, 28*(1), 47–63. doi:10.1177/1075547006291345

Brown, S. (1998). *Peer assessment in practice*. Birmingham, UK: SEDA.

Bruffee, K. A. (1995). Sharing our toys: Cooperative learning versus collaborative learning. *Change, 27*(1), 12–18. doi:10.1080/00091383.1995.9937722

Brusilovsky, P. (2004). Knowledge tree: A distributed architecture for adaptive e-learning. In *Proceedings of the World Wide Web Conference* (pp. 104-113).

Bryan, C., & Clegg, K. (Eds.). (2006). *Innovative Assessment in higher education*. London, UK: Routledge.

Burns, D. (2007). *Systemic action research: A strategy for whole system change*. Bristol, UK: The Policy Press.

Business and Higher Education Round Table (BHERT). (2001). *The critical importance of lifelong learning (BHERT Position Paper No. 4)*. Sydney, Australia: Author.

Butler, P. (2006). *A review of the literature on portfolios and electronic portfolios*. Palmerston North, New Zealand: eCDF ePortfolio Project, Massey University College of Education Licensed under the Creative Commons.

Cambridge, B. L., & Williams, A. C. (1997). *Portfolio learning*. Upper Saddle River, NJ: Prentice Hall.

Cambridge, D. (Ed.). (2009). *E-Portfolios and global diffusion: Solutions for collaborative education*. Hershey, PA: IGI Global.

Cambridge, D., Cambridge, B., & Yancey, K. (2009). *Electronic Portfolios 2.0: Emergent* RESEARCH ON IMPLEMENTATION AND IMPA*ct*. Sterling, VA: Stylus.

Cambridge, D., Cambridge, B., & Yancey, K. B. (2009). Electronic portfolio technology and design for learning. In Cambridge, D., Cambridge, B., & Yancey, K. B. (Eds.), *Electronic Portfolios 2.0: Emergent research on implementation and impact*. Sterling, VA: Stylus.

Campbell, D., Cignetti, P., Melenyer, B., Nettles, D., & Wyman, R. (2004). *How to develop a professional portfolio*. Boston, MA: Pearson Education.

Campbell, J., Smith, D., Boulton-Lewis, G., Brownlee, J., Burnett, P., & Carrington, S. (2001). Students' perceptions of teaching and learning: The influence of students' approaches to learning and teachers' approaches to teaching. *Teachers and Teaching: Theory and Practice*, *7*(2), 173–187.

Canto. (n. d.). *Cumulus*. Retrieved August 28, 2008, from http://www.canto.com

Carnegie Foundation. (1989). *The condition of the professoriate: Attitudes and trends, 1989*. Princeton, NJ: Author.

Carney, J. (2005). *What kind of electronic portfolio research do we need?* Paper presented at the Annual Meeting of the Society for Information Technology and Teacher Education.

Carr, V. H., Jr. (2001). *Technology adoption and diffusion*. Retrieved October 3, 2010, from http://www.au.af.mil/au/awc/awcgate/innovation/adoptiondiffusion.htm

Carrick Institute for Learning and Teaching in Higher Education. (2007). *Research brief: e-portfolios for university students*. Retrieved March 21, 2008, from http://www.carrickinstitute.edu.au/carrick/webdav/site/carricksite/users/siteadmin/public/grants_priority_eportfolios_researchbrief_april2007.pdf

Carson, J., & Nelson, G. (1996). Chinese students' perceptions of ESL peer response group interaction. *Journal of Second Language Writing*, *5*, 1–19. doi:10.1016/S1060-3743(96)90012-0

Centre National de Formation des Formateurs (CENAFFE). (2008). *Ministère de l'éducation*. Retrieved March 19, 2009 from http://www.cenaffe.edunet.tn/index.php

CFCC. (2007). *Journées de réflexion sur l'évaluation du français – Egypte*. Retrieved March 3, 2009, from http://www.ambafrance-eg.org/cfcc/IMG/pdf/Message_d_ouverture_R._Adam.pdf

Challis, D. (2005). Towards the mature ePortfolio: Some implications for higher education. *Canadian Journal of Learning and Technology, 31*(3). Retrieved November 2, 2010, from http://www.cjlt.ca/index.php/cjlt/article/viewArticle/93/87

Chang, C.-C. (2009). Self-evaluated effects of web-based portfolio assessment system for various student motivation levels. *Journal of Educational Computing Research*, *41*(4), 391–405. doi:10.2190/EC.41.4.a

Chang, C.-C., Tseng, K.-H., Yueh, H.-P., & Lin, W.-C. (2010). Consideration factors and adoption of type, tabulation and framework for creating e-portfolios. *Computers & Education, 56*(2).

Chang, K.-E., Sung, Y.-T., & Chen, S.-F. (2001). Learning through computer-based concept mapping with scaffolding aid. *Journal of Computer Assisted Learning*, *17*(1), 21–33. doi:10.1046/j.1365-2729.2001.00156.x

Chang, S.-N. (2007). Externalizing students' mental models through concept maps. *Journal of Biological Education*, *41*(3), 107–112. doi:10.1080/00219266.2007.9656078

Chapelle, C. (1998). Construct definition and validity inquiry in SLA research. In Bachman, L. F., & Cohen, A. D. (Eds.), *Interfaces between second language acquisition and language testing research* (pp. 32–70). Cambridge, UK: Cambridge University Press.

Chen, H. L., Cannon, D., Gabrio, J., Leifer, L., Toye, G., & Bailey, T. (2005). Using Wikis and weblogs to support reflective learning in an introductory engineering design course. In *Proceedings of the American Society for Engineering Education Annual Conference & Exposition*, Stanford, CA.

Chéneau-Loquay, A. (2009). Accès aux nouvelles technologies en Afrique et en Asie: TIC et service universel. In L'Harmattan (Ed.), *Cahiers des sciences socials sur les enjeux des technologies de la communication dans les SUD* (4th ed.). Versailles, France: CEA-CNRS. Retrieved March 22, 2010, from books.google.com

Chen, N.-S., Kinshuk, C.-W. W., & Chen, H.-J. (2008). Mining e-Learning domain concept map from academic articles. *Computers & Education, 50*, 1009–2001. doi:10.1016/j.compedu.2006.10.001

Cheung, H. L., Fisher, D., Pickard, V., & Chan, Y. F. (2009). *Scaffolding student learning: Integrating ePortfolios into the university experience.* Paper presented at the Improving University Teaching International Conference, Burnaby, BC, Canada.

Chuang, H.-H. (2010). Weblog-based electronic portfolios for student teachers in Taiwan. *Educational Technology Research and Development, 58*, 211–227. doi:10.1007/s11423-008-9098-1

Clark, J. E., & Eynon, B. (2009). E-portfolios at 2.0: Surveying the field. *Peer Review, 11*(1), 18-23. Retrieved October 29, 2009, from AAC&U website: http://www.aacu.org/peerreview/pr-wi09/pr-wi09_eportfolios.cfm

Cloutier, M., Fortier, G., & Slade, S. (2006). *Le portfolio numérique, un atout pour le citoyen apprenant. Société de formation à distance des commissions scolaires du Québec (SOFAD) et Cégep@distance. Récupéré le 11 septembre 2009 du site de la SOFAD.* Retrieved from http://www.sofad.qc.ca/pdf/portfolio_numerique.pdf

Cochran-Smith, M. (2005). Studying teacher education. *Journal of Teacher Education, 56*(4), 301–306. doi:10.1177/0022487105280116

Cochran-Smith, M. (2005). Teacher accreditation. *Journal of Teacher Education, 56*(4), 299–300. doi:10.1177/0022487105280117

Commission of the European Communities. (2001). *Making a European area of lifelong learning a reality.* Brussels, Belgium: Author.

Croger Associates Pty Ltd. (2007). *Research report: Interoperability standards across the Australian education and training sector.* Retrieved November 23, 2010, from http://www.aictec.edu.au/aictec/webdav/site/standardssite/shared/ Interoperability%20Standards%20Report.pdf

Curyer, S., Leeson, J., Mason, J., & Williams, A. (2007). *Developing eportfolios for VET: Policy issues and interoperability.* Retrieved November 23, 2010, from http://e-standards.flexiblelearning.net.au/docs/vet-eportfolio-report-v1-0.doc

Danielson, C. (1996). *Enhancing professional practice: A framework for teaching.* Alexandria, VA: Association for Supervision and Curriculum.

Darling-Hammond, L. (2009, November 17). *Lessons from abroad: International standards and assessments.* A webinar presented for Edutopia and the Stanford Center for Opportunity Policy in Education in collaboration with the Council for Chief State School Officers.

Darling-Hammond, L. (2006). Constructing 21st-century teacher education. *Journal of Teacher Education, 57*(3), 300–314. doi:10.1177/0022487105285962

Darling-Hammond, L., & McLaughlin, M. L. (1995). Policies that support professional development in an era of reform. *Phi Delta Kappan, 76*(8), 587–604.

Dearing, R. (1997). *Higher education in the learning society - The report of the National Committee of Inquiry into higher education.* London, UK: HMSO. Retrieved July 20, 2008, from http://www.leeds.ca.uk/educol/ncihe

Dearing, R. (1997). *National Committee of Inquiry into higher education.* Retrieved November 23, 2010, from http://www.leeds.ac.uk/educol/ncihe/

Deneen, P. (2009, March 26). *Against monoculture.* Retrieved October 29, 2009, from http://www.frontporchrepublic.com/?p=1739

Department for Education and Skills. (2005). *Harnessing technology: Transforming learning and children's services*. London, UK: Department for Education and Skills.

Department of Education Employment and Workplace Relations (DEEWR). (2008b). *Digital education revolution: Overview.* Retrieved November 23, 2010, from http://www.digitaleducationrevolution.gov.au/about.htm

Department of Education, Science and Training. (DEST). (2006). *Bologna process and Australia: Next steps.* Retrieved November 23, 2010, from http://www.dest.gov.au/sectors/higher_education/publications_resources/profiles/bologna_process_and_australia.htm

Department of Education. Employment and Workplace Relations (DEEWR). (2008a). *Review of Australian higher education.* Retrieved November 23, 2010, from http://www.deewr.gov.au/highereducation/review/pages/reviewofaustralianhighereducationreport.aspx

Department of Education. Employment and Workplace Relations (DEEWR). (2009). *Transforming Australia's higher education system.* Retrieved November 23, 2010, from http://www.deewr.gov.au/HigherEducation/Pages/TransformingAustraliasHESystem.aspx

Department of Education. Employment and Workplace Relations (DEEWR). (2010a). *Overview*. Retrieved November 23, 2010, from http://www.deewr.gov.au/HigherEducation/Pages/Overview.aspx/

Department of Education. Employment and Workplace Relations (DEEWR). (2010b). *Productivity places program.* Retrieved November 23, 2010, from http://www.deewr.gov.au/Skills/Programs/SkillTraining/ProductivityPlaces/Pages/default.aspx

Department of Education. Training and the Arts (DETA). (2007). *ICT pedagogical license.* Retrieved November 23, 2010, from http://education.qld.gov.au/smartclassrooms/strategy/tsdev_pd-licence.html

DiGiovanni, E., & Nagaswami, G. (2001). Online peer review: An alternative to face-to-face? *EFL Journal, 55*(3), 263–272.

Dishner, E. K., & Readence, J. E. (1973). *A systematic procedure for teaching main idea.* Paper presented at the Annual Meeting of the National Reading Conference.

Dove. (n. d.). *Campaign for real beauty.* Retrieved August 7, 2007, from http://www.campaignforrealbeauty.com.au/self-esteem-fund/why-it-matters.asp

Downes, S. (2006). Learning networks and connective knowledge (Discussion Paper No. 92). In *Proceedings of the Instructional Technology Forum.* Retrieved March 5, 2008, from http://it.coe.uga.edu/itforum/paper92/paper92.html

Dreyfus, S. E. (2004). The five-stage model of adult skill acquisition. *Bulletin of Science, Technology & Society, 24*(3), 177–181. doi:10.1177/0270467604264992

Edgerton, R., Hutchings, P., & Quinlan, K. (1991). *The teaching portfolio: Capturing the scholarship in teaching.* Washington, DC: American Association of Higher Education.

Education en France. (2006). *Plan en faveur des technologies de l'information appliquées à l'éducation.* Retrieved March 19, 2009, from http://www.education.gouv.fr/cid3949/plan-en-faveur-des-technologies-de-l-information-appliquees-a-l-education.html

education.au. (2008a). *National symposium on e-portfolios: Background paper.* Retrieved November 23, 2010, from http://educationau.edu.au/jahia/webdav/site/myjahiasite/shared/papers/eportfolio_background_paper.pdf

education.au. (2008b). *E-portfolio symposium: Draft recommendations.* Retrieved July 20, 2008, from http://educationau.edu.au/jahia/Jahia/pid/637

Edunet. (2008). *Portail Educatif Tunisien.* Retrieved March 19, 2009, from http://www.edunet.tn

EduPortfolio. (2006). *Portfolio de TIC et Education.* Retrieved March 24, 2009, from http://eduportfolio.org/791

Edutopia. (2008, February 28). *Why teach with project learning? Providing students with a well-rounded classroom experience.* Retrieved on November 30, 2009, from Edutopia website: http://www.edutopia.org/project-learning-introduction

Edwards, G. (2000). *Connecting PDP to employer needs and the world of work* (Project Report to QAA). Retrieved July 20, 2008, from http://www.qaa.ac.uk

Eisen, J. (1996). *Creating a teaching portfolio: The SCRIPT model.* Tampa, FL: Center for Teaching Enhancement, University of South Florida.

Elgg. (2008). *Powerful, professional social networking.* Retrieved March 5, 2009, from http://elgg.org/

Elliott, E. (Ed.). (2003). *Assessing education candidate performance: A look at changing practices.* Washington, DC: National Council for Accreditation of Teacher Education.

Elouriachi, M. A. (2005). *Le portfolio numérique en classe.* Retrieved March 5, 2009, from http://www.ibnrochd.ma/gallery_files/porfolio_eleve_inspect_oujda.doc

Emmett, D. J. (2003). *E-portfolios at QUT: Providing the potential for competitive advantage and a motivating learner-centred environment.* Paper presented at the OLT Excellence: Making the Connections Conference, Brisbane, Australia.

Epsilen. (n. d.). *Portfolios.* Retrieved July 30, 2008, from http://www.epsilen.com

Europass. (2004). *Five documents to make your skills and qualifications clearly and easily understood in Europe.* Retrieved September 19, 2008 from http://europass.cedefop.europa.eu

Evans, S., & Green, C. (2007). Why EAP is necessary: A survey of Hong Kong tertiary students. *Journal of English for Academic Purposes, 6,* 3–17. doi:10.1016/j.jeap.2006.11.005

Extensis. (n. d.). *Portfolios.* Retrieved August 25, 2008, from http://www.extensis.com

Falchikov, N. (1995). Peer feedback marking: Developing peer assessment. *Innovations in Education and Training International, 32*(2), 175–187. doi:10.1080/1355800950320212

Fielden, J. (2007). *Global horizons for UK universities.* London, UK: Council for Industry and Higher Education. Retrieved September 9, 2008, from http://www.cihe-uk.com/docs/PUBS/0711IntHEsumm.pdf

Fix, M. (2006). *Texte schreiben: Schreibprozesse im Deutschunterricht.* Paderborn, Germany: Schöningh.

Fleet, J., Goodchild, F., & Zajchowski, R. (1999). *Learning for success: Effective strategies for students* (3rd ed.). Toronto, ON, Canada: Harcourt, Brace.

Fosnot, C. T. (1996). Constructivism: A psychological theory of learning. In Fosnot, C. T. (Ed.), *Constructivism: Theory, perspectives, and practice* (pp. 8–33). New York, NY: Teacher College Press.

Garner, B. K. (2007). *Getting to got it! Helping struggling students learn how to learn.* Alexandria, VA: Association for Supervision and Curricukum Development.

Gathercoal, P., Love, D., Bryde, B., & McKean, G. (2002). *On implementing Web-based electronic portfolios.* Retrieved March 6, 2006, from EDUCAUSE website: http://net.educause.edu/ir/library/pdf/eqm0224.pdf

Gathercoal, P., Love, D., Bryde, B., & McKean, G. (2002). On implementing Web-based electronic portfolios. *EDUCAUSE Quarterly, 25*(2), 29–37.

Gibbs, G. (2006). How assessment frames student learning. In Bryan, C., & Clegg, K. (Eds.), *Innovative assessment in higher education* (pp. 23–36). London, UK: Routledge.

Giest, H., & Lompscher, J. (2003). Formation of learning activity and theoretical thinking in science teaching. In Kozulin, A., Ginidis, B., Ageyev, V., & Miller, S. (Eds.), *Vygotsky's educational theory in cultural contexts* (pp. 267–288). Cambridge, UK: Cambridge University Press.

Gläser-Zikuda, M., & Hascher, T. (Eds.). (2007). *Lernprozesse dokumentieren, reflektieren und beurteilen. Lerntagebuch und Portfolio in Bildungsforschung und Bildungspraxis.* Bad Helbrunn, Austria: Klinkhardt.

GNU Operating System. (2010). *Licenses.* Retrieved from http://www.gnu.org/licenses

Goody, A., & von Konsky, B. (2010). *Giving life to teaching portfolios.* Retrieved February 9, 2011, from http://www.flexiblelearning.net.au/files/EAC2010_Abstracts_eBook_20101109.pdf

Goodyear, P. (1998). New technology in higher education: Understanding the innovation process. In *Proceedings of the Integrating Information and Communication Technology in Higher Education (BITE) Meeting,* Maastricht, The Netherlands. Retrieved January 23, 2005, from http://www.lancs.ac.uk/staff/erapmg

Grant, S. (2005). *Clear e-portfolio definitions: A prerequisite for effective interoperability.* Paper presented at the ePortfolio Conference, Cambridge, UK.

Grant, S., et al. (2010). *Leap2A specification.* Retrieved from http://wiki.cetis.ac.uk/LEAP2A_specification

Graves, A. W., & Levin, J. R. (1989). Comparison of monitoring and mnemonic text-processing strategies in learning disabled students. *Learning Disability Quarterly, 12*, 232–236. doi:10.2307/1510693

Green, C. (1994). *Campus computing report.* Encino, CA: EDUCAUSE. Retrieved January 23, 2005, from http://www.campuscomputing.net/pdf/1994-CCP.pdf

Green, C. (1997). *Campus computing report.* Encino, CA: EDUCAUSE. Retrieved January 23, 2005, from http://www.campuscomputing.net/pdf/1997-CCP.pdf

Green, C. (2003). *Campus computing report.* Encino, CA: EDUCAUSE. Retrieved January 23, 2005, from http://www.campuscomputing.net/pdf/2003-CCP.pdf

Greenberg, G. (2004). The digital convergence: Extending the portfolio model. *EDUCAUSE Review, 39*(4), 28–34.

Greller, W. (2007). A sample e-portfolio service model for higher education. In Griffiths, D., Koper, R., & Liber, O. (Eds.), *Service oriented approaches and lifelong competence development infrastructures* (pp. 68–74). Manchester, UK: TENC.

Grey, D. (1999). *Knowledge mapping: a practical overview.* Retrieved September 14, 2009, from http://www.impactalliance.org/file_download.php?location¼S_U&filename¼10383546681Knowledge_Mapping.htm

Grush, M. (2008). The future of Web 2.0. In *Campus Technology.* Retrieved February 27, 2008, from http://www.campustechnology.com/articles/58872_1/

Gulbahar, Y., & Tinmaz, H. (2006). Implementing project-based learning and e-portfolio assessment in an undergraduate course. *Journal of Research on Technology in Education, 38*(3), 309–327.

Gu, Y., & Johnson, R. K. (1996). Vocabulary learning strategies and language learning outcomes. *Language Learning, 46*(4), 643–679. doi:10.1111/j.1467-1770.1996.tb01355.x

Hafner, C. A., & Miller, L. (2010). *Learner Autonomy and the role of technology.* Seminar presented at the Hong Kong Association of Self-Access and Learner Development, Hong Kong.

Hallam, G., Harper, W., Hauville, K., McAllister, L., & Creagh, T. (2008). *ePortfolio use by university students in Australia: Informing excellence in policy and practice.* Retrieved November 23, 2010, from http://www.eportfoliopractice.qut.edu.au/docs/Aep_Final_Report/AeP_Report_ebook.pdf

Hallam, G., Harper, W., McAllister, L., Hauville, K., & Creagh, T. (2010). *ePortfolio use by university students: Informing excellence in policy and practice. Supplementary report.* Retrieved November 23, 2010, from http://www.eportfoliopractice.qut.edu.au/survey/index.jsp

Hamp-Lyons, L., & Condon, W. (2000). *Assessing the portfolio: Principles for practice, theory and research.* Cresskill, NJ: Hampton Press.

Haney, J. J., & McArthur, J. (2002). Four case studies of prospective science teachers' beliefs concerning constructivist teaching practice. *Science Education, 86*(6), 783–802. doi:10.1002/sce.10038

Hargadon, S. (2008). *Web 2.0 is the future of education.* Retrieved March 4, 2008, from http://www.stevehargadon.com/2008/03/web-20-is-future-of-education.html

Harman, K., & Koohang, A. (2007). *Learning objects -Standards, metadata, repositories, and LCMS.* Santa Rosa, CA: Informing Science Institute.

Hartnell-Young, E., Harrison, C., Crook, C., Joyes, G., Davies, L., & Fisher, T. (2007). *The impact of e-portfolios on learning.* Coventry, UK: British Educational Communications and Technology Agency (Becta).

Haynes, M., & Baker, I. (1993). American and Chinese readers learning from lexical familiarizations in English text. In Huckin, T., Haynes, M., & Coady, J. (Eds.), *Second language reading and vocabulary learning* (pp. 130–152). Norwood, NJ: Ablex.

Heinrich, E., Bhattacharya, M., & Rayudu, R. (2007). Preparation for lifelong learning using ePortfolios. *European Journal of Engineering Education, 32*(6), 653–663. doi:10.1080/03043790701520602

Hillocks, G. Jr. (1995). *Teaching writing as reflective practice*. New York, NY: Teachers College Press.

Himpsl, K., & Baumgartner, P. (2009). Evaluation of e-portfolio software. *International Journal of Emerging Technologies in Learning, 4*(1).

Huang, Y. (2006). Sustaining ePortfolio: Progress, challenges and changing dynamics in teacher education. In Jafari, A., & Kaufman, C. (Eds.), *Handbook of research on eportfolios* (pp. 2150–2162). Hershey, PA: Idea Group. doi:10.4018/978-1-59140-890-1.ch045

IMS Global Learning Consortium Inc. (2008). *IMS global consortium*. Retrieved February 22, 2008, from http://www.imsglobal.org/ep/index.html

IMS. (2007). *ePortfolio best practice and implementation guide*. Retrieved May, 3, 2007, from http://www.imsglobal.org/ep/epv1p0/imsep_bestv1p0.html

Irons, A. (2008). *Enhancing learning through formative assessment and feedback*. London, UK: Routledge.

Irvine, M. (2007, January 8). Survey illuminates teen social networks. *USA Today*. Retrieved from http://www.usatoday.com/tech/news/2007-01-08-teen-networks_x.htm

Ittelson, G. L. (2005, July). *An overview of e-portfolios*. Retrieved January 14, 2008, from EDUCAUSE website: http://net.educause.edu/ir/library/pdf/ELI3001.pdf

Iwan, R. (2006). Wie man schreibend den Weg von der Schule in die Ausbildung finden kann. In Bräuer, G. (Ed.), *Schreiben(d) lernen: Ideen und Projekte für die Schule* (2nd ed., pp. 71–83). Hamburg, Germany: Edition Körber-Stiftung.

Jackson, B. (2003). Education reform as if student agency mattered academic microcultures and student identity. *Phi Delta Kappan, •••*, 84.

Jacobowitz, T. (1990). A metacognitive strategy for constructing the main idea of text. *Journal of Reading, 33*(6), 620–624.

Jafari, A. (2004). The "sticky" eportfolio system: Tackling challenges and identifying attributes. *EDUCAUSE Review, 39*(4), 38–45.

JISC. (2006). *Epics project final report*. Retrieved August 22, 2008, from http://www.jisc.ac.uk/whatwedo/programmes/programme_edistributed/epics.aspx#downloads

JISC. (2007a). *Effective practice with e-assessment*. Retrieved August 22, 2008, from http://www.jisc.ac.uk/media/documents/themes/elearning/effpraceassess.pdf

JISC. (2007b). *ISLE: Individualised support for learning through e-portfolios: All roads lead to enhanced learning?* Retrieved August 22, 2008, from http://www.jisc.ac.uk/media/documents/programmes/elearningsfc/sfcbookletisle.pdf

JISC. (2007c). *epistle: Individualised support for learning through e-portfolios: All roads lead to enhanced learning?* Retrieved August 22, 2008, from http://www.jisc.ac.uk/media/documents/programmes/elearningsfc/sfcbookletisle.pdf

JISC. (2007d). *myWorld final report*. Retrieved August 22, 2008, from http://www.jisc.ac.uk/whatwedo/programmes/programme_edistributed/myworld.aspx

JISC. (2008). *ePortfolio key resources*. Retrieved May 10, 2008, from http://www.jisc.ac.uk/whatwedo/themes/elearning/eportfolios/resources.aspx

JISC. (2008a). *eportfolios Infokit*. Retrieved August 22, 2008, from http://www.jiscinfonet.ac.uk/infokits/e-portfolios/

JISC. (2008b). *Circular 08/08: Projects in the areas of curriculum delivery, assessment and course advertising*. Retrieved August 22, 2008, from http://www.jisc.ac.uk/fundingopportunities/funding_calls/2008/06/circular808.aspx

Johnson, D. (2003). A planning and assessment model for developing effective CMS support. *Online Journal of Distance Learning Administration, 7*(1), 1–9.

Junior Achievement of Middle America. (2009). *Executive summary: Work-readiness impact of JA program participation*. Retrieved January 10, 2010, from http://jamidamerica.org/docs/rf/ExecutiveSummary-Work-ReadinessImpactofJAProgramParticipation.pdf

Junior Achievement of Middle America. (n. d.). *About*. Retrieved January 14, 2005, from http://www.ja.org/about/about.shtml

Kahn, S. (2001). Conclusion: Recommendations. In Cambridge, B. L. (Ed.), *Electronic portfolios: Emerging practices in student, faculty and institutional learning*. Washington, DC: American Association for Higher Education.

Kane, R., Sandretto, S., & Heath, C. (2002). Telling half the story: A critical review of research on the teaching beliefs of university academics. *Review of Educational Research*, *72*(2), 177–228. doi:10.3102/00346543072002177

Kankaanranta, M., Barrett, H. C., & Hartnell-Young, E. (2001). Exploring the use of electronic portfolios in international contexts. In *Proceedings of World Conference on Educational Multimedia, Hypermedia and Telecommunications* (pp. 874-876). Chesapeake, VA: AACE.

Karparov, Y. V. (2003). Vygotsky's doctrine of scientific concepts: Its role for contemporary education. In Kozulin, A., Ginidis, B., Ageyev, V., & Miller, S. (Eds.), *Vygotsky's educational theory in cultural context* (pp. 65–82). Cambridge, UK: Cambridge University Press.

Karsenti, T., & Williams, M. (2008). *EduPortfolio*. Retrieved May 5, 2008 from http://www.eduportfolio.org

Katz, R. (1999). Competitive strategies for higher education in the information age. In R. Katz (Ed.), *Dancing with the Devil: Information technology and the new competition in higher education*. San Francisco, CA: Jossey-Bass.

Kellner, D. (2000). New technologies/new literacies: Restructuring education for the new millennium. *Teaching Education*, *11*(3), 245–265. doi:10.1080/713698975

Kent, D. M., Bradbury, G. G., Kent, M. A., & Hand, R. W. (2010). *Mahara 1.2 ePortfolios: Beginner's guide*. Birmingham, UK: Packt.

Kinchin, I., & Hay, D. (2000). How a qualitative approach to concept map analysis can be used to aid learning by illustrating patterns of conceptual development. *Educational Research*, *42*(1), 143–157. doi:10.1080/001318800363908

Knight, P., & Yorke, M. (2003). *Assessment, learning and employability*. Maidenhead, UK: Open University.

Kong, H.-C. (1996). Teaching college English: From ESL to ESP. *Studies in English Language and Literature*, *1*, 40–45.

Kruse, O. (2006). The origins of writing in the disciplines. *Written Communication*, *23*(3), 331–352. doi:10.1177/0741088306289259

Labissiere, Y., & Reynolds, C. (2004). Using reflective electronic portfolios to enhance student learning. *Creative College Teaching Journal*, *1*(1), 49–61.

Lai, L.-C. (2009). *E-portfolio*. Retrieved October 7, 2010, from http://www.digitimes.com.tw/tw/dt/n/shwnws.asp?CnlID=10&id=0000138304_9A128D2F1YLGAJ3OZJG9N

Lankes, A. M. D. (1998). Portfolios: A new wave in assessment. *T.H.E. Journal*, *25*(9), 18.

Laufer, B. (1997). The lexical plight in second language reading: Words you don't know, words you think you know, and words you can't guess. In Coady, J., & Huckin, T. (Eds.), *Second language vocabulary acquisition: A rationale for pedagogy* (pp. 20–34). New York, NY: Cambridge University Press.

Lave, J., & Wenger, E. (1991). *Situated learning: Legitimate peripheral participation*. Cambridge, UK: Cambridge University Press.

Leece, R. (2005). The role of eportfolios in graduate recruitment. *Australian Journal of Career Development*, *14*(2), 72–79.

Leeson, J. (2008). *ePortfolios: Policy issues and interoperability*. Retrieved November 23, 2010, from http://www.avetra.org.au/AVETRA%20WORK%2011.04.08/CS3.2%20-%20Jerry%20Leeson.pdf

Lenhart, M., & Madden, M. (2007). *55% of online teens use social networks and 55% have created online profiles; older girls predominate*. Retrieved August 1, 2007, from Pew Internet website: http://www.pewinternet.org/Reports/2007/Social-Networking-Websites-and-Teens/Data-Memo/Findings.aspx

Levin, B. B., & Rock, T. C. (2003). The effects of collaborative action research on preservice and experienced teacher partners in professional development schools. *Journal of Teacher Education*, *54*(2), 135–149. doi:10.1177/0022487102250287

Lin, S. S.-J., Liu, E. Z.-F., & Yuan, S.-M. (2001). Web-based peer assessment: feedback for students with various thinking-styles. *Journal of Computer Assisted Learning, 17*, 420–432. doi:10.1046/j.0266-4909.2001.00198.x

Liu, C.-C., & Tsai, C.-M. (2005). Peer assessment through web-based knowledge acquisition: tools to support conceptual awareness. *Innovations in Education and Teaching International, 42*, 43–59. doi:10.1080/14703290500048838

Lorenzo, G., & Ittelson, J. (2005). *An overview of e-portfolios* (pp. 1-28). Washington, DC: Educause Learning Initiative. Retrieved October 11, 2010, from http://www.educause.edu/ir/library/pdf/ELI3001.pdf

Lorenzo, G., & Ittelson, J. (2005). *An overview of e-portfolios*. Washington, DC: EDUCAUSE Learning Initiative. Retrieved October 6, 2010, from http://www.educause.edu/LibraryDetailPage/666?ID=ELI3001

Lougheed, P., Bogyo, B., Brokenshire, D., & Kumar, V. (2005). Formalizing electronic portfolios in the SPARC ePortfolio tool. In *Proceedings of the Applications of Semantic Web Technologies for E-Learning workshop at the Third International Conference on Knowledge Capture.*

Lumsden, J. (2007). Development and implementation of an e-portfolio as a university-wide program. *New Directions for Student Services, 119*, 43–63. doi:10.1002/ss.248

Lyman-Hager, M., Davis, J. N., Burnett, J., & Chennault, R. (1993). Une Vie de Boy: Interactive reading in French. In *Proceedings of the CALICO Annual Symposium on Assessment* (pp. 93-97). Durham, NC: Duke University.

MacLeod, L. (1999). Computer-aided peer review of writing. *Business Communication Quarterly, 62*(3), 87–94. doi:10.1177/108056999906200309

Mandl, H., Gruber, H., & Renkl, A. (2002). Situiertes Lernen in multimedialen Lernumgebungen. In Issing, L. J., & Klimsa, P. (Eds.), *Information und Lernen mit Multimedia und Internet* (3rd ed., pp. 138–148). Winheim, Germany: Beltz Psychologie Verlags Union.

Manifesto. (2000). *The 6 key points.* Retrieved January 14, 2006, from Unesco website: http://www3.unesco.org/manifesto2000/

Mayank, S. (2008). *ELGG social networking.* Birmingham, UK: Packt.

McCowan, C., Harper, W., & Hauville, K. (2005). Student e-Portfolio: The successful implementation of an e-Portfolio across a major Australian university. *Australian Journal of Career Development, 14*(2).

Mehrpour, S., & Rahimi, M. (2010). The impact of general and specific vocabulary knowledge on reading and listening comprehension: A case of Iranian EFL learners. *System, 38*(2), 292–300. doi:10.1016/j.system.2010.01.004

Meyer, E., Abrami, P. C., Wade, C. A., Aslan, O., & Deault, L. (2010). Improving literacy and metacognition with electronic portfolios: Teaching and learning with ePEARL. *Computers & Education, 55*, 84–91. doi:10.1016/j.compedu.2009.12.005

Mhiri, H. (2005). *Cours: Technologie de l'Information et de la communication.* Retrieved March 23, 2009, from http://ut.uvt.rnu.tn/course/category.php?id=12

Mhiri, H. (2005). *Portfolio de Hédia Mhiri Sellami.* Retrieved May 5, 2008, from http://eduportfolio.com/558

Mhiri, H. (2005, July 6). Some difficulties in distance learning in developing countries. In *Proceedings of the IEEE 3rd International Workshop on Technology for Education in Developing Countries,* Kaohsiung, Taiwan.

Mhiri, H. (2007a, May). L'utilisation de l'ePortfolio pour le suivi d'étudiants en formation continue. In *Proceedings of the Congrés de l'Association Internationale de Pédagogie Universitaire,* Montreal, QC, Canada. Retrieved September, 29, 2008, from http://aipu2007.umontreal.ca/appel.php

Mhiri, H. (2007b). One ePortfolio for the life. *In Proceedings of the E-LEARN World Conference on E-Learning in Corporate, Government, Healthcare, and Higher Education.* Retrieved March 20, 2009, from http://www.editlib.org/j/ELEARN/v/2007/n/1

Moses, I. (1986). Promotion of academic staff: Reward and incentive. *Higher Education, 15*(1-2), 135–149. doi:10.1007/BF00138097doi:10.1007/BF00138097

Murray, F. (2005). On building a unified system of accreditation in teacher education. *Journal of Teacher Education, 56*(4), 307–317. doi:10.1177/0022487105279842

Naisbitt, J. (2006). *Mind set!: Reset your thinking and see the future.* New York, NY: HarperCollins.

National Broadband Network (NBN). (2010). *Home page*. Retrieved November 23, 2010 from http://www.nbn.gov.au/

National Center for Educational Statistics. (1997). *United States Department of Education*. Retrieved on January 12, 2005, from http://nces.ed.gov

Nation, P. (2001). *Learning vocabulary in another language*. Cambridge, UK: Cambridge University Press.

Nelson, G., & Carson, J. (1998). ESL students' perceptions of effectiveness in peer response groups. *Journal of Second Language Writing, 7*(2), 113–131. doi:10.1016/S1060-3743(98)90010-8

Nicholson, B. (2004). Course portfolio. In Galbraith, M. (Ed.), *Adult learning methods: A guide for effective instruction* (pp. 321–340). Malabar, FL: Krieger.

Niguidula, D. (1993). *The digital portfolio. A richer picture of student performance*. Providence, RI: Coalition of Essential Schools. Retrieved October 7, 2010, from http://www.essentialschools.org

Nikirk, M. (2008). Digital portfolios. *Tech Directions, 68*(5), 13–15.

Nitsch, K. E. (1977). *Structuring decontextualized forms of knowledge* (Unpublished doctoral dissertation). Vanderbilt University, Nashville, TN.

North, S. (1987). *The making of knowledge in composition: Portrait of an emerging field*. Portsmouth, NH: Heinemann.

Novak, J. D. (1998). *Learning, creating, and using knowledge: concept maps as facilitative tools in schools and corporations*. Mahwah, NJ: Lawrence Erlbaum.

Novak, J., & Gowin, D. (1984). *Learning how to learn*. Cambridge, UK: Cambridge University Press.

O'Donnell, A. M., Dansereau, D. F., & Hall, R. H. (2002). Knowledge maps as scaffolds for cognitive processing. *Educational Psychology Review, 14*(1), 71–86. doi:10.1023/A:1013132527007

O'Neil, M., & Wright, W. (1993). *Recording teaching accomplishment: A Dalhousie guide to the teaching dossier*. Halifax, NS: Office of Instructional Development and Technology, Dalhousie University.

Oliver, B. (2008, July). *Graduate employability as a standard of success in teaching and learning*. Paper presented at the Australian Universities Quality Forum, Canberra, Australia.

Oliver, B., & Nikoletatos, P. (2009). *Building engaging physical and virtual learning spaces: A case study of a collaborative approach*. Paper presented at the Same Places, Different Spaces Ascilite Conference, Auckland, New Zealand. Retrieved from http://www.ascilite.org.au/conferences/auckland09/procs/oliver.pdf

Oliver, B. (2010). *Teaching fellowship: Benchmarking partnerships for graduate employability*. Sydney, Australia: Australian Learning and Teaching Council.

Oliver, B., Jones, S., & Ferns, S. (2010). *Curriculum 2010 final report*. Perth, Australia: Curtin University.

Olson, L., Schroeder, L., & Wasko, P. (2009). Moving eFolio Minnesota to the next generation. In Cambridge, D., Cambridge, B., & Yancey, K. (Eds.), *Electronic portfolios 2.0: Emergent research on implementation and impact* (pp. 165–174). Sterling, VA: Stylus.

Olson, V. L. B. (1990). The revising process of sixth-grade writers with and without peer feedback. *The Journal of Educational Research, 84*, 22–29.

Otieno, D. (2001). *Faculty perceptions of the impact of information technology on tenure and promotion decisions at technologically advanced institutions of higher education: Comparing perceptions of faculty at a teaching university to those of faculty at a research University in the state of New Jersey* (Unpublished doctoral dissertation). New Jersey Institute of Technology, Newark, NJ.

Ovington, J., Diamantes, T., Roby, D., & Ryan, C. (2003). An analysis of prevailing myths regarding tenure and promotion. *Education, 123*(3), 635–637.

Pajares, P., & Schunk, D. H. (2001). *Self-beliefs and school success: Self-efficacy, self concept, and school achievement*. Retrieved October 19, 2010, from Emory University website: http://www.des.emory.edu/mfp/PajaresSchunk2001.html

Pajares, M. F. (1992). Teachers' beliefs and educational research: Cleaning up a messy construct. *Review of Educational Research, 62*, 307–332.

Papadopoulos, P. M., Demetriadis, S. N., Stamelos, I. G., & Tsoukalas, I. A. (2010). The value of writing-to-learn when using question prompts to support web-based learning in ill-structured domains. *Educational Technology Research and Development, •••*, 1–20.

Papanikolaou, K. A., Grigoriadou, M., Magoulas, G. D., & Kornilakis, H. (2002). Towards new forms of knowledge communication: The adaptive dimension of a web-based learning environment. *Computers & Education, 39*, 333–360. doi:10.1016/S0360-1315(02)00067-2

Paqset. (2005). *Professionnalisation des formateurs Tunisiens.* Retrieved August 29, 2009, from http://affinitiz.com/space/professionnalisme/tag/apprentissage

Pare. (2006). *Réforme de l'éducation et innovation Pédagogique en Algérie.* Retrieved March 26, 2009, from http://unesdoc.unesco.org/Ulis/cgi-bin/ulis.pl?catno=158372&set=495A2B23_3_48&gp=1&lin=1

Partnership for 21st Century Skills. (2007). *The intellectual and policy foundations of the 21st century skills framework.* Retrieved March 1, 2009, from http://www.21stcenturyskills.org/route21/images/stories/epapers/skills_foundations_final.pdf

Paulus, T. M. (1999). The effect of peer and teacher feedback on student writing. *Journal of Second Language Writing, 8*(3), 256–289. doi:10.1016/S1060-3743(99)80117-9

Paus-Hasebrink, I., Jadin, T., & Wijnen, C. (2007). *Aktualisierter Bericht zur Evaluation des Projekts "Web 2.0-Klasse."* Retrieved January 19, 2008, from http://beat.doebe.li/bibliothek/b03924.html

Payne, S. J., & Reader, W. R. (2006). Constructing structure maps of multiple on-line texts. *International Journal of Human-Computer Studies, 64*, 461–474. doi:10.1016/j.ijhcs.2005.09.003

Pellegrino, J., Chuowsky, N., & Glaser, R. (Eds.). (2001). *Knowing what students know: the science and design of educational assessment.* Washington, DC: National Academy Press.

Pink, D. (2006). *A whole new mind: Why right-brainers will rule the future.* New York, NY: Penguin.

Plotnick, E. (1997). *Concept mapping: a graphical system for understanding the relationship between concepts: an ERIC digest.* New York, NY: ERIC Clearinghouse on Information and Technology.

Poore, C. (2001). *Building your career portfolio.* Clifton Park, NY: Thomson Delmar Learning.

Portafolio Academico Geatec. (2008). *Mi portafolio.* Retrieved from http://www.geatec.net/portafolio2009/

Portafolio-Asuncion. (n. d.). *Portafolio- Klahowya.* Retrieved January 8, 2010, from http://web.asuncion.edu.gt/portfolio/index.php

Port-Unisa. (2008). *University of South Africa. Your career portfolio.* Retrieved March 9, 2010, from http://www.unisa.ac.za/default.asp?CMD=ViewContent&ContentID=15162

Precision Consultancy. (2007). *Graduate employability skills: Prepared for the business, industry and higher education collaboration council.* Retrieved November 23, 2010, from http://www.dest.gov.au/NR/rdonlyres/E58EFDBE-BA83-430E-A541-2E91BCB59DF1/20214/GraduateEmployabilitySkillsFINALREPORT1.pdf

Prus, R. (2005). Studying human knowing and acting: The interactionist quest for authenticity. In Pawluch, D., Shaffir, W., & Miall, C. (Eds.), *Doing ethnography: Studying everyday life* (pp. 7–23). Toronto, ON, Canada: Canadian Scholars' Press.

Pruyn, M. (1996). *The social construction of critical student agency in one adult literacy classroom* (Unpublished doctoral dissertation). University of California Los Angeles, Los Angeles, CA.

Qian, D.-D. (1999). Assessing the roles of depth and breadth of vocabulary knowledge in reading comprehension. *Canadian Modern Language Review, 56*, 282–308. doi:10.3138/cmlr.56.2.282

Qian, D.-D. (2002). Investigating the relationship between vocabulary knowledge and academic reading performance: an assessment perspective. *Language Learning, 52*, 513–536. doi:10.1111/1467-9922.00193

Qualifications and Curriculum Authority. (2004). *A proposed blueprint for delivering e-assessment.* Retrieved July 20, 2008, from http://www.qca.org.uk/libraryAssets/media/6995_blueprint_for_e-assessment.rtf

Quality Assurance Agency for Higher Education (QAA). (2003). *Learning from subject review 1993-2001.* Retrieved July 20, 2008, from http://www.qaa.ac.uk/reviews/subjectReview/learningfromSubjectReview/learningFromSubjectReview.pdf

Quality Assurance Agency in Higher Education (QAA). (2001). *Guidelines for HE progress files.* Retrieved November 23, 2010, from http://www.qaa.ac.uk/academicinfrastructure/progressFiles/guidelines/progfile2001.asp

Ravet, S. (2007). *For an ePortfolio enabled architecture.* Retrieved June 11, 2007, from http://www.eife-l.org/publications/eportfolio/documentation/positionpaper

Reinking, D., & Schreiner, R. (1985). The effects of computer-mediated text on measures of reading comprehension and reading behavior. *Reading Research Quarterly, 20,* 536–551. doi:10.2307/747941

Richardson, V. (1996). The role of attitudes and beliefs in learning to teach. In Sikula, J. (Ed.), *Handbook of research on teacher education* (pp. 102–119). New York, NY: Macmillan.

Robertson, R. (2006). *Institutional support systems necessary for teacher education unit faculty members to create electronic portfolios for promotion and tenure* (Unpublished doctoral dissertation). Argosy University, Sarasota, FL.

Robinson, P. (2009, March 27). *COMPORT: A comparative study of e-portfolio implementation in work-based learning (Final project report).* Bristol, UK: Joint Information Systems Commission.

Rodgers, C. (2002). Defining reflection: Another look at John Dewey and reflective thinking. *Teachers College Record, 104*(4), 842–866. doi:10.1111/1467-9620.00181

Rodriguez-Farrar, H. (1995). *Teaching portfolio handbook.* Providence, RI: Center for the Advancement of College Teaching, Brown University.

Rogoff, B., Goodman Turkanis, C., & Bartlett, L. (Eds.). (2001). *Learning together: Children and adults in a school community.* New York, NY: Oxford University Press.

Rowntree, D. (1977). *Assessing students: How shall we know them?* London, UK: Harper and Row.

SACE Board of South Australia. (2010). *Personal learning plan.* Retrieved November 23, 2010, from http://www.saceboard.sa.edu.au/newsace/plp.php

Salmon, G. (2002). *E-tivities: a key to active online learning.* London, UK: Routledge.

Salmon, G. (2005). Flying not flapping: a strategic framework for e-learning and pedagogical innovation in higher education institutions. *ALT-J: Research in Learning Technology, 13*(3), 201–218. doi:10.1080/09687760500376439

Salton, G., & McGill, M. J. (1983). *Introduction to modern information retrieval.* New York, NY: McGraw-Hill.

Scheepers, M. D., Jordan, A. J. J., & Mostert, E. (2008). Analysis of three different models used to acquire three e-learning solutions at the same university. *International Journal of Emerging Technologies in Learning, 3*(1).

Schmitt, N. (1997). Vocabulary learning strategies. In Schmitt, N., & McCarthy, M. (Eds.), *Vocabulary: description, acquisition and pedagogy* (pp. 199–228). Cambridge, UK: Cambridge University Press.

Schön, D. A. (1987). *Educating the reflective practitioner: Toward a new design for teaching and learning in the professions.* San Francisco, CA: Jossey-Bass.

Seldin, P. (1993). *Successful use of teaching portfolios.* Bolton, MA: Anker.

Seldin, P. (1997). *The teaching portfolio: A practical guide to improved performance and promotion/tenure decisions.* Bolton, MA: Anker.

Seldin, P. (2000). Teaching portfolio's: A positive appraisal. *Academe, 86*(1), 36–44. doi:10.2307/40252334 doi:10.2307/40252334

Seldin, P. (1991). *The teaching portfolio: A practical guide to improved performance and promotion- tenure decisions.* Bolton, MA: Anker.

Shore, M., et al. (1986). *The teaching dossier.* Montreal, QC, Canada: Canadian Association of University Teachers.

Siemens, G. (2004). *Connectivism: A learning theory for the digital age.* Retrieved March 4, 2008, from http://www.elearnspace.org/Articles/connectivism.htm

Siemens, G. (2006). *Knowing knowledge.* Retrieved December 3, 2009, from http://www.elearnspace.org/KnowingKnowledge_LowRes.pdf

Skills Australia. (2010a). *Australian workforce futures: A national workforce development strategy.* Retrieved November 23, 2010, from http://www.skillsaustralia.gov.au/publications.shtml#workforce-futures

Skills Australia. (2010b). *Creating a future direction for Australian vocational education and training.* Retrieved November 23, 2010, from http://www.skillsaustralia.gov.au/publications.shtml#yoursay

Smith, K., & Sela, O. (2005). Action research as a bridge between pre-service teacher education and in-service professional development for students and teacher educators. *European Journal of Teacher Education, 28*(3), 293–310. doi:10.1080/02619760500269418

Smith, K., & Tillema, H. (2003). Clarifying different types of portfolio use. *Assessment & Evaluation in Higher Education, 28*(6), 625–648. doi:10.1080/0260293032000130252

Soder, R. (1990). The rhetoric of teacher professionalization. In J. I. Goodlad, R. Soder, & K. A. Sirotnik (Eds.), *The moral dimension of teaching* (pp. 35–86). San Francisco, CA: Jossey-Bass.

Soyibo, K. (1995). Using concept maps to analyze text book presentations of respiration. *The American Biology Teacher, 57*(6), 344–351.

Spector-Cohen, E., Kirschner, M., & Wexler, C. (2001). Designing EAP reading courses at the university level. *English for Specific Purposes, 20*, 367–386. doi:10.1016/S0889-4906(00)00019-3

Starett, D. (2004). Reward and conquer. *Campus Technology, 1*(1), 42–46.

Stefani, L. A. J. (1994). Peer, self and tutor assessment: relative reliabilities. *Studies in Higher Education, 19*(1), 69–75. doi:10.1080/03075079412331382153

Stefani, L., Mason, R., & Pegler, C. (2007). *The educational potential of e-portfolios: Supporting personal development and reflective learning.* London, UK: Routledge.

Sternberg, R. (1998). Metacognition, abilities, and developing expertise: What makes an expert student? *Instructional Science, 26*(1-2), 129–140.

Steve, R. J. (1986). *The effects of strategy training on the identification of the main idea of expository passages* (Report No. 4). Washington, DC: Center for Research on Elementary and Middle Schools.

Stoddart, T., Abrams, R., Gasper, E., & Canaday, D. (2000). Concept maps as assessment in science inquiry learning - a report of methodology. *International Journal of Science Education, 22*(12), 1221–1246. doi:10.1080/095006900750036235

Strudler, N. (2002). *Faculty development.* Retrieved April 4, 2005, from http://www.pt3.org/stories/faculty.html

Su, C.-Y., & Wang, T.-I. (2010). Construction and analysis of educational assessments using knowledge maps with weight appraisal of concepts. *Computers & Education, 55*, 1300–1311. doi:10.1016/j.compedu.2010.05.027

Sweller, J. (1988). Cognitive load during problem solving: Effects on learning. *Cognitive Science, 12*, 257–285. doi:10.1207/s15516709cog1202_4

Tecsult. (2008). *Tecsult Group.* Retrieved December 12, 2008 from http://www.tecsult.com

The Association of American Colleges and Universities. (2009). *VALUE: Valid Assessment of Learning in Undergraduate Education.* Retrieved October 29, 2009, from AAC&U website: http://www.aacu.org/value/

Thomas, J. W. (2000). *A review of research on project-based learning.* San Rafael, CA: The Autodesk Foundation.

Tomes, N., & Higgison, C. (1998). *Exploiting the network for teaching and learning in Scottish higher education: Teaching and learning in the Scottish metropolitan area networks.* Edinburg, UK: Scottish Higher Education Funding Council.

Topping, K. J. (1998). Peer assessment between students in colleges and universities. *Review of Educational Research, 68*, 249–276.

Topping, K., Smith, F. F., Swanson, I., & Elliot, A. (2000). Formative peer assessment of academic writing between postgraduate students. *Assessment & Evaluation in Higher Education, 25*(2), 149–169. doi:10.1080/713611428

Tosh, D., Light, T. P., Fleming, K., & Haywood, J. (2005). Engagement with electronic portfolios: Challenges from the student perspective. *Canadian Journal of Learning and Technology, 31*(3). Retrieved September 24, 2008, from http://www.cjlt.ca/content/vol31.3/tosh.html

Treuer, P., & Jenson, J. D. (2003). Electronic portfolios need standards to thrive. *EDUCAUSE Quarterly, 26*(2), 34–42.

Trigwell, K., & Prosser, M. (1999). Relations between teachers' approaches to teaching and students' approaches to learning. *Higher Education, 37*(1). doi:10.1023/A:1003548313194

Trigwell, K., & Prosser, M. (2004). Development and use of the approaches to teaching inventory. *Educational Psychology Review, 16*(4).

Tseng, S.-S., Sue, P.-C., Su, J.-M., Weng, J.-F., & Tsai, W.-N. (2007). A new approach for constructing the concept map. *Computers & Education, 49,* 691–707. doi:10.1016/j.compedu.2005.11.020

Tseng, Y.-H., Chang, C.-Y., Rundgren, C. S.-N., & Rudgren, C.-J. (2010). Mining concept maps from news stories for measuring civic scientific literacy in media. *Computers & Education, 55,* 165–177. doi:10.1016/j.compedu.2010.01.002

Tucker, A. (1996). *Chairing the academic department: Leadership among peers.* New York, NY: Greenwood.

United States Department of Education. (2002). *E-portfolios: Kick it up a notch, taking professional portfolios from black-and-white to 3D color.* Retrieved April 4, 2005, from http://www.pt3.org/stories/eportfolio.html

Universities, U. K. (2007). *Beyond the honours degree classification: The Burgess Group final report.* Retrieved September 10, 2008, from http://bookshop.universitiesuk.ac.uk/downloads/Burgess_final.pdf

University of British Columbia. (n. d.). *Office of learning technology.* Retrieved September 24, 2008, from http://www.olt.ubc.ca

University of Pretoria. (2008a). *Information design.* Retrieved March 24, 2009, from http://web.up.ac.za/sitefiles/File/46/1584/ma_infodesign(2).htm

University of Pretoria. (2008b). *Department of Visual Arts: Selection Procedure for BA Fine Arts.* Retrieved March 24, 2010 from http://web.up.ac.za/sitefiles/file/46/1584/selection%20procedure%20FA%202010.doc

University of Western Australia. (2003). *Guidelines for preparing a teaching portfolio.* Crawley, WA, Australia: Evaluation and Teaching Unit.

Van den Berg, I., Admiraal, W., & Pilot, A. (2006). Design principles and outcomes of peer assessment in higher education. *Studies in Higher Education, 31*(3), 341–356. doi:10.1080/03075070600680836

VanCoillie, M. (2007, October 16-19). Building Europass CV ePortfolio application profiles. In *Proceedings of the First Human Capital and Social Innovation Technology Summit,* Maastricht, The Netherlands.

VET National Data Strategy Action Group. (2010). *A unique student identifier for Australia's vocational education and training system: A consultation paper about introduction a USI in VET.* Retrieved November 23, 2010, from http://www.training.com.au/Documents/Unique+Student+Identifier+consultation+paper-+July+2010.pdf

von Konsky, B., & Comfort, J. (2010). *The iPortfolio: A tool for work integrated learning for health promotion students* Retrieved February 9, 2011, from http://www.flexiblelearning.net.au/files/EAC2010_Abstracts_eBook_20101109.pdf

Vovides, Y., Sanchez-Alonso, S., Mitropoulou, V., & Nickmans, G. (2007). The use of e-learning course management systems to support learning strategies and to improve self-regulated learning. *Educational Research Review,* (2): 64–74. doi:10.1016/j.edurev.2007.02.004

Vygotsky, L. S. (1978). *Mind in society: The development of higher psychological processes.* Cambridge, MA: Harvard University Press.

Wade, A., Abrami, P., & Sclater, J. (2005). An electronic portfolio to support learning. *Canadian Journal of Learning and Technology, 31*(3). Retrieved November 30, 2009, from http://www.cjlt.ca

Ward, R. (2008). *E-Portfolio practice in higher education: (something of) the UK experience.* Paper presented at the Australian ePortfolio Symposium, Brisbane, Australia. Retrieved November 23, 2010, from http://www.eportfoliopractice.qut.edu.au/docs/AeP_presentations_web/AeP_Ward_7Feb08.pdf

Wardlaw, C. (2006, September). *Mathematics in Hong Kong/China: Improving on being first in PISA.* Paper presented at the 50th Annual Meeting of the Australian Mathematical Society, Sydney, Australia.

Watters, D., & Watters, J. (2007). Approaches to learning by students in the biological sciences: Implications for teaching. *International Journal of Science Education, 29*(1), 19–43. doi:10.1080/09500690600621282

Weideman, H., & Strümpfer, C. (2004). The effect of search engine keyword choice and demographic features on Internet searching success. *Information Technology and Libraries*, 56-65.

Wenger, E. (1998). *Communities of practice: Learning, meaning, identity.* New York, NY: Cambridge University Press.

Western Association of Schools and Colleges. (2008). *Program learning outcomes.* Retrieved July 24, 2008 from WASC website: http://www.wascsenior.org/findit/files/forms/Program_Learning_Outcome_Rubric_080430_.pdf

Wetzel, K., & Strudler, N. (2005). The diffusion of electronic portfolios in teacher education: Next steps and recommendations for accomplished users. *Journal of Research on Technology in Education, 38*(2), 231–243.

Wikipedia. (2011). *Mahara architecture introduction.* Retrieved from http://wiki.mahara.org/Developer_Area/Mahara_Architecture_Introduction

Wilcox, B., & Tomei, L. (1999). *Professional portfolios for teachers.* Norwood, MA: Christopher-Gordon.

Wilder, M. V. (n.d.). *Klahowya student portfolio solution.* Retrieved February 2005, from Sourceforge website: http://sourceforge.net/projects/klahowya2/

Williams, A., & Hall, K. (2004). *Creating your career portfolio: At a glance guide.* Upper Saddle River, NJ: Prentice Hall.

Williams, J. P. (1988). Identifying main ideas: A basic aspect of reading comprehension. *Topics in Language Disorders, 8*, 1–13. doi:10.1097/00011363-198806000-00003

Wise, A. (2005). Establishing teaching as a profession. *Journal of Teacher Education, 56*(4), 318–331. doi:10.1177/0022487105279965

Wong, Y. W., Wong, S. K., & Cheung, H. L. (2006). *Adoption of e-learning: From organic to planned.* Paper presented at the International Conference on Improving University Teaching, Dunedin, New Zealand.

Yancey, K. (2008, July). *Outcomes, reflection, electronic portfolios.* Paper presented at the St. Jerome's University Eportfolio Conference, Waterloo, ON, Canada.

Yancey, K. (1996). The electronic portfolio: Shifting paradigms. *Computers and Composition, 13*(13), 259–262. doi:10.1016/S8755-4615(96)90014-6

Ynternet. (2008). *Communication Libre pour une société Libre.* Retrieved November 12, 2008, from http://www.ynternet.org/ynternet.org

York-Barr, J., Sommers, W. A., Ghere, G. S., & Montie, J. K. (2006). *Reflective practice to improve school: An action guide for educators* (2nd ed.). Thousand Oaks, CA: Corwin Press.

Yorke, M., & Knight, P. (2004). *Learning, curriculum and employability in higher education.* London, UK: Routledge Falmer.

Zeichner, K., & Wray, S. (2001). The teaching portfolio in us teacher education programs: What we know and what we need to know. *Teaching and Teacher Education, 17*, 613–621. doi:10.1016/S0742-051X(01)00017-8

Zhou, M., Cheung, H. L., & Wong, M. C. Chan. Y. F., & Pickard, V. (2010, January). *An evaluation of electronic portfolio platforms in higher education.* Paper presented at the e-CASE & e-Tech Conference, Macau, China.

Zimmerman, B. J. (2000). Attaining self-regulation: A social cognitive perspective. In Boekaerts, M., Pintrich, P. R., & Zeidner, M. (Eds.), *Handbook of self-regulation* (pp. 13–39). San Diego, CA: Academic Press.

Zimmerman, B. J., & Kitsantas, A. (1997). Developmental phases in self-regulation: Shifting from process to outcome goals. *Journal of Educational Psychology, 89,* 29–36. doi:10.1037/0022-0663.89.1.29

Zubizarreta, J. (1994). Teaching portfolios and the beginning teacher. *Phi Delta Kappan, 76*(4), 323–326.

Zubizarreta, J., & Millis, B. J. (2009). *The learning portfolio: Reflective practice for improving student learning* (2nd ed.). New York, NY: John Wiley & Sons.

Zuckermann, T. (2007, June 29-July 1). *From journal writing to action research: A step toward systematic reflective writing.* Paper presented at the EATAW Conference, Bochum, Germany.

Related References

To continue our tradition of advancing information science and technology research, we have compiled a list of recommended IGI Global readings. These references will provide additional information and guidance to further enrich your knowledge and assist you with your own research and future publications.

Note: The editor and authors of this publication do not endorse the citations listed below nor are any of the following references necessarily cited in the preceding text.

REFERENCES

Abdullah, S., Siew, N. M., & Abbas, M. (2012). The effectiveness of an inquiry-based computer-simulated lesson in physics. In Alias, N., & Hashim, S. (Eds.), *Instructional technology research, design and development: Lessons from the field* (pp. 401–425). Hershey, PA: IGI Global. doi:10.4018/978-1-61350-198-6.ch024

Abrami, P. C., Savage, R. S., Deleveaux, G., Wade, A., Meyer, E., & LeBel, C. (2010). The learning toolkit: The design, development, testing and dissemination of evidence-based educational software 1. In Zemliansky, P., & Wilcox, D. (Eds.), *Design and implementation of educational games: Theoretical and practical perspectives* (pp. 168–188). Hershey, PA: IGI Global. doi:10.4018/978-1-61520-781-7.ch012

Adán-Coello, J. M., Tobar, C. M., José de Faria, E. S., Serafim de Menezes, W., & Luís de Freitas, R. (2011). Forming groups for collaborative learning of introductory computer programming based on students' programming skills and learning styles. *International Journal of Information and Communication Technology Education, 7*(4), 34–46. doi:10.4018/jicte.2011100104

Adekanmbi, G., & Boitshwarelo, B. (2010). International collaboration in distance education in sub-saharan africa: trends, trials and tomorrow's thrusts. In Mukerji, S., & Tripathi, P. (Eds.), *Cases on interactive technology environments and transnational collaboration: Concerns and perspectives* (pp. 39–55). Hershey, PA: IGI Global. doi:10.4018/978-1-61520-909-5.ch002

Adesope, O. O., & Nesbit, J. C. (2010). A systematic review of reserch on collaborative learning with concept maps. In Lupion Torres, P., & de Cássia Veiga Marriott, R. (Eds.), *Handbook of research on collaborative learning using concept mapping* (pp. 238–255). Hershey, PA: IGI Global. doi:10.4018/978-1-59904-992-2.ch012

Aggarwal, A., Turoff, M., Legon, R., Hackbarth, G., & Fowler, D. (2008). Asynchronous learning: Emerging issues for the 21st century. In Esnault, L. (Ed.), *Web-based education and pedagogical technologies: Solutions for learning applications* (pp. 206–225). Hershey, PA: IGI Global.

Ahamer, G. (2011). How technologies can localize learners in multicultural space: A newly developed "global studies" curriculum. *International Journal of Technology and Educational Marketing, 1*(2), 1–24. doi:10.4018/IJTEM.2011070101

Akyol, Z., & Garrison, D. R. (2011). Learning and satisfaction in online communities of inquiry. In Eom, S., & Arbaugh, J. (Eds.), *Student satisfaction and learning outcomes in e-learning: An introduction to empirical research* (pp. 23–35). Hershey, PA: IGI Global. doi:10.4018/978-1-60960-615-2.ch002

Alavi, M., Dufner, D., & Howard, C. (2009). Collaborative learning technologies. In Rogers, P., Berg, G., Boettcher, J., Howard, C., Justice, L., & Schenk, K. (Eds.), *Encyclopedia of distance learning* (2nd ed., pp. 334–339). Hershey, PA: IGI Global. doi:10.4018/978-1-60566-198-8.ch048

Alegre, O. M., & Villar, L. M. (2011). Faculty professional learning: An examination of online development and assessment environments. In Vincenti, G., & Braman, J. (Eds.), *Teaching through multi-user virtual environments: Applying dynamic elements to the modern classroom* (pp. 66–93). Hershey, PA: IGI Global.

Ali, A. (2009). Modern technology and mass education: A case study of a global virtual learning system. In Rahman, H. (Ed.), *Selected readings on global information technology: Contemporary applications* (pp. 194–204). Hershey, PA: IGI Global.

Alvino, S., & Trentin, G. (2012). Fostering NCL in higher education: New approaches for integrating educational technology instructional design into teachers' practice. In Olofsson, A., & Lindberg, J. (Eds.), *Informed design of educational technologies in higher education: Enhanced learning and teaching* (pp. 331–351). Hershey, PA: IGI Global.

Andresen, B. B. (2007). Web services for learning in educational settings. In Tatnall, A. (Ed.), *Encyclopedia of portal technologies and applications* (pp. 1166–1168). Hershey, PA: IGI Global. doi:10.4018/978-1-59140-989-2.ch190

Annese, S., Traetta, M., & Spadaro, P. F. (2010). Blended learning communities: Relational and identity networks. In Park, J., & Abels, E. (Eds.), *Interpersonal relations and social patterns in communication technologies: Discourse norms, language structures and cultural variables* (pp. 256–276). Hershey, PA: IGI Global. doi:10.4018/978-1-61520-827-2.ch014

Aoki, K. (2009). Cultural issues in global collaborative education 1. In Salmons, J., & Wilson, L. (Eds.), *Handbook of research on electronic collaboration and organizational synergy* (pp. 30–42). Hershey, PA: IGI Global.

Ashcraft, D., & Treadwell, T. (2008). The social psychology of online collaborative learning: The good, the bad, and the awkward. In Orvis, K., & Lassiter, A. (Eds.), *Computer-supported collaborative learning: Best practices and principles for instructors* (pp. 140–163). Hershey, PA: IGI Global. doi:10.4018/978-1-59904-753-9.ch007

Asunka, S. (2011). Collaborative online learning in non-formal education settings in the developing world: A best practice framework. *International Journal of Adult Vocational Education and Technology, 2*(4), 43–57. doi:10.4018/javet.2011100104

Augar, N., Raitman, R., Lanham, E., & Zhou, W. (2009). Building virtual learning communities. In Lytras, M., & Ordóñez de Pablos, P. (Eds.), *Social Web evolution: Integrating semantic Applications and Web 2.0 technologies* (pp. 192–215). Hershey, PA: IGI Global. doi:10.4018/978-1-60566-272-5.ch015

Baltazar, G. (2011). Developing an e-learning course for a global legal firm. In Edmundson, A. (Ed.), *Cases on globalized and culturally appropriate e-learning: Challenges and solutions* (pp. 223–244). Hershey, PA: IGI Global. doi:10.4018/978-1-61520-989-7.ch011

Baten, L., Bouckaert, N., & Yingli, K. (2009). The use of communities in a virtual learning environment. In Thomas, M. (Ed.), *Handbook of research on Web 2.0 and second language learning* (pp. 137–155). Hershey, PA: IGI Global. doi:10.4018/978-1-60566-190-2.ch008

Beck, D. E., & Normann, S. A. (2009). Implementing successful online learning communities. In Rogers, P., Berg, G., Boettcher, J., Howard, C., Justice, L., & Schenk, K. (Eds.), *Encyclopedia of distance learning* (2nd ed., pp. 1134–1141). Hershey, PA: IGI Global. doi:10.4018/978-1-60566-198-8.ch161

Berger, O., Bac, C., & Hamet, B. (2009). Integration of Libre software applications to create a collaborative work platform for researchers at GET. In Alkhatib, G., & Rine, D. (Eds.), *Integrated approaches in information technology and Web engineering: Advancing organizational knowledge sharing* (pp. 1–17). Hershey, PA: IGI Global. doi:10.4018/jitwe.2006070101

Bhattacharya, M. (2009). Introducing integrated e-portfolio across courses in a postgraduate program in distance and online education. In Spratt, C., & Lajbcygier, P. (Eds.), *E-Learning technologies and evidence-based assessment approaches* (pp. 243–253). Hershey, PA: IGI Global. doi:10.4018/978-1-60566-410-1.ch014

Bishop, J. (2011). The role of augmented e-learning systems for enhancing pro-social behaviour in socially impaired individuals. In Theng, L. (Ed.), *Assistive and augmentive communication for the disabled: Intelligent technologies for communication, learning and teaching* (pp. 248–272). Hershey, PA: IGI Global. doi:10.4018/978-1-60960-541-4.ch009

Bodomo, A. B. (2010). Evaluating learning technologies. In Bodomo, A. (Ed.), *Computer-mediated communication for linguistics and literacy: Technology and natural language education* (pp. 291–313). Hershey, PA: IGI Global.

Bondarouk, T., & Sikkel, K. (2007). The relevance of learning processes for IT implementation. In Khosrow-Pour, M. (Ed.), *Emerging information resources management and technologies* (pp. 1–23). Hershey, PA: IGI Global. doi:10.4018/978-1-59904-286-2.ch001

Bondarouk, T., & van Riemsdijk, M. (2009). Successes and failures of SAP implementation: A learning perspective. In Zaphiris, P., & Ang, C. (Eds.), *Cross-disciplinary advances in human computer interaction: User modeling, social computing, and adaptive interfaces* (pp. 338–357). Hershey, PA: IGI Global. doi:10.4018/978-1-60566-142-1.ch021

Bonk, C. J., Lee, S., Lin, X., & Su, B. (2007). Awareness design in online collaborative learning: A pedagogical perspective. In Neto, F., & Brasileiro, F. (Eds.), *Advances in computer-supported learning* (pp. 251–273). Hershey, PA: IGI Global.

Borton, S., Frost, A., & Warrington, K. (2009). Assessing the composition program on our own terms. In Schreiner, C. (Ed.), *Handbook of research on assessment technologies, methods, and applications in higher education* (pp. 167–184). Hershey, PA: IGI Global. doi:10.4018/978-1-60566-667-9.ch010

Bouras, C., Giannaka, E., & Tsiatsos, T. (2010). Exploiting virtual environments and Web 2.0 immersive worlds to support collaborative e-learning communities. In Karacapilidis, N. (Ed.), *Novel developments in Web-based learning technologies: Tools for modern teaching* (pp. 20–45). Hershey, PA: IGI Global. doi:10.4018/978-1-60566-938-0.ch002

Bowers, C., Smith, P. A., & Cannon-Bowers, J. (2009). Social psychology and massively multiplayer online learning games. In Ferdig, R. (Ed.), *Handbook of research on effective electronic gaming in education* (pp. 702–718). Hershey, PA: IGI Global. doi:10.4018/978-1-59904-808-6.ch040

Brack, C. (2009). Collaborative e-learning using wikis: A case report. In Spratt, C., & Lajbcygier, P. (Eds.), *E-learning technologies and evidence-based assessment approaches* (pp. 37–54). Hershey, PA: IGI Global. doi:10.4018/978-1-60566-410-1.ch003

Braidic, S. (2011). Brain based learning environments in an online setting. In Tomei, L. (Ed.), *Online courses and ICT in education: Emerging practices and applications* (pp. 90–98). Hershey, PA: IGI Global. doi:10.4018/978-1-60960-150-8.ch007

Braidic, S. L. (2009). Fostering successful learning communities to meet the diverse needs of university students by creating brain based online learning environments. *International Journal of Information and Communication Technology Education*, 5(4), 18–25. doi:10.4018/jicte.2009041002

Brammer, C., & Parker, R. (2009). Workshops and e-portfolios as transformational assessment. In Schreiner, C. (Ed.), *Handbook of research on assessment technologies, methods, and applications in higher education* (pp. 281–289). Hershey, PA: IGI Global. doi:10.4018/978-1-60566-667-9.ch017

Branco Neto, W. C. (2007). Using semantic Web technologies within e-learning applications. In Neto, F., & Brasileiro, F. (Eds.), *Advances in computer-supported learning* (pp. 173–201). Hershey, PA: IGI Global. doi:10.4018/978-1-59904-355-5.ch008

Brézillon, P. (2011). Context and explanation in e-collaborative work. In Daniel, B. (Ed.), *Handbook of research on methods and techniques for studying virtual communities: Paradigms and phenomena* (pp. 285–302). Hershey, PA: IGI Global.

Brochado, M. R., & Caulliraux Pithon, A. J. (2008). Collaborative techniques in customer's involvement. In Putnik, G., & Cruz-Cunha, M. (Eds.), *Encyclopedia of networked and virtual organizations* (pp. 252–260). Hershey, PA: IGI Global. doi:10.4018/978-1-59904-885-7.ch034

Brooke, S. L. (2008). The case method and collaborative learning. In Orvis, K., & Lassiter, A. (Eds.), *Computer-supported collaborative learning: Best practices and principles for instructors* (pp. 66–88). Hershey, PA: IGI Global. doi:10.4018/978-1-59904-753-9.ch004

Brown, E., Hobbs, M., & Gordon, M. (2010). A virtual world environment for group work. In Karacapilidis, N. (Ed.), *Novel developments in Web-based learning technologies: Tools for modern teaching* (pp. 233–244). Hershey, PA: IGI Global. doi:10.4018/978-1-60566-938-0.ch013

Brunvard, S., Luera, G. R., Marra, T., & Peet, M. (2011). Implementing an open source ePortfolio in higher education: Lessons learned along the way. In Czerkawski, B. (Ed.), *Free and open source software for e-learning: Issues, successes and challenges* (pp. 132–146). Hershey, PA: IGI Global.

Bubb, T. E., McDonald, D., & Crawford, C. M. (2012). Meaningful connections: "Going the distance" in distance learning through the design and generation of community building online learning interactions. In Wang, H. (Ed.), *Interactivity in e-learning: Case studies and frameworks* (pp. 274–304). Hershey, PA: IGI Global.

Buchan, J. (2011). Developing a dynamic and responsive online learning environment: A case study of a large Australian university. In Czerkawski, B. (Ed.), *Free and open source software for e-learning: Issues, Successes and challenges* (pp. 92–109). Hershey, PA: IGI Global.

Bunse, C., Peper, C., Grützner, I., & Steinbach-Nordmann, S. (2009). Applying blended learning in an industrial context: An experience report. In Ellis, H., Demurjian, S., & Naveda, J. (Eds.), *Software engineering: Effective teaching and learning approaches and practices* (pp. 213–232). Hershey, PA: IGI Global.

Caballé, S., Daradoumis, T., & Xhafa, F. (2008). A generic platform for the systematic construction of knowledge-based collaborative learning applications. In Pahl, C. (Ed.), *Architecture solutions for e-learning systems* (pp. 219–242). Hershey, PA: IGI Global. doi:10.4018/978-1-59904-633-4.ch012

Caladine, R. (2008). A review of methods for selecting learning technologies. In Caladine, R. (Ed.), *Enhancing e-learning with media-rich content and interactions* (pp. 42–66). Hershey, PA: IGI Global. doi:10.4018/978-1-59904-732-4.ch004

Caladine, R. (2008). The learning activities model. In Caladine, R. (Ed.), *Enhancing e-learning with media-rich content and interactions* (pp. 75–100). Hershey, PA: IGI Global. doi:10.4018/978-1-59904-732-4.ch006

Caladine, R. (2008). The learning technologies model. In Caladine, R. (Ed.), *Enhancing e-learning with media-rich content and interactions* (pp. 101–133). Hershey, PA: IGI Global. doi:10.4018/978-1-59904-732-4.ch007

Cameron, B. (2008). IS project and portfolio management. In Kidd, T., & Song, H. (Eds.), *Handbook of research on instructional systems and technology* (pp. 476–496). Hershey, PA: IGI Global. doi:10.4018/978-1-59904-865-9.ch034

Cameron, B. H. (2009). IT portfolio management: Implementing and maintaining IT strategic alignment. In Tan, A., & Theodorou, P. (Eds.), *Strategic information technology and portfolio management* (pp. 352–377). Hershey, PA: IGI Global. doi:10.4018/978-1-59904-687-7.ch019

Carlén, U., & Lindström, B. (2012). Informed design of educational activities in online learning communities. In Olofsson, A., & Lindberg, J. (Eds.), *Informed design of educational technologies in higher education: Enhanced learning and teaching* (pp. 118–134). Hershey, PA: IGI Global. doi:10.4018/978-1-61350-080-4.ch007

Carter, P. (2007). Experiential group learning for developing competencies in usability practice. In Lowry, G., & Turner, R. (Eds.), *Information systems and technology education: From the university to the workplace* (pp. 242–263). Hershey, PA: IGI Global. doi:10.4018/978-1-59904-114-8.ch011

Carvalho, A. A., Lustigova, Z., & Lustig, F. (2009). Integrating new technologies into blended learning environments. In Stacey, E., & Gerbic, P. (Eds.), *Effective blended learning practices: Evidence-based perspectives in ICT-facilitated education* (pp. 79–104). Hershey, PA: IGI Global. doi:10.4018/978-1-60566-296-1.ch005

Catterick, D. (2007). Do the philosophical foundations of online learning disadvantage non-western students? In Edmundson, A. (Ed.), *globalized e-learning cultural challenges* (pp. 116–129). Hershey, PA: IGI Global. doi:10.4018/978-1-59904-301-2.ch007

Chang, K. T., Lim, J., & Zhong, Y. (2008). Web-based interface elements in team interaction and learning: Theoretical and empirical analysis. In Esnault, L. (Ed.), *Web-based education and pedagogical technologies: Solutions for learning applications* (pp. 56–87). Hershey, PA: IGI Global.

Charles, D., Fyfe, C., Livingstone, D., & Mc-Glinchey, S. (2008). Reinforcement learning. In Charles, D., Fyfe, C., Livingstone, D., & Mc-Glinchey, S. (Eds.), *Biologically inspired artificial intelligence for computer games* (pp. 202–226). Hershey, PA: IGI Global.

Chen, S., Caropreso, E., & Hsu, C. (2008). Designing cross-cultural collaborative online learning. In Kidd, T., & Song, H. (Eds.), *Handbook of research on instructional systems and technology* (pp. 952–971). Hershey, PA: IGI Global. doi:10.4018/978-1-59904-865-9.ch067

Cho, H., & Gay, G. (2009). The effect of communication styles on computer-supported collaborative learning. In Mourlas, C., Tsianos, N., & Germanakos, P. (Eds.), *Cognitive and emotional processes in Web-based education: Integrating human factors and personalization* (pp. 357–374). Hershey, PA: IGI Global. doi:10.4018/978-1-60566-392-0.ch017

Chorney, T. T. (2009). The World Wide Web and cross-cultural teaching in online education. In Khosrow-Pour, M. (Ed.), *Encyclopedia of information science and technology* (2nd ed., pp. 4146–4154). Hershey, PA: IGI Global. doi:10.4018/978-1-60566-652-5.ch078

Clark, D., & Baillie-de Byl, P. (2009). Enhancing the IMS QTI to better support computer assisted marking. In Syed, M. (Ed.), *Methods and applications for advancing distance education technologies: International issues and solutions* (pp. 174–189). Hershey, PA: IGI Global. doi:10.4018/978-1-60566-342-5.ch014

Clark, D., Sampson, V., Stegmann, K., Marttunen, M., Kollar, I., & Janssen, J. …Laurinen, L. (2010). Online learning environments, scientific argumentation, and 21st century skills. In B. Ertl (Ed.), *E-Collaborative knowledge construction: learning from computer-supported and virtual environments* (pp. 1-39). Hershey, PA: IGI Global. doi:10.4018/978-1-61520-729-9.ch001

Clohesy, B., Frye, A., & Redpath, R. (2011). Conceptual business service: An architectural approach for building a business service portfolio. In Polgar, J., & Adamson, G. (Eds.), *New generation of portal software and engineering: Emerging technologies* (pp. 174–190). Hershey, PA: IGI Global. doi:10.4018/978-1-60960-571-1.ch014

Cochrane, T., & Bateman, R. (2009). Transforming pedagogy using mobile Web 2.0. *International Journal of Mobile and Blended Learning*, *1*(4), 56–83. doi:10.4018/jmbl.2009090804

Coleman, H., Dickerson, J., & Kubasko, D. (2010). Electronic portfolios in teacher education: Practical reflections and insights from a systemic implementation. In Yamamoto, J., Penny, C., Leight, J., & Winterton, S. (Eds.), *Technology leadership in teacher education: Integrated solutions and experiences* (pp. 196–213). Hershey, PA: IGI Global. doi:10.4018/978-1-61520-899-9.ch012

Colfax, R., & Perez, K. (2007). Global organizational fit pyramid for global IT team selection. In Law, W. (Ed.), *Information resources management: Global challenges* (pp. 373–385). Hershey, PA: IGI Global. doi:10.4018/978-1-59904-102-5.ch018

Collis, B., & Moonen, J. (2009). Collaborative learning in a contribution-oriented pedagogy. In Rogers, P., Berg, G., Boettcher, J., Howard, C., Justice, L., & Schenk, K. (Eds.), *Encyclopedia of distance learning* (2nd ed., pp. 327–333). Hershey, PA: IGI Global. doi:10.4018/978-1-60566-198-8.ch047

Connolly, T., Gould, C., Baxter, G. J., & Hainey, T. (2012). Learning 2.0: Using Web 2.0 technologies for learning in an engineering course. In Babo, R., & Azevedo, A. (Eds.), *Higher education institutions and learning management systems: Adoption and standardization* (pp. 50–73). Hershey, PA: IGI Global.

Conté, E., & Gouardères, G. (2009). E-Portfolio to promote the virtual learning group communities on the grid. In Alkhatib, G., & Rine, D. (Eds.), *Agent technologies and Web engineering: Applications and systems* (pp. 117–133). Hershey, PA: IGI Global. doi:10.4018/978-1-60566-618-1.ch007

Cooper, L., & Burford, S. (2010). Collaborative learning: Using group work concepts for online teaching. In Martin, J., & Hawkins, L. (Eds.), *Information communication technologies for human services education and delivery: Concepts and cases* (pp. 37–52). Hershey, PA: IGI Global.

Corbitt, B., Holt, D. M., & Segrave, S. (2008). Strategic design for Web-based teaching and learning: Making corporate technology system work for the learning organization. In Esnault, L. (Ed.), *Web-based education and pedagogical technologies: Solutions for learning applications* (pp. 280–302). Hershey, PA: IGI Global.

Coutinho, C. P. (2010). Challenges for teacher education in the learning society: Case studies of promising practice. In Yang, H., & Yuen, S. (Eds.), *Handbook of research on practices and outcomes in e-learning: Issues and trends* (pp. 385–401). Hershey, PA: IGI Global.

Creed, A., Zutshi, A., & Ross, J. (2008). E-Learning and knowledge management in the global context. In Zhao, F. (Ed.), *Information technology entrepreneurship and innovation* (pp. 329–343). Hershey, PA: IGI Global. doi:10.4018/978-1-59904-901-4.ch017

Crichton, S. (2009). Linking individual learning plans to ePortfolios. In Khosrow-Pour, M. (Ed.), *Encyclopedia of information science and technology* (2nd ed., pp. 2426–2430). Hershey, PA: IGI Global.

Cunha, M. M., & Putnik, G. D. (2009). A changed economy with unchanged universities? A contribution to the university of the future. In Syed, M. (Ed.), *Methods and applications for advancing distance education technologies: International issues and solutions* (pp. 246–267). Hershey, PA: IGI Global. doi:10.4018/978-1-60566-342-5.ch019

Cunningham, M., Robbins, R., & Buell, D. (2008). Learning villages network and its computer components. In Kidd, T., & Song, H. (Eds.), *Handbook of research on instructional systems and technology* (pp. 287–299). Hershey, PA: IGI Global. doi:10.4018/978-1-59904-865-9.ch021

Cunningham, T., McDonnell, C., McIntyre, B., & McKenna, T. (2009). A reflection on teachers' experience as e-learners. In Donnelly, R., & McSweeney, F. (Eds.), *Applied e-learning and e-teaching in higher education* (pp. 56–84). Hershey, PA: IGI Global. doi:10.4018/978-1-59904-814-7.ch004

D'Angelo, B., & Maid, B. (2009). Assessing outcomes in a technical communication capstone. In Schreiner, C. (Ed.), *Handbook of research on assessment technologies, methods, and applications in higher education* (pp. 152–166). Hershey, PA: IGI Global. doi:10.4018/978-1-60566-667-9.ch009

D'Urso, S. C., & Scott, C. R. (2012). Engaging the digitally engaged student: Comparing technology-mediated communication use and effects on student learning. In Ferris, S. (Ed.), *Teaching, learning and the Net generation: Concepts and tools for reaching digital learners* (pp. 150–170). Hershey, PA: IGI Global.

Daradoumis, T., & Kordaki, M. (2011). Employing collaborative learning strategies and tools for engaging university students in collaborative study and writing. In Pozzi, F., & Persico, D. (Eds.), *Techniques for fostering collaboration in online learning communities: Theoretical and practical perspectives* (pp. 183–205). Hershey, PA: IGI Global. doi:10.4018/978-1-61692-898-8.ch011

Dawley, L. (2007). Assessment and survey tools. In Dawley, L. (Ed.), *The tools for successful online teaching* (pp. 171–204). Hershey, PA: IGI Global. doi:10.4018/978-1-59140-956-4.ch008

Dawley, L. (2007). Small group learning. In Dawley, L. (Ed.), *The tools for successful online teaching* (pp. 98–120). Hershey, PA: IGI Global. doi:10.4018/978-1-59140-956-4.ch005

de Cássia Veiga Marriott, R. (2010). Collaborative learning and concept mapping for language teaching. In Lupion Torres, P., & de Cássia Veiga Marriott, R. (Eds.), *Handbook of research on collaborative learning using concept mapping* (pp. 13–34). Hershey, PA: IGI Global. doi:10.4018/978-1-59904-992-2.ch002

de Vreede, G., Briggs, R. O., & Kolfschoten, G. L. (2008). Collaboration engineering for designing self-directed group efforts. In Kock, N. (Ed.), *Encyclopedia of e-collaboration* (pp. 60–67). Hershey, PA: IGI Global. doi:10.4018/978-1-59904-000-4.ch010

Dewever, F. (2008). Opportunities for open source e-learning. In Esnault, L. (Ed.), *Web-based education and pedagogical technologies: Solutions for learning applications* (pp. 252–265). Hershey, PA: IGI Global.

DiMarco, J. (2009). Toward an increase in student Web portfolios in New York colleges and universities. In Tomei, L. (Ed.), *Information communication technologies for enhanced education and learning: Advanced applications and developments* (pp. 204–218). Hershey, PA: IGI Global. doi:10.4018/978-1-60566-150-6.ch015

Dixon, K. (2009). Capacity of an electronic portfolio to promote professionalism, collaboration and accountability in educational leadership. In Salmons, J., & Wilson, L. (Eds.), *Handbook of research on electronic collaboration and organizational synergy* (pp. 328–348). Hershey, PA: IGI Global. doi:10.4018/978-1-60566-106-3.ch022

Diziol, D., & Rummel, N. (2010). How to design support for collaborative e-learning: A framework of relevant dimensions. In Ertl, B. (Ed.), *E-Collaborative knowledge construction: Learning from computer-supported and virtual environments* (pp. 162–179). Hershey, PA: IGI Global. doi:10.4018/978-1-61520-729-9.ch009

Donnelly, R. (2009). Transformative potential of constructivist blended problem-based learning in higher education. In Payne, C. (Ed.), *Information technology and constructivism in higher education: Progressive learning frameworks* (pp. 182–202). Hershey, PA: IGI Global. doi:10.4018/978-1-60566-654-9.ch012

Donnelly, R., & Portimojärvi, T. (2009). Shifting perceptions within online problem-based learning. In Rogers, P., Berg, G., Boettcher, J., Howard, C., Justice, L., & Schenk, K. (Eds.), *encyclopedia of distance learning* (2nd ed., pp. 1865–1875). Hershey, PA: IGI Global. doi:10.4018/978-1-60566-198-8.ch276

Downing, K. F., & Holtz, J. K. (2008). Knowledge transfer and collaboration structures for online science. In Downing, K., & Holtz, J. (Eds.), *Online science learning: Best practices and technologies* (pp. 98–119). Hershey, PA: IGI Global. doi:10.4018/978-1-59904-986-1.ch006

Du, J., Harvard, B., Adams, J., Ding, G., & Yu, W. (2007). Project-based online group collaborative learning characteristics. In Tomei, L. (Ed.), *Integrating information & communications technologies into the classroom* (pp. 188–202). Hershey, PA: IGI Global.

Du, J., Liu, Y., & Brown, R. L. (2010). The key elements of online learning communities. In Yang, H., & Yuen, S. (Eds.), *Handbook of research on practices and outcomes in e-learning: Issues and trends* (pp. 61–75). Hershey, PA: IGI Global. doi:10.4018/978-1-60566-788-1.ch004

Du, J., & Pate, G. (2008). Implementing varied discussion forums in e-collaborative learning environments. In Kock, N. (Ed.), *Encyclopedia of e-collaboration* (pp. 370–376). Hershey, PA: IGI Global. doi:10.4018/978-1-59904-000-4.ch057

Dufner, D., Alavi, M., & Howard, C. (2009). Evolving technologies supporting of collaborative learning. In Rogers, P., Berg, G., Boettcher, J., Howard, C., Justice, L., & Schenk, K. (Eds.), *Encyclopedia of distance learning* (2nd ed., pp. 987–994). Hershey, PA: IGI Global. doi:10.4018/978-1-60566-198-8.ch139

Dyson, L. E., & Litchfield, A. (2011). Advancing collaboration between m-learning researchers and practitioners through an online portal and Web 2.0 technologies. *International Journal of Mobile and Blended Learning*, 3(1), 64–72. doi:10.4018/jmbl.2011010104

Dziuban, C., Hartman, J., Cavanagh, T. B., & Moskal, P. D. (2011). Blended courses as drivers of institutional transformation. In Kitchenham, A. (Ed.), *Blended learning across disciplines: Models for implementation* (pp. 17–37). Hershey, PA: IGI Global. doi:10.4018/978-1-60960-479-0.ch002

Eberle, J. H., & Childress, M. D. (2007). Universal design for culturally-diverse online learning. In Edmundson, A. (Ed.), *Globalized e-learning cultural challenges* (pp. 239–254). Hershey, PA: IGI Global.

Ekúndayò, O. T., & Tuluri, F. (2011). Learner management systems and environments, implications for pedagogy and applications to resource poor environments. In Lazarinis, F., Green, S., & Pearson, E. (Eds.), *Handbook of research on e-learning standards and interoperability: Frameworks and issues* (pp. 499–525). Hershey, PA: IGI Global. doi:10.4018/978-1-61692-789-9.ch025

Erkunt, H. (2009). Developing electronic portfolios in a computer supported collaborative learning environment. In Chang, M., & Kuo, C. (Eds.), *Learning culture and language through ICTs: Methods for enhanced instruction* (pp. 209–226). Hershey, PA: IGI Global. doi:10.4018/978-1-60566-166-7.ch013

Erlich, Z. (2009). Integrating new technologies to promote distance learning. In Rogers, P., Berg, G., Boettcher, J., Howard, C., Justice, L., & Schenk, K. (Eds.), *Encyclopedia of distance learning* (2nd ed., pp. 1228–1243). Hershey, PA: IGI Global. doi:10.4018/978-1-60566-198-8.ch177

Evangelou, C. E., Tzagarakis, M., Karousos, N., Gkotsis, G., & Nousia, D. (2007). Augmenting collaboration with personalization services. *International Journal of Web-Based Learning and Teaching Technologies*, *2*(3), 77–89. doi:10.4018/jwltt.2007070105

Evoh, C. J. (2009). Collaborative partnerships and the application of ICTs in secondary education in South Africa. In Salmons, J., & Wilson, L. (Eds.), *Handbook of research on electronic collaboration and organizational synergy* (pp. 103–129). Hershey, PA: IGI Global. doi:10.4018/978-1-60566-106-3.ch008

Finger, G., McGlasson, M., & Finger, P. (2007). Information and communication technologies: Towards a mediated learning context. In Inoue, Y. (Ed.), *Technology and diversity in higher education: New challenges* (pp. 81–103). Hershey, PA: IGI Global.

Flanigan, E. J. (2008). Digital business portfolios: Categories, content, and production. In Tomei, L. (Ed.), *Encyclopedia of information technology curriculum integration* (pp. 221–227). Hershey, PA: IGI Global. doi:10.4018/978-1-59904-881-9.ch036

Ford, N. (2008). ICT developments: Learning design and teaching. In Ford, N. (Ed.), *Web-based learning through educational informatics: Information science meets educational computing* (pp. 191–241). Hershey, PA: IGI Global. doi:10.4018/978-1-59904-741-6.ch006

Ford, N. (2008). Learning: Basic processes. In Ford, N. (Ed.), *Web-based learning through educational informatics: Information science meets educational computing* (pp. 1–38). Hershey, PA: IGI Global. doi:10.4018/978-1-59904-741-6.ch001

Ford, N. (2008). Learning: Individual differences. In Ford, N. (Ed.), *Web-based learning through educational informatics: Information science meets educational computing* (pp. 39–74). Hershey, PA: IGI Global. doi:10.4018/978-1-59904-741-6.ch002

Ford, N. (2008). Real world learning. In Ford, N. (Ed.), *Web-based learning through educational informatics: Information science meets educational computing* (pp. 326–352). Hershey, PA: IGI Global. doi:10.4018/978-1-59904-741-6.ch009

Forment, M. A., Casany Guerrero, M. J., & Poch, J. P. (2010). Towards mobile learning applications integration with learning management systems. In Goh, T. (Ed.), *Multiplatform e-learning systems and technologies: Mobile devices for ubiquitous ICT-based education* (pp. 182–194). Hershey, PA: IGI Global. doi:10.4018/978-1-60566-703-4.ch011

Fuchs-Kittowski, F., & Siegeris, E. (2012). An integrated collaboration environment for various types of collaborative knowledge work. In Kock, N. (Ed.), *Advancing collaborative knowledge environments: New trends in e-collaboration* (pp. 102–113). Hershey, PA: IGI Global. doi:10.4018/jec.2010040103

Garrison, D. R. (2009). Blended learning as a transformative design approach. In Rogers, P., Berg, G., Boettcher, J., Howard, C., Justice, L., & Schenk, K. (Eds.), *Encyclopedia of distance learning* (2nd ed., pp. 200–204). Hershey, PA: IGI Global. doi:10.4018/978-1-60566-198-8.ch028

Garrison, D. R. (2009). Communities of inquiry in online learning. In Rogers, P., Berg, G., Boettcher, J., Howard, C., Justice, L., & Schenk, K. (Eds.), *Encyclopedia of distance learning* (2nd ed., pp. 352–355). Hershey, PA: IGI Global. doi:10.4018/978-1-60566-198-8.ch052

Gay, G. R., Salomoni, P., & Mirri, S. (2008). E-Learning. In Freire, M., & Pereira, M. (Eds.), *Encyclopedia of Internet technologies and applications* (pp. 179–184). Hershey, PA: IGI Global.

Geer, R. (2009). Strategies for blended approaches in teacher education. In Stacey, E., & Gerbic, P. (Eds.), *Effective Blended Learning Practices: Evidence-based perspectives in ICT-facilitated education* (pp. 39–61). Hershey, PA: IGI Global. doi:10.4018/978-1-60566-296-1.ch003

Ghosh, S., & Majumdar, S. K. (2011). Portfolio selection models and their discrimination. *International Journal of Operations Research and Information Systems, 2*(2), 65–91. doi:10.4018/joris.2011040104

Giambona, G. J., & Birchall, D. W. (2010). Collaborative e-Learning and ICT tools to develop SME managers: An Italian case. *International Journal of Distributed Systems and Technologies, 1*(3), 71–82. doi:10.4018/IJDST.2010070105

Goh, D. H. (2007). Learning geography with the G-Portal Digital Library. In Tatnall, A. (Ed.), *Encyclopedia of portal technologies and applications* (pp. 547–553). Hershey, PA: IGI Global. doi:10.4018/978-1-59140-989-2.ch092

Gomez, E. A., Wu, D., Passerini, K., & Bieber, M. (2007). Utilizing Web tools for computer-mediated communication to enhance team-based learning. *International Journal of Web-Based Learning and Teaching Technologies, 2*(2), 21–37. doi:10.4018/jwltt.2007040102

Gouardères, G., & Conté, E. (2009). E-Portfolio to promote virtual learning group communities on the grid. In Wang, L., Chen, J., & Jie, W. (Eds.), *Quantitative quality of service for grid computing: Applications for heterogeneity, large-scale distribution, and dynamic environments* (pp. 320–337). Hershey, PA: IGI Global. doi:10.4018/978-1-60566-370-8.ch017

Graham, C. G., & Allen, S. (2009). Designing blended learning environments. In Rogers, P., Berg, G., Boettcher, J., Howard, C., Justice, L., & Schenk, K. (Eds.), *Encyclopedia of distance learning* (2nd ed., pp. 562–570). Hershey, PA: IGI Global. doi:10.4018/978-1-60566-198-8.ch082

Grippa, F., De Maggio, M., & Corallo, A. (2012). Observing the evolution of a learning community using social network analysis. In Safar, M., & Mahdi, K. (Eds.), *Social networking and community behavior modeling: Qualitative and quantitative measures* (pp. 215–231). Hershey, PA: IGI Global.

Gulbahar, Y. (2009). Usage of electronic portfolios for assessment. In Tan Wee Hin, L., & Subramaniam, R. (Eds.), *Handbook of research on new media literacy at the K-12 Level: Issues and challenges* (pp. 702–719). Hershey, PA: IGI Global. doi:10.4018/978-1-60566-120-9.ch044

Gündogan, M. B. (2011). 'O' is for organic: An ecological perspective for online learning. In Kurubacak, G., & Yuzer, T. (Eds.), *Handbook of research on transformative online education and liberation: Models for social equality* (pp. 425–438). Hershey, PA: IGI Global.

Gunn, C., & Blake, A. (2009). Blending technology into an academic practice qualification for university teachers. In Stacey, E., & Gerbic, P. (Eds.), *Effective blended learning practices: Evidence-based perspectives in ICT-facilitated education* (pp. 259–279). Hershey, PA: IGI Global. doi:10.4018/978-1-60566-296-1.ch014

Gupta, S., & Bostrom, R. (2008). E-Collaboration technologies impact on learning. In Kock, N. (Ed.), *Encyclopedia of e-collaboration* (pp. 191–197). Hershey, PA: IGI Global.

Gütl, C. (2011). The support of virtual 3D worlds for enhancing collaboration in learning settings. In Pozzi, F., & Persico, D. (Eds.), *Techniques for fostering collaboration in online learning communities: Theoretical and practical perspectives* (pp. 278–299). Hershey, PA: IGI Global. doi:10.4018/978-1-61692-898-8.ch016

Hai-Jew, S. (2009). Why "cultural sensitivities" and "localizations" in global e-learning? In Demiray, U., & Sharma, R. (Eds.), *Ethical practices and implications in distance learning* (pp. 155–197). Hershey, PA: IGI Global.

Hai-Jew, S. (2010). Capturing and authoring tools for graphics in e-learning. In Hai-Jew, S. (Ed.), *Digital imagery and informational graphics in e-learning: Maximizing visual technologies* (pp. 118–141). Hershey, PA: IGI Global. doi:10.4018/978-1-60566-972-4.ch006

Hai-Jew, S. (2010). Maximizing collaborative learning and work in digital libraries and repositories: A conceptual meta-case. In Russell, D. (Ed.), *Cases on collaboration in virtual learning environments: Processes and interactions* (pp. 169–192). Hershey, PA: IGI Global.

Hai-Jew, S. (2011). Staying legal and ethical in global e-learning course and training developments: An exploration. In Wang, V. (Ed.), *Encyclopedia of information communication technologies and adult education integration* (pp. 958–970). Hershey, PA: IGI Global.

Hai-Jew, S. (2011). Virtual collaboration. In Wang, V. (Ed.), *Encyclopedia of information communication technologies and adult education integration* (pp. 876–895). Hershey, PA: IGI Global.

Hai-Jew, S. (2012). Taking public health learning global through branding and identity management. In Kapoor, A., & Kulshrestha, C. (Eds.), *Branding and sustainable competitive advantage: Building virtual presence* (pp. 24–45). Hershey, PA: IGI Global.

Häkkinen, P., Arvaja, M., Hämäläinen, R., & Pöysä, J. (2010). Scripting computer-supported collaborative learning: A review of SCORE studies. In Ertl, B. (Ed.), *E-Collaborative knowledge construction: Learning from computer-supported and virtual environments* (pp. 180–194). Hershey, PA: IGI Global. doi:10.4018/978-1-61520-729-9.ch010

Hall, R., Mackenzie, S., & Hall, M. (2010). The impact of interactive and collaborative learning activities on the personalised learning of adult distance learners. In O'Donoghue, J. (Ed.), *Technology-supported environments for personalized learning: Methods and case studies* (pp. 128–148). Hershey, PA: IGI Global. doi:10.4018/978-1-60566-884-0.ch008

Hao, Y. (2010). Integrating blogs in teacher education. In Kidd, T., & Keengwe, J. (Eds.), *Adult learning in the digital age: Perspectives on online technologies and outcomes* (pp. 134–147). Hershey, PA: IGI Global.

Harrer, A., & Hoppe, H. U. (2008). Visual modelling of collaborative learning processes: Uses, desired properties, and approaches. In Botturi, L., & Stubbs, T. (Eds.), *Handbook of visual languages for instructional design: Theories and practices* (pp. 280–297). Hershey, PA: IGI Global.

Harvard, B., Du, J., & Olinzock, A. (2007). Task-orientation online discussion: A practical model for student learning. In Tomei, L. (Ed.), *Integrating information & communications technologies into the classroom* (pp. 154–166). Hershey, PA: IGI Global.

Haythornthwaite, C., Lunsford, K. J., Bowker, G. C., & Bruce, B. C. (2006). Challenges for research and practice in distributed, interdisciplinary collaboration. In Hine, C. (Ed.), *New infrastructures for knowledge production: Understanding e-science* (pp. 143–166). Hershey, PA: IGI Global. doi:10.4018/978-1-59140-717-1.ch007

Heinrich, E., & Bozhko, Y. (2012). The role of institutions in creating student-focused virtual learning spaces with ePortfolio systems. In Keppell, M., Souter, K., & Riddle, M. (Eds.), *Physical and virtual learning spaces in higher education: Concepts for the modern learning environment* (pp. 119–135). Hershey, PA: IGI Global. doi:10.4018/978-1-60960-114-0.ch008

Heinze, A., & Procter, C. (2012). The significance of the reflective practitioner in blended learning. In Parsons, D. (Ed.), *Refining current practices in mobile and blended learning: New applications* (pp. 175–187). Hershey, PA: IGI Global. doi:10.4018/978-1-4666-0053-9.ch012

Hennis, T., Lukosch, S., & Veen, W. (2012). Reputation in peer-based learning environments. In Santos, O., & Boticario, J. (Eds.), *Educational recommender systems and technologies: Practices and challenges* (pp. 95–128). Hershey, PA: IGI Global.

Hepburn, G. (2008). Preparing for the virtual workplace in the educational commons. In Zemliansky, P., & St.Amant, K. (Eds.), *Handbook of research on virtual workplaces and the new nature of business practices* (pp. 334–344). Hershey, PA: IGI Global. doi:10.4018/978-1-59904-893-2.ch024

Hobbs, M., Brown, E., & Gordon, M. (2009). Learning and assessment with virtual worlds. In Spratt, C., & Lajbcygier, P. (Eds.), *E-Learning technologies and evidence-based assessment approaches* (pp. 55–75). Hershey, PA: IGI Global. doi:10.4018/978-1-60566-410-1.ch004

Hogan, R. (2012). How to be a transnational distance learning winner. In Hogan, R. (Ed.), *Transnational distance learning and building new markets for universities* (pp. 260–279). Hershey, PA: IGI Global. doi:10.4018/978-1-46660-206-9

Holland, J. L. (2009). A scale of affective satisfaction in online learning communities. In Whitworth, B., & de Moor, A. (Eds.), *Handbook of research on socio-technical design and social networking systems* (*Vol. 1-2*, pp. 651–668). Hershey, PA: IGI Global. doi:10.4018/978-1-60566-264-0.ch043

Holt, D., Segrave, S., & Cybulski, J. L. (2012). E-Simulations for educating the professions in blended learning environments. In Holt, D., Segrave, S., & Cybulski, J. (Eds.), *Professional education using e-simulations: Benefits of blended learning design* (pp. 1–23). Hershey, PA: IGI Global.

Holt, L., & Ziegler, M. F. (2011). Promoting team learning in the classroom. *International Journal of Adult Vocational Education and Technology*, *2*(3), 1–11. doi:10.4018/javet.2011070101

Howell-Richardson, C. (2010). A pragmatic approach to analysing CMC discourse. In Taiwo, R. (Ed.), *Handbook of research on discourse behavior and digital communication: Language structures and social interaction* (pp. 759–775). Hershey, PA: IGI Global. doi:10.4018/978-1-61520-773-2.ch049

Hribernik, K. A., Thoben, K., & Nilsson, M. (2008). A generic definition of collaborative working environments. In Kock, N. (Ed.), *Encyclopedia of e-collaboration* (pp. 308–313). Hershey, PA: IGI Global. doi:10.4018/978-1-60566-652-5.ch009

Hribernik, K. A., Thoben, K., & Nilsson, M. (2008). Technological challenges to the research and development of collaborative working environments. In Kock, N. (Ed.), *Encyclopedia of e-collaboration* (pp. 612–617). Hershey, PA: IGI Global. doi:10.4018/978-1-60566-652-5.ch030

Hricko, M. (2011). Social networks: Implications for education. In D'Agustino, S. (Ed.), *Adaptation, resistance and access to instructional technologies: Assessing future trends in education* (pp. 216–234). Hershey, PA: IGI Global.

Hron, A., Cress, U., & Neudert, S. (2011). Using and acquiring shared and unshared knowledge in collaborative learning and writing. In Pozzi, F., & Persico, D. (Eds.), *Techniques for fostering collaboration in online learning communities: Theoretical and practical perspectives* (pp. 49–63). Hershey, PA: IGI Global. doi:10.4018/978-1-61692-898-8.ch004

Hsu, P., & Chang, T. (2011). A new process phase diagnostic technique: Visualized interface for diagnosing learning progress. In Jin, Q. (Ed.), *Distance education environments and emerging software systems: New technologies* (pp. 138–150). Hershey, PA: IGI Global. doi:10.4018/978-1-60960-539-1.ch009

Hsu, P., & Chang, T. (2011). Validation of learning effort algorithm for real-time non-interfering based diagnostic technique. *International Journal of Distance Education Technologies, 9*(3), 31–44. doi:10.4018/jdet.2011070103

Hu, C. (2010). When cultures meet in blended learning: What literature tells us. In Ng, E. (Ed.), *Comparative blended learning practices and environments* (pp. 278–300). Hershey, PA: IGI Global.

Huett, J. B., Sharp, J. H., & Huett, K. C. (2011). What's all the FOSS? How freedom and openness are changing the face of our educational landscape. In Czerkawski, B. (Ed.), *Free and open source software for e-learning: Issues, successes and challenges* (pp. 24–38). Hershey, PA: IGI Global.

Hughes, G. D., & Tsemunhu, R. (2011). Avoiding isolation through collaborative learning and lecture videos. In Huffman, S., Albritton, S., Wilmes, B., & Rickman, W. (Eds.), *Cases on building quality distance delivery programs: Strategies and experiences* (pp. 232–246). Hershey, PA: IGI Global. doi:10.4018/978-1-60960-111-9.ch016

Hwang, G., Cheng, H., Chu, C. H., Tseng, J. C., & Hwang, G. (2009). Development of a Web-based system for diagnosing student learning problems on english tenses. In Syed, M. (Ed.), *Methods and applications for advancing distance education technologies: International issues and solutions* (pp. 324–341). Hershey, PA: IGI Global. doi:10.4018/978-1-60566-342-5.ch022

Hwang, S., & Plankis, B. (2012). Individual e-portfolios: Can a classic tool for teachers and students be merged with Web 2.0 tools for reflective learning? In Yang, H., & Yuen, S. (Eds.), *Handbook of research on practices and outcomes in virtual worlds and environments* (pp. 706–721). Hershey, PA: IGI Global.

Hwang, Y., & Chen, M. (2011). Adopting Web 2.0 in English writing course: A collaborative learning approach in NPO-Universities in Taiwan. In Chen, T. (Ed.), *Implementing new business models in for-profit and non-profit organizations: Technologies and applications* (pp. 133–154). Hershey, PA: IGI Global.

Ikeya, N., Awamura, N., & Sakai, S. (2010). Why do we need to share information? Analysis of collaborative task management meetings. In Foster, J. (Ed.), *Collaborative information behavior: User engagement and communication sharing* (pp. 89–108). Hershey, PA: IGI Global. doi:10.4018/978-1-61520-797-8.ch006

Immonen-Orpana, P., & Åhlberg, M. (2010). Collaborative learning by developing (LbD) using concept maps and vee diagrams. In Lupion Torres, P., & de Cássia Veiga Marriott, R. (Eds.), *Handbook of research on collaborative learning using concept mapping* (pp. 215–237). Hershey, PA: IGI Global. doi:10.4018/978-1-59904-992-2.ch011

Inan, F. A., & Lowther, D. (2007). A comparative analysis of computer-supported learning models and guidelines. In Neto, F., & Brasileiro, F. (Eds.), *Advances in computer-supported learning* (pp. 1–20). Hershey, PA: IGI Global. doi:10.4018/978-1-59904-355-5.ch001

Inoue, A. B. (2009). The technology of writing assessment and racial validity. In Schreiner, C. (Ed.), *Handbook of research on assessment technologies, methods, and applications in higher education* (pp. 97–120). Hershey, PA: IGI Global. doi:10.4018/978-1-60566-667-9.ch006

Iyamu, E. O., & Ukadike, J. O. (2007). Perception of self-directed cooperative learning among undergraduate students in selected Nigerian universities. *International Journal of Information and Communication Technology Education, 3*(4), 13–20. doi:10.4018/jicte.2007100102

Jimoyiannis, A., Gravani, M., & Karagiorgi, Y. (2012). Teacher professional development through virtual campuses: Conceptions of a 'new' model. In Yang, H., & Yuen, S. (Eds.), *Handbook of research on practices and outcomes in virtual worlds and environments* (pp. 327–347). Hershey, PA: IGI Global.

Johnson, T. E., Ifenthanler, D., Pirnay-Dummer, P. N., & Spector, J. M. (2010). Using concept maps to assess individuals and teams in collaborative learning environments. In Lupion Torres, P., & de Cássia Veiga Marriott, R. (Eds.), *Handbook of research on collaborative learning using concept mapping* (pp. 358–381). Hershey, PA: IGI Global. doi:10.4018/978-1-59904-992-2.ch018

Joia, L. A., & Costa, M. F. (2008). Some key success factors in Web-based corporate training in Brazil: A multiple case study. *International Journal of Web-Based Learning and Teaching Technologies, 3*(4), 1–28. doi:10.4018/jwbltt.2009092201

Jones, F. S. (2008). The perceptions of collaborative technologies among virtual workers. In Zemliansky, P., & St.Amant, K. (Eds.), *Handbook of research on virtual workplaces and the new nature of business practices* (pp. 150–166). Hershey, PA: IGI Global. doi:10.4018/978-1-59904-893-2.ch012

Jones, S. A., Green, L., Hodges, C. B., Kennedy, K., Downs, E., Repman, J., & Clark, K. F. (2012). Supplementing the learning management system: Using Web 2.0 for collaboration, communication, and productivity in the preparation of school technology leaders. In Polly, D., Mims, C., & Persichitte, K. (Eds.), *Developing technology-rich teacher education programs: Key issues* (pp. 118–134). Hershey, PA: IGI Global.

Jong, T. D., Fuertes, A., Schmeits, T., & Specht, M. (2010). A contextualised multi-platform framework to support blended learning scenarios in learning networks. In Goh, T. (Ed.), *Multiplatform e-learning systems and technologies: Mobile devices for ubiquitous ICT-based education* (pp. 1–19). Hershey, PA: IGI Global. doi:10.4018/978-1-60566-703-4.ch001

Juang, Y. (2010). Blended learning in engineering curricula through the meaningful use of ICT tools. In Luppicini, R., & Haghi, A. (Eds.), *Cases on digital technologies in higher education: Issues and challenges* (pp. 202–216). Hershey, PA: IGI Global. doi:10.4018/978-1-61520-869-2.ch015

Juneau, K. R. (2008). Varieties of authentic assessment. In Tomei, L. (Ed.), *Encyclopedia of information technology curriculum integration* (pp. 936–942). Hershey, PA: IGI Global. doi:10.4018/978-1-59904-881-9.ch146

Kamthan, P. (2007). A perspective on software engineering education with open source software. In St. Amant, K., & Still, B. (Eds.), *Handbook of research on open source software: Technological, economic, and social perspectives* (pp. 690–702). Hershey, PA: IGI Global. doi:10.4018/978-1-59140-999-1.ch054

Kanev, K., & Kimura, S. (2011). Collaborative learning in dynamic group environments. In Jin, Q. (Ed.), *Distance education environments and emerging software systems: New technologies* (pp. 1–14). Hershey, PA: IGI Global. doi:10.4018/978-1-60960-539-1.ch001

Kaun, K., & Arora, P. (2010). Global education greenhouse: Constructing and organizing online global knowledge. In Mukerji, S., & Tripathi, P. (Eds.), *Cases on technology enhanced learning through collaborative opportunities* (pp. 208–222). Hershey, PA: IGI Global. doi:10.4018/978-1-61520-751-0.ch012

Kaur, K. (2009). Enlivening the promise of education: Building collaborative learning communities through online discussion. In Lytras, M., Tennyson, R., & Ordóñez de Pablos, P. (Eds.), *Knowledge networks: The social software perspective* (pp. 257–279). Hershey, PA: IGI Global.

Kautz, K. (2009). Towards an integrated model of knowledge sharing in software development: Insights from a case study. In Lytras, M., Tennyson, R., & Ordóñez de Pablos, P. (Eds.), *Knowledge networks: The social software perspective* (pp. 280–307). Hershey, PA: IGI Global.

Kawachi, P. (2009). Ethics in interactions in distance education. In Demiray, U., & Sharma, R. (Eds.), *Ethical practices and implications in distance learning* (pp. 24–34). Hershey, PA: IGI Global.

Kazmer, M. M. (2009). Online learning community. In Rogers, P., Berg, G., Boettcher, J., Howard, C., Justice, L., & Schenk, K. (Eds.), *Encyclopedia of distance learning* (2nd ed., pp. 1506–1511). Hershey, PA: IGI Global. doi:10.4018/978-1-60566-198-8.ch219

Keegan, H., & Lisewski, B. (2009). Living, working, teaching and learning by social software. In Hatzipanagos, S., & Warburton, S. (Eds.), *Handbook of research on social software and developing community ontologies* (pp. 208–221). Hershey, PA: IGI Global. doi:10.4018/978-1-60566-208-4.ch015

Kenny, R. F. (2007). Using problem-based learning in online courses: A new hope? In Bullen, M., & Janes, D. (Eds.), *Making the transition to e-learning: Strategies and issues* (pp. 243–265). Hershey, PA: IGI Global.

Kenon, V. H. (2011). Global education access utilizing partnerships and networked global learning communities. *International Journal of Cyber Ethics in Education, 1*(3), 40–49. doi:10.4018/ijcee.2011070104

Keppell, M. J. (2007). Instructional designers on the borderline: Brokering across communities of practice. In Keppell, M. (Ed.), *Instructional design: Case studies in communities of practice* (pp. 68–89). Hershey, PA: IGI Global. doi:10.4018/978-1-59904-322-7.ch004

Khan, B. A., & Matskin, M. (2010). A platform for actively supporting e-learning in mobile networks. *International Journal of Mobile and Blended Learning, 2*(1), 55–79. doi:10.4018/jmbl.2010010104

Khoroshilov, A., Kuliamin, V., Petrenko, A., Petrenko, O., & Rubanov, V. (2011). Building open learning environment for software engineering students. In Czerkawski, B. (Ed.), *Free and open source software for e-learning: Issues, successes and challenges* (pp. 110–119). Hershey, PA: IGI Global. doi:10.4018/978-1-61520-917-0.ch007

Kim, S., Kim, M., & Hong, J. (2010). Integrated design of Web-platform, offline supports, and evaluation system for the successful implementation of University 2.0. In Song, H., & Kidd, T. (Eds.), *Handbook of research on human performance and instructional technology* (pp. 533–551). Hershey, PA: IGI Global. doi:10.4018/978-1-60566-782-9.ch032

Kinash, S., & Crichton, S. (2011). Blended learning internationalization from the commonwealth: An Australian and Canadian collaborative case study. In Edmundson, A. (Ed.), *Cases on globalized and culturally appropriate e-learning: Challenges and solutions* (pp. 141–167). Hershey, PA: IGI Global. doi:10.4018/978-1-61520-989-7.ch007

King, K. P. (2009). Blended learning. In Rogers, P., Berg, G., Boettcher, J., Howard, C., Justice, L., & Schenk, K. (Eds.), *Encyclopedia of distance learning* (2nd ed., pp. 194–199). Hershey, PA: IGI Global. doi:10.4018/978-1-60566-198-8.ch027

Kismihók, G., & Vas, R. (2011). Empirical research on learners' thoughts about the impact of mobile technology on learning. *International Journal of Mobile and Blended Learning, 3*(1), 73–88. doi:10.4018/jmbl.2011010105

Kissel, B. (2012). Weebly, wikis, and digital storytelling: The potential of Web 2.0 tools in writing classrooms. In Polly, D., Mims, C., & Persichitte, K. (Eds.), *Developing technology-rich teacher education programs: Key issues* (pp. 288–298). Hershey, PA: IGI Global.

Kitchenham, A. (2009). Electronic portfolios in teacher education. In Rogers, P., Berg, G., Boettcher, J., Howard, C., Justice, L., & Schenk, K. (Eds.), *Encyclopedia of distance learning* (2nd ed., pp. 877–884). Hershey, PA: IGI Global. doi:10.4018/978-1-60566-198-8.ch123

Kitchenham, A. (2009). E-Professional development and rural teachers: Finding the blend. *International Journal of Mobile and Blended Learning, 1*(3), 70–85. doi:10.4018/jmbl.2009092204

Kitchenham, A. (2011). Blending professional development for rural educators an exploratory study. In Parsons, D. (Ed.), *Combining e-learning and m-learning: New applications of blended educational resources* (pp. 225–238). Hershey, PA: IGI Global. doi:10.4018/978-1-60960-481-3.ch014

Kock, N. (2008). A basic definition of e-collaboration and its underlying concepts. In Kock, N. (Ed.), *Encyclopedia of e-collaboration* (pp. 48–53). Hershey, PA: IGI Global. doi:10.4018/978-1-60566-652-5.ch001

Kolfschoten, G. L., Briggs, R. O., & Vreede, G. D. (2010). A technology for pattern-based process design and its application to collaboration engineering. In Rummler, S., & Ng, K. (Eds.), *Collaborative technologies and applications for interactive information design: Emerging trends in user experiences* (pp. 1–18). Hershey, PA: IGI Global. doi:10.4018/978-1-60566-727-0.ch001

Kong, S. C. (2008). Collaborative learning in a mobile technology supported classroom. In Lumsden, J. (Ed.), *Handbook of research on user interface design and evaluation for mobile technology* (pp. 270–285). Hershey, PA: IGI Global. doi:10.4018/978-1-59904-871-0.ch017

Kong, S. C. (2010). A multiplatform e-learning system for collaborative learning: The potential of interactions for learning fraction equivalence. In Goh, T. (Ed.), *Multiplatform e-learning systems and technologies: Mobile devices for ubiquitous ICT-based education* (pp. 244–259). Hershey, PA: IGI Global.

Konstantinidis, A., Tsiatsos, T., Demetriadis, S., & Pomportsis, A. S. (2011). Collaborative e-learning techniques: Learning management systems vs. multi-user virtual environments. In Vincenti, G., & Braman, J. (Eds.), *Multi-user virtual environments for the classroom: Practical approaches to teaching in virtual worlds* (pp. 101–114). Hershey, PA: IGI Global. doi:10.4018/978-1-60960-545-2. ch008

Kopp, B., Germ, M., & Mandl, H. (2010). Supporting virtual learning through e-tutoring. In Ertl, B. (Ed.), *E-Collaborative knowledge construction: Learning from computer-supported and virtual environments* (pp. 213–231). Hershey, PA: IGI Global. doi:10.4018/978-1-61520-729-9.ch012

Kopp, B., & Mandl, H. (2011). Supporting virtual collaborative learning using collaboration scripts and content schemes. In Pozzi, F., & Persico, D. (Eds.), *Techniques for fostering collaboration in online learning communities: Theoretical and practical perspectives* (pp. 15–32). Hershey, PA: IGI Global. doi:10.4018/978-1-61692-898-8. ch002

Krpan, D., Tomaš, S., & Vladušic, R. (2010). Using effect size for group modeling in e-learning systems. In Stankov, S., Glavinic, V., & Rosic, M. (Eds.), *Intelligent tutoring systems in e-learning environments: Design, implementation and evaluation* (pp. 237–257). Hershey, PA: IGI Global. doi:10.4018/978-1-61692-008-1.ch012

Kukulska-Hulme, A. (2009). Group leadership in online collaborative learning. In Rogers, P., Berg, G., Boettcher, J., Howard, C., Justice, L., & Schenk, K. (Eds.), *Encyclopedia of distance learning* (2nd ed., pp. 1052–1059). Hershey, PA: IGI Global. doi:10.4018/978-1-60566-198-8.ch149

Kukulska-Hulme, A., Pettit, J., Bradley, L., Carvalho, A. A., Herrington, A., Kennedy, D. M., & Walker, A. (2011). Mature students using mobile devices in life and learning. *International Journal of Mobile and Blended Learning, 3*(1), 18–52. doi:10.4018/jmbl.2011010102

Kukulska-Hulme, A., Sharples, M., Milrad, M., Arnedillo-Sanchez, I., & Vavoula, G. (2009). Innovation in mobile learning: A European perspective. *International Journal of Mobile and Blended Learning, 1*(1), 13–35. doi:10.4018/jmbl.2009010102

Kulyk, O., van Dijk, B., van der Vet, P., Nijholt, A., & van der Veer, G. (2009). Situational awareness in collaborative work environments. In Whitworth, B., & de Moor, A. (Eds.), *Handbook of research on socio-technical design and social networking systems* (*Vol. 1-2*, pp. 636–650). Hershey, PA: IGI Global. doi:10.4018/978-1-60566-264-0.ch042

Kumar, R., Ajjan, H., & Niu, Y. (2010). Information technology portfolio management: Literature review, framework, and research issues. In Khosrow-Pour, M. (Ed.), *Global, social, and organizational implications of emerging information resources management: Concepts and applications* (pp. 446–470). Hershey, PA: IGI Global.

Labour, M., & Kolski, C. (2010). A pedagogic pattern model of blended e-learning: A step towards designing sustainable simulation-based learning. In Tzanavari, A., & Tsapatsoulis, N. (Eds.), *Affective, interactive and cognitive methods for e-learning design: Creating an optimal education experience* (pp. 114–137). Hershey, PA: IGI Global. doi:10.4018/978-1-60566-940-3.ch006

Lacouture, J., & Aniorté, P. (2011). Self-adaptable discovery and composition of services based on the semantic CompAA approach. *International Journal of Adaptive, Resilient and Autonomic Systems, 2*(4), 54-73. Hershey, PA: IGI Global. doi:10.4018/jaras.2011100104

Laffey, J. M., Schmidt, M., & Amelung, C. J. (2011). Open for social: How open source software for e-learning can take a turn to the social. In Czerkawski, B. (Ed.), *Free and open source software for e-learning: Issues, successes and challenges* (pp. 187–202). Hershey, PA: IGI Global.

Lai-Chen, L., & Ching-Long, Y. (2010). Collaborative e-learning using semantic course blog. In Syed, M. (Ed.), *Technologies shaping instruction and distance education: New studies and utilizations* (pp. 67–76). Hershey, PA: IGI Global.

Lajbcygier, P., & Spratt, C. (2009). The validity of group marks as a proxy for individual learning in e-learning settings. In Spratt, C., & Lajbcygier, P. (Eds.), *E-Learning technologies and evidence-based assessment approaches* (pp. 136–150). Hershey, PA: IGI Global. doi:10.4018/978-1-60566-410-1.ch008

Lajbcyier, P., & Spratt, C. (2007). Using "blended learning" to develop tertiary students' skills of critique. In Tomei, L. (Ed.), *Integrating information & communications technologies into the classroom* (pp. 1–18). Hershey, PA: IGI Global.

Lam, W., Kong, E., & Chua, A. (2008). Managing online discussion forums for collaborative learning. In Kock, N. (Ed.), *Encyclopedia of e-collaboration* (pp. 437–443). Hershey, PA: IGI Global. doi:10.4018/978-1-59904-000-4.ch067

Lambropoulos, N. (2007). User-centered design of online learning communities. In Lambropoulos, N., & Zaphiris, P. (Eds.), *User-centered design of online learning communities* (pp. 1–28). Hershey, PA: IGI Global.

Lambropoulos, N. (2011). The sense of e-learning community index (SeLCI) for computer supported collaborative e-learning (CSCeL). In Daniel, B. (Ed.), *Handbook of research on methods and techniques for studying virtual communities: Paradigms and phenomena* (pp. 672–698). Hershey, PA: IGI Global. doi:10.4018/978-1-60960-040-2.ch040

Larson, D. (2011). Inter-organization partnership and collaborative work tools. In Milhauser, K. (Ed.), *Distributed team collaboration in organizations: Emerging tools and practices* (pp. 212–223). Hershey, PA: IGI Global. doi:10.4018/978-1-60960-533-9.ch013

Lavigne, S., & Sanchez, S. (2007). Modeling an artificial stock market. In Rennard, J. (Ed.), *Handbook of research on nature-inspired computing for economics and management* (pp. 909–925). Hershey, PA: IGI Global.

Law, E. L., & Hvannberg, E. T. (2007). Quality models of online learning community systems: Exploration, evaluation and exploitation. In Lambropoulos, N., & Zaphiris, P. (Eds.), *User-centered design of online learning communities* (pp. 71–101). Hershey, PA: IGI Global.

Lee, C. (2009). Instructional technology theory for online teaching/learning system. In Chao, L. (Ed.), *Utilizing open source tools for online teaching and learning: Applying Linux technologies* (pp. 28–59). Hershey, PA: IGI Global. doi:10.4018/978-1-60566-376-0.ch002

Lee, D., & Boreland, S. (2007). Implementing computer-supported learning in corporations. In Neto, F., & Brasileiro, F. (Eds.), *Advances in computer-supported learning* (pp. 228–250). Hershey, PA: IGI Global.

Lee, H., Davis, R. A., & Chi, Y. (2011). Integrating XML technologies and open source software for personalization in e-learning. In Ng, E., Karacapilidis, N., & Raisinghani, M. (Eds.), *Dynamic advancements in teaching and learning based technologies: New concepts* (pp. 216–231). Hershey, PA: IGI Global. doi:10.4018/jwbltt.2009090803

Lee, H., & Herner-Patnode, L. (2011). Reflecting on portfolio development: How does the portfolio facilitate a preservice teacher's growth? *International Journal of Online Pedagogy and Course Design, 1*(1), 64–78. doi:10.4018/ijopcd.2011010105

Lee, L., & Hung, J. C. (2011). Effect of teaching using whole brain instruction on accounting learning. In Jin, Q. (Ed.), *Distance education environments and emerging software systems: New technologies* (pp. 261–282). Hershey, PA: IGI Global. doi:10.4018/978-1-60960-539-1.ch016

Lee, T., Shen, P., & Tsai, C. (2012). Enhance students' computing skills via web-mediated self-regulated learning with feedback in blended environment. In Mesquita, A. (Ed.), *Human interaction with technology for working, communicating, and learning: Advancements* (pp. 149–166). Hershey, PA: IGI Global.

Lee, Y., Junginger, M., & Geller, J. (2003). High performance publisher/subscriber communication for adaptive, collaborative Web-based learning. *International Journal of Distance Education Technologies, 1*(3), 14–27. doi:10.4018/jdet.2003070102

Leng, J., & Sharrock, W. (2010). Collaborative practices in computer-aided academic research. In Portela, I., & Cruz-Cunha, M. (Eds.), *Information communication technology law, protection and access rights: Global approaches and issues* (pp. 249–270). Hershey, PA: IGI Global. doi:10.4018/978-1-61520-975-0.ch016

Li, B., & Gillam, L. (2010). Grid service level agreements using financial risk analysis techniques. In N. Antonopoulos, G. Exarchakos, M. Li, & A. Liotta (Eds.), *Handbook of research on P2P and grid systems for service-oriented computing: Models, methodologies and applications* (pp. 686-710). Hershey, PA: IGI Global. doi:10.4018/978-1-61520-686-5.ch029

Li, F. W., Lau, R. W., & Dharmendran, P. (2012). An adaptive course generation framework. In Jin, Q. (Ed.), *Intelligent learning systems and advancements in computer-aided instruction: Emergings* (pp. 76–93). Hershey, PA: IGI Global.

Lien, W., Kuo, R., & Chang, M. (2009). Using blended learning to teach foreign brides Chinese. In Chang, M., & Kuo, C. (Eds.), *Learning culture and language through ICTs: Methods for enhanced instruction* (pp. 120–137). Hershey, PA: IGI Global. doi:10.4018/978-1-60566-166-7.ch008

Lim, H. L. (2009). Understanding group interaction and knowledge building in virtual learning environments. In Wang, V. (Ed.), *Handbook of research on e-learning applications for career and technical education: Technologies for vocational training* (pp. 312–328). Hershey, PA: IGI Global. doi:10.4018/978-1-60566-739-3.ch025

Lim, H. L., & Sudweeks, F. (2008). Discourse and network analyses of learning conversations. In Kelsey, S., & St.Amant, K. (Eds.), *Handbook of research on computer mediated communication* (pp. 451–476). Hershey, PA: IGI Global. doi:10.4018/978-1-59904-863-5.ch034

Lim, H. L., & Sudweeks, F. (2009). Constructivism and online collaborative group learning in higher education: A case study. In Payne, C. (Ed.), *Information technology and constructivism in higher education: Progressive learning frameworks* (pp. 231–246). Hershey, PA: IGI Global. doi:10.4018/978-1-60566-654-9.ch015

Lim, J., Yang, Y. P., & Zhong, Y. (2009). Group support systems as collaborative learning technologies: A meta-analysis. In Karacapilidis, N. (Ed.), *Solutions and innovations in Web-based technologies for augmented learning: Improved platforms, tools, and applications* (pp. 79–108). Hershey, PA: IGI Global. doi:10.4018/978-1-60566-238-1.ch006

Lin, C., & Yang, S. (2011). The effects of videoconferenced distance-learning instruction in a taiwanese company. *International Journal of Distance Education Technologies*, 9(2), 52–64. doi:10.4018/jdet.2011040105

Lin, C. S., & Chou, C. C. (2007). APEC Cyber Academy: Integration of pedagogical and HCI principles in an international networked learning environment. In McKay, E. (Ed.), *Enhancing learning through human computer interaction* (pp. 154–177). Hershey, PA: IGI Global. doi:10.4018/978-1-59904-328-9.ch009

Ling, L. H., & Sudweeks, F. (2008). Chatting to Learn: A Case Study on Student Experiences of Online Moderated Synchronous Discussions in Virtual Tutorials. In Negash, S., Whitman, M., Woszczynski, A., Hoganson, K., & Mattord, H. (Eds.), *Handbook of Distance Learning for Real-Time and Asynchronous Information Technology Education* (pp. 170–191). doi:10.4018/978-1-59904-964-9.ch009

Liu, L., & D'Andrea, L. (2011). Initial stages to create online graduate communities: Assessment and development. In Wang, V. (Ed.), *Encyclopedia of information communication technologies and adult education integration* (pp. 911–926). Hershey, PA: IGI Global.

Liu, X., & Magjuka, R. J. (2011). Learning in cross-cultural online MBA courses: Perceptions of Chinese students. In Edmundson, A. (Ed.), *Cases on globalized and culturally appropriate e-learning: Challenges and solutions* (pp. 168–186). Hershey, PA: IGI Global. doi:10.4018/978-1-61520-989-7.ch008

Liu, Y. (2007). Designing quality online education to promote cross-cultural understanding. In Edmundson, A. (Ed.), *Globalized e-learning cultural challenges* (pp. 35–59). Hershey, PA: IGI Global. doi:10.4018/978-1-59904-301-2.ch003

Lobry de Bruyn, L. (2011). Testing strategies to enhance online student collaboration in a problem-based learning activity. In Pozzi, F., & Persico, D. (Eds.), *Techniques for fostering collaboration in online learning communities: Theoretical and practical perspectives* (pp. 99–123). Hershey, PA: IGI Global. doi:10.4018/978-1-61692-898-8.ch007

Löfstrand, M. (2009). Functional product development challenges collaborative work practices. In Kock, N. (Ed.), *Virtual team leadership and collaborative engineering advancements: Contemporary issues and implications* (pp. 203–216). Hershey, PA: IGI Global. doi:10.4018/978-1-60566-110-0.ch014

Lowe, M. A. (2010). Developing electronic portfolios. In Seok, S., Meyen, E., & DaCosta, B. (Eds.), *Handbook of research on human cognition and assistive technology: Design, accessibility and transdisciplinary perspectives* (pp. 251–263). Hershey, PA: IGI Global. doi:10.4018/978-1-61520-817-3.ch017

Lowry, P. (2010). Instructional strategy approaches with technology. In Song, H. (Ed.), *Distance learning technology, current instruction, and the future of education: Applications of today, practices of tomorrow* (pp. 216–229). Hershey, PA: IGI Global.

Luppicini, R. (2008). Conversational pragmatics and learning in virtual organizations. In Putnik, G., & Cruz-Cunha, M. (Eds.), *Encyclopedia of networked and virtual organizations* (pp. 337–345). Hershey, PA: IGI Global. doi:10.4018/978-1-59904-885-7.ch045

Luppicini, R. (2009). Conversation ethics for online learning communities. In Demiray, U., & Sharma, R. (Eds.), *Ethical practices and implications in distance learning* (pp. 98–107). Hershey, PA: IGI Global.

Lygo-Baker, S., & Hatzipanagos, S. (2012). Enabling professional development with e-portfolios: Creating a space for the private and public self. *International Journal of Online Pedagogy and Course Design*, *2*(1), 37–52. doi:10.4018/ijopcd.2012010103

Lyman, C. (2010). Facilitating virtual collaborative writing through informed leadership. In Hewett, B., & Robidoux, C. (Eds.), *Virtual collaborative writing in the workplace: Computer-mediated communication technologies and processes* (pp. 144–157). Hershey, PA: IGI Global. doi:10.4018/978-1-60566-994-6.ch008

Lynch, K., Heinze, A., & Scott, E. (2009). Scholarly collaboration across time zones. In Salmons, J., & Wilson, L. (Eds.), *Handbook of research on electronic collaboration and organizational synergy* (pp. 237–249). Hershey, PA: IGI Global.

Mackay, S., & Fisher, D. (2012). Web conferencing and remote laboratories as part of blended learning in engineering and science: A paradigm shift in education or more of the same? In Lê, T., & Lê, Q. (Eds.), *Technologies for enhancing pedagogy, engagement and empowerment in education: Creating learning-friendly environments* (pp. 246–263). Hershey, PA: IGI Global.

Mackey, J. (2009). Virtual learning and real communities: Online professional development for teachers. In Stacey, E., & Gerbic, P. (Eds.), *Effective blended learning practices: Evidence-based perspectives in ICT-facilitated education* (pp. 163–181). Hershey, PA: IGI Global. doi:10.4018/978-1-60566-296-1.ch009

Manathunga, C., & Donnelly, R. (2009). Opening online academic development programmes to international perspectives and dialogue. In Donnelly, R., & McSweeney, F. (Eds.), *Applied e-learning and e-teaching in higher education* (pp. 85–109). Hershey, PA: IGI Global. doi:10.4018/978-1-59904-814-7.ch005

Mandasari, V., Lu, M. V., & Theng, L. B. (2011). 2D animated social story for assisting social skills learning of children with autism spectrum disorder. In Theng, L. (Ed.), *Assistive and augmentive communication for the disabled: Intelligent technologies for communication, learning and teaching* (pp. 1–24). Hershey, PA: IGI Global. doi:10.4018/978-1-60960-541-4.ch001

Marshall, K. (2008). E-Portfolios in teacher education. In Putnik, G., & Cruz-Cunha, M. (Eds.), *Encyclopedia of networked and virtual organizations* (pp. 516–523). Hershey, PA: IGI Global. doi:10.4018/978-1-59904-885-7.ch068

Martin, J. B., & Collins, R. A. (2011). Evaluating teaching in adult education. In Wang, V. (Ed.), *Encyclopedia of information communication technologies and adult education integration* (pp. 824–837). Hershey, PA: IGI Global.

Martins, H. F., & Ferro, M. J. (2008). Interaction in cooperative learning. In Putnik, G., & Cruz-Cunha, M. (Eds.), *Encyclopedia of networked and virtual organizations* (pp. 735–744). Hershey, PA: IGI Global. doi:10.4018/978-1-59904-885-7.ch097

Massey, A. P., Montoya, M. M., & Bartelt, V. (2011). Cross-university collaborative learning: Extending the classroom via virtual worlds. In Vincenti, G., & Braman, J. (Eds.), *Multi-user virtual environments for the classroom: Practical approaches to teaching in virtual worlds* (pp. 333–347). Hershey, PA: IGI Global. doi:10.4018/978-1-60960-545-2.ch021

Mathur, R., & Oliver, L. (2010). Building relationships in an international blended learning program: Opportunities and challenges in a Central American Country. In Mukerji, S., & Tripathi, P. (Eds.), *Cases on technology enhanced learning through collaborative opportunities* (pp. 329–341). Hershey, PA: IGI Global. doi:10.4018/978-1-61520-751-0.ch019

Matuga, J. M. (2007). Self-regulation and online learning: Theoretical issues and practical challenges to support lifelong learning. In Inoue, Y. (Ed.), *Online education for lifelong learning* (pp. 146–168). Hershey, PA: IGI Global. doi:10.4018/978-1-59904-319-7.ch007

McClelland, R. J. (2010). Using virtual learning environments to present different learning blends. In Kidd, T., & Keengwe, J. (Eds.), *Adult learning in the digital age: Perspectives on online technologies and outcomes* (pp. 219–238). Hershey, PA: IGI Global. doi:10.4018/978-1-60566-828-4.ch019

McGhie-Richmond, D., & Winter, E. (2011). Considerations for effective collaborative practice: A reflection on the use of case studies in on-line teacher education learning spaces. In Pozzi, F., & Persico, D. (Eds.), *Techniques for fostering collaboration in online learning communities: Theoretical and practical perspectives* (pp. 124–145). Hershey, PA: IGI Global.

McGrath, O. (2011). Data mining user activity in Free and Open Source Software (FOSS)/ open learning management systems. In Czerkawski, B. (Ed.), *Free and open source software for e-learning: Issues, successes and challenges* (pp. 120–131). Hershey, PA: IGI Global. doi:10.4018/jossp.2010010105

McInnerney, J. M., & Roberts, T. S. (2009). Collaborative and cooperative learning. In Rogers, P., Berg, G., Boettcher, J., Howard, C., Justice, L., & Schenk, K. (Eds.), *Encyclopedia of distance learning* (2nd ed., pp. 319–326). Hershey, PA: IGI Global. doi:10.4018/978-1-60566-198-8.ch046

McKenna, G. F., & Stansfield, M. (2012). The development of e-portfolio evaluation criteria and application to the blackboard LMS e-portfolio. *International Journal of Virtual and Personal Learning Environments, 3*(1), 19–36. doi:10.4018/jvple.2012010102

McLoughlin, C. (2011). Leading pedagogical change with innovative Web tools and social media. *International Journal of Adult Vocational Education and Technology, 2*(1), 13–22. doi:10.4018/javet.2011010102

Mengel, S., Kuszpa, M., & de Witt, C. (2010). Mobile learning: didactical scenarios in the context of learning on the Job. In Ebner, M., & Schiefner, M. (Eds.), *Looking toward the future of technology-enhanced education: Ubiquitous learning and the digital native* (pp. 223–244). Hershey, PA: IGI Global. doi:10.4018/978-1-61520-678-0.ch026

Metcalf, D., Graffeo, C., & Read, L. (2011). Fundamental design elements of pervasive games for blended learning. In Kitchenham, A. (Ed.), *Blended learning across disciplines: Models for implementation* (pp. 148–172). Hershey, PA: IGI Global. doi:10.4018/978-1-60960-479-0.ch009

Milanovic, N., & Malek, M. (2008). Adaptive search and learning-based approaches for automatic Web service composition. In Zhang, L. (Ed.), *Web services research and practices* (pp. 135–188). Hershey, PA: IGI Global. doi:10.4018/978-1-59904-904-5.ch006

Miliszewska, I. (2009). Federated agent-based architecture for collaborative education model. In Syed, M. (Ed.), *Strategic applications of distance learning technologies* (pp. 84–95). Hershey, PA: IGI Global. doi:10.4018/978-1-59904-480-4.ch006

Miranda Correia, P. R., & Infante-Malachias, M. E. (2010). Expanded collaborative learning and concept mapping: A road to empowering students in classrooms. In Lupion Torres, P., & de Cássia Veiga Marriott, R. (Eds.), *Handbook of research on collaborative learning using concept mapping* (pp. 283–300). Hershey, PA: IGI Global.

Mochizuki, T., Kato, H., Fujitani, S., Yaegashi, K., Hisamatsu, S., & Nagata, T. (2007). Promotion of self-assessment for learners in online discussion using the visualization software. In Lambropoulos, N., & Zaphiris, P. (Eds.), *User-centered design of online learning communities* (pp. 365–386). Hershey, PA: IGI Global. doi:10.3115/1149293.1149351

Moncallo, N. J., Herrero, P., & Joyanes, L. (2009). Applying a teaching strategy to create a collaborative educational mode. In Khosrow-Pour, M. (Ed.), *Encyclopedia of information science and technology* (2nd ed., pp. 193–199). Hershey, PA: IGI Global. doi:10.4018/978-1-60566-026-4.ch034

Mouzakis, C., & Bourletidis, C. (2010). A blended learning course for teachers' ongoing professional development in Greece. In Yamamoto, J., Kush, J., Lombard, R., & Hertzog, C. (Eds.), *Technology implementation and teacher education: Reflective models* (pp. 1–24). Hershey, PA: IGI Global. doi:10.4018/978-1-61520-897-5.ch001

Mowbray, M. (2009). Designing online learning communities to encourage cooperation. In Lytras, M., & Ordóñez de Pablos, P. (Eds.), *Social Web evolution: Integrating semantic applications and Web 2.0 yechnologies* (pp. 177–191). Hershey, PA: IGI Global. doi:10.4018/978-1-60566-272-5.ch014

Munro, M., & McMullin, B. (2009). E-Learning for all? Maximizing the impact of multimedia resources for learners with disabilities. In Donnelly, R., & McSweeney, F. (Eds.), *Applied e-learning and e-teaching in higher education* (pp. 154–179). Hershey, PA: IGI Global. doi:10.4018/978-1-59904-814-7.ch008

Murphy, K. L., Gazi, Y., & Cifuentes, L. (2009). Intercultural collaborative project-based learning in online environments. In Chang, M., & Kuo, C. (Eds.), *Learning culture and language through ICTs: Methods for enhanced instruction* (pp. 286–297). Hershey, PA: IGI Global. doi:10.4018/978-1-60566-166-7.ch017

Nanclares, N. H. (2008). Evaluation and effective learning: Strategic use of e-portfolio as an alternative assessment at university. In García-Peñalvo, F. (Ed.), *Advances in e-learning: Experiences and methodologies* (pp. 264–278). Hershey, PA: IGI Global. doi:10.4018/978-1-59904-756-0.ch015

Ng, E. M. (2010). Comparing IT and non-IT faculty and students' perceptions on blended learning. In Ng, E. (Ed.), *Comparative blended learning practices and environments* (pp. 365–388). Hershey, PA: IGI Global. doi:10.4018/978-1-60566-852-9.ch018

Ng, E. M. (2011). An exploratory study of blended learning activities in two classes. *International Journal of Web-Based Learning and Teaching Technologies*, 6(1), 14–23. doi:10.4018/jwltt.2011010102

Ng, F. F. (2008). Dialogue mapping and collaborative learning. In Luppicini, R. (Ed.), *Handbook of conversation design for instructional applications* (pp. 403–418). Hershey, PA: IGI Global. doi:10.4018/978-1-59904-597-9.ch023

Ng, W., & Hanewald, R. (2010). Concept maps as a tool for promoting online collaborative learning in virtual teams with pre-service teachers. In Lupion Torres, P., & de Cássia Veiga Marriott, R. (Eds.), *Handbook of research on collaborative learning using concept mapping* (pp. 81–99). Hershey, PA: IGI Global. doi:10.4018/978-1-59904-992-2.ch005

Ng, W., Nicholas, H., Loke, S., & Torabi, T. (2010). Designing effective pedagogical systems for teaching and learning with mobile and ubiquitous devices. In Goh, T. (Ed.), *Multiplatform e-learning systems and technologies: Mobile devices for ubiquitous ICT-based education* (pp. 42–56). Hershey, PA: IGI Global. doi:10.4018/978-1-60566-703-4.ch003

Nikolaidou, M., Sofianopoulou, C., Alexopoulou, N., Abeliotis, K., Detsis, V., Chalkias, C., & Lasaridi, K. (2012). The blended learning ecosystem of an academic institution in Greece. In Ng, E., Karacapilidis, N., & Raisinghani, M. (Eds.), *Evaluating the impact of technology on learning, teaching, and designing curriculum: Emerging trends* (pp. 173–194). Hershey, PA: IGI Global. doi:10.4018/jwltt.2010070102

Ninomiya, T., Anma, F., & Okamoto, T. (2010). An organizational knowledge circulation management system for universities. In Karacapilidis, N. (Ed.), *Web-based learning solutions for communities of practice: Developing virtual environments for social and pedagogical advancement* (pp. 143–155). Hershey, PA: IGI Global. doi:10.4018/978-1-60566-711-9.ch011

Nouri, J., Cerratto-Pargman, T., Eliasson, J., & Ramberg, R. (2011). Exploring the challenges of supporting collaborative mobile learning. *International Journal of Mobile and Blended Learning*, 3(4), 54–69. doi:10.4018/jmbl.2011100104

November, N. (2010). Integrating online group work into first-year music studies in New Zealand: 'This IS a University. In Ragusa, A. (Ed.), *Interaction in communication technologies and virtual learning environments: Human factors* (pp. 314–330). Hershey, PA: IGI Global. doi:10.4018/978-1-60566-874-1.ch020

Oehl, M., & Pfister, H. (2010). E-Collaborative knowledge construction in chat environments. In Ertl, B. (Ed.), *E-Collaborative knowledge construction: Learning from computer-supported and virtual environments* (pp. 54–73). Hershey, PA: IGI Global. doi:10.4018/978-1-61520-729-9.ch003

Okamoto, T., Ninomiya, T., Kayama, M., & Nagata, N. (2008). Collaborative e-learning system and e-pedagogy: Learning resource infrastructure for distributed knowledge sharing. In Pahl, C. (Ed.), *Architecture solutions for e-learning systems* (pp. 24–43). Hershey, PA: IGI Global.

Olaniran, B. (2007). Challenges to implementing e-learning in lesser developed countries. In Edmundson, A. (Ed.), *Globalized e-learning cultural challenges* (pp. 18–34). Hershey, PA: IGI Global. doi:10.4018/978-1-59904-301-2.ch002

Olivares, O. J. (2008). Collaborative vs. cooperative learning: The instructor's role in computer supported collaborative learning. In Orvis, K., & Lassiter, A. (Eds.), *Computer-supported collaborative learning: Best practices and principles for instructors* (pp. 20–39). Hershey, PA: IGI Global. doi:10.4018/978-1-59904-753-9.ch002

Olla, P. (2007). Open source e-learning systems: Evaluation of features and functionality. In St. Amant, K., & Still, B. (Eds.), *Handbook of research on open source software: Technological, economic, and social perspectives* (pp. 638–648). Hershey, PA: IGI Global. doi:10.4018/978-1-59140-999-1.ch049

Olla, P., & Crider, R. (2007). Open-source online knowledge portals for education. In Tatnall, A. (Ed.), *Encyclopedia of portal technologies and applications* (pp. 684–688). Hershey, PA: IGI Global. doi:10.4018/978-1-59140-989-2.ch113

Olvera-Lobo, M. D., Castro-Prieto, R. M., Quero-Gervilla, E., Muñoz-Martín, R., Muñoz-Raya, E., & Murillo-Melero, M. (2008). Collaborative work training in higher education. In Putnik, G., & Cruz-Cunha, M. (Eds.), *Encyclopedia of networked and virtual organizations* (pp. 261–268). Hershey, PA: IGI Global. doi:10.4018/978-1-59904-885-7.ch035

Orito, Y., Kambayashi, Y., Tsujimura, Y., & Yamamoto, H. (2011). An agent-based model for portfolio optimization using search space splitting. In Chen, S., Kambayashi, Y., & Sato, H. (Eds.), *Multi-agent applications with evolutionary computation and biologically inspired technologies: Intelligent techniques for ubiquity and optimization* (pp. 19–34). Hershey, PA: IGI Global. doi:10.4018/978-1-60566-898-7.ch002

Ortega Gil, P., & Arcos García, F. (2011). Blended learning revisited: How it brought engagement and interaction into and beyond the classroom. In Kitchenham, A. (Ed.), *Blended learning across disciplines: Models for implementation* (pp. 58–72). Hershey, PA: IGI Global. doi:10.4018/978-1-60960-479-0.ch004

Özkan, B. C. (2010). Implementing e-learning in University 2.0: Are universities ready for the digital age? In Yang, H., & Yuen, S. (Eds.), *Handbook of research on practices and outcomes in e-learning: Issues and trends* (pp. 278–293). Hershey, PA: IGI Global.

Paechter, M., Kreisler, M., & Maier, B. (2010). Supporting collaboration and communication in videoconferences. In Ertl, B. (Ed.), *E-Collaborative knowledge construction: Learning from computer-supported and virtual environments* (pp. 195–212). Hershey, PA: IGI Global. doi:10.4018/978-1-61520-729-9.ch011

Palma de Schrynemakers, G. (2011). Lessons from constructivist theories, open source technology, and student learning. In Czerkawski, B. (Ed.), *Free and open source software for e-learning: Issues, successes and challenges* (pp. 39–54). Hershey, PA: IGI Global. doi:10.4018/978-1-61520-917-0.ch003

Parchoma, G. (2007). Visualizing ICT change in the academy. In McKay, E. (Ed.), *Enhancing learning through human computer interaction* (pp. 1–20). Hershey, PA: IGI Global. doi:10.4018/978-1-59904-328-9.ch001

Parchoma, G. (2011). Toward diversity in researching teaching and technology philosophies-in-practice in e-learning communities. In Daniel, B. (Ed.), *Handbook of research on methods and techniques for studying virtual communities: Paradigms and phenomena* (pp. 61–86). Hershey, PA: IGI Global. doi:10.4018/978-1-60960-040-2.ch004

Pawlowski, J. M., & Kozlov, D. (2010). Analysis and validation of learning technology models, standards and specifications: The reference model analysis grid (RMAG). *International Journal of IT Standards and Standardization Research, 8*(2), 1–19. doi:10.4018/jitsr.2010070101

Pei-Jin, T., Gwo-Jen, H., Judy, C. T., & Gwo-Haur, H. (2010). A computer-assisted approach to conducting cooperative learning process. In Syed, M. (Ed.), *Technologies shaping instruction and distance education: New studies and utilizations* (pp. 50–66). Hershey, PA: IGI Global. doi:10.4018/978-1-60566-934-2.ch004

Pelliccione, L., Pocknee, C., & Mulvany, J. (2010). The use of social interaction technologies in e-portfolios. In Dumova, T., & Fiordo, R. (Eds.), *Handbook of research on social interaction technologies and collaboration software: Concepts and trends* (pp. 233–244). Hershey, PA: IGI Global. doi:10.4018/978-1-60566-368-5.ch021

Peristeras, V., Martínez-Carreras, A., Gómez-Skarmeta, A. F., Prinz, W., & Nasirifard, P. (2012). Towards a reference architecture for collaborative work environments. In Kock, N. (Ed.), *Advancing collaborative knowledge environments: New trends in e-collaboration* (pp. 11–24). Hershey, PA: IGI Global. doi:10.4018/jec.2010091102

Peters, G. B. (2008). Chat as new pedagogy: The emerging communities of learners in higher education. In Tomei, L. (Ed.), *Encyclopedia of information technology curriculum integration* (pp. 93–98). Hershey, PA: IGI Global. doi:10.4018/978-1-59904-881-9.ch015

Petrina, S. (2007). Assessment and evaluation. In Petrina, S. (Ed.), *Advanced teaching methods for the technology classroom* (pp. 280–321). Hershey, PA: IGI Global.

Pettipiece, D., Ray, T., & Everett, J. (2009). Redefining writing reality multi-modal writing and assessment. In Schreiner, C. (Ed.), *Handbook of research on assessment technologies, methods, and applications in higher education* (pp. 298–316). Hershey, PA: IGI Global. doi:10.4018/978-1-60566-667-9.ch019

Petty, G. C., & Brewer, E. W. (2011). Comparing lecturing and small group discussions. In Wang, V. (Ed.), *Encyclopedia of information communication technologies and adult education integration* (pp. 396–414). Hershey, PA: IGI Global.

Pieper, S., Edwards, E., Haist, B., & Nolan, W. (2009). A survey of effective technologies to assess student learning. In Schreiner, C. (Ed.), *Handbook of research on assessment technologies, methods, and applications in higher education* (pp. 47–64). Hershey, PA: IGI Global. doi:10.4018/978-1-60566-667-9.ch003

Pincham, L. B. (2011). A dinosaur hatches its eggs: Using technology as a pedagogical tool. In D'Agustino, S. (Ed.), *Adaptation, resistance and access to instructional technologies: Assessing future trends in education* (pp. 256–272). Hershey, PA: IGI Global.

Piotrowski, M. (2011). QTI: A failed e-learning standard? In Lazarinis, F., Green, S., & Pearson, E. (Eds.), *Handbook of research on e-learning standards and interoperability: Frameworks and issues* (pp. 59–82). Hershey, PA: IGI Global.

Portimojärv, T., & Vuoskoski, P. (2009). The alliance of problem-based learning, technology, and leadership. In Donnelly, R., & McSweeney, F. (Eds.), *Applied e-learning and e-teaching in higher education* (pp. 310–326). Hershey, PA: IGI Global. doi:10.4018/978-1-59904-814-7.ch015

Powell, S. R. (2011). On the internationalization of the wireless telecommunications industry: A market-based analysis of six European service providers. In Bartolacci, M., & Powell, S. (Eds.), *Interdisciplinary and multidimensional perspectives in telecommunications and networking: Emerging findings* (pp. 197–215). Hershey, PA: IGI Global. doi:10.4018/978-1-60960-505-6.ch013

Powell, S. R. (2012). An analysis of the Latin American wireless telecommunications market portfolios of Telefonica and America Movil. In Bartolacci, M., & Powell, S. (Eds.), *Research, practice, and educational advancements in telecommunications and networking* (pp. 267–284). Hershey, PA: IGI Global. doi:10.4018/jitn.2010100104

Pozzi, F. (2009). Supporting group and individual processes in Web-based collaborative learning environments. In Mourlas, C., Tsianos, N., & Germanakos, P. (Eds.), *Cognitive and emotional processes in Web-based education: Integrating human factors and personalization* (pp. 396–413). Hershey, PA: IGI Global. doi:10.4018/978-1-60566-392-0.ch019

Praeg, C. (2011). Framework for IT service value engineering: Managing value and IT service quality. In Praeg, C., & Spath, D. (Eds.), *Quality management for IT services: Perspectives on business and process performance* (pp. 274–297). Hershey, PA: IGI Global.

Prinz, W., Martínez-Carreras, M. A., & Pallot, M. (2010). from collaborative tools to collaborative working environments. *International Journal of e-Collaboration*, *6*(1), 1–13. doi:10.4018/jec.2010091101

Prisk, J., & Lee, K. (2012). How to utilize an online community of practice (Cop) to enhance innovation in teaching and learning. In Wang, V. (Ed.), *Encyclopedia of e-leadership, counseling and training* (pp. 532–544). Hershey, PA: IGI Global. doi:10.4018/978-1-61350-068-2.ch039

Proske, A., Narciss, S., & Körndle, H. (2011). Exploring the effects of an optional learning plan tool in technology-enhanced learning. In Dettori, G., & Persico, D. (Eds.), *Fostering self-regulated learning through ICT* (pp. 315–333). Hershey, PA: IGI Global. doi:10.4018/978-1-61692-901-5.ch019

Qiu, L. (2010). Computer support in e-collaborative learning-by-doing environments. In Ertl, B. (Ed.), *Technologies and practices for constructing knowledge in online environments: Advancements in learning* (pp. 1–24). Hershey, PA: IGI Global. doi:10.4018/978-1-61520-937-8.ch001

Rahman, H. (2011). Collaborative learning: An effective tool to empower communities. In Chhabra, S., & Rahman, H. (Eds.), *Human development and global advancements through information communication technologies: New initiatives* (pp. 75–103). Hershey, PA: IGI Global. doi:10.4018/978-1-60960-497-4.ch006

Rahschulte, T. (2011). The evolution of collaborative work. In Milhauser, K. (Ed.), *Distributed team collaboration in organizations: Emerging tools and practices* (pp. 15–31). Hershey, PA: IGI Global. doi:10.4018/978-1-60960-533-9.ch002

Reddy, M. C., Jansen, B. J., & Spence, P. R. (2010). Collaborative information behavior: Exploring collaboration and coordination during information seeking and retrieval activities. In Foster, J. (Ed.), *Collaborative information behavior: User engagement and communication sharing* (pp. 73–88). Hershey, PA: IGI Global. doi:10.4018/978-1-61520-797-8.ch005

Reiff-Marganiec, S., Hong, Y., Qing Yu, H., Dustdar, S., Dorn, C., & Schall, D. (2009). Context aware collaborative working environments. In Khalil, I. (Ed.), *Handbook of research on mobile multimedia* (2nd ed., pp. 702–717). Hershey, PA: IGI Global.

Rejas-Muslera, R. J., García-Tejedor, A. J., & Rodriguez, O. P. (2010). Open educational resources in e-Learning: Standards and environment. *International Journal of Open Source Software and Processes, 2*(4), 1–12. doi:10.4018/IJOSSP.2010100101

Remtulla, K. (2007). E-Learning and the global workforce: Social and cultural implications for workplace adult education and training. In St. Amant, K. (Ed.), *Linguistic and cultural online communication issues in the global age* (pp. 276–305). Hershey, PA: IGI Global. doi:10.4018/978-1-59904-213-8.ch017

Remtulla, K. A. (2009). E-Learning adaptability and social responsibility. In Khosrow-Pour, M. (Ed.), *Encyclopedia of information science and technology* (2nd ed., pp. 1323–1328). Hershey, PA: IGI Global.

Remtulla, K. A. (2010). Towards more socio-culturally sensitive research and study of workplace e-learning. *International Journal of Adult Vocational Education and Technology, 1*(3), 27–45. doi:10.4018/javet.2010070103

Rice, R. (2012). ePortfolios and the communicative intellect in online education. In S. Kelsey & K. St. Amant (Eds.), *Computer-mediated communication: Issues and approaches in education* (pp. 62-73). Hershey, PA: IGI Global. doi:10.4018/978-1-61350-077-4.ch005

Riedl, R. E., Gilman, R., Tashner, J. H., Bronack, S. C., Cheney, A., Sanders, R., & Angel, R. (2008). Teaching IT through learning communities in a 3D immersive world: The evolution of online instruction. In Negash, S., Whitman, M., Woszczynski, A., Hoganson, K., & Mattord, H. (Eds.), *Handbook of distance learning for real-time and asynchronous information technology education* (pp. 65–82). Hershey, PA: IGI Global. doi:10.4018/978-1-59904-964-9.ch003

Rigou, M., Sirmakessis, S., Stavrinoudis, D., & Xenos, M. (2007). Tools and methods for supporting online learning communities and their evaluation. In Lambropoulos, N., & Zaphiris, P. (Eds.), *User-centered design of online learning communities* (pp. 215–237). Hershey, PA: IGI Global. doi:10.4018/978-1-59904-358-6.ch010

Rimor, R., & Rosen, Y. (2010). Collaborative knowledge construction in online learning environment: Why to promote and how to investigate. In Mukerji, S., & Tripathi, P. (Eds.), *Cases on transnational learning and technologically enabled environments* (pp. 190–212). Hershey, PA: IGI Global. doi:10.4018/978-1-61520-749-7.ch010

Ritzhaupt, A. D., Parker, M. A., & Ndoye, A. (2012). ePortfolio integration in teacher education programs: Does context matter from a student perspective? In D. Polly, C. Mims, & K. Persichitte (Eds.), *Developing technology-rich teacher education programs: Key issues* (pp. 250-264). Hershey, PA: IGI Global. doi:10.4018/978-1-4666-0014-0.ch017

Riverin, S. (2009). Blended learning and professional development in the K-12 sector. In Stacey, E., & Gerbic, P. (Eds.), *Effective blended learning practices: Evidence-based perspectives in ICT-facilitated education* (pp. 182–202). Hershey, PA: IGI Global. doi:10.4018/978-1-60566-296-1.ch010

Robbins, R., & Cunningham, M. (2010). Project learning, the linked course, and ramifications for global research. In Mukerji, S., & Tripathi, P. (Eds.), *Cases on transnational learning and technologically enabled environments* (pp. 288–301). Hershey, PA: IGI Global. doi:10.4018/978-1-61520-749-7.ch016

Rozar, N. B., Ibrahim, A. B., & Razik, M. A. (2011). Comparing effectiveness of e-learning training and traditional training in industrial safety and health. *International Journal of Online Marketing*, *1*(3), 46–61. doi:10.4018/ijom.2011070105

Salmons, J. E. (2008). Taxonomy of collaborative e-learning. In Tomei, L. (Ed.), *Encyclopedia of information technology curriculum integration* (pp. 839–846). Hershey, PA: IGI Global. doi:10.4018/978-1-59904-881-9.ch132

Saltiel, I. M., Witte, M. M., & Witte, J. E. (2009). Supervising projects and dissertations. In Wang, V. (Ed.), *Handbook of research on e-learning applications for career and technical education: Technologies for vocational training* (pp. 180–191). Hershey, PA: IGI Global. doi:10.4018/978-1-60566-739-3.ch014

Samarawickrema, G. (2009). Blended learning and the new pressures on the academy: Individual, political, and policy driven motivators for adoption. In Stacey, E., & Gerbic, P. (Eds.), *Effective blended learning practices: Evidence-based perspectives in ICT-facilitated education* (pp. 222–238). Hershey, PA: IGI Global. doi:10.4018/978-1-60566-296-1.ch012

Sari, E., & Lim, C. P. (2012). Online learning community: Building the professional capacity of indonesian teachers. In Jia, J. (Ed.), *Educational stages and interactive learning: From kindergarten to workplace training* (pp. 451–467). Hershey, PA: IGI Global. doi:10.4018/978-1-4666-0137-6.ch024

Schwier, R. A., & Daniel, B. K. (2007). Did we become a community? Multiple methods for identifying community and its constituent elements in formal online learning environments. In Lambropoulos, N., & Zaphiris, P. (Eds.), *User-centered design of online learning communities* (pp. 29–53). Hershey, PA: IGI Global. doi:10.4018/978-1-59904-358-6.ch002

Segrave, S., & Rice, M. (2012). The challenge of investigating the value of e-simulations in blended learning environments: A case for design-based research. In Holt, D., Segrave, S., & Cybulski, J. (Eds.), *Professional education using e-simulations: Benefits of blended learning design* (pp. 394–414). Hershey, PA: IGI Global.

Sharma, R. C., & Mishra, S. (2007). Global e-learning practices: An introduction. In Sharma, R., & Mishra, S. (Eds.), *Cases on global e-learning practices: Successes and pitfalls* (pp. 1–12). Hershey, PA: IGI Global.

Shaw, P. A., & Slick, S. (2009). Creating an electronic student teaching portfolio. In Rogers, P., Berg, G., Boettcher, J., Howard, C., Justice, L., & Schenk, K. (Eds.), *Encyclopedia of distance learning* (2nd ed., pp. 510–516). Hershey, PA: IGI Global. doi:10.4018/978-1-60566-198-8.ch074

Shen, C., & Wu, C. (2011). An exploration of students' participation, learning process, and learning outcomes in Web 2.0 computer supported collaborative learning. *International Journal of Online Pedagogy and Course Design*, *1*(2), 60–72. doi:10.4018/ijopcd.2011040105

Shen, P., & Tsai, C. (2009). Exploring the effects of Web-enabled self-regulated learning and online class frequency on students' computing skills in blended learning courses. *International Journal of Mobile and Blended Learning*, *1*(3), 1–16. doi:10.4018/jmbl.2009092201

Sherman, G., & Byers, A. (2011). Electronic portfolios in the professional development of educators. In D'Agustino, S. (Ed.), *Adaptation, resistance and access to instructional technologies: Assessing future trends in education* (pp. 429–444). Hershey, PA: IGI Global. doi:10.4018/978-1-61692-854-4.ch025

Sitzmann, T., Ely, K., & Wisher, R. (2008). Designing Web-based training courses to maximize learning. In Orvis, K., & Lassiter, A. (Eds.), *Computer-supported collaborative learning: Best practices and principles for instructors* (pp. 1–19). Hershey, PA: IGI Global. doi:10.4018/978-1-59904-753-9.ch001

Sivakumar, S. C. (2011). E-Learning for knowledge dissemination. In Schwartz, D., & Te'eni, D. (Eds.), *Encyclopedia of knowledge management* (2nd ed., pp. 249–262). Hershey, PA: IGI Global.

Slick, S., & Shaw, P. A. (2009). Teacher electronic portfolios. In Rogers, P., Berg, G., Boettcher, J., Howard, C., Justice, L., & Schenk, K. (Eds.), *Encyclopedia of distance learning* (2nd ed., pp. 2032–2039). Hershey, PA: IGI Global. doi:10.4018/978-1-60566-198-8.ch299

Sluijsmans, D. M., & Strijbos, J. (2010). Flexible peer assessment formats to acknowledge individual contributions during (Web-based) collaborative learning. In Ertl, B. (Ed.), *E-Collaborative knowledge construction: Learning from computer-supported and virtual environments* (pp. 139–161). Hershey, PA: IGI Global. doi:10.4018/978-1-61520-729-9.ch008

Smith, P. J., Stacey, E., & Ha, T. S. (2009). Blending collaborative online learning with workplace and community contexts. In Stacey, E., & Gerbic, P. (Eds.), *Effective blended learning practices: Evidence-based perspectives in ICT-facilitated education* (pp. 125–143). Hershey, PA: IGI Global. doi:10.4018/978-1-60566-296-1.ch007

So, H. (2008). Designing interactive and collaborative e-learning environments. In Kidd, T., & Song, H. (Eds.), *Handbook of research on instructional systems and technology* (pp. 596–613). Hershey, PA: IGI Global. doi:10.4018/978-1-59904-865-9.ch042

Soares Martins, A. C., & de Carvalho Fidelis Braga, J. (2009). The emergence of social presence in learning communities. In de Cássia Veiga Marriott, R., & Lupion Torres, P. (Eds.), *Handbook of research on e-learning methodologies for language acquisition* (pp. 22–38). Hershey, PA: IGI Global. doi:10.4018/978-1-59904-994-6.ch002

Söderström, T. (2011). Teaching online: The handbook dilemma in higher education. *International Journal of Cyber Ethics in Education, 1*(4), 10–21. doi:10.4018/ijcee.2011100102

Soon, L. (2011). E-Learning and m-learning: Challenges and barriers in distance education group assignment collaboration. *International Journal of Mobile and Blended Learning, 3*(3), 43–58. doi:10.4018/jmbl.2011070104

Soon, L., & Fraser, C. (2011). E-Learning for ICT group work in a blended learning environment. *International Journal of Quality Assurance in Engineering and Technology Education, 1*(2), 50–60. doi:10.4018/ijqaete.2011070105

Spiliotopoulos, V. (2011). Towards a technology-Enhanced university education. In Kitchenham, A. (Ed.), *Blended learning across disciplines: Models for implementation* (pp. 1–16). Hershey, PA: IGI Global. doi:10.4018/978-1-60960-479-0.ch001

Stacey, E., & Gerbic, P. (2009). Introduction to blended learning practices. In Stacey, E., & Gerbic, P. (Eds.), *Effective blended learning practices: Evidence-based perspectives in ICT-facilitated education* (pp. 1–19). Hershey, PA: IGI Global. doi:10.4018/978-1-60566-296-1.ch001

Stamelos, I. (2009). Teaching software engineering with Free/Libre open source projects. *International Journal of Open Source Software and Processes, 1*(1), 72–90. doi:10.4018/jossp.2009010105

Steger, H. (2011). Open source for mobile devices and mobile learning. In Chao, L. (Ed.), *Open source mobile learning: Mobile Linux applications* (pp. 84–92). Hershey, PA: IGI Global. doi:10.4018/978-1-60960-613-8.ch006

Stepich, D., Chyung, S. Y., & Smith-Hobbs, A. (2009). Research on cultural factors in global e-learning. In Rogers, P., Berg, G., Boettcher, J., Howard, C., Justice, L., & Schenk, K. (Eds.), *Encyclopedia of distance learning* (2nd ed., pp. 1758–1765). Hershey, PA: IGI Global. doi:10.4018/978-1-60566-198-8.ch259

Stoicovy, C. E., & Sanchez, J. (2007). Crossing the digital divide: Online portfolios in a diverse student environment. In Inoue, Y. (Ed.), *Technology and diversity in higher education: New challenges* (pp. 65–80). Hershey, PA: IGI Global.

Stone, A. (2010). The holistic model for blended learning: A new model for K-12 district-level cyber schools. In Tomei, L. (Ed.), *ICTs for modern educational and instructional advancement: New approaches to teaching* (pp. 200–213). Hershey, PA: IGI Global.

Strang, K. D. (2010). Multicultural e-Education: Student learning style, culture and performance. In Song, H., & Kidd, T. (Eds.), *Handbook of research on human performance and instructional technology* (pp. 392–412). Hershey, PA: IGI Global.

Strijbos, J., Ochoa, T. A., Sluijsmans, D. M., Segers, M. S., & Tillema, H. H. (2009). Fostering interactivity through formative peer assessment in (Web-based) collaborative learning environments. In Mourlas, C., Tsianos, N., & Germanakos, P. (Eds.), *Cognitive and emotional processes in Web-based education: Integrating human factors and personalization* (pp. 375–395). Hershey, PA: IGI Global. doi:10.4018/978-1-60566-392-0.ch018

Swanson, K. W., & Kayler, M. (2009). Self-assessment in building online communities of learning. In Wang, V. (Ed.), *Handbook of research on e-learning applications for career and technical education: Technologies for vocational training* (pp. 431–443). Hershey, PA: IGI Global. doi:10.4018/978-1-60566-739-3.ch034

Swanson, K. W., & Kayler, M. (2011). Blended learning: The best of both worlds. In Wang, V. (Ed.), *Encyclopedia of information communication technologies and adult education integration* (pp. 795–809). Hershey, PA: IGI Global.

Syrris, V. (2009). Information technology portfolio management: A meta-heuristic optimization approach. In Tan, A., & Theodorou, P. (Eds.), *Strategic information technology and portfolio management* (pp. 118–149). Hershey, PA: IGI Global. doi:10.4018/978-1-59904-687-7.ch007

Tam, M. (2012). The outcomes-based approach: Concepts and practice in curriculum and educational technology design. In Olofsson, A., & Lindberg, J. (Eds.), *Informed design of educational technologies in higher education: Enhanced learning and teaching* (pp. 21–37). Hershey, PA: IGI Global.

Tennyson, R., & Jorczak, R. L. (2011). Benefits of CSCL for learners with disabilities. In Ordóñez de Pablos, P., Zhao, J., & Tennyson, R. (Eds.), *Technology enhanced learning for people with disabilities: Approaches and applications* (pp. 1–9). Hershey, PA: IGI Global. doi:10.4018/978-1-61520-923-1.ch001

Thomas, P. (2010). Opportunities and challenges of emerging technologies in higher education: Future directions. *International Journal of Innovation in the Digital Economy*, *1*(4), 27–40. doi:10.4018/jide.2010100103

Thompson, T. L., & Kanuka, H. (2009). Establishing communities of practice for effective and sustainable professional development for blended learning. In Stacey, E., & Gerbic, P. (Eds.), *Effective blended learning practices: Evidence-based perspectives in ICT-facilitated education* (pp. 144–162). Hershey, PA: IGI Global. doi:10.4018/978-1-60566-296-1.ch008

Thoms, B., Garrett, N., & Ryan, T. (2010). Enhancing scholarly conversation through an online learning community. In Tomei, L. (Ed.), *ICTs for modern educational and instructional advancement: New approaches to teaching* (pp. 68–81). Hershey, PA: IGI Global. doi:10.4018/978-1-60566-936-6.ch007

Thornton, K., & Yoong, P. (2010). The application of blended action learning to leadership development: A case study. In Yoong, P. (Ed.), *Leadership in the digital enterprise: Issues and challenges* (pp. 163–180). Hershey, PA: IGI Global.

Tinnerman, L. S., & Johnson, J. (2011). The integration of social networking in creating collaborative partnerships in education. In D'Agustino, S. (Ed.), *Adaptation, resistance and access to instructional technologies: Assessing future trends in education* (pp. 235–255). Hershey, PA: IGI Global. doi:10.4018/978-1-61692-854-4.ch015

Tomei, L. A. (2010). Methodologies for assessing the adult learner. In Tomei, L. (Ed.), *Designing instruction for the traditional, adult, and distance learner: A new engine for technology-based teaching* (pp. 244–260). Hershey, PA: IGI Global.

Torres-Coronas, T., & Vidal-Blasco, M. A. (2011). Promoting digital competences through social software: A case study at the Rovira i Virgili University. In Wang, V. (Ed.), *Encyclopedia of information communication technologies and adult education integration* (pp. 204–225). Hershey, PA: IGI Global.

Torrisi-Steele, G. (2011). Blended learning primer. In Wang, V. (Ed.), *Encyclopedia of information communication technologies and adult education integration* (pp. 521–538). Hershey, PA: IGI Global.

Tsai, C. (2012). Facilitating students to earn computing certificates via blended learning in online problem-solving environment: A cross-course-orientation comparison. In Tomei, L. (Ed.), *Advancing education with information communication technologies: Facilitating new trends* (pp. 112–125). Hershey, PA: IGI Global.

Tsai, P., Hwang, G., Tseng, J. C., & Hwang, G. (2008). A computer-assisted approach to conducting cooperative learning process. *International Journal of Distance Education Technologies*, *6*(1), 49–66. doi:10.4018/jdet.2008010104

Tscholl, M., & Dowell, J. (2010). Collaborative knowledge construction: Examples of distributed cognitive processing. In Ertl, B. (Ed.), *E-Collaborative knowledge construction: Learning from computer-supported and virtual environments* (pp. 74–90). Hershey, PA: IGI Global. doi:10.4018/978-1-61520-729-9.ch004

Tsiatsos, T., Konstantinidis, A., Terzidou, T., Ioannidis, L., & Tseloudi, C. (2011). CSCL techniques in collaborative virtual environments: The case of Second Life. In Vincenti, G., & Braman, J. (Eds.), *Teaching through multi-user virtual environments: Applying dynamic elements to the modern classroom* (pp. 139–156). Hershey, PA: IGI Global.

Tzikopoulos, A., Manouselis, N., & Vuorikari, R. (2009). An overview of learning object repositories. In Halpin, T. (Ed.), *Selected readings on database technologies and applications* (pp. 85–94). Hershey, PA: IGI Global.

Uden, L., & Wojnar, L. (2007). Group process and trust in group discussion. In Tomei, L. (Ed.), *Integrating information & communications technologies into the classroom* (pp. 135–153). Hershey, PA: IGI Global. doi:10.4018/978-1-59904-258-9.ch009

Usoro, A., Majewski, G., & Bloom, L. (2010). Individual and collaborative approaches in e-learning design. In Tzanavari, A., & Tsapatsoulis, N. (Eds.), *Affective, interactive and cognitive methods for e-learning design: Creating an optimal education experience* (pp. 51–71). Hershey, PA: IGI Global. doi:10.4018/978-1-60566-940-3.ch003

Valenti, S., Falsetti, C., Ramazzotti, S., & Leo, T. (2008). Reshaping the structure of learning objects in the light of metacognition. In Esnault, L. (Ed.), *Web-based education and pedagogical technologies: Solutions for learning applications* (pp. 226–246). doi:10.4018/jwltt.2006010102

Valeria, N., Lu, M. V., & Theng, L. B. (2011). Collaborative virtual learning for assisting children with cerebral palsy. In Theng, L. (Ed.), *Assistive and augmentive communication for the disabled: Intelligent technologies for communication, learning and teaching* (pp. 127–158). Hershey, PA: IGI Global. doi:10.4018/978-1-60960-541-4.ch005

Van Haneghan, J. P. (2011). The impact of technology on assessment and evaluation in higher education. In Surry, D., Gray, R. Jr, & Stefurak, J. (Eds.), *Technology integration in higher education: Social and organizational aspects* (pp. 222–235). Hershey, PA: IGI Global. doi:10.4018/978-1-60960-147-8.ch016

Vat, K. H. (2008). E-Portfolio and pedagogical change for virtual universities. In Putnik, G., & Cruz-Cunha, M. (Eds.), *Encyclopedia of networked and virtual organizations* (pp. 508–515). Hershey, PA: IGI Global. doi:10.4018/978-1-59904-885-7.ch067

Vat, K. H. (2009). An e-portfolio scheme of flexible online learning. In Rogers, P., Berg, G., Boettcher, J., Howard, C., Justice, L., & Schenk, K. (Eds.), *Encyclopedia of distance learning* (2nd ed., pp. 941–949). Hershey, PA: IGI Global. doi:10.4018/978-1-60566-198-8.ch132

Vat, K. H. (2009). Developing REALSpace: Discourse on a student-centered creative knowledge environment for virtual communities of learning. *International Journal of Virtual Communities and Social Networking*, *1*(1), 43–74. doi:10.4018/jvcsn.2009010105

Vat, K. H. (2010). Developing student e-portfolios for outcomes-based assessment in personalized instruction. In Kats, Y. (Ed.), *Learning management system technologies and software solutions for online teaching: Tools and applications* (pp. 259–290). Hershey, PA: IGI Global. doi:10.4018/978-1-61520-853-1.ch015

Vat, K. H. (2010). The e-governance concerns in information system design for effective e-government performance improvement. In Rahman, H. (Ed.), *Handbook of research on e-government readiness for information and service exchange: Utilizing progressive information communication technologies* (pp. 48–69). Hershey, PA: IGI Global. doi:10.4018/978-1-60566-671-6.ch003

Vat, K. H. (2012). Innovating elite undergraduate education through quality continuous improvement: A learning enterprise's e-transformation perspective. In Rahman, H., & Ramos, I. (Eds.), *SMEs and open innovation: Global cases and initiatives* (pp. 146–182). Hershey, PA: IGI Global.

Vivitsou, M., Lambropoulos, N., Papadimitriou, S., & Gkikas, A. (2009). Web 2.0 collaborative learning tool dynamics. In Lytras, M., Tennyson, R., & Ordóñez de Pablos, P. (Eds.), *Knowledge networks: The social software perspective* (pp. 105–130). Hershey, PA: IGI Global. doi:10.4018/978-1-59904-976-2.ch009

Vlachos, K. (2010). Comparing face-to-face with blended learning in the context of foreign language education. In Ng, E. (Ed.), *Comparative blended learning practices and environments* (pp. 250–276). Hershey, PA: IGI Global. doi:10.4018/978-1-60566-852-9.ch013

Voulgari, I., & Komis, V. (2011). Collaborative learning in massively multiplayer online games: A review of social, cognitive and motivational perspectives. In Felicia, P. (Ed.), *Handbook of research on improving learning and motivation through educational games: Multidisciplinary approaches* (pp. 370–394). Hershey, PA: IGI Global. doi:10.4018/978-1-60960-495-0.ch018

Vuorikari, R., & Sarnow, K. (2007). European national educational school authorities' actions regarding open content and open source software in education. In Lytras, M., & Naeve, A. (Eds.), *Open source for knowledge and learning management: Strategies beyond tools* (pp. 245–265). Hershey, PA: IGI Global. doi:10.4018/978-1-59904-117-9.ch008

Walker, R., & Baets, W. (2009). Instructional Design for Class-Based and Computer-Mediated Learning: Creating the Right Blend for Student-Centred Learning. In Donnelly, R., & McSweeney, F. (Eds.), *Applied E-Learning and E-Teaching in Higher Education* (pp. 244–264).

Wallace, R. (2011). Empowered learner identity through m-learning: Representations of disenfranchised students' perspectives. *International Journal of Mobile and Blended Learning*, *3*(1), 53–63. doi:10.4018/jmbl.2011010103

Wang, L., & Chang, H. (2011). Improve oral training: The method of innovation assessment on English speaking performance. *International Journal of Distance Education Technologies*, *9*(3), 56–72. doi:10.4018/jdet.2011070105

Wang, S. (2011). Benefits and challenges of e-learning: University student perspectives. In Matsuo, T., & Fujimoto, T. (Eds.), *E-Activity and intelligent Web construction: Effects of social design* (pp. 203–215). Hershey, PA: IGI Global. doi:10.4018/978-1-61520-871-5.ch017

Wang, S., & Turner, S. (2008). How students learned in creating electronic portfolios. In Tomei, L. (Ed.), *Adapting information and communication technologies for effective education* (pp. 245–256). Hershey, PA: IGI Global. doi:10.4018/978-1-59904-922-9.ch019

Wang, X. (2008). What factors promote sustained online discussions and collaborative learning in a Web-based course? In Negash, S., Whitman, M., Woszczynski, A., Hoganson, K., & Mattord, H. (Eds.), *Handbook of distance learning for real-time and asynchronous information technology education* (pp. 192–211). Hershey, PA: IGI Global. doi:10.4018/978 1 59904 964 9.ch010

Wang, Y. (2009). Classification based on supervised learning. In Wang, Y. (Ed.), *Statistical techniques for network security: Modern statistically-based intrusion detection and protection* (pp. 305–347). Hershey, PA: IGI Global.

Wang, Y. (2009). Classification based on unsupervised learning. In Wang, Y. (Ed.), *Statistical techniques for network security: Modern statistically-based intrusion detection and protection* (pp. 348–395). Hershey, PA: IGI Global.

Wang, Y. J., Zheng, X., & Coenen, F. (2009). Mining allocating patterns in investment portfolios. In Rahman, H. (Ed.), *Data mining applications for empowering knowledge societies* (pp. 110–135). Hershey, PA: IGI Global.

Wasko, P. (2009). Implementing a statewide electronic portfolio infrastructure. In Rogers, P., Berg, G., Boettcher, J., Howard, C., Justice, L., & Schenk, K. (Eds.), *encyclopedia of distance learning* (2nd ed., pp. 1117–1124). Hershey, PA: IGI Global. doi:10.4018/978-1-60566-198-8.ch159

Watson, C. E., Zaldivar, M., & Summers, T. (2010). ePortfolios for learning, assessment, and professional development. In R. Donnelly, J. Harvey, & K. O'Rourke (Eds.), *Critical design and effective tools for e-learning in higher education: Theory into practice* (pp. 157-175). Hershey, PA: IGI Global. doi:10.4018/978-1-61520-879-1.ch010

Watson, W. R., Lee, S., & Reigeluth, C. M. (2007). Learning management systems: An overview and roadmap of the systematic application of computers in education. In Neto, F., & Brasileiro, F. (Eds.), *Advances in computer-supported learning* (pp. 66–96). Hershey, PA: IGI Global.

Weber, I., & Evans, P. (2011). E = Mportfolios2? Challenges and opportunities in creating mobile electronic portfolio systems for lifelong learning. *International Journal of Web Portals, 3*(2), 1–13. doi:10.4018/jwp.2011040101

Webster-Smith, A. (2011). The third time's for charm: A three-semester journey of learning to facilitate relational, online learning communities. In Huffman, S., Albritton, S., Wilmes, B., & Rickman, W. (Eds.), *Cases on building quality distance delivery programs: Strategies and experiences* (pp. 200–216). Hershey, PA: IGI Global.

West, C., Slatin, C., Sanborn, W., & Volicer, B. (2011). computer-based simulation in blended learning curriculum for hazardous waste site worker health and safety training. In L. Tomei (Ed.), *Online courses and ICT in education: Emerging practices and applications* (pp. 230-241). Hershey, PA: IGI Global. doi:10.4018/978-1-60960-150-8.ch018

Whitehouse, P., McCloskey, E., & Ketelhut, D. J. (2010). Online pedagogy design and development: New models for 21st century online teacher professional development. In Lindberg, J., & Olofsson, A. (Eds.), *Online learning communities and teacher professional development: Methods for improved education delivery* (pp. 247–262). Hershey, PA: IGI Global.

Wieseman, K. C. (2009). Electronic portfolios. In Rogers, P., Berg, G., Boettcher, J., Howard, C., Justice, L., & Schenk, K. (Eds.), *Encyclopedia of distance learning* (2nd ed., pp. 870–876). Hershey, PA: IGI Global. doi:10.4018/978-1-60566-198-8.ch122

Wiesner-Steiner, A., Wiesner, H., & Luck, P. (2009). Distance education teaching methods in childcare management. In Khosrow-Pour, M. (Ed.), *Encyclopedia of information science and technology* (2nd ed., pp. 1168–1173). Hershey, PA: IGI Global. doi:10.4018/978-1-60566-026-4.ch185

Williams, P. (2010). Beyond control: Will blended learning subvert national curricula? In Ng, E. (Ed.), *Comparative blended learning practices and environments* (pp. 1–19). Hershey, PA: IGI Global.

Williams van Rooij, S. (2011). Higher education and FOSS for e-learning: The role of organizational sub-cultures in enterprise-wide adoption. In Czerkawski, B. (Ed.), *Free and open source software for e-learning: Issues, successes and challenges* (pp. 55–74). Hershey, PA: IGI Global.

Williamson, T. B., Hauer, G. K., & Luckert, M. K. (2011). Economic concepts, methods, and tools for risk analysis in forestry under climate change. In Olej, V., Obršálová, I., & Krupka, J. (Eds.), *Environmental modeling for sustainable regional development: System approaches and advanced methods* (pp. 303–326). Hershey, PA: IGI Global. doi:10.4018/978-1-60960-156-0.ch015

Wilson, G. (2009). Case studies of ICT-enhanced blended learning and implications for professional development. In Stacey, E., & Gerbic, P. (Eds.), *Effective blended learning practices: Evidence-based perspectives in ICT-facilitated education* (pp. 239–258). Hershey, PA: IGI Global. doi:10.4018/978-1-60566-296-1.ch013

Wu, Y. L. (2012). A research of applying learning diagnosis diagram in online learning diagnosis. In Jin, Q. (Ed.), *Intelligent learning systems and advancements in computer-aided instruction: Emerging studies* (pp. 305–322). Hershey, PA: IGI Global.

Yang, H. H. (2010). Blogging minds on web-based educational projects. In Song, H., & Kidd, T. (Eds.), *Handbook of research on human performance and instructional technology* (pp. 195–209). Hershey, PA: IGI Global.

Yaniv, H. (2008). ThinkTeam: GDSS methodology and technology as a collaborative learning task. In Adam, F., & Humphreys, P. (Eds.), *Encyclopedia of decision making and decision support technologies* (pp. 872–881). Hershey, PA: IGI Global. doi:10.4018/978-1-59904-843-7.ch098

Yee, G., Xu, Y., Korba, L., & El-Khatib, K. (2007). Privacy and security in e-learning. In Shih, T., & Hung, J. (Eds.), *Future directions in distance learning and communication technologies* (pp. 52–75). Hershey, PA: IGI Global.

Yen, N. Y., Shih, T. K., Jin, Q., Hsu, H., & Chao, L. R. (2010). Trend of e-learning: the service mashup. *International Journal of Distance Education Technologies*, 8(1), 69–88. doi:10.4018/jdet.2010010105

Yilmaz, L. (2008). Collaborativet: Improving team cooperation and awareness in distance learning for IT education. In Negash, S., Whitman, M., Woszczynski, A., Hoganson, K., & Mattord, H. (Eds.), *Handbook of distance learning for real-time and asynchronous information technology education* (pp. 157–169). Hershey, PA: IGI Global. doi:10.4018/978-1-59904-964-9.ch008

Yoon, K. S. (2012). Measuring the influence of expertise and epistemic engagement to the practice of knowledge management. *International Journal of Knowledge Management*, 8(1), 40–70. doi:10.4018/jkm.2012010103

Yuen, S. C., & Yang, H. H. (2010). Using blogfolios to enhance interaction in e-learning courses. In Yang, H., & Yuen, S. (Eds.), *Handbook of research on practices and outcomes in e-learning: Issues and trends* (pp. 455–470). Hershey, PA: IGI Global. doi:10.4018/978-1-60566-788-1.ch027

Yukselturk, E., & Cagiltay, K. (2008). Collaborative work in online learning environments: Critical issues, dynamics, and challenges. In Orvis, K., & Lassiter, A. (Eds.), *Computer-supported collaborative learning: Best practices and principles for instructors* (pp. 114–139). Hershey, PA: IGI Global. doi:10.4018/978-1-59904-753-9.ch006

Zhan, H. (2012). Collaborative learning: A way to transform learning and instruction in online courses. In Yang, H., & Yuen, S. (Eds.), *Handbook of research on practices and outcomes in virtual worlds and environments* (pp. 491–513). Hershey, PA: IGI Global.

Zhang, Y. (2009). Collaborative learning in a Web-based environment: A COMPARISON STUDY. In Mourlas, C., Tsianos, N., & Germanakos, P. (Eds.), *Cognitive and emotional processes in Web-based education: Integrating human factors and personalization* (pp. 343–356). Hershey, PA: IGI Global. doi:10.4018/978-1-60566-392-0.ch016

Zhong, Y., & Lim, J. (2008). Perceptions in computer-supported collaborative learning: Interaction of cultural diversity, group size, and leadership. In Khosrow-Pour, M. (Ed.), *Innovative technologies for information resources management* (pp. 182–199). Hershey, PA: IGI Global.

Zhong, Y., & Lim, J. (2009). Cultural diversity in collaborative learning systems. In Khosrow-Pour, M. (Ed.), *Encyclopedia of information science and technology* (2nd ed., pp. 852–857). Hershey, PA: IGI Global.

Zhu, C., Valcke, M., & Schellens, T. (2010). E-Learning in higher education in China and Belgium: Student, teacher, contextual variables. In Mukerji, S., & Tripathi, P. (Eds.), *Cases on transnational learning and technologically enabled environments* (pp. 136–157). Hershey, PA: IGI Global. doi:10.4018/978-1-61520-749-7.ch008

Zygouris-Coe, V. I., & Swan, B. (2010). Challenges of online teacher professional development communities: A statewide case study in the United States. In Lindberg, J., & Olofsson, A. (Eds.), *Online learning communities and teacher professional development: Methods for improved education delivery* (pp. 114–133). Hershey, PA: IGI Global.

About the Contributors

Darren Cambridge is senior consultant at the American Institutes for Research in Washington, DC, USA, where he serves as project director and principal investigator for the U.S. Department of Education's Connected Online Communities of Practice project. He was previously a faculty member at George Mason University, a director at the American Association for Higher Education, and a fellow with EDUCAUSE. He co-leads the Inter/National Coalition for Electronic Portfolio Research and serves on the board of the Association for Authentic, Experiential, and Evidence-Based Learning. He has developed technical specifications IMS Global Learning Consortium and open source eportfolio software through the Sakai Foundation. His work appears in a range of scholarly journals and books. He is author of *Electronic Portfolios for Lifelong Learning and Assessment* (Jossey-Bass, 2010) and co-editor of *Electronic Portfolios 2.0: Emergent Research on Implementation and Impact* (Stylus, 2009).

* * *

Gabriela Alpírez is a technology integration consultant at Instituto Experimental de la Asunción in Guatemala, where she has worked for the last ten years. She researches new approaches to technology in education and management, and current developments on hardware, software, network and digital services, and is currently working on the design of an eportfolio system for Spanish-speaking college students that allow them to reflect on their internships. She has been a Humphrey Fellow at Pennsylvania State University and is a certified Global Career Development Facilitator.

Ashley Ater-Kranov is managing director of professional services at ABET in the USA. Her department is responsible for ensuring the quality training of program evaluators, partnering with faculty and industry to conduct robust and innovative technical education research, and providing educational opportunities on sustainable assessment processes for program continuous improvement worldwide. She is Principal Investigator of a NSF-funded validity study of her direct method for teaching and measuring the ABET engineering professional skills and is adjunct associate professor in the School of Electrical Engineering and Computer Science at Washington State University where she co-teaches the senior design capstone sequence. During her more than 21 years as a higher education administrator and professional educator, Ater-Kranov has led university-wide assessment initiatives, coordinated regional and professional accreditation activities, taught at the undergraduate and graduate levels, and conducted faculty development workshops on teaching and assessment worldwide.

Igor Balaban works at the Faculty of Organization and Informatics at the University of Zagreb, Croatia, as a researcher. He has published more than 30 scientific papers and three book chapters. His main areas of interest are information system success and advanced learning technologies, especially online learning systems and eportfolios. He has presented several workshops and talks regarding the eportfolio usage and implementation. He is a member of ePForum2012 organizational committee and reviewer for the *International Journal of ePortfolios*. Professionally, he works with open source technologies.

Gerd Bräuer is director of training and projects at the Freiburg Writing Center hosted at the University of Education, Freiburg, Germany. In 2006-2008 he was the head of the European Writing Centers Association (EWCA). After more than ten years of teaching at U.S. universities and promotion to associate professor at Emory University, in 2004 he returned to his native country, Germany. Since then he has facilitated the development of portfolio systems, writing curricula, and writing/reading centers throughout secondary and higher education in Europe. His latest initiative, www.international-literacy-management.org, is focusing on the training of people in how to set up modes of reflective practice (e.g. ePortfolios) as a means of longterm institutional development.

Gary Brown directs the Center for Online Learning at Portland State University in the USA. He is co-director of the Association for Authentic Experiential and Evidence-Based Learning and a senior fellow with the Association for American Colleges and Universities, where he serves as assessment fellow on the new *Quality Collaboratives* project, a national initiative in collaboration with the Lumina Foundation designed to pilot strategies for using competencies to guide student transfer between two- and four-year institutions. Brown has written and presented extensively on undergraduate learning, assessment, and technology. He was the lead developer for the FIPSE-funded WSU Critical Thinking Project, and, work with the EDUCAUSE Learning Initiative (ELI) and a variety of professional associations on the Evidence of Impact project. Gary's teams have received six NUTN best research awards. He was a National Learning Communities fellow and the assessment section editor for *Innovate*.

Vicky Chan obtained an M.Sc. in Library and Information Management in the University of Hong Kong and a BSc (Hons) in Computer Studies in 2010 and 2006 respectively. Before joining the Chinese University of Hong Kong as an assistant computer officer in the Department of Ophthalmology and Visual Sciences, she worked in the Office of Education Development and Gateway Education (EDGE) at City University of Hong Kong as a research assistant on a number of eportfolio research projects.

Josephine Chen studied Anthropology at the Oxford University and Chinese University of Hong Kong. She has conducted extensive research in Shanghai on migrants and social status. When she worked at City University of Hong Kong, Josephine promoted the use of eportfolios and, with her team, contributed to the creation of an institution-wide impact on using eportfolios to enhance learning and employability. Currently, Josephine is a training officer at Gucci Hong Kong Ltd.

Hokling Cheung is an education development officer in the Office of Education Development and Gateway Education (EDGE) at City University of Hong Kong. She has been one of the core members in the implementation of institutional wide e-learning strategies at the University since 1999. In 2005, she introduced new ideas and related tools of Web 2.0 to the University for teaching and learning enhancement. In the same year, she started collaborating with teachers and staff from different departments as the co-principal investigator researching eportfolio technologies and pedagogies, which she sees as involving a paradigm shift of learning and education technology in which learners are empowered to direct their own learning and collaborate effectively with other facilitators and learners. She enjoys investigating and promoting creative and pedagogical applications of the latest available technologies for effective teaching and learning.

YoonJung Cho is assistant professor in the School of Applied Health and Educational Psychology at Oklahoma State University. Her research is focused on students' achievement motivation and self-regulated learning process and teachers' motivation and its impact on instructional practices, both in traditional classroom settings and online instruction.

Ruth Cox coordinates the ePortfolio Initiative at San Francisco State University in the USA, working campus-wide with faculty on comprehensive assessment strategies using student electronic portfolios, and teaches Masters of Public Health (MPH) students in the Health Education Department. Cox has designed and implemented curriculum and educational programming in academic and corporate settings since 1989. She has taught a range of courses using distance education strategies at SF State and Santa Clara University. As a visiting scientist at Cisco Systems, she advised the World Wide Education Group on new collaborative learning software and online teaching solutions for K-12 and higher education applications.

Blazenka Divjak is a full professor of mathematics and information science at the University of Zagreb, Croatia. Besides pure mathematics, her research interests are e-learning, strategic decision-making, and project management. She published more than 70 scientific and professional papers and six books. Additionally, she is involved in international R&D projects in the area of informatics and e-learning. She is currently vice-rector for students and study programs and a Croatian Bologna expert.

Shona Ellis is a senior instructor in the Department of Botany at the University of British Columbia, in Vancouver, Canada. She was one of the first lecturers at UBC to use websites for her courses starting with the beta version of WebCT. She has been involved with numerous pilot projects that deal with incorporating technology into the classroom to promote a better learning and teaching environment. Ellis has received two university-wide Killam Teaching Awards.

Dean Fisher is an associate head in the English Language Centre at City University of Hong Kong. He has worked as a teacher in France, the UK, Japan, Turkey, Singapore, and Argentina. In 2008 he was presented with City University's Teaching Excellence Award. His professional interests include self-directed learning, which is where his passion for eportfolios originated; curriculum design; creative and critical thinking; teacher education; and research. He was a co-principal investigator of a university project entitled "ePortfolios for All: A Roadmap for Success."

Eleanor J. Flanigan is professor of management and Information Systems in the School of Business at Montclair State University in New Jersey, USA. Her business experiences include serving as international marketing manager for Ashton-Tate/MultiMate in the United Kingdom, Western Europe, and

SouthEast Asia. She was a systems analyst for General Electric Company, director of the Anti-Poverty Action Commission for the Archdiocese of Philadelphia, and General Electric Company corporate advisor to Philadelphia Model Cities Programs. Flanigan was chosen as University Teacher of the Year at Montclair State University as well as being voted Educator of the Year by the Eastern Business Education Association.

Darko Grabar works at the Faculty of Organization and Informatics as a head of Application Development Centre at the University of Zagreb, Croatia. The main responsibilities of Application Development Centre are providing e-learning support, application development and ICT support for Faculty of Information activities; cooperation with SMEs; and involvement in ICT related projects. Since 2007, he has been the Faculty's representative for e-learning at the University. He has extensive experience managing and running different LMS and eportfolio systems. He also actively participates in international Open Source communities and, since 2009, has been a member of the HrOpen (Croatian Society for Open Systems and Internet) Steering Committee.

Gillian Hallam is adjunct professor with Queensland University of Technology, Brisbane, Australia. From 2007-2010, she was project leader for the Australian ePortfolio Project, a national research initiative to investigate eportfolio practice in higher education in Australia funded by the Australian Learning and Teaching Council. After ten years of academic life, Gillian currently provides consultancy services to the library and information services sector, building on her research experience in the areas of workforce planning and evidence based practice. She also works with the International Federation of Library Associations (IFLA) to develop and run training programs internationally.

Wendy Harper is the director of both the eLearning Services Department and the ePortfolio Initiatives team at Queensland University of Technology in Australia. Harper has over 25 years' broad experience in the tertiary sector, with a particular interest in the application of technology in learning and teaching contexts. Harper's work in the field of eportfolios has acquired international standing, and she has been invited to speak both nationally and internationally in government, tertiary, and secondary fora. In 2010, the QUT Student ePortfolio Program received national recognition from the Australian Learning and Teaching Council for Services Supporting Student Learning.

Elizabeth Hartnell-Young is an educator who has written extensively on portfolio development, for over a decade, including *Digital Portfolios: Powerful Tools for Professional Growth and Reflection* (2nd ed., Corwin, 2007). In 1997, she established women@the cutting edge, a project developing digital portfolios with teachers to support learning through technology, funded by AT&T (USA). In 2007-2008, she was an expert consultant for the Joint Information Systems Committee (JISC) in the UK's Higher Education sector, while a Research Fellow at the Learning Sciences Research Institute at the University of Nottingham. She currently manages research for the Department of Education and Early Childhood Development in Victoria, Australia, and is also an Honorary Fellow at The University of Melbourne.

Yi Huang currently serves as vice president for accreditation at the National Council for Accreditation of Teacher Education. She holds an M.A. and a Ph.D. in Ethnomusicology, an M.A. and two post baccalaureate certificates in Instructional Systems Development, Training Systems and Computer/

Web-Based Training from University of Maryland Baltimore County, and a professional certificate in Integrated Planning and Assessment from the Society for College and University Planning. The recipient of numerous awards for her achievements in music and dance, she has performed at diplomatic and public events around the world.

Gordon Joyes is associate professor in e-learning at the University of Nottingham, UK, and holds the Dearing Award for Excellence in Teaching and Learning. He is an accomplished director of international e-learning projects involving both research and innovation, and he is also an experienced online course developer and tutor. He has used portfolios extensively in his teaching and has been involved in researching their use in the UK for Becta, which long was the UK government agency promoting the use of information and communications technology in schools. From 2007 to 2009, he was an expert consultant for the Joint Information Systems Committee (JISC) evaluating e-portfolio use across the higher education sector and advising on policy and practice.

Kevin Kelly is director of Wiley Learning Institute, a new business venture focused on professional development in higher education in the USA. He joined this endeavor after 12 years at San Francisco State University, where he managed two units—Online Teaching & Learning and Media Distribution and Support Services. In these roles, he was responsible for professional development for faculty, curriculum redesign support, program assessment support, accreditation preparation support, academic technology integration, eportfolio planning and implementation, and instructional consultation related to teaching and learning in both face-to-face and online environments. Kevin continues to teach at SF State, and is a lead editor of a new book about eLearning, *Education for a Digital World 2.0: Innovations in Education* (2011), collaboratively authored and peer reviewed by almost 100 practitioners in 15 countries. He received his Ed.D. in Organization and Leadership at University of San Francisco in 2009.

Lynn McAllister currently works with eLearning Services at Queensland University of Technology in Australia. She is the senior support officer for the QUT ePortfolio program. Her areas of interest include critical reflective practice and eLearning design, and, in particular, development and support of reflective practice through the QUT Student ePortfolio approach. The program aims to enhance students' learning outcomes in line with the focus on "real world learning" at QUT. Lynn enjoys sharing reflective practice and eportfolio experiences through conference presentations. Her approach to professional practice has been recognized through an individual award in the 2007 QUT Vice-Chancellor's Excellence Award for professional staff.

Joanne Nakonechny, an educational anthropologist, was director and research associate at the Science Centre for Learning and Teaching at the University of British Columbia in Canada during the research and writing of this chapter. She worked with science faculty to research how students learn and to promote effective teaching strategies. Currently an educational consultant, Nakonechny is working on a project to facilitate engineering students' understanding of appropriate socio-technical problem solving approaches locally and globally.

Judith Patton and Candace Reynolds have been involved in the improvement of undergraduate education including the design and implementation of eportfolios for student learning and institutional and program assessment for over 16 years. They are early pioneers in the development of using ePortfolios for both student learning and program assessment. In their administrative and teaching roles in University Studies at Portland State University, Patton and Reynolds were leaders in developing and teaching in the nationally recognized general education program that integrated eportfolios for learning and for program assessment into the curriculum. Both have been involved in eportfolio projects through organizations such as the Association of American Colleges and Universities, the Carnegie Foundation for the Advancement of Teaching, the Inter/National Coalition for Electronic Portfolio Research, and the Pew Charitable Trust. They have published over 20 articles on ePortfolios and pedagogical practices in higher education in peer-reviewed journals. They have been frequent speakers at conferences on eportfolios as well as served as consultants to over 30 institutions developing eportfolio programs. Currently, Patton and Reynolds are co-principle investigators for Portland State in the Lifelong Learning Curriculum Transformation Project.

Valerie Pickard is currently a freelance consultant for independent learning, eportfolios and I.T. in education. She has taught English in the UK, Sweden, Denmark, Egypt, Kuwait, and Hong Kong, where she has worked for over 20 years. In addition to using eportfolios in her teaching, she successfully applied her conceptual understanding and practical experience to the creation of her own eportfolios for her recent M.Sc. studies in Library and Information Management with the University of Hong Kong.

Royce Robertson is the director of assessment, educator licensing programs, for the Richard W. Riley College of Education and Leadership at Walden University. Prior to Walden, Robertson was assistant professor of Education and Technology at Plymouth State University (NH). His research interests include eportfolios, teacher education, and assessment systems.

Hédia Mhiri Sellami has been an associate professor at the Higher Institute of Management at the University of Tunis in Tunisia since 1994. She earned her diploma of engineering in Computer Sciences in 1986 from the Faculty of Sciences of Tunis. She completed her thesis in the Computer Sciences in 1996. Her research focus is on ICT, elearning, and eportfolios.

Brady J. Spangenberg earned his Ph.D. in Comparative Literature from Purdue University in May 2011. His dissertation, *Civil Death in Early Modern Europe from Jack Cade to Luther, Raleigh and Hamlet*, explores the practical and metaphoric consequences of the legal designation civil death. He earned his Master's in Comparative Literature from Purdue and his Bachelor of Arts in English and Religion from Simpson College. He currently lives and works in Ludwigshafen, Germany.

Anthony Wong is currently a postgraduate student in the University of Hong Kong, where his studies focus on the e-commerce and Internet computing. He is also a graduate from City University of Hong Kong and holds a bachelor's degree with honors in Engineering. Wong believes technology can change people's lives, and he is actively helping different universities, such as Hong Kong Baptist University and City University of Hong Kong, to build in-house, tailor-made systems. His primary research interest is how learning can be effectively enhanced with cloud computing and mobile devices.

Yu-Fen Yang is a professor in the Graduate School of Applied Foreign Languages at National Yunlin University of Science and Technology in Taiwan. Her research focus is mainly on learning psychology of reading and writing, computer-assisted language learning, language education for special needs, and language assessment. She has published many articles in journals such as the *British Journal of Educational Technology, Computers and Education, Computers in Human Behavior, Educational Technology and Society*, and *Computer-Assisted Language Learning*.

Hui-chin Yeh is an associate professor in the Graduate School of Applied Foreign Languages at National Yunlin University of Science and Technology in Taiwan. Her research expertise centers on EFL teacher education, computer assisted language learning, and EFL reading and writing. She has published many articles in *Educational Technology Research & Development, Educational Technology and Society, Asia-Pacific Education Researcher*, and *Asia Pacific Education Review*.

Bojan Zugec is a junior researcher in the field of Mathematics at the Faculty of Organization and Informatics, University of Zagreb, Croatia. He is a graduate of both Faculty of Science programs, holding a Master's of Science in Applied Mathematics and a Master's of Education in Mathematics, and is currently finishing his doctoral study there. His other interest is e-learning, and he is tutoring as an external associate at CARNet's (Croatian Academic and Research Network) E-learning Academy, an annual institute on the management, design, and delivery of e-learning programs. He and his team members won the first prize for the best e-learning course at University of Zagreb for the academic year 2008-2009.

Index

CPSIA information can be obtained at www.ICGtesting.com
Printed in the USA
BVOW051707200212

283235BV00002B/6/P